EL GRECO

BY ANTONINA VALLENTIN

EL GRECO

THE DRAMA OF ALBERT EINSTEIN

H. G. WELLS

THIS I SAW: A LIFE OF GOYA

MIRABEAU

LEONARDO DA VINCI

FRUSTRATION: STRESEMANN'S RACE WITH DEATH

POET IN EXILE: THE LIFE OF HEINRICH HEINE

1. St. Martin and the Beggar. c. 1597–99

ANTONINA VALLENTIN

EL GRECO

TRANSLATED FROM THE FRENCH
BY ANDREW RÉVAI AND
ROBIN CHANCELLOR

DOUBLEDAY & COMPANY, INC., 1955

GARDEN CITY, NEW YORK

Library of Congress Catalog Card Number 55–7010

First published in the United States in 1955

Copyright, 1954, by Antonina Vallentin
All Rights Reserved
Printed in the United States
at
The Country Life Press, Garden City, N.Y.
Designed by Alma Reese Cardi
First Edition

CONTENTS

ILLUSTRATIONS

EL GRECO

In mezzo mar si'ede un paese guasto,
Diss' egli allora, che s'appella Creta.

DANTE; INFERNO, CANTO XIV

CHAPTER

ONE

A LAND

IN DECAY

CRETE rises up from the blue sea with her thick green woods and glittering mountain peaks. Ancient Mount Ida, "pointed like a fir cone and vast in extent," as Pierre Belon du Mans described it,[1] dominates the bay of Canea, capped with eternal snow. The climate is mild, there are springs in plenty, and a popular saying has it that "though fair flowers may grow elsewhere in the world, the fairest grow in Crete."

The same French traveller also extols the soil, for, though not naturally fertile, it is furrowed with streams "which enable the inhabitants to plant many beautiful gardens and orchards of surpassing loveliness which bring them much profit, and some are so pleasing that a man never wearies of admiring them."

The French naturalist knew the island in the years between 1540 and 1550, and the landscape he saw was the same that first greeted the eyes of El Greco on his birth in 1541.

Legend held Crete to be the land of abundance. It was here, in a field thrice turned by the plough, that Ceres gave birth to Pluto. The course of centuries had obliterated passing civilizations. The peasants had retained their ancient manner of dress and mode of life. Their hair, shaved close above the brow, hung down over their white shirts; their boots reached up to the waist; and they carried bows slung over their shoulders, with quivers of arrows on their backs and rapiers at

[1] *Les observations de plusieurs singularités et choses mémorables trouvées en Grèce, Asie, Judéa, Egypte, Arabie et autres pays estranges redigées en trois livres par Pierre Belon du Mans, à Paris, 1553.*

their sides. "The Cretans were justly dedicated of old to Diana," reported the Frenchman, "for even to-day they still follow this ancient cult and apply themselves from childhood as by a natural instinct to drawing the Scythian bow. Even an infant in his cradle, crying in a fit of rage, can be calmed merely by being shown a bow or given an arrow to hold."

But this warlike spirit in a people who could on occasion defend themselves better "even than the Turks" derived less from ancient tradition than from the insecurity of their age.

The Cretans had lost their mastery of the sea and their reputation for commercial genius, so envied by their rivals that a Greek writer had stated: "Avarice and love of gold are so much part of their lives that the Cretans alone in all the world consider no gain unlawful." Their shrewdness survived in the classic example of the syllogism: Epimenides used to say that all Cretans were liars, but Epimenides was a Cretan, therefore he was a liar, etc. But towards the middle of the sixteenth century, Crete, which had been "rich and opulent of old" and had held sway over a large part of the world, "as fortune permits of sudden changes is now reduced to such a state that there is not one single foot of earth left which is not a tributary under the Turkish yoke or Venetian bondage."

Crete was no longer that cradle of civilization which had astonished the first Greeks to land on her soil with her system of canalization and drainage, and her baths, for which they still had no words in their own language. Crete was no longer Hecatopolis—the island of a hundred towns. Belon found no more than three towns "of any considerable size." The capital was Candia, and this name was used by the Venetians to designate the whole island—"regno di Candia." And at Candia, Domenico Theotocopuli was born. Scholars have discovered in the little town of Fodele the existence of a family called Theotokis and the ruins of a large house, still known as the Archonticon: the House of the Lords. They have sought to establish Fodele as El Greco's birthplace, and the University of Valladolid has even presented the town with a commemorative plaque set up in its main square. In all probability a branch of the Theotokis family did exist in Fodele, as there did in other parts of the island, for traces of a Marino Theotocopuli have been found in the village of Kenurio, and of a Mourinos Theotocopuli at Gortyna. But against all assumptions, however well founded, stands the testimony of El Greco himself. He states his birthplace unequivocally. And, in accordance with the psychology of all exiles, even voluntary ones, Domenico Theotocopuli was deeply attached to his origins. When signing his pictures, always in Greek lettering, he often placed the definition "Cretan" after his name; and when, towards the end of his life, he painted the series of Apostles, he depicted St. Paul with a letter to Titus, the first bishop of Crete, placed ostentatiously between his fingers, brandished like a manifesto, a letter glaring white against the metallic blue of his clothing. Like every man who has left his native land in early youth, who can never return and who has made his life elsewhere but nevertheless failed to root himself completely in foreign soil, El Greco cherished his memories and continually referred to his origins with an insistence reflecting the nostalgia of the homeless. When, after El Greco's death, Brother Hortensio Felix Paravicino collected together everything he knew regarding the fame of his friend, he stressed the following, probably often repeated, fact: "Crete gave him his life and his brushes." When he was questioned, in his capacity of interpreter, by the Tribunal of the Inquisition, El Greco explicitly stated that he "was born in the town of Candia." One hardly makes a mistake on such an occasion; even less does one deceive so formidable a tribunal.

"Candia is a beautiful, well-built town on the sea," said a German pilgrim at the end of the fifteenth century. "But for one who has never seen the like, the houses are strange, for they have no proper roofs, these being flat." The town with its terraced roofs recalled its former Arabic character, from the time when it was known as Khandak. It seemed more marked by that period of Saracen domination than by its ancient origins. But after the Fourth Crusade, Crete fell in 1204 to the "Most Illustrious Republic." The Venetians hastened to fortify the town on the landward side, and the same German pilgrim saw them still zealously constructing its defence walls. A citadel rose up at the mouth of the harbour, and a crenellated rampart enclosed the centre of the town, extending over the hill. Seen from the sea, it resembled one of those landscape backgrounds in Byzantine paintings which stretch upwards in height instead of receding in depth.

It suffered severely in the earthquake of 1508. Domenico Trevesan, who visited the island a few years later, saw the effects of the disaster: crumbled palaces, gutted houses—a sight so terrifying "that it could be likened to the Roman ruins."

After the catastrophe the town was rebuilt, but slowly and never completely. In 1549, when El Greco was eight years old, it was again shaken by an earthquake, which fissured the walls of the governmental

palaces built by the Venetians and revived the inhabitants' feeling
of insecurity and of a constant threat to their existence. A German
pilgrim who passed through Candia towards the middle of the sixteenth century was astonished by its poverty-stricken appearance and
by its houses, all very low except for the palaces of the nobles, "for
they have not enough beams to build with." The nobles themselves
allowed their homes to fall into ruin and retired to their huge estates
in the country. Moreover, as soon as they had sufficiently exploited the
soil and the serfs, they left Crete to enjoy the splendours of Venice,
until only the poorest descendants of the former settlers remained in
the island; these, although they still bore the great Venetian names of
Cornaro or Dandolo, were now mere peasants who had forgotten even
their mother tongue.

Venice needed Crete as a base for her ships, where they could re-
plenish their stores of fresh food and drinking water *en route* for
Egypt or Syria. They also took shelter there to repair damage or to
evade the pirates. In view of the island's importance Venice spent
200,000 ducats a year on its administration. But the Venetians despised the people they had subjugated. When trouble broke out in the
island and the Cretans proposed to send to Venice twenty experts,
known in the language of the day as "Sages," a minister of the Grand
Council mockingly asked: "Are there so many sages in Crete?" The
government of the island was modelled on that of the mother city,
with the Duke of Candia at its head and a few local variations in the
lower ranks, such as the official in charge of the mortality of livestock
(*officialis de morte animalium*), whose duty it was to prevent the
slaughter of cattle.

The laws promulgated were designed above all to benefit the Most
Illustrious Republic, such as that compelling the sale of all the corn
destined for the Venetian government and ships at a specified place
in the capital, in order to prevent a rise in prices. "The Cretans,"
stated a French traveller, "are such slaves to the Venetians that they
neither possess nor enjoy anything except that which the said masters
graciously concede to them."

Clear-sighted Venetians reported to the authorities the grievances
of the people and the abuses of the nobles, who had made the Cretans
"enemies of the very name of Venice." But in Venice the views of the
advocates of a strong-arm policy prevailed. Fra Paolo Sarpi recommended "that the Candians be treated like wild beasts, so that they
may not give free rein to their savage instincts." He particularly ad-

vised against arming them on the pretext that they might be useful in time of war. In fact the Cretans became so desperate that the whole population, except for the privileged persons, longed, according to one Venetian nobleman, for a change of government and, although the only other hands they could fall into were those of the Turks, they believed they could fare no worse under their tyrannical rule.

Not daring to arm the population, Venice sent troops to protect the island. Crete swarmed with foreign soldiers, volunteers rushed to its defence, Bulgarian, Armenian, Albanian, German and Czech mercenaries of the Republic. The foreigners sometimes settled there, but the Venetian soldiers thought only of returning to their own country.

The declining town sank into a state of neglect. Contemporary travellers unanimously deplored its filth. A main artery—the Corso— divided it into two, but the streets, for the most part narrow and tortuous, were choked with excrement and teeming with pigs which jostled passers-by and rummaged in the stinking garbage. Swarms of mosquitoes hung in the air, which reeked from the open sewers; even in cold weather they did not disappear as in other countries— according to the complaints of one exasperated traveller.

Throughout its decline something still lingered on from the heritage of the past, although the simple people no longer knew whether it was myth or reality. In the first place it was an awareness of their religious faith, made all the keener by the ever-present threat of assault from the Infidel. The coast was ceaselessly haunted by Mohammedan corsairs. In 1537 Kheyr-ed-Din Barbarossa succeeded in invading the island, but he was swiftly repulsed. Against the common peril the faithful united. Their two cults existed side by side and on occasion even intermingled. Behind this division lay the usual phenomenon of the influence exerted by a subject people over their conquerors. The descendants of those few hundred Venetian families who had occupied and colonized the island in 1204 allowed themselves to be rapidly imbued with the remains of Hellenic civilization; those living in the country spoke Greek like the rural population and often adopted even the Orthodox practices. When, in 1363, a revolt broke out against Venetian domination, it was not only a struggle against the oppression of foreign bureaucrats and for self-government, but also a fight for the equality of the two cults. This rebellion, which lasted two years, was led under the banner of St. Titus against the banner of St. Mark and ended in victory for the rebels. The former patron saint of the island ousted the apostolic protector of the Venetians and equal rights were granted to the two cults.

In the towns the Latin cult remained predominant. Government buildings, the palaces of the Venetian nobles, walls, and fountains bore the lion of St. Mark; there was a wealth of Latin inscriptions; the Catholic churches were vast and spacious, surmounted by tall belfries; the Greek churches, Byzantine in style, although numerous, were small and wretched. In the country, on the other hand, the Greek churches ruled unchallenged, sometimes set up inside natural grottoes. The countless monasteries were overcrowded, monks and coenobites formed whole settlements around reputedly miraculous grottoes, and throughout the countryside one could have sought in vain for Latin inscriptions or the lion of St. Mark. The Most Illustrious Republic constantly opposed the permanent establishment of a Greek bishop on the island. Yet the descendants of her former colonists, who had become Greek in speech, dress and religion, knew no better way of expressing their sense of peril, their anxiety for salvation, or sometimes their pride or economic rivalry than by building Orthodox churches or monasteries which, to the annoyance of the Italian Catholics, sprang up like mushrooms on all sides.

It was sometimes enough for Orthodox priests to show a purely formal submission to the Pope in order to be considered, along with their flocks, as Greek Catholics. But, even without this concession, they pursued their cult in close proximity. A Polish prince, passing through Candia on a pilgrimage, saw one day in the same church a Latin priest and a Greek pope officiating simultaneously at either side of the common altar.

One saint intimately united the two rites: the "Poverello" of Assisi. In one rustic church a ruined fifteenth-century fresco of pure Byzantine technique and faithfully following the Greek iconography depicted amongst others a large figure of St. Francis with a Latin inscription in Gothic lettering. The poor peasants of Crete offered ex-votos to St. Francis for the recovery of their kinsfolk and wrapped their sick sons in rough Franciscan homespun. The monastery of St. Francis in Candia was the most important and most celebrated of all the monasteries on the island. It was in its church that the schismatics, thanks to a special dispensation obtained from the Pope, held a service in his honour on his feast day, according to their own rite. The high walls of the monastery dominated all the other buildings in the town. Its sumptuous gateway anticipated the luxury of the altar, adorned with precious chalices, the work of Venetian goldsmiths. Cretan pride as well as piety fostered the cult of the saint. From this Franciscan monastery came the Cretan Pietro Filargo, who assumed the tiara in 1409 under the name of Alexander V. This Pope forgot neither his native island nor his monastery. He enlarged the church and showered the monastery with gifts, to which wealthy Cretans continuously added, partly out of devotion and partly to acquire some slight reflection of its ancient glory, for, the more drab and disappointing the present was, the more vividly they recalled the past.

The figure of the saint of Assisi dominated the childhood of El Greco—that great figure of reconciliation between believers divided by schism and a reminder, too, of an exceptional destiny. No saint was to be painted by El Greco so often, with such affection, almost with such frenzy, as St. Francis. It was as if he wanted to wrest from him the secret of his meditations, the mystery of his ecstasies. At each stage of his life El Greco returned to him as a man returns to a safe and familiar refuge. His vision of him was always the same, but, at the same time, different; and these effigies of the saint reflect the curves of his own evolution. There exist today over one hundred twenty paintings of St. Francis of Assisi by El Greco; they were doubtless much in demand, as if the simplehearted believers, like the connoisseurs, had felt that a particular bond of intimacy existed between the artist and his subject.

Apart from St. Francis another object of devotion united the two creeds which shared the island: the image of the Virgin in the cathedral in Candia. This cathedral, dedicated to St. Titus, was the proud possessor of relics of its patron saint, as well as those of St. Stephen, St. Martin, and St. Lucia, but its real glory was the miraculous image of the Virgin, worshipped by the faithful of both denominations, heaped with gifts by both the rich Venetians and the poor people of Crete. Rebuilt towards the middle of the fifteenth century, the cathedral endured the earthquakes and in 1544 was ravaged by a terrible fire, but the miraculous Virgin protected it and the holy relics, herself escaping from the flames. This famous icon of the *Messopanditissa* probably did not date from much earlier than the twelfth century, but its glory seemed to be of all time. It derived, in the purity of its Byzantine type, from some antique model, the first portrait of the Virgin, believed to have been painted by St. Luke. The *Messopanditissa* was one of the Cretans' most treasured possessions, and when the island was threatened it was taken for safety to Venice.

It was to this eternal Virgin, this miraculous Mother of God, victorious over the flames, that the infant Greco raised his eyes. The Cretans, like the Byzantine people down the ages, appealed to Virgins of the distant past—always the same ones, to whom their ancestors had prayed. The sacred images were not allowed to be altered by any human quality. The less they evoked either woman or mother, the less they resembled any of the faithful kneeling before them, the more they were venerated. Like the Byzantines, who had set aside the more intimate respresentations of the Virgin, such as that depicting her while suckling the Holy Child, their descendants in Crete chose for preference the *Glykophilousa,* the Virgin of Tenderness; the *Eleousa,* the Virgin of Pity; and the Virgin of the Passion, so popular in Crete, known as the *Cardiotissa.* The Latin and Greek churches alike had inherited the common and immutable artistic tradition; a church, even if built by the Venetians, would have seemed incomplete without its Byzantine elements.

Crete seems to have been too poor to allow herself the luxury of decoration in mosaic, or else her fresco painters were so skilled in their art that they gave complete satisfaction, for no traces of mosaics have been found save on the paved floors of the churches. The interiors, however, are wholly covered with frescoes, as if, from the thirteenth century onwards, these formed an integral part of each building. The frescoes, moreover, were all alike, so that it was said that if one saw one church, one had seen them all. Not only was the technique Byzantine in the churches of both cults, but also the iconography. Realism crept in shyly on the side, in the portraits of the founders— alone or with their families. Their features are barely given any individuality, less, one would say, through any lack of experience or skill than through a desire not to create too wide a divergence between the men depicted and the saints they worshipped. Their costumes, sometimes extravagant, are on the other hand painted with immense attention to detail: warriors armed with bows, belted with swords or daggers; women in white robes or in mourning.

Occasionally realism slipped into some lay model. Thus, in a representation of the Last Judgment which employed a several-centuries-old formula, the anonymous painter of a country church depicted a completely rustic hell with damned souls of lowly origin, whose sins were intelligible to the congregation—the tailor who has spoilt a suit of clothes being tormented by the devil; the peasant who has trespassed on a neighbour's field and fallen under the plough bestridden by the figure of evil; the mother who has refused to suckle her children having her breasts bitten by snakes.

In these humble attempts Cretan art reflected, with the backwardness of its provincial status, the tendency which had appeared in Byzantine art two centuries earlier; that new tide surging towards realism whilst at the same time safeguarding tradition, as if it were menaced and could only survive by taking fresh root in the lives of the people. This Cretan art was not, however, given its most complete expression in the island itself, perhaps too poor, too exhausted, or too subjugated by a foreign civilization to be still capable of autonomous manifestations. It was at Mistra, the ancient capital of the Peloponnese, that the school was born which took its name from the island or, rather, from one artist. Theophanes the Greek, a native of Crete, the presumed painter of the pictures in the monastery of the Peribleptos, built in the second half of the fourteenth century. Another artist who became the true leader of this school, Theophanes of Crete, worked with the help of his son, Simon, in the monastery on Mt. Athos towards the middle of the sixteenth century. Strangely, at this time, the artistic activity of the island itself was suddenly interrupted, almost cut short, for no known reason, material or otherwise. There is no fresco in Crete dating from the second half of this century. Was the habit abruptly lost? Had the island's impoverishment suddenly made itself felt? But at the same time Cretan artists went to work abroad, as did Theophanes and his son, Michele Damascenos, Zorzi of Crete, and the prolific Andrea Rico of Candia.

This migratory movement, this desire to go abroad, sprang from a dual source: ambition to leave a threatened land and the seeking of assured success. The poor Cretans went to work abroad before they were forced to flee from their native island. Artistic activity ceased in Crete at a moment when the threat of invasion was neither more serious nor more acute than during the preceding years, when the painting of frescoes flourished in every Cretan church of both cults. What was the contribution of this art which departed rather because it was needed elsewhere than because it was obliged to do so? What were the teachings of that school which was also El Greco's when he first began? A contribution hard to trace in a transplantation as radical as that which El Greco underwent, through his successive stages of assimilation. But a definite contribution it was, and one very evident to his contemporaries; a contribution which El Greco never ceased to emphasize when talking to his friends. For a time debate regarding it revolved round a comma in Paravicino's famous line. Should it read: "Crete gave him life, and his brushes Toledo"? Or should the comma be placed before the word "Toledo"? But Toledo, at the time when El Greco settled there, had neither a tradition nor artistic activity, nor a school capable of passing on its teachings to the newcomer. These brushes absent from Spain were meanwhile at work in Crete and spreading throughout the world the heritage of their tradition. A thousand-year-old tradition, simply altered to become more convincing, to establish its enduring quality.

Cretan art, even if expressed through frescoes, was an art of icon painting applied to architectural decoration. Its spiritual roots reached far back into that struggle in which the iconoclasts opposed worship of the saints; into that affirmation of the Council of Nicoea which decreed that "whoever worships an image worships the person it represents." All the main religious and philosophical trends of Byzantium supported the zeal of simple worshippers, the neo-Platonic contribution of the pseudo-Dionysius the Areopagite, who maintained that all things perceived by the eye impress themselves more strongly on the soul, and likewise the profession of faith of the patriarch Nicephores: "Things seen lead better to belief than things heard."

This power attributed to images, this quality of maximum efficacy, was supported by the belief in the divine origin of the effigy addressed. Those first paintings incorporated into the cult—such as the Virgin attributed to St. Luke, said to have been sent from Jerusalem to Pulcheria by the Empress Eudokia—"were not made by the hand of man." The icon of Edessa was supposed to be the cloth on which Jesus imprinted his features—the *mandylion*—the Holy Face impressed on the sudary of St. Veronica. To make any alteration in a model of such origins would have been inconceivable, and the Cretan school remained particularly true to the purity of the tradition. Even when they widened the scope of their representations of the divine, even when they varied their subjects, they maintained the old formal austerity, with the full frontal position of the figures, the two-dimensional presentation, and the hieratic gestures. This school was so opposed to all Western influence that it seemed to ignore the existence of any world of form other than its own. At the time when Theophanes of Crete was painting his frescoes on Mt. Athos—towards 1546 —the West had experienced the great revolution of the Renaissance, the discovery of man and of space, the exploration of reality, and was even moving on to another stage. In that Italy so short a distance away Leonardo da Vinci had long since died, while Michelangelo had just completed his "Last Judgment"; and in that Venice to which the little island was subject Titian was painting his "Ecce Homo" and "Danaë." The hermetic world of Byzantine formalism had deliberately returned to the past, resolutely denying the present.

The Cretan school, a prisoner of inherited forms, employed all its inventive subtlety to perfect a technique which distinguished it immediately from every other Byzantine school. It was characterized by the minuteness of detail, the calligraphy of the drawing, and the technique of "open painting," which, instead of filling in all the outlines with paint, left the initial stages visible between the successive layers, between the thin and close-set brush strokes laid on in parallel lines. But above all it shone through its sumptuous colouring: that rare quality of precious stone or enamel, glowing crimsons, red-browns, deep lilacs, made all the more intense by the way in which the colour now plunged into shadow, now emerged into the light, to produce its whole iridescent effect. As the years rolled by, the memory of this pictorial effect became ever keener with El Greco. He himself used it frequently, in the same way as a man recovers an ancient heritage.

The influence of the Cretan school was not, however, confined to a partially adopted technical process. Its particular contribution, neglected at the outset, dwelt on in him, submerged by other interests, until the day when it was to coincide with his own evolution. These qualities which he took so long to recognize were, nevertheless, merely those self-same ones to which those Cretan painters who, during his youth, had left for other lands owed their success. Italian art had long since cast off the last shackles of Byzantinism, but the Cretan painters found an eager clientele by perpetuating a thousand-year-old tradition at the very time when the Byzantine Empire was collapsing. With the fall of Byzantium this diffusion grew in importance, as if even the humblest of these artists had a special message to pass on.

Venice remained easily accessible for the Cretan painters. They took their icons there, for the most part those so-called "Black" Virgins, as dark as if they had been given a patina by the centuries, which earned them in Italy the name of Madonna painters—*madonneri*. These primitive and archaic icons seemed valueless as works of art, especially in the eyes of those giants who dominated artistic life. Yet at the same time Titian was insisting that the old mosaics in St. Mark's be destroyed and replaced with works by his own followers (El Greco was already in Venice), the Cretan painters Andrea Rico of Candia,

Michele Damascenos, and many other *madonneri,* often anonymous, found a wide field of activity. The Orthodox Greeks, many of whom had fled to Venice, evidently demanded these icons, to which they were accustomed. But the clientele of the *madonneri* did not consist of the followers of the Greek cult alone. The rich patrons, like the common people, gave their admiration to the grandiose works of the masters who were the pride of Venice and the envy of the whole world; in the sumptuous churches they knelt before glittering and recognizable saints; but at home they prayed to those strange "Black Virgins" who seemed to offer a surer pledge of intercession on behalf of the faithful. When it came to their private devotions, not only the common people, but also the wealthy patricians and the better educated preferred these to the fair, largely naked flesh of their accustomed Madonnas. In many of the inventories of noble families the list of works of art includes a "Candian picture of Our Lady" (*quadro de Nostra Dama Candioto*).

The popularity of these Cretan artists owed much to that anxiety which had taken hold of men's souls in the second half of the century, an anguish which fissured the world, a need for a faith, for a fervour which would triumph over doubt, a yearning for stability in all things. But it was also caused to some extent by a literary craze, to the prestige enjoyed by everything that derived from the Greek heritage. The gilded youths of Venice, the idle nobles in search of distraction, strove to talk Greek among themselves. The *madonneri,* too, benefited from this fashion, and when they signed their pictures, unlike the Byzantine artists who never appended their signatures, they did so most frequently in Greek, just as Domenico Theotocopuli was to do as soon as he began to work in Venice.

The Renaissance had commenced with the revelation of the antique, which for its art was a road to realism. It had assimilated the formal elements of the classical vision, but it was only after the fall of the Byzantine Empire that, according to one of the best historians of this period, Byzantium really bestowed its intellectual heritage on the West. It was in the first thirty years of the sixteenth century that Hellenism finally conquered Europe. In this expansion of a materially vanished but spiritually victorious world, Crete, that Byzantine enclave under Venetian rule, played a considerable part. Forced to choose between the Latin culture of her rulers and a most ancient tradition, she opted in favour of her Byzantine heritage. "The authors of all good sources and disciplines which we may see to-day have for the main part come from Greece," wrote Pierre Belon. But this intellectual elite was sparse, the people uneducated, and there was no university in the island to enable the young men to pursue their studies. The universities had been replaced by religious colleges. Their teaching cannot have been inferior to the general level of the day: one Cretan monk, Joseph Bryenna, born at Mistra, who at the beginning of the fifteenth century won an immense reputation as a scholar and orator, became official preacher to the court. He reorganized the educational system at Constantinople and, after failing in his efforts to achieve religious union, returned to end his days on the island. The basis of all teaching, for the colleges of both cults, was Greek. It was in one of these religious foundations that Domenico Theotocopuli learned to write Greek, in a copper-plate style of almost ostentatious elegance. To this college he also owed his wide culture, the culture of an erudite man rather than that of an adolescent obsessed by the visual and absorbed by his artistic vocation. It was the culture of the son of a well-to-do family, of a young man with varied interests, the leisure for serious reading, and the means to acquire the books he wanted. He appears to have taken these books, or at least a number of them, with him on his wanderings, on his migrations from country to country. His library, an inventory of which was drawn up after his death, contained many Greek books. His son listed twenty-six of these, and the selection, doubtless a fragmentary one, a mere fraction of what he possessed in his youth, offers a guide to the intellectual debt which he owed to his native island. Among them was that indispensable working equipment of every educated man—a lexicon. The foundation of his religious education also derived from Greek sources: his Bible (both Old and New Testaments), which he knew so well, was a Greek edition in five volumes. There were also the Lives of the Apostles in Greek, a work which the creator of the *Apostolados* must often have consulted; the Sermons of St. John Chrysostom; the Homilies of St. Basil; a collection of the latter's ethical sermons; and a life of St. Justin Martyr. There was also a publication in Greek on the Council of Trent, one of those many comforting writings which reaffirmed the faith of men distressed by the religious revolt and steered them between the reefs of controversy.

In this list, which, incidentally, was drawn up in haste, one is particularly struck by one name, to which no details are attached—Artemidorus. Was this the geographer who left fragmentary writings on aspects of the earth? We have no other indication of El Greco's curiosity about the problems of the world's development. It is much

more likely that this refers to Artemidorus of Ephesus, a contemporary
of Marcus Aurelius, and his work *Oneikritis*—the interpretation of
dreams. It was part of the Byzantine tradition to attach a great importance to dreams. This passion for piercing the veil of the future was
a heritage from the East, a passion nurtured on a variety of superstitions, on a belief in oracles, and consultations with astrologers and
seers. Several other keys to dreams in current use in Byzantium were
widespread among Greek-speaking peoples. But this book by Artemidorus was especially popular in Crete: the two manuscripts now in
Venice were copied by a refugee from Byzantium towards the middle
of the fifteenth century in Crete, while he was "dying there of hunger."
The key to dreams contained a host of immemorial symbols: its interpretations had the ambiguity of the Delphic oracle. For they changed
their meanings according to the sex, age, and social status of the
dreamer. It needed all the subtlety of the Greek dialecticians to draw
a specific interpretation from them, but this subtlety El Greco possessed. The book must have been familiar to him; he was doubtless a
man who had vivid dreams and who sought for a meaning to apparently incoherent visions.

As a man of general education, El Greco possessed a Homer, a
Euripides, and a Lucian in two volumes, together with Aesop's *Fables*.
It would be quite natural for him to take an interest in the human body
—the interest of a painter, no doubt, but perhaps also that of a man
of delicate constitution, for besides a Hippocrates in Greek, he owned
a volume in Italian entitled *The Art of Preserving the Health*. Stranger,
in an artist's library, seems the presence of works by the great masters
of Greek eloquence, Isocrates and Demosthenes; but those who knew
El Greco well in later years have stressed his verbal facility, his dia-
lectical subtlety, and even when he was a physically weakened old man
Pacheco recorded his mental acuity and taste for striking expressions—
agudos dichos. Particularly remarkable in El Greco was his pronounced
interest in history. His library included Josephus' *War of the Jews*,
Arrian's *Anabasis of Alexander*, Xenophon, and Plutarch's *Lives*.
Pacheco described him as "a great philosopher" and in his library
philosophy—a neat guiding thread throughout his spiritual life—played
a large part. He possessed the *Moral Philosophy*, also by Plutarch; two
copies of Aristotle's *Politics* and also his *Physics*. But there was no book
by Plato, so one might well believe that in his youth he had come under
the influence of some Aristotelian master, for he also owned the works
of Philoponos, the great commentator on Aristotle, here listed under

the title of *The Books of the Soul*. His philosophical preoccupations, however, in so far as they are revealed by his choice in books, finally led him in an opposite direction, as is made plain by the presence of "St. Dionysius," represented by two works, including *The Celestial Hierarchy*. This Neo-Platonist turned Christian wrote under the celebrated name of Dionysius, the only member of the Areopagus whom St. Paul had succeeded in converting—thus creating perhaps the first resounding case of a fraud in the history of letters. This man who so strongly affected the spiritual life of Byzantium seems also to have exerted a great influence over El Greco. The mystique of the pseudo-Dionysius the Areopagite, who was to nurture Byzantine theology on Neo-Platonic ideas, must have left a strong mark on the minds of young men torn between a love of tradition and the need for renewal, by reconciling the revered paganism of the antique with the strict demands of dogma, and the lucidity of the Greek philosophers with the tendency towards spiritual abandon. His Neo-Platonic *mystique* did not demonstrate truth, but laid it bare beneath all the symbols.

Once outlined, this thread of evolution seems to have been followed through to the end by El Greco, for the only philosopher of his time whose work he possessed was Francisco Patrizzi, a passionate advocate of Neo-Platonism.

The progress of El Greco's thought, as it appears through his choice of books, was necessarily to lead him to repudiate the dogmas of Aristotle, on whom he seems to have been nurtured at the outset: first he rejected only his theory, but later on the contribution of the classical philosophers altogether. Pacheco heard him with surprise rise up "against Aristotle and all the antique world," and this confirmed him in his opinion that Domenico Theotocopuli was a "singular" man.

Yet this repudiation was merely a form of contradictory dialogue with his own youth, a way of disposing of his first spiritual attainments. This early knowledge he acquired was important, perhaps decisive. At the moment when Domenico Theotocopuli left his native island, he was in full possession of it. It is not known when he left Crete—left forever. In fact nothing is known of him, nothing of his family, of the impressions of his childhood, of the vicissitudes of his youth. Nothing of his origins apart from what he admitted himself, and he was sparing of personal information, jealous of his privacy, extremely sensitive over any incursion into his private affairs. But his life, reconstructed backwards, seems to have flowed from that dual spring which nourished his youth, a burning faith, the faith of threatened men, and the spiritual heritage of a civilization which had foundered but which in so doing had illuminated the world.

Crete, at the time of El Greco's departure, was a mere memory of the past, a subjugated and discontented province, a vast agricultural estate with scarce, deserted towns. She offered no future for an ambitious young man whose vocation seemed already decided upon. It was perhaps the migration of the *madonneri* which showed him the way to Venice, but it was neither in pursuit of this outmoded art nor in search of a modest career that he set out for the unknown. He had his eye resolutely fixed on the future. Like so many other Candians of good family, he wanted his share of the splendours of Venice; he also wanted fame and fortune. He wanted to win these by the means which Venice offered to her sons, at the price of assimilation. He was a Venetian subject, but his physique most likely, and certainly his manner, marked him so strongly as a foreigner that he was from the start called "The Greek." It was an Oriental who set out to conquer the West, in full awareness of himself and of the task he had set himself.

CHAPTER
TWO
A YOUNG
MAN
OF MERIT

ACCORDING to Vasari, "Titian has been favoured
beyond the lot of most men, and has received from
Heaven only favours and blessings."

Just as Michelangelo dominated Rome through the power of his
genius, his single-mindedness of purpose, and also by his longevity,
Titian ruled over the artistic life of Venice. A young artist such as
Domenico Theotocopuli was bound to make first for the studio of the
great old man, whose reputation had spread all over Europe. Foreigners thronged there, talented artists who were anxious to assert themselves, young noblemen whose ambition was to shine in the master's
reflected glory, and even great ladies.

Domenico Theotocopuli was about twenty years old when he arrived
in Venice. The immigration from Crete had been on the increase for
some time. Within a century the small colony of about five hundred
Cretans had grown to fourteen thousand, the majority of whom were
of Orthodox faith. The colony included many painters, several of
whom were called "Greco" or "delle Greche." A certain Domenico
delle Greche had also been a pupil of Titian's for some time. The majority, however, worked in those studios which preserved the ancient
Byzantine art, with a few timid concessions to Occidental perspective.
Domenico Theotocopuli apparently did not mix much with his compatriots. His name does not appear on any register, neither on those of
the religious community—he did not belong to the Orthodox faith—
nor in the Cretan archives, which were partially transferred to Venice
when the Turks conquered the island. He was absolutely determined

to adapt himself to the Western world. He was open to every influence, responded to every source of inspiration, took advantage of everything which he thought could be of use to him. Everything he encountered he absorbed like a sponge. Perhaps it was because in his beginnings he stripped himself so completely of all individuality that he was later to develop such an entirely uncompromising character.

The multitude of influences reflected in his first works has led some to wonder whether he was in fact an apprentice in the master's studio. Yet his first patron referred to him as "Titian's disciple" and the influences which can be detected in his work rule out any further doubt in spite of their variety. Still, even if he submerged himself in this, for him so novel, world of art to the extent that only strongly developed, firm characters can when they decide to efface themselves and completely abandon their own personalities, he could not allow himself to be dominated by a single man or by one creative conception alone, even if it were imposed upon him with such an impact, by such a forceful reputation, and such calculated principles as those of Titian.

There was a fundamental discrepancy between the two men, made the more poignant by the difference in their ages and the uncertain life of a homeless emigrant. When Domenico Theotocopuli arrived in Venice, Titian was at least eighty and more likely eighty-three years old. But old age seemed to have no hold over him; it was as if his power had been crystallized for all time, braving decline and death. In fact nothing short of an epidemic of the plague, which ravaged Venice and claimed fifty thousand victims, managed to remove him, together with his son, when he was on the threshold of his centenary. El Greco saw him as he had painted himself at various periods in his life—portraits in which the essentials of his physiognomy had barely changed. A solid block of a man, as if sculpted from the rock of his native mountains. A wide forehead, not the dome of a thinker, but a still-smooth wall reflecting concentrated energy. In the self-portrait in the Prado (Plate 2), painted shortly after this time, the temples are growing faintly hollow, but the carriage of the head is still erect, and apparently so by nature, not as the result of a momentary effort. The whole strength of the man lies in the keenness of his sight. The eyes, still broadly carved under the projecting eyebrows, hold an eternally eager and scrutinizing glance, a look which—according to Titian's own admission—had never been cast on a woman without laying bare her sensual and lascivious qualities. His sensuality is revealed by his mouth: the lips are those of a pleasure-seeker who has never denied himself any worldly joy. Even in the late portrait, in which the mouth sinks in as if the teeth were gone, the lips are still firm. The strongly modelled head of the ageing man is dominated by the aquiline nose, revealing his passion for hoarding, his obstinacy and his stubbornness. It is the hooked nose of a miser, whose sensuality, however, just saved him from meanness. The whole is held together by a long, silky beard flowing down over his breast and, even if the hair is thinning at the temples, this beard retains all its opulence. The hands complete the impression of triumphant strength; they are the hands of a peasant or woodcutter, resting weightily before him, the fingers so strong that they could easily crush not only paints but a bar of iron. The ravages of time on this face, the deep wrinkles, the sagging flesh, are but the wear and tear of hard work; the exhaustion that the face reflects is that of creative labour. No spiritual disquiet has touched those features, no doubts impaired that mordant glance. It is the face of a man who has had to pay the price but who has succeeded in reaching his goal.

It was given to him to live in an age which looked kindly on success. He came down from his mountains to Venice, a city that knew, better than any other in the world, how to make the most of its power and enjoy all the opportunities that power offered. There developed a rare understanding between the man, his desires, his extraordinary means of achieving them and the atmosphere of his environment. His ambition was as inordinate as that of the still sovereign Republic. He became enamoured of luxury, of the external trappings of his rank, equal to that of a Venetian patrician. Yet he was as calculating as those merchants who had given the Republic her greatness. He gave himself up to the pleasures of the day without remorse or regret, but he was also influenced by that slightly pagan indulgence of Venice which captivated all foreigners.

Yet, towards the middle of the century, Venice ceased to be an uncontested empire. Since the discovery of America and of the sea route to India her unique position as mistress of the seas had been shaken. Her decline was slow—a gradual crumbling in which she herself did not entirely believe. But since 1540, when she lost her third war against the Turks and was deprived of several of her Eastern colonies, she had resigned her political and commercial sovereignty. Her somewhat barbaric splendour, however, still gave the impression that nothing had changed. According to a French traveller Venice was "still the most populous city one is like to see, with the most beautiful shops offering the greatest variety of merchandise one is like to find."

But it was not only material power the survival of which was confined to an artificial façade. Something closely connected with it, a perfect harmony with the age, the ability to enjoy worldly things, was crumbling as well. The shadows were lengthening on the horizon; they were weighing heavily on men's souls. It was the hour of the Council of Trent, of spiritual mobilization in defence of a threatened Church. Venice was less affected by that great anguish than the other artistic centres. The throbbing anxieties of the age seemed to be appeased at her gates, at that opening onto the marriage of heaven and earth in a glow of opalescent light. Conflicts lost some of their bitterness in the face of that lust for life which persisted as if by the force of inertia. But the century had suffered a severe shock, and all the charms of life in Venice were unable to remedy it. Titian, too, felt that something had changed. He was not a man to speculate over the problems of the next world; he was far too preoccupied by those of his own. He suffered no spiritual upheaval; he changed none of his ways. No scruples were to prevent him, for example, from completing an allegorical painting begun for Alphonso of Ferrara, a painting of a nude woman imploring the protection of the goddess Minerva, by transforming it into "Religion Saved by Spain" in fulfilment of an important commission from his powerful patron, Philip II. Thus Minerva became Spain, the nude the symbol of religion, the Neptune the Turk. Yet, although he was barely aware of the transformation which art was undergoing and far from being a moralist, he more or less consciously responded to the anxieties of the age. He was a painter, no more and no less; his way of response was to change his manner of painting. His new manner reflected the innate perplexities of his time, a new vision of things more temporary and fragmentary than hitherto. His old admirers, the conservatives of his age, were horrified. Vasari voiced their disappointment:

His mode of procedure in these last-mentioned works is very different from that pursued by him in those of his youth, the latter being executed with a certain care and delicacy which renders the work equally effective, whether seen at a distance or examined closely; while those of the later period, executed with bold strokes and dashes, can scarcely be distinguished when the observer is near them, but if viewed from the proper distance they appear perfect.

The Spaniards who saw his latest works to arrive at the court of Philip II were also shocked by this new manner, and Francisco

Pacheco, in his *Dialogue on Painting,* spoke of these *"borrones"* (thick blobs of paint) of Titian's—the same expression he was later to employ when defining El Greco's manner.

Domenico Theotocopuli's arrival in Venice more or less coincided with this change in Titian's style. With his technique his colours changed as well. The shadows oppressing the world seemed to darken his palette. The pale tints identified with the light of Venice, the reds saturated with gold, the strident blues, the sumptuosity of the velvets, the flashing silks, that voluptuous greed for colour gave way to more sparing and twilight values. As a man of visual impressions, Titian achieved by means of form and surface, instead of through content, a growing intensity, a foreknowledge of the drama which was in fact alien to him.

His personal life, however, continued, as in the past, as if nothing had changed. He still lived in the large house into which he had settled some thirty years before, at Biri Grande, opposite Murano. His big studio on the first floor had a view over the sea and its boundless horizon. And on clear days, looking landward, he could even see the distant peaks of the Dolomites reaching up to the sky. There was a garden in front of the house in which an old, sombre tree raised black, twisted limbs against the iridescent clouds. Titian painted this tree as one paints a familiar face, whenever a scene of martyrdom or violence required a tragic note. The dramatic atmosphere which could be produced by the writhing branches of a single tree outlined against a stormy sky must have remained in El Greco's memory up to the end of his days, and it was also to Titian that he was altogether indebted for his feeling for landscapes, a feeling quite alien to him during his Byzantine training.

In fact he had everything to learn; and also everything to forget. The Cretan artists painted almost without exception on panels and in tempera. The technique of oil painting revealed to him undreamed-of possibilities, a new creative process with a different rhythm. For him the manner in which Titian painted was a revelation in itself. Titian, who was barely affected by religious conflicts and spiritual upheavals, took his profession more seriously than anything else in the world. It was for him a permanent struggle with his material, a frantic, almost tragic struggle, the only one he had ever known. Although nothing is known of El Greco's personal life while he was working in Titian's studio—he was much too obscure a young man to arouse any interest —we do know in full detail what he saw while watching the master at

work. This was described by Palma Giovane as follows: "He begins
by applying to the canvas an indistinguishable mass of paint, which
serves as a background for the figures to be modelled. He makes decisive strokes with a brush thick with paint, sometimes a scumble of
pure 'terra rossa' which serves him, so to speak, as a half-tint; sometimes a layer of white. Then, with the same brush saturated with red,
black or yellow, he models the relief of the flesh, sketching in with
four brush strokes the promise of a rare body. He turns his paintings
to the wall and leaves them there, sometimes for months, without
looking at them. And when he wants to resume work on them, he ex-
amines the canvases with rigorous care, as if they were his mortal
enemies, to see whether he can find any faults in them. And if he dis-
covers something which disagrees with his delicate conception, he
treats his canvas as a benevolent surgeon treats his patient, removing
some tumour or growth of the flesh, or straightening an arm. . . .
The final garnishing, the last retouching, consists for him in rubbing
the surface of the flesh tones with quivering fingers, or bringing them
close together with half-tints and fusing them into a harmonious whole.
Or sometimes, by rubbing with his fingers, he applies a stroke of
shadow to some corner . . . some glaze of red, like a small drop of
blood, to intensify a superficial expression."

All this was very new and disconcerting for the young Cretan. His
inherited technique was a fluid and supple way of painting; he preferred thin brushes which could follow the drawn contours, whereas
he saw his master handling brushes "as thick as brooms." None of these
lessons was lost on him, however, even if he could not assimilate them
all at once: neither those patches of independent colour which, from a
distance, looked perfect, nor even those drops of blood, those reds
rubbed in, which were later to be found in El Greco's paintings and
which render the flesh almost transparent. At that time these technical
refinements were still beyond him. There was too much for him to
learn. Nevertheless some rare indications prove that he had the will
to succeed. He tried everything. Like a good pupil, he strove to copy
his master. In actual fact he was never to be a faithful copyist of anyone
but himself. His own particular quality was always to shine through his
work, almost without his knowing it. But in his beginnings he was so
undecided that the copies attributed to him are neither faithful render-
ings of the originals nor endowed with a sufficiently distinctive personal
style to enable one to establish their authenticity. The "Mater Dolorosa" at Lugano (Thyssen Collection), the "Portrait of a Woman" in

the Contini Bonacossi Gallery, and the "Portrait of a Boy" in Roberto
Longhi's collection at Bologna, all attributed to El Greco by August
L. Mayer, could all have been copied after Titian's originals by any
other of the master's pupils. The "Portrait of an Unknown Man," in
Vienna, mentioned by Cossio as El Greco's work, painted in Titian's
early manner, a portrait of a pale, red-bearded, Nordic type, with that
fragmentary Latin inscription which seems to attribute it to El Greco,
is even more alien to him. The first entirely authentic attribution is
that of a drawing in the Print Room in Munich (Plate 8). The sheet
bears the name of Domenico Greco and an indication that it belonged
to Vasari. It is a copy of Michelangelo's sculpture "The Day." The
young Cretan must have realized that, in order to acquire a strict foundation in drawing, he would have to turn elsewhere than to his aged
master. Michelangelo, after meeting Titian in Rome, himself revealed
this weakness by saying to Vasari that "the manner and colouring of
that artist pleased him greatly, but that it was a pity the Venetian did
not study drawing more, for if this artist had been as aided by art and
knowledge of design as he was by nature, more especially in imitating
life, he would have produced works which none could surpass."

The sculpture copied by the young El Greco was not the marble
monument in Florence, but a small model distinguished by the fact
that its left foot was missing. The drawing is notable for the seriousness with which the young man pursued his apprenticeship, his determination to seek what he lacked from varied sources. It is also a
valuable chronological indication, a landmark on the uncertain road
of his youth.

The model of "The Day" was at that time in Venice, where it was
sold to a Bolognese dealer on May 20, 1563. The drawing shows the
young Cretan already in full possession of everything he could learn
from Western technique. The lines are clear and sharp, drawn force-
fully by a confident hand. But it was not only technique which El
Greco had assimilated. He had also fathomed the feeling of movement,
that movement in spirals which enlivens Michelangelo's sculptures,
that sense of resilient strength flowing from muscle to muscle. Greco
had left far behind him the hieratic saints of his native land, who knew
only an upward surge, who existed but never developed. This education could not have been completed in a short time. El Greco must already have spent several years in Venice when the opportunity arose
for him to copy this model before it was sold.

He continued to look for what was to become the elements of his future work in as many, often contradictory, directions as possible. He sensed that Titian's art, despite its grandeur, had it limitations; that it had ceased to express fully the aspirations of his time. The various artistic trends of that period display a similar impatience to El Greco's; they were all variants of a single thirst for something new.

The grand manner of religious paintings, with their frozen formalism, their heroic postures, their demigods which might today be holy martyrs, tomorrow mythological lovers, appears hollow in spite of their crowded compositions. One trend of the time introduced the new element of anecdotal painting in order to humanize pictorial art through everyday reality. This trend, which had its origin in Flemish painting, with its predilection for depicting familiar details and still-lifes became widespread in Italy, particularly through Jacopo da Ponte and his family. These men worked together in their studio at Bessano with the diligence of good craftsmen and with considerable success. The wealth of Venetian forms blends badly with the attention to minute detail; the grandiose arrangement of the composition, designed to be embraced in a single glance, accords ill with the scattered rendering of a story, each detail of which is intended to be read in succession. But the picturesque costumes, the ground strewn with animals and homely objects, the nocturnal lighting transforming things all too familiar diverted a public already satiated with pictorial perfection, and the works of the Bassani were much in demand both in Italy and abroad.

This intrusion of the element of reality and the anecdotal must have particularly baffled an Oriental brought up on the negation of everyday motifs. Perhaps these elements in the work of the Bassani attracted him all the more, because he found them not only alien, but even adverse, in his early beginnings. He was to introduce them into his very first paintings, only to eliminate them later on as something he was unable to assimilate. The influence of the Bassani is so obvious that it has led to the thesis (for which there is, however, no factual support) that El Greco paid a prolonged visit to their studio at Bassano. During the years which he is supposed to have spent there, between 1562 and 1569, an undeniable change took place in Jacopo da Ponte's style. A new influence was at work, which fined down the plump forms, elongated the hitherto squat figures, endowing them with flowing movements and precious gestures. It would be most tempting to conjecture an interplay of reciprocal influences; technical achievements imparted by an accomplished master, familiar with all the mysteries of his craft, in exchange for a spiritual deepening contributed by a disciple thirty years younger than himself. But in fact this spiritualization, this elongation which seemed to relieve Bassano's figures of their heavy materialism, was purely formal. It was neither dictated by a new spiritual need, nor was it the outcome of a change of ideology.

It was another trend of the time, and not the hypothetical presence of a young foreigner in the Bassani studio, which caused this change in their style. Among the many artists of that age in search of some form of escapism there was one group known under the vague name of Mannerists. The origin and inspiration of Mannerism were purely cerebral. As so often happens in times of unrest, it is the intellect which recovers first and, by abandoning the overfamiliar, paves the way for a reasoned transformation towards the unexpected. It was, in fact, a new idiom and not a new content. Parmigianino, who influenced Bassano, and his numerous imitators introduced those silhouettes elongated out of all proportion, those figures seemingly bent by a non-existent wind, those too small heads affectedly borne on overlong necks, those undulating arms, those too slender hands with outspread fingers grasping at space with feverish gestures. This canon of elongation must have been particularly familiar to the young Cretan. *The Guide to Painting* elaborated by the monk, Dionysius of Fourna, taught the Byzantine disciples "that the body of a man should be nine heads high," whereas the normal proportion is one to seven.

El Greco himself came under the influence of the Italian Mannerists, but more indirectly, with delayed results, and this influence was confined to the most external elements of Italian Mannerism. Their path was not the one he was seeking on his quest for Western vision. If Titian's frank sensuality was alien to him, he was even more bewildered by the vaguely erotic refinement of the Mannerists, a kind of frigid eroticism.

There was, however, one painter in Venice whose art would seem to be most akin to El Greco's and whose influence over him must have come first and foremost. Giacomo Robusti, known as "Il Tintoretto," was his elder by twenty years. He also had worked in Titian's studio, but not for long. His fierce independence rebelled against the firm hold which the aged master tried to maintain over his disciples. When El Greco arrived in Venice, Tintoretto was already a famous painter. The son of a simple dyer, whose profession became his byname, he pursued his aims with full consciousness and lucidity, with the obsession of a bourgeois who seemed to deny the frantic quality of his art.

This "furioso," as he was also called, knew exactly what he wanted
and how to attain it. His ambition was to reconcile Michelangelo's
power with Titian's pictorial richness. One of those studio stories which
are more convincing than the truth has it that he inscribed in huge
letters in his studio, as his working motto, "Titian's colouring and
Michelangelo's design." This ambition of his became so exacerbated
that he made an offer to the Prior of Santa Maria dell' Orto to paint a
"Last Judgment" for the chancel of his church for 100 ducats. He was
quite uninterested in financial gain and only spurred on by his desire
to compete with the giant of the Sistine Chapel. In fact he was close
enough to Michelangelo in his violence of temperament, but with him
it was only a pictorial violence in which he was not spiritually involved.
He is revealed as such by his self-portrait, described by one historian as
"the face of a man who is terribly determined but at the same time indifferent." With him everything was the result of meditation and calculation, both his passion for innovation and his frenzied pursuit of
originality. This visionary who with breathless impatience covered
endless yards of canvas on which everything was entangled—bodies
projected through space, stormy lights, violent foreshortenings of perspective directing all movement into an abyss—was at heart a realist,
because (as Fosca, one of his most penetrating biographers, has said)
he was not voluptuous. In this he was a man of his age; he wanted to
touch the hearts of believers by his religious paintings, by depicting
sacred subjects with the utmost possible realism. To this end he used
the charm of the familiar, that epic trivality which heralded the
baroque.

About the time El Greco arrived in Venice, Tintoretto experienced
an inner evolution which expressed itself, as with Titian, by a darken-
ing of his palette. He passed from what has been called his "golden
manner" to his "green manner." Reality became dimmed in this
crepuscular light, but it lost nothing of its heavy material substance. A
broad green ray of light, slanting down across his canvas, seems as
tangible as a beam of wood catapulted through the abyss in the background. Apart from this predilection for the dramatic there is no deep
affinity between Tintoretto and El Greco. And even Tintoretto's rendering of the dramatic differs fundamentally from that which was
later, much later, to haunt Domenico Theotocopuli. With Tintoretto
the miraculous seems to break into men's lives, crashing down amidst
the drabness of everyday existence. The miracle becomes flesh, the invisible assumes substance. But El Greco, apart from his early efforts,

never sought to give it the solid density of reality. The supernatural
does not crash down on men, but dissolves beings of flesh and blood
from within, melts them into invisibility. The creative temperaments
of the two men were as divergent as their aims; they were even antagonistic. El Greco's borrowings from Tintoretto were but formal
ones. They are very much in evidence in his early years, and so numerous that they have led to the belief that he worked for some time in
Tintoretto's studio as well. That he knew Tintoretto's studio is beyond
doubt. It was there that he saw those wax models, made by Tintoretto
himself, suspended by strings from the ceiling and lit by a lamp. It was
from Tintoretto that he must have borrowed a similar procedure: he
too made use of sculptured models to the end of his life. But there is
no reason to believe that he was his pupil; no eyewitness ever mentioned his working in Tintoretto's studio. Nevertheless his borrowings
are precise and definite: sometimes he transferred entire groups from
one of Tintoretto's canvases; and very frequently he borrowed one of
those figures called "reversed" which so easily created a link between
the two halves of a picture. These borrowings exist in El Greco's early
work side by side with others taken from Raphael or Michelangelo.
He collected them with the unconcern customary in an age when even
the greatest artists took whatever they could find, either from nature
or from the work of some other master. With El Greco this need to
appropriate everything accessible was all the more pressing because at
that time he was acquiring an entirely new vision. He differed from
the majority of the young pupils arriving in a famous studio in that he
had not only much to learn but also much to forget.

Recent discoveries have revealed what are believed to be his first
paintings. They throw light on the beginnings of a period which, however imperfect its achievements, explains a great deal of his future development—explains perhaps everything. Those first pictures reflect a
deep conflict, almost one might say a clash between his past attainments and those of the present.

The "Adoration of the Magi" painted in tempera on wood, now in
the Benakis Museum in Athens, has been credited as one of his first
Italian pictures, and the abbreviated inscription "Mater Theou . . ."
has been interpreted as an illusion to his own name. But this painting
is still so indefinite in character that it could just as well have come
from one of those Venetian studios which blended the influences of
East and West for the sake of an easy sale.

His first signed Italian painting preserved for us, bearing his name

"Domenico" in Greek capital letters, is the Modena altarpiece (Plates 4–7). This establishes definite knowledge about his beginnings in place of vague conjecture. The outer measurements of this small portable altar are only 16 by 9 inches. This kind of altarpiece was customarily used for travelling in Flanders, Spain, and also the East, but it is rarely found in Italian art. One visualizes it being ordered by some pious patron, perhaps a rich compatriot, whom El Greco was anxious to please with these reminders of Byzantine elements. The six scenes painted on both sides of the triptych are not unlike a sample collection of everything El Greco had so far acquired as new means of expression, and of everything he had retained from his past. To the first category belongs a wing with a ᵃ ᵇ ᵈ scale—"God the Father Appearing before Adam and Eve in the Garden of Eden"; another wing depicting the "Annunciation," based on a lost work of Titian; and the "Adoration of the Shepherds," the motifs of which were borrowed from no less than three different engravings. This utilization of engravings was a frequent habit, particularly at that time of weariness with outworn representations, which led to a search for new means of expression. Use of these engravings, which could travel across frontiers without difficulty, often led to an unexpected and disconcerting blend of varied styles. El Greco must have made considerable use of them in his beginnings. He had never been, and never was to become, a storyteller. Therefore, when, in his youth, he had to set out a narrative, he must have looked elsewhere for the thread. His "Adoration of the Shepherds" was taken in particular from an engraving of the monogramist "L.B.," but it also drew on an engraving by Bonasone and on one by Parmigianino.

A wing depicting the "Baptism of Christ" represents a transition between his two styles. Whereas the two figures are Venetian in type, the traditional scheme of Byzantine compositions shines through with the insistence of a tracing which has not been obliterated by forgetfulness.

The panel representing "Mount Sinai" is an undimmed memory of his native land. Those mountains, with their abrupt peaks; those slabs of rocks with their hollow cavities, resembling petrified waves in their schematic undulation; the Convent of St. Catherine—a rectangular block set in a hollow, seen from above, as if from a bird's-eye view— all these had their origins in those engravings so popular among Oriental pilgrims, which could then be bought as easily as holy images and plaster figures can be today at places of pilgrimage.

The print of Mt. Sinai seems to have haunted El Greco, as if he knew it from early childhood. He was to repeat this landscape several times, mainly while he was painting in Italy, as if his nostalgia were still quite fresh. He faithfully reproduced the original model. Yet, even though he retained the sombre outlines first drawn by some humble anonymous artist, those desolate rocks already bear his stamp. Something indefinable took place during this transposition: it is as if El Greco had found in this subject a short cut to his own individuality, an outlet for his haunting memories.

The repetition of this view of Mt. Sinai, painted a few years later on a small panel (ex-Hatvany Collection, Budapest strikes one as a purified and intensified vision of the Modena wing. It is a volcanic landscape in which no tree, no blade of grass, can grow—a landscape evocative of the end of the world. Even the clouds seem to be petrified. At the same time, by some strange effect, one gets an impression of impenetrable space, of the confines of the world extending to infinity. This small picture, although copied from an old and well-known design, radiates a feeling for landscape which is very close to us, a sort of anguish of our present day. A direct line of evolution leads from Mt. Sinai to the Toledo landscapes. Between the two there was a whole life to be lived, and a whole life's work to be done.

The sixth scene of the Modena altarpiece also discloses his heritage from the past, which shows through the Venetian forms, such as the rock peaks under a layer of green. It is of Christ, with his triumphant banner unfurled, crowning a holy warrior, perhaps St. Theodore. He rises up above a moon borne by the symbols of the four Evangelists. His feet rest on the outstretched body of the devil, who hangs, frenziedly writhing, over a human skeleton. It is the triumph announced in the Epistle to the Corinthians: "Death is swallowed up in victory. O death, where is thy sting? O grave, where is thy victory?" The hell which yawns below the feet of Christ is depicted as the mouth of a monster, a representation familiar in Cretan imagery and which also appears in the frescoes on Mt. Athos. This was a permanent motif, to be repeated by El Greco many years later in "The Dream of Philip II," a picture commissioned by Philip II for the Escorial and therefore executed with particular care.

The young El Greco, however, does not seem to have been aware of his own characteristic features, nor did he suspect the value he was to attach one day to these permanent motifs. Perhaps he even despised them as a young provincial, both dazzled and confused. A new period of his life was beginning, dominated by the effort to become assimilated at all costs. A number of paintings characterize this stage, when he was trying to lose rather than to find himself. This deliberate absence of a physiogonomy of his own has baffled even his most competent biographers to such an extent that certain paintings which previously figured under the name of either one or other of the Bassani have been attributed to him, only to be again deleted from the list of his works after a period of hesitation. Thus the "Adoration of the Magi" in the Vienna Museum and two other paintings of the same subject in the Borghese Gallery in Rome suffered this changing fate. The Vienna picture, known since the seventeenth century as the work of the young Bassano, Leandro da Ponte, was attributed to El Greco by the first of his biographers, only to be taken away again by his most recent one. Less typical of the Bassani, yet still rather close to them, are the pictures in the Borghese Gallery. The fact that all three pictures draw on sources ranging from an engraving by Dürer to Parmigianino would speak more in favour of attribution to the young El Greco than against it. The doubts of the experts, however, are based on a very convincing argument: the fact that the subject never reappears in El Greco's work, whereas the other iconographic subjects of his early years recur again and again. These never ceased to purify and intensify, each new version becoming a new stage in his evolution until sometimes—not until quite late—he achieved what was to be for him a definitive version.

To this confusion of works which cannot easily be accepted belong the two small pictures in Strasbourg: "The Feast at Cana" and "The Woman Taken in Adultery." Also "The Flight into Egypt" in the Andrews Collection in London, certain elements in which seem to justify its attribution to the young El Greco, even though this subject does not recur in his later work either. The "Christ in the House of Mary and Martha" in a New York private collection (formerly Collection J. Brass, Venice) does to a certain extent anticipate El Greco, yet it was probably painted by one of his Mannerist predecessors. "The Adoration of the Shepherds" in the Willumsen Collection had to undergo the same fluctuations of assessment. Its owner, a Danish painter, concentrated with considerable ingenuity and also imagination on El Greco's early works and did in fact succeed in discovering a number of important keys to his early output and above all to his pictorial technique. But the "Adoration" attributed by him to El Greco contains several elements which were alien to him, even during this period of assimilation, such as the two figures at the window, which never reappeared in his later work.

The first of his signed paintings of this period is probably the picture in the Cook Collection in Richmond—"The Cleansing of the Temple" (Plate 9). It is signed neatly and clearly in Greek letters: "Domenico Theotocopuli, Cretan, fecit." The Cretan character of the work is, however, confined to his signature. If this did not exist and the attribution were to be based solely on El Greco's later works, probably no one would have dreamed of assigning it to him. The picture is painted on wood, a material which at that time was perhaps more familiar to him than canvas. The colours are laid on thickly over a brownish underpaint, and the brushes trace sinuous strokes almost in relief. Here and there one can find a touch of the fingers, with which certain roughnesses have been smoothed out. A typically Occidental technique. The work is ostensibly Venetian. A work of its time, a meeting place of contemporary influences; almost, one might say, of current fashions. The work of a young man anxious to please, who is playing all his trump cards.

The subject is typical of the man who chose it, and who signed it with his name and birthplace—both often indications of the importance he attached to a painting. A subject which must have impressed itself upon him in the bustling life of the public squares of this mercantile city, where the merchants spread their wares so close to the church of St. Mark that their barrows scratched the marble and scraped the sculptures. Christ in his anger has seized the whip: "My house shall be called the house of prayer; but ye have made it a den of thieves." But the young El Greco still lacked the necessary means of expression for the violent emotion of such a subject. The agitation remains purely superficial. The depth he sought to create by opening up vistas in the background, as an Oriental who had just discovered the mysteries of perspective, seems quite artificial. The main group is bunched restlessly on the left side of the picture, with a false feeling of balance, in front of a monumental arch and a patch of stormy sky; whereas on the right-hand side a colonnade recedes into spaces. The figure of Christ is so hemmed in that it fails to dominate the crowd. He has no room to wield His whip; but the young Cretan seems to have been proud to paint vigorous male torsos and to trace diagonals made up of segments of legs, backs, and arms. The figures outside the main group are totally indifferent to the drama. In the foreground a woman selling pigeons reclines on a step, displaying a beautiful leg, naked to the thigh, sloping shoulders, a bosom bursting out of her draperies and a small curly head turned in profile—the expectant profile of a Danaë or a Venus lying on her couch. In front of the colonnade, prominently placed, the figure of a woman borrowed from Raphael after an engraving by Parmigianino, with outthrust breasts and bare shoulders, quietly goes on her way, with her back turned to the central scene, carrying her pails and leading her naked child by the hand. On the steps leading to the heavily accentuated colonnade another naked child is lying on the marble floor; also a chest, which seems to have fallen out of nowhere, a lamb tied to a stick, and a bird, which links up in the lower foreground with some guinea pigs, rabbits, and a basket of pigeons belonging to a merchant sitting on the steps. Like a clumsy storyteller, El Greco embarked on an anecdote only to lose himself in pointless detail. But he only did so for an instant.

"The Cleansing of the Temple" is a sort of balance sheet. El Greco had appropriated the fullness of Venetian flesh, the sumptuous colouring, the taste for picturesque costumes, and the play of light falling full, now on the bare shoulder of a young girl, now on the bald head of an old man. The most important item in this balance sheet of the young Cretan's acquisitions is the feeling for architecture which is manifest in the arrangement of the arch, the heaviness of its curve, the sharp outlines of the cornices, and the smooth roundness of the columns spreading out into the leaves of Corinthian capitals; one feels straightaway that here is a man with a passion for architecture who, the day he is called upon to build, will choose a classical order.

If El Greco already knew a great deal about the relationships of the elements of architecture, he still did not know those of the human body, whose proportions he perverted. If the reclining woman, the naked child or the old seated merchant were to stand up, they would be giants. Neither had he a feeling for space; and although he know how to calculate the gaps between the receding columns, he was unable to measure the distances between the figures placed at different levels. In fact El Greco was never completely to assimilate this sense of space; nor was he to incorporate in his Oriental vision the sequence of the various planes. Indeed he hardly made any very great effort to acquire this sense, except during the time of his apprenticeship. The exigencies of perspective did not form part of his creative vision and barely entered into his conception of the universe.

From the Venetian period also dates the "Healing of the Blind

Man" in the Dresden Gallery (Plate 13), an incontestable attribution, thanks to a later, fully signed replica. The picture is not much later than the first version of the "Cleansing of the Temple." It, too, is painted on a panel of wood. In the meantime, however, El Greco had learned better how to distribute the groups of his composition, and how and what to accentuate. The division of space falls in the centre. The figure of Christ is sufficiently isolated to appear the principal actor. He has just rubbed the blind man's eyes. A miracle has occurred. The Apostles are arguing about it with Latin vehemence. But they are arguing, nonetheless. One old man, anxiously frowning, gazing fixedly at the ground, has spread out both his hands as if the explanation were beyond him. Other Apostles seem reasonably interested. In the far background two figures are deep in private conversation. This picture also bears the hallmarks of Venetian origin: in the bearded heads of the Apostles, as in the face of Christ, with His rich red-gold hair and soft, imperturbable features; in the richness of the colours; in the architectural background, which seems to have been inspired by some building El Greco had seen, perhaps a villa by Palladio. He was quick to learn his lesson. But the proportions remain uncertain. El Greco still believed he had to fill the foreground with anecdotal details. He set the whole scene on a platform, with a step hollowed out in the lower right foreground, and on this step a dog is sniffing interestedly at the bundle and water jug of the blind man.

Another version of the same subject in the Pinacoteca at Parma (Plate 14) must have been painted only two or three years later. But the progress of El Greco's evolution was rapid. The composition indicates a very marked advance. The empty space in the centre is reduced to a minimum; the architecture has ceased to have an autonomous existence as decoration only and, compressed and foreshortened, is integrated into the whole. The step leading as if up on to a stage has disappeared. There are no more indifferent spectators or private conversations. A young man in the foreground, with his back turned, is pointing to the sun, which the blind man is about to see for the first time. This young man seen from the back marks the first appearance of those commentators of the drama who were later to play such an important part in El Greco's foregrounds, like the leaders of the chorus in Greek tragedy. The silhouette itself, with its muscular calves and bare back, is familiar to Italian painting, but, a curious detail, this vanishing profile and the back of the head have something vaguely foreign about them; the cap of hair is not rounded at the base but

descends low down the neck, to end in a point in a manner frequently
found amongst Orientals. The Oriental note is also to be seen in the
woman with the turban. But apart from these slight exotic touches
something indefinable has entered into the picture, a certain separation
of the optical vision from its general mood. A separation which, however, was unintentional. El Greco, on the contrary, seems to have
striven after current conceptions. One of the faces in the background
is an almost exact copy of a portrait by Titian. But the conventional
seems to slip through his fingers, to veer from the regular and opulent
beauty typical of Venice towards a certain characteristic ugliness
which humanizes his figures. Yet he seems to have mistrusted his own
tendency to draw out the proportions and fine down the features. The
Christ of the Parma version is the most thick-set of all the representations of Christ which El Greco was to paint thereafter. Yet, in comparison with the Dresden picture His features are thinner and His hair
smooth, in place of the former abundant curls. The face is oval, rapidly tapering to the slender, pointed beard. This is the first time El
Greco's endeavours to remove the solid strength from masculine
beauty become apparent. The picture is painted on canvas, thickly
and with strokes of white in relief. But at the same time it is painted
with extremely thin brushes and with as much attention to detail as
if it were a miniature, following the manner in which the young Cretan
must have painted in his youth.

The few discordant notes are, however, drowned in the ensemble,
which is dominated by the artist's effort at adaptation. The sombre
colouring and the mellowness of the flesh are those of Titian's later
style. This affinity, which one feels to be deliberate, even forced, has
led El Greco's more recent biographers to presume that it was mainly
towards the end of his stay in Venice that he worked in Titian's studio.
It is conceivable that he worked there more persistently at that time.
It is also likely that he deliberately sought to suppress the remnants
of independence and to impose a stricter discipline on himself, the
more he felt himself yielding to a certain impatience. Or perhaps his
wish was to please his master, who at that time held the keys to the
success of his career. If Titian's teaching seemed to weigh heavily on
him despite the eagerness he displayed, if the two men belonged to
two different, fundamentally hostile worlds, El Greco was nevertheless
to learn from Titian more than technical skill, more than mere mastery
of the material. The impact made on him by Titian during their period
of work together was the lesson of a lifetime.

Domenico Theotocopuli saw Titian living after the fashion of the privileged, in the luxurious atmosphere of his great house, filled with works of art; a taste for luxury was perhaps the only characteristic these two men had in common. He also saw him administering his artistic heritage with skill and circumspection. He saw how he made use of unusual means, and of such men as Aretino, and this in an unusual way. Although Aretino had been dead for some years, El Greco saw this first pamphleteer, this forerunner of modern publicity, as he emerged from the accounts of his contemporaries. When Aretino wrote his letters (one is tempted to call them advertising puffs) on each of Titian's works, he would boldly exclaim: "Everyone knows how far he has gone, thanks to me." El Greco was to remember this later and value the homage (so much more subtle) paid him by the poets of Spain.

El Greco must have been aware of Titian's efforts to acquire his immense fortune and to keep it. The old man, according to a balance sheet drawn up by himself in 1566, owned property almost everywhere —real estate, houses and cottages, lagoons and dams in Venezia, woods he exploited, pastures on which he raised sheep—and all this list of his possessions was merely intended to continue his exemption from the tax for which he was then being assessed. It was even rumoured, very likely with good reason, that Titian lent money—and malicious tongues added that he charged usurious rates. He traded jewellery with the German banker Fugger and dealt in works of art with a Venetian dealer, who described him as "avarice incarnate." This terms recurs in the writings of all those who knew him. "Titian is the greediest man ever produced by nature," wrote the envoy of the Duke of Urbino. When talking of his works, he would praise their beauty only in order to obtain a higher price. Any means of procuring a commission was justified. He would promise to portray a woman as more beautiful than she was, provided that his fee was granted; in fact, through the magic of his brush, Isabella d'Este, when almost sixty years old, was reborn in the full glamour of her youth. He multiplied replicas of his works, especially of those which were in princely hands, thus adroitly exploiting the snobbishness of his clients. "For money," said the Spanish envoy, "he would do anything."

El Greco was never to set about amassing a fortune following Titian's example. Lessons in prudence and cunning were lost on him; Titian's cupidity must have repelled him, for he seems to have been born a spendthrift. But perhaps it was to Titian that he owed his sense of the commercial value of his work and the bitterness with which he fought for a just price. To him he most likely owed the calculating side of his nature, which appeared from time to time, quite alien to his customary improvidence. He was never to be haunted, as Titian was, by fear of a needy old age and, instead of being in a position to lend money, he was to be compelled to borrow. Yet the language he used towards recalcitrant clients was to echo the intransigence of the old peasant from Pieve de Cadore. Titian's private life and his contempt for social conventions may also have left their mark on the young Cretan, for Titian married his mistress, who ran his house for him, only in order to legitimatize his son. But the most important lesson he can have taught an ambitious young man was conscious pride in the high rank it had been possible for him to attain.

The language Titian used towards his patrons was sometimes as whining, obsequious and humble as that of a peasant in the market place. Yet his ambitions aimed very high, at a state of equality with those born mighty. By the time El Greco arrived in Venice, Titian had already been given the order of the Golden Spur; he was Count Palatine and Aulic Counsellor; thanks to the warrant conferred on him by Charles V he was authorized to appoint notaries and judges, to legitimatize illegitimate children, free slaves, and wear a military sword. El Greco must have seen this warrant, with the preamble in which the sovereign of two worlds called Titian "the apostle of the century" and stressed his excellent virtues, which made him worthy to be elected as his painter by the successor of Alexander the Great and the divine Augustus. This encounter with fame was, in fact, the chief event of El Greco's Venetian period. Perhaps he later aimed so high because he had been so close to fame and to all that goes with it. Probably it had a decisive influence on him, that Titian's most powerful client, the monarch on whom he placed his highest hopes, was Philip II. Indeed El Greco's fateful meeting with Spain and her ruler took place in Titian's studio. There he doubtless saw some copy of the portrait which Titian painted of the heir to the throne of Spain. Perhaps it was the fierce sketch of the Prado portrait, drawn from life without any embellishment, with its pallid mask, jutting lower jaw, spongy lips, and pale protuberant eyes, as slimy as a snail. Although this face, frozen into one unchanging expression, deprived of all emotion from early youth, may have repelled a sensitive young artist, it was also deified by boundless power beyond human limitations. The Italy to which the young Cretan had come in search of fame and fortune was either wholly or partially subservient to the Spanish monarch.

The Most Illustrious Republic, which had shown itself so cunning in its domination of the kingdom of Candia, assumed towards Spain a position of humble dependency; dukes, princes, doges, and even the Pope himself only retained their power thanks to the King of Spain; they were more sovereigns in name than independent rulers.

Philip II also ruled to some extent over Titian's studio. For twenty-five years the master had devoted almost all his activities to the House of Austria, as he himself wrote to Philip. He also wrote that "so long as he could make use of his limbs, now bent by age, they would still work for him." Yet he continued to complain that his canvases were not paid for. The all-powerful monarch called Titian *"mio amado"* (my beloved), and with him this was not one of the empty superlatives of the time. When a fire broke out in the Prado, destroying a large number of pictures, Phillip II consoled himself for their loss with the knowledge that Titian's "Venus" had been saved. "It is possible to recreate the others, but the Venus is unique and irreplaceable."

In this bond, which united a great artist to an absolute ruler, an old peasant to a young religious fanatic, there was one rather equivocal feature. The robust youth of Philip II concealed a generous share of sensuality, which remained unsubdued either by reasons of state or religious piety. The old man, with his peasant cunning, seems to have discovered this carefully hidden side of Philip's nature, this secret predilection. His Prado "Venus" was not to be the only erotic painting especially destined for the young King. He sent him a Danaë, a Calypso pregnant with Jupiter's child, a Europa being carried off by the bull, a nude woman with a satyr, and a Venus courted by an Adonis whose masculine attractions Titian did not fail to stress in his letters to his royal patron. But it was only secretly that he could flatter this inclination, for he was at the same time the intermediary between Philip II and his devotions.

At the moment of El Greco's arrival in Venice, Titian had been working for some time (since 1558) on a canvas destined for the Escorial, to which Philip attached particular importance: "The Martyrdom of St. Lawrence." The work was progressing but slowly. Titian soothed the King, directly he had finished the painting, by writing to him, on December 2, 1567, that he had been aided in this task by a certain young disciple of great merit: *"molto valente giovane mio discepolo."* El Greco's most competent biographers have believed that they could identify him as this young disciple of merit. Every psychological probability speaks in favour of this identification. Titian's picture itself, with its energetic treatment, its fiery brush strokes, seems to bear the hallmark of the young El Greco.

Was it Titian's intention to recommend to the King of Spain this young disciple whose name, incidentally so hard to pronounce, he withheld? Did El Greco thenceforward count on being called to work for the Escorial? The credit of Titian himself was on the decline during these years. The Spanish envoys described him to the King as a decrepit old man no longer in full possession of his faculties. Philip II's suspicious nature was always ready to accept any form of mistrust. Titian himself offered to paint a whole series depicting the life of St. Lawrence for the Escorial, but Philip did not accept the old man's proposal. Did he also refuse to employ the young disciple recommended to him? Was this why El Greco left Venice, to seek favourable opportunities for winning fortune and renown elsewhere? He does not seem to have looked for a new master, despite his continued lack of self-assurance. His years of apprenticeship were over, although it was still to take him a long time to find his true face. At this stage with his still hybrid art he nursed aspiration beyond his power to achieve. Venice was scarcely propitious ground for a young, unknown painter. However lavish she may have been towards the great, however ready to serve as a springboard for every kind of success and to extend reputations already made, she mistrusted and was hard on the promise shown by youthful talents, too excessive in number and over-eager in their aspirations. It needed the tenacity of a son of the people, the self-abnegation of a young Tintoretto, or, for a foreigner, a persistence in the face of misfortune such as Schiavone possessed to attain success. The beginnings of both these artists shed a crude light on the struggle which even men of exceptional talent had to wage in Venice. They would haunt that sort of market set up in the open under the arcades of St. Mark's Square, the *banche per le dipintori,* where poor, unknown artists exhibited their works and solicited commissions. It was there, in the Merceria, that Tintoretto hung two canvases with the object of catching the attention of passers-by: his portrait of himself, and that of his brother playing the guitar. It was there he succeeded in obtaining commissions such as the one from the carpenters of the arsenal. But when commissions were not forthcoming, he and Schiavone made friends with the masons, who would notify them directly a house was to be built. They would then call on the owner and offer to decorate the façade with frescoes; they were willing to execute these sometimes for the price of a few sacks of lime and sand, and the paints used.

Domenico Theotocopuli was born in an easygoing atmosphere, which had not made him adaptable to this kind of life; he must also have inherited every prejudice against manual labour and contacts with artisans or needy artists. At no time in his life was he ever to display patience, or present himself in the guise of a humble petitioner. He can never, even in his youth, have had much power of endurance. One day he left Venice; it is not known when or why.

CHAPTER
THREE
IN THE SHADOW
OF THE PAST

Every foreigner passing through one of the great
gates of Rome towards this second half of the sixteenth
century must have felt like Joachim du Bellay:

> *The newcomer who seeketh Rome in Rome,*
> *And nought of Rome in Rome can he perceive.*[1]

Of classical Rome he could still see the sombre ruins, ancient monuments, triumphal arches upholding a "dusty honour." Renaissance Rome, too, survived in the pride of her cupolas, in stone and marble, yet as a former capital city of literature and the arts she was a mere empty shell still echoing with the tumultuous splendours of her past.

Her churches and palaces were built to defy eternity, but the cobbles of her streets could recall how they had been trampled by foreign troops, who came to pillage and set fire to the sacred city like any other conquered town. Those who experienced the sack of Rome were never to forget—like all who have lived through a time of terror—that their lives and possessions had been at the mercy of fate, and the rest of their days were to be spent frozen round that time of horror.

Rome vulnerable, Rome humiliated since the last revolt against Spanish supremacy, led by that great hater Pius IV, had been shattered with the defeat of the French before St. Quentin, and had been reduced, as a temporal power, to a petty principality. Her treasury was exhausted by war, her farms ruined by the laying waste of the countryside, her prestige abolished.

[1]*Antiquités de Rome,* by Joachim du Bellay (1524–60), French poet.

Through her hapless wars, her trials, and her religious strife which rent the world, Rome had developed the state of mind of a beleaguered citadel. The Holy Office implacably tracked down every weak spot in the armour of faith. Since the Council of Trent, in its eighteenth session, had decided to place not only heretical treatises but also immoral writings on the *Index,* the Inquisition had carefully inspected all private libraries, consigning to the flames those books which the Italians held most dear, Machiavelli as well as the *Decameron,* books which even the most pious handed over with regret. Sometimes their owners, such as one unfortunate possessor of the works of Machiavelli, were tortured for having shown insufficient zeal in adding them to the pyre. "By the way, in what corner of the world are you living?" an Italian scholar wrote at that time to a foreign colleague. "If in an inhabited country, have you not heard of the peril which threatens every kind of book? This wrecking, this burning of books will discourage many from writing in your country too, I think."

As in all periods troubled by suspicion, informers held themselves to be the servants of truth. Scholars denounced each other for heretical passages or errors of faith. The prisons of the Holy Office lay in wait for those accused out of malevolence, even falsely, and only released them when broken in spirit and with their careers ruined. The atmosphere in Rome became heavy for all those who had learned to breathe freely.

The fine arts were subjected to the same discipline as letters. They were even, one might say, in the forefront of the battle. It was at them that the accusation of idolatry laid against the Church of Rome was directed. The Council of Trent regarded the problem as so thorny that it set it aside for its final session, at which it nevertheless confined itself to reiterating the doctrine affirmed in the Second Council of Nicaea on "the intercession of the Saints, the invocation and veneration of relics and the permissible use of images." The Council declared itself ready to uphold tradition with the following reservations: "If some abuses have insinuated themselves into these pious and salutary observances, the Holy Council is keenly desirous that they should be totally abolished. It forbids the setting up in churches of any images related to erroneous dogma and which might lead humble believers astray. All impurities are to be avoided, and no images should be given any provocative attraction."

The immediate repercussions could not be compared with the constraint which clamped down on the world of letters, shackling all thought. The disasters which had shaken Rome, and her material decline, had awakened that sense of peril which leads to severe self-examination, to a loss of freedom from care, and to an obscure feeling of sins to be expiated and punishment deserved. The creative spirit recaptured its eternal anguish, hitherto obscured by intoxication with its own power. The greatest of the giants of an age which had barely evolved, Michelangelo, died also in a strange state of searching for his soul, with that desperate confession which he wished to have carved on his tomb, as if he were renouncing the tempestuous purpose of a life-time:

> *Imagination's sensuous delight,*
> *Which made of art my idol and my queen,*
> *I know how fraught with error it hath been. . . .*[2]

The triumphant Rome where art was an idol and a king was no more. Those Popes who vied with each other in building imperishable monuments to survive them had been succeeded since 1566 by Pius V, a former Dominican monk and member of the Inquisition. The most powerful patrons in the world, who had wished to dazzle the whole of Christendom with their glory, had been followed by a man who detested all luxury and prided himself on his byname—the Father of Poverty (*Padre de la Povertà*). His creation was to be the Palace of the Holy Office. The giants of the Sistine Chapel no longer offended a new feeling of decency with their provocative charms, since Michelangelo had barely closed his eyes before one of his pupils was charged with covering the powerful thighs of his athletes with absurd draperies. The people of Rome had not, however, lost their caustic sense of humour. They called this zealous disciple *Il Braghettone,* the Tailor of Cod-pieces.

In the Vatican and its gardens there still stood antique statues, the first to be delivered up by Italian soil. Pius V had these Venuses and Apollos removed. He presented them to the magistrates of Rome, who used them to adorn the Capitol. Among these statues was the Laocoön group and it was here that El Greco saw it. Doubtless he was seeing Rome for the first time. He had not come there, like so many others, in search of her glorious past. He had come from a land whose age-old glories had died with the relentless passage of time. The oblivion of centuries and the sight of ancient ruins crumbling into dust

[2]Sonnet LXIV, from the translation by S. Elizabeth Hall.

was nothing new to him. He had come to Rome as he had gone to Venice, in search of the present and, no doubt, of his own future. And from whence he came to meet this present day of a militant and threatened faith the road was not a long one. Turkish assaults on the shores of Crete had created the same state of mind of a beleaguered citadel which he found in Rome as the result of assaults by heretics against the Church. For him emancipation from the yoke of convention was not the same imperious need as it was for the elite of Italy, with their bitter struggles to escape from an enclosed and hermetic world, the spiritual and moral yoke of the Middle Ages. The battle for the sovereignty of Man, typified by the Renaissance, was not his personal battle. There seems to have been a link missing in his evolution, with regard to the surroundings in which he found himself. Oriental in his upbringing, he held curiosity about and conquest of the outside world to be less important than self-exploration, contemplation, and the inner life. Much that afflicted the survivors from a time of absolute freedom and plenty was no privation for him. The forbidden books were not his spiritual inheritance. He had never turned to Boccaccio for distraction, nor to Machiavelli for moral instruction. He was so deeply rooted in the Byzantine tradition that the artists' winning of independence for their art, that great achievement of the Renaissance, had not the same meaning for him as it had for the followers of Leonardo da Vinci and Michelangelo. Artistic creation, which could never have become for him either an idol or a king, was a means of stimulating man's sensibility, of engendering in him a mood which extended beyond the narrow confines of self-interest, leading him on to something greater than himself, to a zeal surging upwards towards the light or towards God.

The triumph of Man and his potentialities, that lesson which Michelangelo revealed in his world of giants, was not entirely comprehensible to El Greco, and his sensibility even shied away from it instinctively. His Oriental vision was shocked by this material and plastic quality, which interposed itself like an unduly thick screen between Man and his vision of the divine. The Occidental method of presenting space and the human body, that new world of forms which he was still busy assimilating, was in truth merely a means for him to acquire his own mastery of expression. He was at this time rather like a foreigner setting out to learn the local language, not in order to express himself like those who speak it fluently, but to impart to them in their own tongue his own personal message.

Even if he did not yet know himself what his own message was to be, he instinctively selected those elements which he wished to preserve whilst in Rome. When his gaze rested on the statues of antiquity, it was not the strength flowing from Apollo's thighs, not the wave of sensuality flooding the body of some Venus, that impressed itself upon his memory. It was the Laocoön group (Plate 82) before which he dreamed so long, that evocation of anguish which binds the human bodies, helpless in the embrace of a terrible death. Its memory was long to remain with him, with the insistence of a symbol which he was to interpret in his own way through a slow process of thought, perhaps as Man's surrender to the forces of evil, or the subjection of every creature to the fate which, in his blindness, he believes he can defy. Perhaps it was that feeling of uneasiness to which all human beings are subject, that feeling of anguish in the face of the inexplicable, which El Greco saw incarnated in the Laocoön and which particularly moved him, as if he had found in it the expression of a familiar state of mind, the mood of his age. New social and moral forces had steeped the world in fire and blood. This upheaval often caught men unawares in the middle of their lives, with their pasts still intact within them. They could surmount it only with difficulty, through self-abnegation or an outburst of zealous ardour. An age in which new spiritual weapons were being forged required men to forget former habits of tolerance and intellectual ease.

Art, too, was seeking a new discipline, a departure from that serenity which marks amongst others, the *Stanze* in the Vatican. Painters no longer trusted their inner certitudes; before embarking on a large-scale work they would request theologians for the most detailed instructions. As always in a time when creative inspiration lacks self-confidence, it saw itself dissected, directed, and regimented. Rarely have so many disputes arisen about art or so many treatises on painting been produced. These were often inspired by princes of the Church who, in the previous century, would merely have been patrons and who henceforth decreed "the true Christian manner of seeing things" in the execution of paintings, both those destined for the churches and those for the intimacy of the home. Art became sombre and cruel. The authors of the treatises demanded scenes of martyrdom with gaping wounds, and of the chastisement of heretics, well suited to inspire fear. Physical torment became the prelude to ecstasy. The dripping blood congealed on the body of the dying Jesus, for, according to precept, the traces of the lash must remain visible on the crucified Saviour.

Artists adapted themselves to this new aspect whilst continuing to employ yesterday's forms to express today's emotions. Domenico Theotocopuli, on the other hand, seems to have been predestined by his origins, his nature, and his peculiar sensibility to find this expression of his time. If a distinct art could have been born of the atmosphere created by the Council of Trent, El Greco would have been the one to initiate it. The still-unknown foreigner who came to Rome could have become the leader of a new school there. Through him the Counter Reformation could have materialized in art. His limitations as an Oriental, even the uncertainties of his youth, would have served in his stead. He had everything necessary to express his century, down to an overriding ambition. He only lacked the opportunity.

On leaving Venice, Domenico Theotocopuli stopped at Reggio. There, in the chapel of the church of St. Prosper, he saw Correggio's "Night." He stayed to copy the picture. A strange halt, and a further proof of his harmony with his time. "All the images of the seventeenth and eighteenth centuries," said Francastel, one of the subtlest art historians, "find their direct source in Correggio." El Greco realized how close Correggio's art was to the soul of the people, how well suited it was to appeal to the faith of simple minds through its rather affected sweetness. This man who sought to acquire every means at the command of Western art was attracted by the effect produced by a single source of light, as well as by its novelty. Yet, in copying this picture, he did so in his own way. Typical of him are the serving maid leaning on the column, with the pointed fold of veil on her forehead, and the wiry legs of the angels cleaving the sky.

This copy inaugurated a theme on which El Greco was to compose endless variations as if, with each new version, he had still not fathomed its true meaning. The Holy Child is born—born in darkness. The light of the salvation of the world filters down through the night. It shifts the proportions of temporal reality. It even challenges the facts and dramatizes the astonishment of the simple onlookers, the wonder of the shepherds.

El Greco was also to copy another of Correggio's pictures: "The Virgin and Child with St. Catherine and St. Sebastian." He took this copy with him to Spain, for it was hung in the Escorial and contemporaries extolled its "sweet beauty."

This encounter with the work of Correggio, a prelude to El Greco's arrival in Rome, was in a certain sense decisive for him. It confirmed him in his purpose. The road was not his own, but it showed him the path along which he was to travel in search of it.

Domenico Theotocopuli does not seem to have come to Rome by chance, as the result of a sudden inspiration. Impulsive as he seems to have been, this prodigal, as he later appeared, was at the same time an anxious, prudent man who prepared each stopping place before setting out towards the next in an uncertain future.

The numerous foreigners in Italy felt themselves to be bound together by a solidarity which perhaps consisted solely of memories of their own difficult beginnings, and they were glad to help each other even if they had no common origins. One of these foreigners, who had achieved success and who was willing to help, was Giulio Clovio. El Greco must have been recommended to him, possibly by one of the Slavs who frequented Titian's studio—natives of countries which the Italians lumped together under the title *Slavonia*. He could have met him early in his stay in Venice, when Giulio Clovio came there to place himself in the hands of a doctor who had been particularly recommended to him. A nephew of Giulio Clovio who was a captain in the Venetian Army must also have served as an intermediary. El Greco, even though still little known and friendless (no protector later stepped forward to claim knowledge of him) managed to arouse the keenest interest in this celebrated man. Vasari called Giulio Clovio "the little Michelangelo" and "the magnificent." Lomazzo[3] described him as unique and others as "the Raphael of miniaturists" and even as "the renovator of all the arts." Only a period of epigoni, of suppressed individuality, and uncertain judgments would have bestowed such flashy fame on this man. His destiny above all was typical of his epoch—a sort of cross section of all its upheavals.

Giulio Clovio, whose real name was Juraj Glovicic, was born in the village of Grizano, near the Adriatic coast. His unusual signature, *Crovato*, was a reminder of his Croatian origin. To avoid his name, which the Italians found unpronounceable, he was first called *Il Macedone*. He came very young to Italy and worked for a while in the studio of Giulio Romano. In his native land he must have acquired those notions of Byzantine art meted out by the local schools— scrupulously detailed drawing, delicate brushwork, and patient submission to traditional patterns. This early training left him ill-prepared for the virtuoso technique of his master, whom contemporaries had

[3]*Trattato della Pittura,* by Giovanni Paolo Lomazzo (1538–?), painter and scholar.

called "Fa Presto." But if his gifts were restricted, he nevertheless possessed the virtues of his limitations—precision, tenacity, and a sure
feeling for quality. He was always seeking something beyond his
power, copying the paintings of Titian as if, by so doing, he could
penetrate the arcana of creative inspiration; throughout his life he
never ceased to draw (for himself) in imitation of the works of
Raphael and even more of Michelangelo. If his master was unable to
turn him into a painter of large mural surfaces, he did him the immense service of guiding him towards his true vocation, that of a
miniaturist. The very technique which was to bring him fame—
stippling, minute strokes of colour which a contemporary called
"atoms"—was perhaps not entirely his own, but of Flemish inspiration.
In Italy, however, he was regarded as an innovator, and the most famous patrons and collectors competed for his works.

In 1524 he was in the service of Louis II of Hungary. He was caught
up in the toils of war, witnessed the terrible victories of the Turks, and
made his painful way through to his native village, only to find it also
occupied by the enemy. He managed to escape across the pillaged
countryside and took refuge in Rome. The world was a prey to the
powers of evil. Men who were conscious of its distress forgathered, in
common concern for a bewildered mankind, in the house of Vittoria
Colona. There the Croatian painter met the man he most admired,
Michelangelo, he too, gloomy and embittered. For the witness of the
Turkish atrocities this respite was to be brief. Barely a year after his
return to Rome Giulio Clovio experienced the sack of the city. He saw
old men and children massacred, women of all ages raped, the streets
littered with their blood-stained corpses, and his artist friends robbed
and tortured. He himself fell into the hands of the Spanish troops.
Beaten, with both legs broken, starving, near unto death, in the city
swept by the plague, he vowed to take holy orders if he succeeded in
escaping from prison. He too was to be marked forever by the terror
through which he had lived. The order he chose was that of the
Flagellants—*the Scopettini*—and in memory of his master he adopted
the name of Giulio. However, Cardinal Mariano Grimani, one of his
former protectors, snatched him away from his monastic life, emphasizing that it was every man's duty to put the gifts he had received
from God to the best possible use, for the benefit of his fellow men.
With the permission of the Pope, Don Giulio Clovio, as he called
himself from now on, returned to Rome and entered the service of
Cardinal Alessandro Farnese. As the best employment of his gifts and

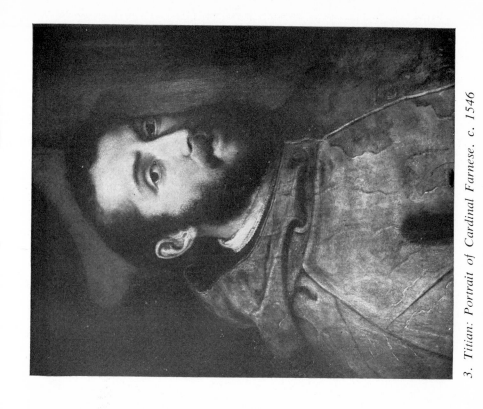

2. *Titian: Self-portrait. c. 1562–70*

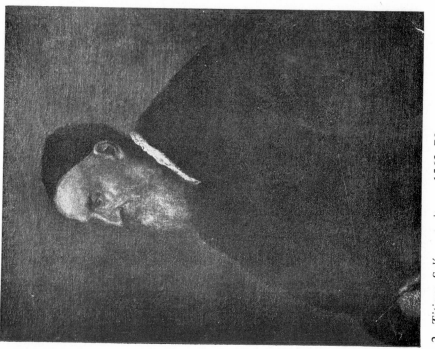

3. *Titian: Portrait of Cardinal Farnese. c. 1546*

5. *The Baptism of Christ. c. 1563–67*

4. *Adoration of the Shepherds. c. 1563–67*

7. *Mt. Sinai. c. 1563–67*

6. *Christ Crowning St. Theodore. c. 1563–67*

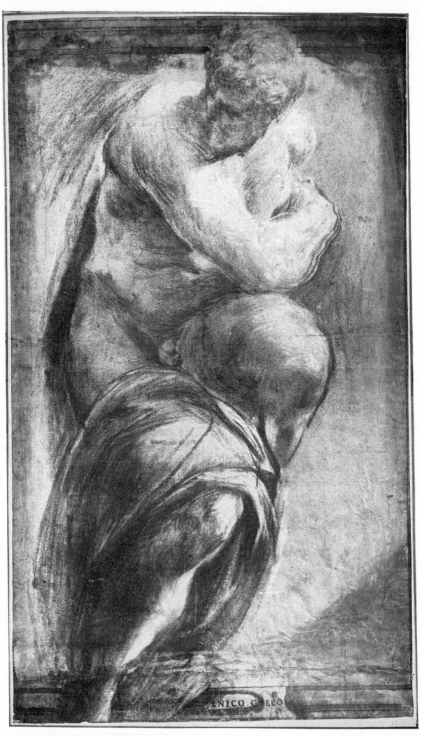

8. *The Day—drawing in black and white chalk on blue paper after Michelangelo's sculpture. c. 1563–65*

9. *The Cleansing of the Temple. c. 1568–70*

10. *The Cleansing of the Temple. c. 1572–76*

11. *Portrait of Giulio Clovio. c. 1570*

12. *The Four Artists, detail from Plate 10*

13. *Healing of the Blind Man. c. 1568–70*

14. *Healing of the Blind Man. c. 1572–74*

FRÁ VINCENTIO
ANASTAGI DOPPÒ
ESSERE STATO GO
VERNATORE DELA
CITTÁ VECCHA DI
MALT ET HAVER CO
MÁDAT NELL ASSE
DIO DELLA MED ISOIA
AD VN DELE DVE
COMPAGNIE DE CA
VALI CHE DENTRO SI
TROVARONO E AD VN
CÔPAGNI DI FANTI COSÁ
DÓ PIÚ VOLTE AD ALTRE
COMPAGNE DI FATÍA JA
FV SARGENTE MAGIOR
DELA MARCA E V HONORAT
IN PIÚ VOLTE DAL GRAN
MASTRO DI TRE COMENDI
E MORI IN MALTA CRD ELLA
CRP DELE GAERE IL ANO
NO 1586 E DELE ETS VA

15. *Vincentio Anastagi. c. 1572*

to the glory of the Farnesi, he painted the Office of the Virgin in twenty-six miniatures, depicting scenes from the Old and New Testaments face to face. The meticulous care of the work, to which he devoted nine years, the minute strokes with which he painted even the details of the liveries worn by the Cardinal's retainers, aroused as much enthusiasm as the real quality of design and the brilliance of the colouring. Cardinal Farnese was to refer in his will to the Office of the Virgin as a unique treasure.

Giulio Clovio was harassed with commissions from collectors; the Viceroy of Milan requested from him a portrait of Philip II which he sent as a gift to his sovereign—a gift doubtless highly appreciated, for Philip II, who was busy building up that library in the Escorial which contemporaries called the graveyard of books, strongly pressed Giulio Clovio to come to Spain. The old man who had come from so far had no further desire to travel or to serve a new patron. His eyesight was worn out by the minuteness of his work; he had had to undergo an operation and, at the age of seventy-one, he complained of his poor sight and enfeebled hands. It was at this time (probably about the year 1569) that El Greco painted his portrait (Naples Museum) (Plate 11). He took great pains over this, for he knew how precious the support of a man of such high standing was for him. He painted him as his model would have wished, in that manner of Titian's which he admired, in tones of black and white of a grey background. He also painted him invested with that calm authority of a man who has been heaped with honours beyond his due. A thick-set figure, a head round as a cannon ball, set almost without transition on sloping shoulders; a wide, square forehead growing hollow at the temples; round, close-set eyes under the straight line of the eyebrows; and a rectangular beard masking a prominent and determined chin. It is the face of a man who has pursued his path with patience and tenacity. With pliancy, too, for the direct and heavy gaze tells all he knew of men; the long nose and the mouth with lips one can guess to have been straight and thin reveal a certain sly wisdom. Short hands with powerful, spatulate thumbs and thick palms, the hands of a craftsman, echo the same note of obstinate strength. Age and suffering have caused the flesh to sink in, lined the temples, and set pouches under the eyes. There is a slight asymmetry in the gaze; the right eye seems clouded. But this gaze remains vigilant and the forefinger of his right hand points with authority at the book which he holds open in his left, his masterpiece, the Office of the Virgin. El Greco reproduced the two miniatures thus displayed

in their blaze of yellows and reds. He also let a window into the monochrome background, with a luminous view of a turbulent landscape,
lashed by the wind, with scudding clouds. This landscape, which is a
memory of Venice, is contrasted (no doubt deliberately) with the massive figure, with its head shorter and squarer than the one in Giulio
Clovio's self-portrait, with the body sunk deep into a chair, forming
a horizontal block, and the cloak thrown over the back of it accentuating still further the broad base of the pyramid.

El Greco did here violence to his innate and traditional inclination
for upright pictures with vertically elongated proportions: he was
anxious to succeed at all costs by falling in with the taste of his sitter.
And succeed he did. Giulio Clovio already had confidence in him
before having himself painted, for he had seen Greco's own self-portrait and had recognized its exceptional worth.

When El Greco arrived in Rome, probably about 1569, he brought
with him several pictures painted in Venice, and also that self-portrait,
now unfortunately lost, which would have been the true revelation
of his youth. Giulio Clovio was not the only one to be impressed by it.
As he wrote, then interceding on El Greco's behalf, and not without
a touch of contempt for his Roman colleagues, this portrait "is stupe-
fying all the painters in Rome" (*fa stupire tutti questi Pittori di Roma*).

It might at first seem strange that the work of an unknown man, of
a Greek who had come via Venice, should create such a sensation in
Rome. But it was above all in the domain of portraiture that the artistic aridity made itself felt—the deficiency of a cerebral art with a
pre-established programme, dominated by theories. In fact the art of
Venice, with its abundant vigour, its taste for the visual, the sensuous-
ness of its materials, had remained still attached to representation of
the human individual, close to reality, even when expanding it in its
own spectacular fashion. But the art of Rome scorned portraiture as
an inferior art. In one of the countless treatises so much in fashion,
which appeared under the title of *The True Precepts of Painting* (*Veri
precetti della pittura*), Giovanni Battista Armenini explained that it
required far more knowledge, effort, and intelligence to paint one or
more nudes in such a way that they stood out in full relief before the
spectator than it did to acquire those few notions necessary to paint a
portrait. When it was a question of a likeness, he added, a mediocre
painter would always triumph over a great master. Like art in general,
portraiture was subjected to the taste for the monumental; it, too,
formed part of a *décor*.

A true portrait (and the one of Giulio Clovio is known to have been an excellent likeness) which was at the same time of a convincing quality must necessarily have caused surprise and drawn attention to the newcomer. But this *succès d'estime* was not accompanied by material success. El Greco had not yet even found means to lodge himself. Giulio Clovio then came to his aid. On November 16, 1570, he applied to his protector, doubtless as the result of an appeal from El Greco, for he wrote from Viterbo to Cardinal Farnese to commend to him "a young Candian, a pupil of Titian, who, in my opinion, is exceptionally gifted in painting." To back up his claims, he referred to the effect produced by the young artist's portrait in Rome. This laudatory introduction was designed to procure El Greco a lodging. "I should like to have him under the protection of Your Most Illustrious and Most Reverend Lordship." As one inured to dealing with the mighty, Giulio Clovio knew that it was fatal to ask too much and, in this letter to one of the richest men in Rome, he made it clear in advance that he was merely soliciting a room in the Palazzo Farnese for his protégé and not means of subsistence (*senza spesa altra de vivere*), and that he was only requesting this "for a short while," until the Candian could find lodgings for himself. Giulio Clovio also knew that a favour of this kind must not cause any inconvenience to a very busy man, not even the trouble of seeing to it in person. It would be sufficient, he wrote, if he would instruct his major-domo, Ludovico, to be so good as to fix his protégé up with a room, any room, at the top of the palace. In conclusion he assured the Cardinal that this would be "a deserving act, worthy of you" and one for which he would hold himself particularly in his debt.

El Greco's stay in Rome began with this humble petition from a man who, although influential in his day, has only been saved from oblivion by this same act of intervention. Thanks to him, El Greco now found himself in the centre of the contemporary intellectual world. "He who goes to Rome," wrote Aldo Manuzio[4] the Younger, "and does not first kiss the hand of Cardinal Farnese must confess that he does not know what the city contains."

Alessandro Farnese (Plate 3) was in fact to a high degree representative of his time. Moreover, through his origins and his position, he was in himself an epitome of the history of a whole century. The

---

[4]Aldo Manuzio the Younger (1547–97), grandson of the famous printer and humanist of the same name and himself an erudite historian and director of the Vatican printing press.

Cardinal, a Legate at Avignon and Monreale and Vice-Chancellor of
the Holy See, was a grandson of Pope Paul III. The foundations of
the Farnese fortune reached back into the days of Rome's licentiousness; Pope Paul III himself had earned a reputation in his youth for
chasing petticoats, and his sister, the lovely Giulia, had been the
titular mistress of the Borgia Pope Alexander VI, the mother of this
man's daughter, and an unchallenged queen of Roman society, whom
the panegyrists unblushingly called the "bride of Christ." The Papal
Legate's father, Pier Luigi, Duke of Parma and Piacenza, the natural
son of Pope Paul III, was the embodiment of violence, arrogance,
rapacity, and cold, dispassionate debauchery even in the eyes of his
contemporaries, who were used to the moral deviations of the great.
He has passed down to posterity in the sinister portrait drawn of him
by Benvenuto Cellini (whom he had cast into the dungeons of the
Castello di Sant' Angelo) in which a love of art wars with avarice,
a love of danger with deceit. But the times were no longer propitious
for either the rebellious or the rapacious. The son of this father, who
had ended as the victim of a savage murder, was merely the sagacious
preserver of the family fortune. And this fortune was considerable.
Towards the middle of the century the Cardinal's income stood at
60,000 crowns; his retinue, excluding his servants (or family as they
were called in Rome), numbered 391 mouths to be fed, including six
prelates. Alessandro Farnese, born in the shadow of St. Peter's, possessed all the ease conferred by the Cardinal's purple, which he had
worn from the age of fourteen: Rabelais called him *"le cardinalicule."*
Contemporaries extolled his majestic bearing as a prince of the Church.
He also possessed the ease of a man of the world; at the court of
France he was said to be "quick with the fluency of his tongue." He
was, at heart, a man of the Renaissance which spiritually nourished
him. The great humanist, Peter Vittori, praised his profound knowledge of Greek and Latin authors, his amazing memory, his love of
letters and the arts, the all-embracing protection he gave to the scholars and poets with whom he liked to surround himself and who spread
the fame of his family and exalted his own importance. For a man of
the Renaissance, Alessandro Farnese was without prejudices, had a
frank sensuality, and in his private circle a charm based more on refinement than on frivolity.

   Libertarian poets gravitated around him in his youth. Francesco
Maria Molza, whom he had taken into his palace in spite of his scandalous ways; Giovanni della Casa, who, although the author of li-

centious poetry, was invested with the rank of Archbishop and Papal Nuncio thanks to the protection of the Farnesi; Annibale Caro, who had in his youth written erotic plays and who became his secretary, confidant, and friend. But times were changing. Most of these people were now dead, their works burnt in the public squares. Alessandro Farnese did not unreservedly approve of the discipline imposed by the Council of Trent. But he adapted himself to the change in morals. Henceforward he provided refuge in his palace for men of letters, ecclesiastics, and authors of edifying works.

Following the taste of the day and for the patron's greater glory, literature was replaced by scholarship. Under the same roof as Domenico Theotocopuli there had lodged for many years a scholar also known as "El Greco," Matheos Devaris, a native of Corfu, who was employed by the Cardinal to search out Greek manuscripts and copy those which he could not acquire. The fashionable learning of the day was above all in religious matters. Another Greek copy maker in the Cardinal's service, Giovanni Onorio d'Otrante, was one of the most eminent of hagiographers. The Cardinal's sagest counsellor and keeper of his collections was Fulvio Orsini, illegitimate son of the illustrious family, who, from being a poor relation taken into the palace, had become to some extent the dictator of arts and letters there. He had amassed an important library of his own, together with antique sculptures and inscriptions; he also possessed a gallery of his own pictures. He was especially renowned as an almost infallible expert on classical manuscripts; the King of Poland was to try in vain to persuade him to enter his service. He had all the fanaticism and also all the jealousy of a passionate collector; when Cardinal Borromeo asked him one day how one distinguished an authentic manuscript from a copy, Orsini closed one of the beautiful examples he was holding and changed the subject.

Fulvio Orsini was probably one of El Greco's first clients in Rome and, it seems, initially on his own account. The little picture of "Mt. Sinai" (ex-Hatvany Collection, Budapest) figures in the inventory of the collection as "a walnut frame with a landscape of Mt. Sinai by the hand of a Greek disciple of Titian." He was also a client on his master's behalf; several pictures have been traced as having belonged to the Cardinal. Giulio Clovio's recommendation, modest in its immediate aim, was in fact designed to attract the Cardinal's attention to his protégé. This interest, once aroused, justified the most ambitious hopes.

Alessandro Farnese had kept up with the times. He had protected the Jesuits from the very outset. In this year of 1569, when El Greco arrived in Rome, the first stone of the Church of Jesus (the Gesù) was laid, thanks to his financial assistance. The Great Cardinal, as he was called, was one of the most active builders of his time. Caprarola, his country villa built by Vignola, was to strike Montaigne as the most beautiful house he had seen in Italy. As if he had not enough already, with the palace of San Giorgio which he occupied in his capacity as Chancellor of the Church, his magnificent family residence of Caprarola, and his *casino* on the Palatine Hill, the Cardinal bought the villa of Agostino Chigi, with the Raphael frescoes, which was henceforth to bear the name of La Farnesina.

He protected musicians, whom he loved to bring together on the Palatine. He protected painters like Vasari, whom he encouraged in his memorable undertaking *The Lives of the Painters,* and the Zuccaro brothers, who covered with frescoes the salons of Caprarola, which were as spacious as those of a royal dwelling. A patron in a bygone age's meaning of the word, Farnese seems to have been sufficiently adapted to the mentality of his time to encourage a man as well able to express it as Domenico Theotocopuli. For the moment he kept him busy. He made him copy the portrait Titian painted of his brother Ranuccio, Cardinal of Sant' Angelo, Latin Patriarch of Constantinople, who had recently died. He made him execute four medallions bearing the portraits of his brother, Pope Marcello, Cardinal Bessarion, and himself. He purchased from him the pictures which he brought from Venice, such as the second version of the "Healing of the Blind Man." El Greco still waited for the big commissions to come in. Meanwhile he lodged in the Palazzo Farnese.

For him this was not only a temporary refuge but also a centre for meetings—primarily meetings with the splendours of Rome's past, a sort of cross section of her history. In the main court, under the arcades, stood two statues of Hercules, found during the excavations of the Thermae of Caracalla—the Greek original and its Latin copy; two giants, all flesh and muscle, with heads too small for their huge bodies. From the same excavations came also the group known in Rome as *"la maravigliosa machina del Toro,"* that mountain of marble, richest in figures of all antique monuments. Like the tragedy of Laocoön, this was also a great drama frozen in stone, the drama of Dirce, lashed to the horns of a gigantic bull by the sons of Antiope in revenge for the outrages committed on their mother; a mass of animal force against which the frailty of the human body struggles in vain. From the formal viewpoint it was a skilfully orchestrated display of flesh, an exaltation of it, and the whole as unfamiliar as could be to the mentality of an Oriental.

This palace courtyard which El Greco was now to see every day also spoke to him of a triumphal past still quite recent in time. The architect of the Palazzo Farnese, San Gallo, had left it, on his death in 1546, surmounted by a nondescript cornice, and all Rome agreed on its inadequacy for so grand a building. For this was a period when the whole of Rome could grow passionate about an architectural detail, the result of that mania for buildings which these people had and also of the way in which men grow impassioned over pure questions of form in times of stress, when so many spiritual problems appear insoluble. Paul III had invited all the great artists in Rome to make designs and had chosen that of Michelangelo. Michelangelo considered the task so important that he had a model made of wood and the outcome of this model became a major event in Rome. He worked on the palace for several years, modifying the arrangement of the courtyard, gathering it up into a single façade with a flat surface, with windows set between double pilasters, whose relief is prodigiously enhanced by the Roman sun, with the wind blowing freely through the open colonnades. "Thus the efforts and ingenuity of this man," said Vasari, "have made it the most beautiful courtyard now in Europe."

These daily meetings of El Greco with Michelangelo's work in the courtyard of the Palazzo Farnese were only the prelude to his later encounters with Michelangelo's gigantic shadow which was to haunt him throughout his stay in Rome.

In the Palazzo Farnese he also rubbed elbows with the Roman present. He saw the great salon almost entirely painted over by Francesco Salviati, Giulio Clovio's pupil. The Farnesi did all they could to glorify their house; they had books written about the family's exploits, and had their ancestors painted in the best heroic tradition. This was epigonus art in its stalest form of servility. Salviati did not hesitate to paint Ranuccio, the founder of the family, in a pose copied from Michelangelo's "Guiliano di Medici." Even if the gods of Olympus no longer peopled a Christian heaven, the allegorical figures which, in the apotheosis of Pope Paul III, bore the tiara up to the clouds, were still pagan goddesses with almost naked breasts.

El Greco also saw the works of Taddeo Buccaro, who, following Salviati's death, replaced him in the service of the Farnesi. Taddeo

painted for the Cardinal the pictures at Caprarola, following the
minutely detailed instructions of Annibale Caro—the *invenzione,* inspired by Alessandro Farnese himself. Taddeo and his younger brother
Federigo were the most characteristic representatives of this period of
transition which, in matters of form, drew inspiration from Raphael's
stanze but subjected these borrowed forms to the ideology of the time.
Vasari described Taddeo Zuccaro as a needy artisan who, on suddenly achieving fame, still retained memories of an impoverished childhood and remained "so grasping that he would accept any commission
whatsoever, simply to make money." His fame was great. When he
died in 1566 he was buried near Raphael's tomb. However alien this
rhetorical art was to El Greco, he was considerably influenced by it,
just as he was by the art of the Bassani during his stay in Venice. For
him it was a foreign language which had to be learned. He himself was,
and always would be, lacking in inventiveness. The devices of skilful
composition which he acquired from the artists of Rome were to serve
him all his life; for example, the division of the canvas into different
planes, the spacing out of the figures, and the oval circuit which gives
clarity to a turbulent composition. Even the iconographical motifs, as
he saw them treated in Rome, remained for him a sort of everlasting
groundwork on which he ceaselessly embroidered. He eventually took
away with him from Rome, as it were, the materials for his future con-
structions, to be adapted after his own fashion.

He was still engaged in completing his apprenticeship, in acquiring a variety of means which would set him on an equal footing with
the virtuosi of Western art. He developed the ideas he received as and
how they came to him. The strong impression made on him by Correggio's "Night" was perhaps reinforced by a meeting which took
place in the Palazzo Farnese, thanks to his protector Giulio Clovio,
who, in his old age, and in spite of his great fame, had remained open
to every form of influence; he found inspiration in Raphael and
Michelangelo, whose drawings he bought; but he also owned paintings
by Pieter Brueghel, with whom he was personally connected. Clovio's
fame attracted young foreign artists to his studio and Rome was still
a place of artistic pilgrimage for foreigners. It must have been through
Giulio Clovio that El Greco had his first direct encounter with Flemish
realism; hitherto he had known it only through popular engravings or
even more indirectly through the Bassani's translation of it into Italian
art.

One of his works, "Boy Blowing on Charcoal" in Naples (Plate 28), which reflects this encounter, figured in the inventory of the Farnese collection under the name of Giulio Clovio, whose long sojourn in the palace left more lasting traces than the brief passage of El Greco. It is in truth a work made up of borrowed elements; a deliberate effort at adaptation to an alien vision. The relief is accentuated, contrary to his own predilection for linear planes; the figure of the boy is hunched and thick-set; like that of Giulio Clovio in his portrait the roundness of the flesh is emphasized with a sensuality foreign to El Greco. The single light which transfigures beings, one of the revolutionary experiments of his time, has here both a realistic and a familiar source. This choice of a *genre* scene, of a glimpse of daily life, reveals a desire in El Greco to approach reality as closely as possible. He was following the teachings of Flemish naturalism. A street urchin, his heavy features coarsened by the light, his lips made even thicker by holding his breath, his stubby hands with their thick palms, all this seems to be drawn from life, from the reality of the moment. One gesture alone betrays El Greco; the manner in which the urchin holds the charcoal on which he is blowing, with the tips of his fingers with the forefinger extended. These tapering fingers, which seem to shrink from the objects they ought to be grasping firmly, were one of his peculiar characteristics— almost his secret signature.

Just as El Greco adhered strictly to this concentrated and plastic vision, he also made himself lay the paint thickly on to rather coarse canvas, instead of a panel of smooth wood. But the picture as a whole suppressed his intentions. The brilliant colours, like enamel or precious stone, are almost drowned in a flood of gold which orchestrates the little picture in broad planes. The yellow garment, the collar of yellowish-white linen, the golden flesh, the black background through which shine drops of gold, all give it a monochrome effect which partly annuls the plasticity of an illuminated figure thrown up by the shadows.

This little picture from the Farnese collection must have met with considerable success. There is one replica of it in New York and another, which was perhaps the first version, in Bologna. El Greco took up again the theme of light from a single source on a larger canvas with several figures. A woman is lighting a candle by blowing on a lump of charcoal; a smiling man with protruding teeth and a monkey on a chain both watch her with almost the same curiosity. This too is a *genre* scene and the man's negroid type and battered hat put one in mind of Spanish gypsies. It has been called (erroneously) a Spanish proverb: the devil, in the guise of a monkey, stirs up fire between a married

couple. The earliest versions of this subject date, however, from his
Italian period, and it was also used by Honthorst. El Greco did not
hesitate to copy the young woman from his urchin in the Farnese collection, even down to the identical gesture of the fingers holding the
charcoal. He stressed the vulgarity in the man's face. From the technical standpoint it is a marked advance. Reality is followed even more
closely; the reliefs of the flesh, like the eyebrows, cast upward shadows.
The painting is smooth, as if El Greco no longer needed the help of
clotted colour to animate the surfaces. His mastery of the material is
more pronounced. This picture met with such success that he made
several replicas of it, the most beautiful of the signed ones being in the
collection of the Earl of Harewood.

At this time he seems to have been seeking variety in his subjects.
Concentration on a few main themes was to be a feature of his maturity. One of his permanent themes, the Annunciation, harks back to
the Roman period—some have even thought a picture in Barcelona to
be a Venetian prelude to it, yet it is so very Venetian that doubts are
now being cast on its authenticity. Repetitions were to become more
frequent the older El Greco grew, as if he wanted to purify the mystery
of the Annunciation of all the traces of earthly dross it might contain.
The first versions (Contini Bonacossi and the Prado) are strongly influenced by Roman plasticity, whereas their colouring recalls his
Venetian apprenticeship. They are marked by a striving after monumentality of form—grandeur at that time found its expression with
El Greco in the powerful build of a body accentuated by flowing robes,
the maturity of the faces, heavy hands and material density.

One influence in particular shines through. Michelangelo was present in Rome at almost every turn of the road. El Greco felt this presence, at once antagonistic and unavoidable. There is one picture into
which he introduced what might almost be a section of his autobiography. After the manner of people deeply aware of what is happening
to them on the spiritual plane El Greco paused at a stage in his evolution and threw a backward glance. He took clear account of the influences which had swayed him, of all that had aided him and guided him
along his path. He drew up a balance sheet, as it were, of his artistic
assets and of the debts of gratitude he had contracted. Debts of gratitude towards the great who were dead as well as those living.

In the replica of his picture "The Cleansing of the Temple" (Plate
10), painted in Rome (today in Minneapolis), he did not go to much

trouble to vary the composition. He may have been asked for a faithful copy. The woman selling pigeons is still there in the left foreground, but in spite of her almost identical pose she is no longer quite a Venus or a Danaë reclining on her couch; her arms and legs are more sturdy, swollen with those straining muscles of the Sybils in the Sistine Chapel, and she clasps the drapery higher to her bosom. The woman carrying water, however, goes her way with the same indifference and the same heavy, protruding breasts. The technical advance is all the plainer since the general composition is almost identical. It is the same story, told first by a still stammering youth and later by a self-confident narrator. Like all progress in any sphere of artistic creation, the purification is brought about through the elimination of unnecessary detail. Of all the still-lifes which El Greco had amassed at the foot of the picture only the basket of pigeons remains. The same applies to the upper part of the picture. There are no more sculptures in the niches, no more architectural details; the setting is no longer a back cloth existing in its own right; the heavy columns cut off below the capitals advance to form part of the picture. Through the covered archway of the temple, on the other hand, an impression of Rome breaks into the scene—buildings with arcades and narrowing upper storeys, and in the far distance a splendid open loggia with a projecting architrave. With that peculiar lucidity of his El Greco was anxious to distinguish between his debt to Rome and his borrowings from his old Venetian master. Into the foreground he introduced four portraits, somewhat after the fashion of the donors of altarpieces. These four portraits (Plate 12) have no common link between them; the heads are set one in front of the other and they avoid each other's eyes, gazing either into the distance or straight at the spectator. In front is Titian; his head, topped by his customary skullcap, haughty and thrown back, his temples hollow, his nose drooping. Behind him is Michelangelo, after his well-known portrait, with deep-set, brooding eyes like relentless gimlets. Superimposed on him is Giulio Clovio, his face longer than in El Greco's portrait of him and filled with a resigned sorrow. The fourth portrait is hard to identify; the long, straight hair, wide-set and luminous eyes evoke Raphael, but the face is fuller and the nose more curved than in the known portraits of him. Did El Greco make use of some lost portrait or did he wish to introduce an unknown figure into this gallery of the great of his time? Raphael would seem to have his place in this balance sheet, drawn up by a man still imbued with his past, but already on the way to surmounting it.[5]

According to the promise made by Giulio Clovio, El Greco did not long remain a guest of the Palazzo Farnese. His success in Rome, which was considerable, enabled him to set up on his own. A belated testimony confirms and also explains the reason for this success. It was made by a learned doctor who—almost at the moment when El Greco was dying in a distant land—undertook to describe the riches of Rome, for the benefit of foreign visitors, one might say. Following the mood of the day, which had made biographies fashionable, Giulio Cesare Mancini added to the description of his journey to Rome certain notes on the painters who had worked there. He must have questioned the artists, connoisseurs, and initiates of the epoch which had just ended. Amongst the survivors none still remembered the barbaric name of a foreigner. In his manuscript,[6] which was never published in his lifetime, Mancini left a blank space for the name, as if he had meant to seek the information from some competent authority.

Under the Pontificate of Pius V of holy memory, there came to Rome ——, who, owing to his origins, was commonly known as "The Greek." Having studied in Venice, particularly the works of Titian, he had attained great distinction in his profession and in this method of work. Coming to Rome at a time when there were not many men whose manner was as distinctive and as fresh as his, he acquired a high reputation, the more so as he caused great satisfaction with certain works painted for private persons, one of which can be seen today in the house of the lawyer Lancilotti, which certain people consider to be by Titian.

This belated echo, sifted through other memories, through a choice of retrospective impressions, reflects as much the aridity of Rome's artistic life as it does El Greco's personal contribution, which Mancini called freshness and distinctiveness. There is no precise information as to the works by El Greco which were in private hands in Rome. The succeeding centuries tarnished the fame which he enjoyed, his name fell into oblivion, and the heirs of his Roman patrons must have got rid of the works that were once so appreciated. The few rare pic-

---

[5]According to Edgar Wind, the fourth portrait, of the man pointing to himself with the typical gesture of self-portraits, may be El Greco himself. (*Journal of the Warburg and Courtauld Institutes, 1939–40.*)

[6]*Alcune considerazione appartenenti alla pittura* . . . MS. No. 5571, Biblioteca Marciana, Venice.

tures which have come down to us are principally portraits, which
families were in the habit of keeping, even through the eclipses of an
artist's fame, and he must have had numerous commissions after the
success met with by his own self-portrait and the one of Giulio Clovio.

When in Rome, El Greco undoubtedly consorted with an intellectual
elite, a society for which he was predestined by his wide culture and
multiplicity of interests. As a native of the Kingdom of Candia, he
would have spoken passable Italian. He continued to perfect his mastery of the language. Amongst the Italian books in his library were a
vocabulary and a grammar by Alberto Accarigio, *Vocabulario colla
grammatica e l'ortografia della lingua volgare,* published in 1543. In
his Italian books one finds the same interests as his choice of Greek
ones reveals. He was, in the first place, passionately addicted to history. He owned an Italian translation of the *Life of Alexander the
Great,* by Quintus Curtius, probably the one made by Pier Candido
Dicembrio, for he does not seem to have possessed any books in
Latin. As a conscientious man he wanted to familiarize himself with
the country he was living in. He also had a *Description of Italy* and a
History of Italy, both quoted by his son without the authors' names.

Had he at that time already been in touch with one who was his
exact contemporary and as characteristic of the spirit of the age as he
himself—the Jesuit Giovanni Botero? Historian, economist, geographer, political writer, great traveller, and harsh critic of Machiavelli,
whose doctrine he challenged in his book *Reason of State,* countering
him with a new science and morality of statecraft based on Christianity and with a just and liberal prince as opposed to the latter's totali-
tarian ruler, Botero owed his reputation to a vast work entitled *Universal Relationships,* in which he described the geography, history,
religion, commerce, and customs of the countries he had visited in
both hemispheres. *Universal Relationships,* mentioned amongst El
Greco's books, was not, however, published until 1592 and he must
therefore have procured it when he was already in Spain, out of curiosity over its subject or perhaps over its author. More strange in an
artist's library appears a book listed under the title of *Military Discipline* without any author's name. This was probably the treatise published by Alfonso Adriani under his own name, though it was in fact
the work of the Cavaliere Aurelio Cicuta. To the same sphere of interest seems to belong a book entitled *Justification of Captain Francesco Pinero.* Camillus Agrippa, another writer of military works,
especially on naval strategy, is mentioned in El Greco's library, but

without any specific title. Agrippa was also a mathematician, a philosopher, and an architect, and was summoned to Rome to build an aqueduct over the Monte Pincio.

Being an artist, El Greco naturally possessed one of the treatises on painting then so fashionable. Judging from its title—*A Treatise on the Art of Painting*—it may have been Lomazzo's but the first edition of this work was not published until 1584, and El Greco must have obtained it in Spain.

The "Moral Philosophy," which his son lists without any name attached, may have been the *Treatise on Moral Philosophy,* by Alessandro Piccolomini; one of the men of encyclopædic knowledge of the bygone century; poet, playwright, translator from the Latin and the Greek, skilled astronomer and geologist, he too was a typical representative of a period of transition. He began by writing licentious works and became, after public repentance, a professor of moral philosophy at Padua. Had El Greco's son made the list of his father's Italian library in less haste, adding the authors' names to the titles of the books, we might have had precious indications as to the men El Greco probably knew, for he bought books by even little-known contemporaries in the way one acquires those written by friends or acquaintances. Another book listed, under its title only—*The Art of Preserving the Health*—may well have been the work of the celebrated Venetian doctor, Tommaso da Ravenna, known as *Il Filologo,* who, according to legend, lived to the age of one hundred twenty, and whom El Greco could have met in Venice, where *Il Filologo,* despite his advanced age, was still practising medicine and anatomy.

Could El Greco, either in Venice, in Rome, or even in Spain, have met Francesco Patrizzi, whose *Ten Dialogues* (probably those on philosophy) he possessed? Born on the island of Cherso and originally named Petris, he was one of those foreigners of Italian culture who played the role of innovators in the country of their adoption. Patrizzi was to make a deep mark on his century. He had that encyclopædic knowledge, a heritage of the Renaissance, which not only enabled him to write treatises of geometry, history, music, and strategy, and to shine as an orator, but also to seek out new paths off the beaten track in philosophy, history, and poetry; he was a man who felt that his epoch needed yeast to make the heavy dough of its intellectual anguish rise. Patrizzi was one of those who fought with the greatest determination against the Aristotelian theory of substance and form, even to the point of exhorting the Pope to forbid the teaching of this philosophy as being irreconcilable with Christianity. He must have reinforced an ideological trend in El Greco which harked back to his youth. He may even have had some influence on his artistic creation. Patrizzi had managed not only to reconcile faith with the theories of Plato, a path along which so many others had preceded him, but also to develop a doctrine of his own, the centre of which was light, for according to him it was not the Prime Mover which engendered all things, as Aristotle taught, but the divine light, the first work of the Creator, towards which every soul ascended.

To El Greco's old preoccupations as revealed by his choice in books, one finds the addition of a new, absorbing interest. Books on architecture occupied an excessive amount of space in his library; his son listed nineteen out of a total of sixty-seven Italian books, but gave details concerning only a few of them.

El Greco had not lost his taste for poetry: his son found seventeen books of "romances" in his library. He mentioned a Petrarch and an Ariosto but no Dante. As one who kept up with his times, El Greco possessed one of the most popular works of the day, published in 1560—Bernardo Tasso's *Amadis*. This epic of "the perfect deed of man," based on an old Spanish romance in which, according to the prevailing taste, the reader does not find himself solely diverted by the loves of the hero, by the abundance of wonders, dreams and apparitions, magicians and fairies, but also nourished by erudition and moralities.

As a man who closely followed the literary and philosophic trends of his time and who was a Greek scholar besides, Domenico Theotocopuli took an active part in his friends' discussions. Such an exchange of ideas seems caught to the life in a curious group representing three men arguing round a table with a child, a picture attributed to Andrea Schiavone which formerly hung in an English private collection. The principal character, doubtless a person of note, is a young man clad in a cloak with a fur collar—an astronomer to judge from the globe he holds in his hands. His face is tense, as if he were in deep thought. On his right is another figure holding a book in one hand and a pen in the other, and next to him an older man, with heavy-looking eyes, as if they were exhausted from long nights of study. But even if the faces of the first two might have justified the attribution to Schiavone, only El Greco could have painted the hands of the man on the left, a dialectician's hands. The child, who is bringing in three notebooks, is as little childlike, with his adult gaze, as all those (with a few rare exceptions) which El Greco introduced into his pictures. There is such a pronounced atmosphere about this strange gathering that it has been called "The Humanists" and attributed to El Greco, for he alone was perhaps capable of portraying men wrestling with great intellectual problems.

There is one odd fact, however. The figures immediately strike one as men of standing. One would imagine them to be humanists of wide repute. But no celebrity of the time, whether great or small, has been recognized amongst them. From now on one comes up against the difficulty of identifying El Greco's characters. No painter of the time painted so many anonymous figures. From the intellectuals of Rome to Spanish noblemen one finds onself in the presence of en-gaging personalities whom one can guess to be singled out for a re-markable, often enigmatic, destiny, individuals who doubtless be-longed to the elite of their day and yet who are not the illustrious ones whose features are familiar.

The signed portrait in the State Gallery of Copenhagen of a man with his right hand raised and his left resting on a book laid on a table, has been thought to represent Palladio, whom El Greco fervently ad-mired and whom he could have met in Venice. But the model's fea-tures hardly correspond with the engraved portraits of the great archi-tect. Despite the care with which the realistic details of the portrait are executed, the model evokes that atmosphere of intellectual preoccupa-tion which El Greco knew so well how to create. One senses that he was a scholar. But it has been pointed out that the gesture of a raised hand is that of an orator, of a man whose business it is to persuade. The drooping nose and moody eyes are those of an Oriental. Some have supposed him to be a rabbi addressing the faithful, with his hand on the Bible. But the man lacks that fervour with which El Greco knew how to illumine even the sternest countenance. He is more like a pro-fessor, Jewish or Greek, brooding darkly on the problems of his calling.

In one portrait alone from this period (in the Frick Collection, New York) can the sitter be identified through a later inscription, but is is merely a name without significance, dragged out of oblivion (Plate 15). Did some foreigner passing through Rome and drawn by El Greco's reputation commission this portrait, or was it painted later, during his voyage to Spain, when he may have stopped at Malta? This full-length portrait is the apotheosis of an unknown man. The inscrip-tion on the high added stele bears information as to the titles of Fra Vincentio Anastagi, a Knight of Malta, the esteem in which he was held by the Grand Master, the battles against the Turks in which he took part and his death in a full naval engagement on the flagship. The Maltese archives further state that, having entered the order "without rank," he distinguished himself in the cavalry engagements which repulsed the violent attacks of the Turks against the island in 1565. Fra Vincentio Anastagi was perhaps a hero in the manner of so many anonymous heroes of his day. If he desired to pass down to posterity as such, his expectations were more than fulfilled. El Greco's Roman contemporaries, too, could have placed an important figure before a curtain (which with them would have become a theatrical back cloth), with the white cross of Malta plainly showing on his breast, sword in hand, with full breeches and strongly pronounced calves. But it was from their great predecessors that El Greco had learned this science of composition, this impressive fall of red hangings which cuts across the white wall to emphasize the lines of the arm and the sword. No Roman of his day could have painted the glitter of the armour, the reflected light breaking up the steel, or that green shining forth against the white with such sensitivity of detail and yet at the same time such subordination to the whole. The technical virtuosity, that Italian eloquence which El Greco had already made his own, is combined with a skilful realism which he owed to his knowledge of the Flemish painters, for it was only with the latter that this preoccupation with minute detail, those small leaded windowpanes, that caress of the brush round an object such as the helmet on the ground, could be found—a preoccupation which in El Greco's case, however, in no way detracted from his psychological penetration of the model.

El Greco was deeply aware both of what he had acquired from outside sources and of his own personal contribution. Success had come to confirm his proud inner certainty. Commissions poured in (not without arousing the envy of his Roman colleagues), to the extent that he began to train a disciple to help him in his work. His choice was typical of the demands he made on his fellow-men, of the value he attached in this age of threatened faith to strength of character and sincerity of convictions. Lattantio Bonastri was born at Lusignano of "honest and respectable" parents. According to the learned Dr. Mancini, one of his brothers was a Capuchin. He had "a most Christian character and was so reserved that he appeared rather stern and austere to the world, but he was not so in truth, for amongst his friends he displayed an extreme gentleness although, by holding himself aloof and withdrawn, he may have given an impression of severity." This brief sketch well describes a man who can be easily imagined to have been closely acquainted with El Greco. Lattantio Bonastri's austerity does not seem to have been merely a façade which he displayed to the world. The taste for solitude which Mancini noted, his fierce independence, and that slight tendency to secretiveness must only have been strengthened by his association with his master. According to the same authority, he made such progress in the sphere of art that he was summoned to Siena (probably after El Greco had left Rome) for a particularly honourable task. The memory of St. Catherine still lived on there with the force of an actual presence when Bonastri was charged with painting a fresco in the house in which she was born and the shop kept by her father, set up as a place of pilgrimage by the brotherhood of the saint. Mancini extolled in Bonastri's painting "the manner of Titian, the composition and the colouring, and the emotion which emanates from the picture, all so appropriate to the subject." He also praised his portraits. Bonastri must have acquired a sufficient mastery of portraiture from El Greco for his own to appear "wonderful." The young man of such promising talent attracted so much attention that Bartolommeo Neroni, called Il Riccio, the famous Sienese architect and painter, himself a son-in-law of Sodoma, offered him the hand of his daughter in marriage, being anxious to perpetuate an artistic dynasty. He was to die very young, crushed by a scaffolding, and only his brief association with El Greco has saved his name from oblivion.

El Greco, conscious of his superiority over his colleagues in Rome, cherished great hopes. In Rome he had initiated himself into the mysteries of composition. Although he partially adopted certain technical achievements, he rejected the superficial excitement, the overemphatic gestures, and exaggerated heroic postures, just as he rejected the false, tinsel emotions, the pretended fervours, the cold violence, and affected piety. One picture he painted, probably towards the end of his stay in Rome, illustrates this divergence between the religious imagery of Rome and his own sensibility. It marks the level which he had attained at that time, above all thanks to its choice of subject—St. Francis of Assisi, the patron saint of his native island. One of the first of an endless series of pictures of this saint is perhaps the one in the Zuloaga collection at Zumaya (Plate 16). Another early version is in the Donà Collection in Paris.

El Greco must have stopped one day at Assisi and seen there

amongst the frescoes that figure of St. Francis which purports to be
his authentic portrait. The picture he painted is partly a religious one
and partly an imaginary portrait. It may even have been painted
from a living model—one, as his disciple Brother Masseo said, "neither
handsome, learned, nor of noble birth"—with a low forehead en-
croached upon by thick, bushy hair, a heavy nose between eyes too
closely set, hollow cheeks covered by a wiry beard, and thick, strongly
defined lips, a sensuous and sad upper one projecting over the lower.
This head, seemingly consumed by an internal fever, is set too small
on an overlong and overrobust neck. The long hands marked with the
stigmata could never have belonged to the same body as the powerful
column of the neck—hands with fingers so thin and tapering that the
small nails cover the tips entirely, without even a narrow rim of flesh
to overlap them. There is a strong quality of Flemish attention to detail in this portrait-picture; the moulding of the lips, the relief of the
nostrils, the wrinkled joints of the thin fingers, and the polished skull
with the gaping caverns of its eye sockets turned towards the spectator.
El Greco's contemporaries usually preferred to paint saints gazing up
to heaven with eyes swimming in tears. The only feature common to
El Greco's saint and those of conventional saints in prayer is this movement of the eyes. But the thick eyebrows which shelter them are
frowning with such intensity that the brow is furrowed; the large eyes
protrude between their thin lids and the pupils, so uneven in size that
the saint seems to squint, are so filled with light that his gaze alone
dominates the whole picture. It is a light of gentle and sorrowful
prayer, a light which compels forgiveness from Heaven.

This was indeed the *Poverello* of Assisi whom El Greco painted the
way one paints a familiar friend—the saint who loved all things
warmed by the brotherly sun, every humble and dumb thing living
on this earth, so hospitable to the lowliest of creatures, the companion
saint of men wandering on the roads of the world, but also the saint
who, through his joyful and pure passion for all created things, whether
birds, flowers, or gushing springs, held direct colloquies with the Lord.
But the hands to which El Greco gave such prominence, with their
fingers spread out fanwise in the manner of prodigals who let everything slip through their fingers, are already the hands of all his saints
and martyrs in their total abandon to divine mercy. Beside the skull
runs the signature in Greek capital letters, forming part of the picture
in its ornamental perfection, the signature of a learned man who wishes
to leave no doubt as to his erudition.

The antagonism between El Greco and the atmosphere of Rome was not only a conflict between the living but also a struggle against one of the great dead. Michelangelo's presence continued to oppress him. One small painting dating from these last days in Rome reveals the extent to which he felt this influence. At the time of his arrival in Rome he was still able to see in a garden on Monte Cavallo a work epitomizing the spiritual torment which had racked the great old man's last years. In this torment, which led him to question the ideal he had pursued all his life and to repudiate his own creative effort, Michelangelo faced the shadow of death, and he who had dreamed of so many grandiose sepulchres turned his thoughts to a monument for his own tomb. But this Pietà, with the lifeless Christ slipping heavily from Joseph of Arimathea's arms into those of the Virgin, did not satisfy him; in one of his fits of rage he broke up the still-unfinished group and made a present of it to his servant. With this "Pietà (Plate 18) Michelangelo buried a whole epoch which he had borne on his shoulders—the heroic athletes who, thanks to him, had scaled the heavens, the mighty Man who had defied the universe. This crumpled Christ, with His head lolling on His shoulder, His lifeless hand turned inwards, His body, with its long unbroken line flowing from the armpit to the bent knee, so akin to Gothic saints, was the Christ of the new era; was according to Michelangelo himself:

That divine love which spread out its arms on the Cross to enfold us.

The mutilated group, restored by a sculptor to whom Michelangelo's servant sold it, passed on its message to a foreign artist. El Greco seems to have interpreted this message in his own way on a small wooden panel now in Philadelphia (Plate 17). From the formal viewpoint he borrowed from Michelangelo the acutely triangular composition, with the compact mass of the figures and the long, flowing lines which throw it up sharply, even if this sharpness leads to a confusion of interlaced arms and draperies billowing round a void at the base. He also borrowed the powerful arms, swelling neck, and square face of the Virgin, so close to the Delphic Sibyl. But El Greco imbued his formal borrowings with a new sensitivity. The pyramid no longer terminates in Joseph of Arimathea, but in the Holy Virgin, calling on heaven to witness her grief. Michelangelo had himself felt that this grief of the Virgin should be the main features of so great a mourning, for, in another Pietà, also unfinished, it is the Virgin who clasps the dead body of Christ, supporting it with a strength unleashed by despair. El Greco's Virgin, although she has borrowed the features of the Sibyl, has a wholly personal stamp; her mouth is twisted in a groan, her eyebrows rise like circumflex accents and there is a tortured look in her sunken eyes. It is through the manner in which El Greco reshaped the most flagrant borrowings that he fully revealed himself . . . revealed his limitations as much as his new contributions. Drawing his inspiration from a piece of sculpture, he nevertheless deprived it of all its plasticity, almost of its third dimension; in spite of its internal shadows the group seems flat, like a cutout silhouette. The background encroaches on the figures; but this same background, through its overemphasis, creates a depth of emotion instead of a recession into space. A devastated landscape with desertlike hollows, as if scooped out with a spoon, a landscape akin to that of "Mount Sinai," is overhung by a stormy sky, a sky of doomsday, towards which the three abandoned crosses rise up like phantoms.

The small "Pietà" in Philadelphia, which seems to have been followed by the one belonging to the Hispanic Society in New York, is in a sense a debate between El Greco and Michelangelo, a passionate argument in a mixture of rage and admiration. Two epochs stand face to face. However impressed El Greco may have been by the grandeur of the past, he knew it to be gone forever and that he was standing on the threshold of a new era. Many years later he was to recall his youthful revolt against an artistic vision alien to his own, and was to say grumblingly of Michelangelo: "He was a good man, but he couldn't paint."

However, he was not to wait for the creative affirmation of a lifetime to arrive at this judgment. He used to talk just as freely in Rome of that great, barely extinguished glory; he was as biting in his criticism then, while he was still disputing with Michelangelo's shade, as he was to be at the height of his own fame. His self-awareness had doubtless been awakened from the moment he took up a brush for the first time. His vocation and his pride in it were born simultaneously. Nothing ever shook his creative certainty, even when this surpassed his means. In the artistic circles of Rome, doubtless made touchy by his success, echoes of his inordinate pride long persisted in an exaggerated and distorted form. Many years later Dr. Mancini still heard his artist friends protesting indignantly over El Greco's presumptuous remarks. One day, while discussing the display of nudes in Michelangelo's "Last Judgment," which offended the new era of austerity, El Greco abruptly threw himself into the conversation, saying that "if all this work was

flung down to the ground, he could redo it with honesty and decency
and it would be in no way inferior in the quality of its painting." There
is in this reported statement an undeniable accent of truth, precisely because of its exaggerated nature, which a man like Mancini, with his
terse way of expressing himself, would have been incapable of in-
venting. At some moment in a conversation with more or less
mediocre artists El Greco had left himself go so far as to disclose his
innermost thoughts, for it was these that his remark betrayed. He was
hardly a man to be impelled to gratuitous assertions, even by irrita-
tion. On the contrary, everything known about him denotes an innate reserve, a shy sensitivity, even a taste for secrecy. This remark
which escaped him was a mature reflection and not a momentary
impulse. There was nothing on the surface to justify his inner certitude. He had not yet tackled any large wall surface and yet he felt
himself capable of redoing one of the most grandiose frescoes in the
world. El Greco, heir to a tradition of minutely detailed icons, and
also of the great Byzantine decorative painting, was a born fresco
painter. He was one of those who have no need to put themselves to
the test in order to discover their strength. He was certain of his ability to compete with the greatest glory of his century. He did not merely
talk of it as one does of a vague project. At the moment of uttering
those words which so scandalized his audience he had no doubt already roughed out the fresco which was to replace Michelangelo's.
This sketch (Plate 19), painted in oils on a panel of wood barely
twelve inches by nine and today in a German collection, is in fact infused with a mighty aspiration. El Greco's remarks may have seemed
insanely ambitious, but this little panel, conceived to fill a vast space, is
like an infinitely suggestive crystallization of this inordinate dream.
The notion of flinging Michelangelo's fresco "to the ground" smacks
of artistic blasphemy, of an unparalleled act of vandalism, enough to
make one shiver. But this idea was born in a time of exaltation which
gave reign to every kind of fanaticism and intransigence. The old
moulds were broken, the old framework had collapsed, and through
the wreckage a new concept of the spiritual unity of the world was
being forged. El Greco's project was an expression of this. It was
conceived in defiance, in deliberate opposition to the conception of
Michelangelo. But in so far as it was a revision of a grandiose (and, in
El Greco's eyes, erroneous) design, his sketch reveals an implacable
inner logic. It is no longer earth which has invaded heaven with its
flesh triumphant even in damnation; clouds no longer stand out on an

opaque and distant horizon like blocks of marble capable of supporting the weight of athletes. El Greco's heaven is a truly interstellar
space submerged in flashing lights. Michelangelo painted his "Last
Judgment" (Plate 20) when already under the shadow of that religious crisis which rent the world, in the desperate fervour of his own
soul-searching. But this fervour expressed itself through forms that
were familiar to him. Despite the stigmata, his Christ in Judgment is
really Jupiter brandishing a thunderbolt with his muscular arm. El
Greco's Christ is no longer of this world. Seated on a rainbow, with
the globe of the earth beneath his feet, He is the Saviour who has
taken heaven for a throne, the earth for a footstool, and whose empire
is the abyss. This rainbow overhangs the great drama of the ultimate
division into the saved and the damned. It is one stable thing, the sole
permanent material object in the midst of a world in upheaval. At the
foot of the picture reigns the terrible horror of the damned, the chaos
of perdition—a mass of white, ghostly bodies recoiling in terror from
the assault of black demons. The monster's jaws, with their fiery reflections, are opened to engulf them. A wave of what seems to be greenish
mud is swallowing up those who flee. But the angels have come down
from heaven to these desperate mortals, angels in red robes, with great
wings powerful enough to carry them and their burden of saved souls.
The Archangel Gabriel has also flung himself down from heaven with
such fury that he and his flaming sword form a line of demarcation
between the two worlds. Above the rainbow the excitement is almost
as intense as the battle for salvation continues. The Virgin, who inter-
venes with her Son, has flung back her arm in a frenzy of pity to point
towards the escort of ghostly martryrs behind her. St. John the Baptist,
the interceder for souls according to Byzantine tradition, has raised
towards Christ his hands clasped in such fervour that he seems to be
seeking to compel mercy. Behind him a column of prophets rises up to
heaven. Amongst them is Moses with the Tablets of the Law in a white,
luminous robe and a red cloak. In the centre of all this gyratory movement shines the immense gloriole of Christ, greenish round the edge
and dotted with the heads of cherubs as transparent as jellyfish in deep
water. The host of saved souls blends with the clouds; the interstellar
space is filled with angels bearing instruments of torture. Everything
in this tiny picture reflects fervour, ecstasy, and excess. But everything
is balanced round the light emanating from Christ like a whirlwind.
The composition, although fragmentary in its details, is as a whole a
grandiose arrangement conceived in truth for an immense surface. The

colours of the upper part have the transparency of glass, as if the human gaze were to plunge through it into infinity, to see heaven opening up before it, whereas earth and hell are engulfed in the scarlet of perdition. There is, in this little sketch, everything the great fresco he planned was intended to convey.

His contemporaries, however, saw nothing in his remarks about the "Last Judgment" but their unspeakable audacity. Like every city peopled with ambitious men, Rome had remained as sensitive as she had always been. The artists of Rome must have given vent to all the sarcasm called for by this challenge. In echoing an already ancient quarrel Mancini built it up into a drama round El Greco's person. "It was on account of these words," he wrote, "that he found all the painters and lovers of art opposed to him and was thus forced to leave Rome for Spain." Time had done its work of exaggeration by the time Mancini wrote these lines. A conspiracy of envious men was certainly formed, incited by El Greco's haughty demeanour. Perhaps there was also a drama by way of prelude to his departure for Spain, but one of another kind. Did El Greco really expect his idea to be accepted? More likely it was one of many stillborn dreams. Despite the protection of Giulio Clovio and the initial good will of Cardinal Farnese the great commissions were still not forthcoming. Under the gloom and constraint which oppressed the city, and in spite of the stiffening of men's spirits, Rome had not yet found a clearly defined creative purpose, that unity of artistic direction which had imbued her in the time of the Renaissance. And far away a monarch was building a lavish yet austere sanctuary for a militant religion. Nothing precise is known about El Greco's reasons for leaving Rome. Mancini wrote: "With all this, he was, in the prime of his life, a man to be placed amongst the best of his century."

CHAPTER
FOUR
THE CITY
OF GENERATIONS

ACCORDING to an ancient legend, Toledo was founded by the Jews who fled from Nebuchadnezzar. They are said to have named it Toledoth, the city of generations. Indeed, in this city poised on its rock, there is not one inch of soil that has not been trodden by either the triumphal march of conquerors or the flight of the vanquished. One conquest succeeded another, each leaving traces of its passage. Each steep and narrow street seems like a dry stream bed along which great events have flowed. Each square recalls either a victory or a defeat. Toledo's history lives also in the imposing aspect she has carved out of the rock and not only in memories obscured by the eclipse of most ancient splendour.

Toledo, rising starkly from its rocky foundations up to heaven, is all pride. Moreover its grandeur is still so spectacular that it does not seem to belong to the past alone. In about 1560 the ancient city, said a historian, was the capital of Spain, but it might have been that of the entire world. According to some, its inhabitants numbered 80,000, according to others, 100,000, hemmed into a small space by the steep banks of the river Tagus, as it were inside a horseshoe. It stood in the heart of a vast agricultural region; and this purple soil, called *La Sagra,* was, according to a contemporary witness, the most fertile and best suited for the cultivation of fruit in the whole of Spain. Toledo, in fact, rose up amidst the silver foliage of olive trees, vineyards, and the pink foam of almond blossom. Friuts and vegetables as well as corn abounded within a stone's throw of the city. But those cornfields and market gardens irrigated by the Tagus, those mulberry plantations and rich orchards, belonged mostly to the Church, the monastic orders, and fraternities. The farmers, poor and often starving, had to seek work in the town. The silk industry, the most important in Toledo, could absorb a considerable amount of labour. It was renowned all over the world for the beauty of its products, its velvets, damasks, and taffetas. Very ancient and important too was the wool industry; Toledan cloth was much appreciated throughout the realm of Spain. The hosiery trade flourished there as well; cheap goods and tarbooshes were exported to Africa and Turkey. A great many candles were manufactured in view of the numerous churches; but in this by no means austere city confections prospered as well, and their marzipan enjoyed a particular reputation.

In the sixteenth century the fame of the weapons manufactured at Toledo eclipsed that of all its other industrial products. The name of a Toledan blade had become synonymous with a thin blade of exquisite workmanship. The master armourers, renowned in every court, were favoured with royal privileges. In times of peace between wars, they also made cutlery in their workshops: table sets of the finest quality. Toledo was in this sixteenth century one of the foremost commercial centres of the empire. Men traded there with buyers from every country and exported their wares to the New World.

At the time of El Greco's arrival in Toledo, probably about 1577, the city was still in its full glory; foreigners still flocked there, following an established trend. They intended to come for a few days or weeks, but stated a Spaniard, they stayed for years, sometimes forever. El Greco came there too for a temporary visit, for a specific purpose. But he was never to leave it again.

Toledo had, however, ceased to be the head of the kingdom. The court had left the city in 1561, when Philip II chose Madrid for his capital. Toledo did not offer sufficiently spacious accommodation for the proud courtiers; there were no thoroughfares wide enough for their sumptuous coaches. The climate was harsh, with scorching summers and bitter winters, but it was Toledan pride above all which no longer accorded with the new spirit with which Philip II, as an absolute ruler, imbued his entourage.

The son of Charles V, who had a vindictive memory, had perhaps not forgotten that forty years earlier the revolt of the *comuñeros* had raged through the city and had resisted the armies of the Emperor for over a year. But even if he no longer remembered this, he himself was to come up against the Toledan's fierce spirit of independence when, in 1560, he was engaged in a violent quarrel with the chapter of the cathedral, who reproached him with having violated the right of sanctuary granted by the Church to a man condemned for murder.

Though the court had gone (temporarily, it was believed), Toledo did not become empty overnight. Its population, on the contrary, rose even higher; Moorish converts and people not only from Galicia and Asturia but also from France still came to the city. There was something in this savage soil which acted as a magnet on adventurers, restless spirits, and men aspiring towards a more intense spiritual life or troubled by a vague curiosity. The simple fortune hunters went to Seville or embarked for the New World in pursuit of fabulous treasures; the ambitious haunted Madrid in quest of royal favours; but it was at Toledo that, according to a Spanish observer, souls and swords were tempered.

The city of generations was perhaps more suited than any other to serve as a refuge for all uprooted people. A friend of El Greco's was to write one day that it became for him "a better fatherland." Every foreigner seemed to feel that one of his distant forebears must have dwelt in this city, that some blood akin to his own had flowed between its deep cobblestones, for much blood had been spilt in its steep streets.

Both Carthage and Rome had contended for this region with the Celtiberi; the Romans had been the first to elevate Toledo into the capital of the colony they called Carpetania. Like El Greco's native island, Toledo too had its roots in the great past of ancient Rome. The famous Cave of Hercules seems to have had its origins in the foundations of a temple of Jupiter; the remains of an important aqueduct are still visible in the rocks below the Alcázar; outside the city a semicircular enclosure, built by the Romans but probably never completed, is called the Circus Maximus. But at the time of El Greco's arrival the great encircling walls served for the stakes of the Inquisition, for the city remembered above all her ancient Christian tradition, her militant faith, and the fact that her first bishop, St. Eugene, had been a disciple of St. Paul.

The flood of vandal invasions had raged in vain round the walls of Toledo. The kingdom of the Visigoths had set up its capital there; the most powerful of rulers who held his luxurious court in the city assumed the title of King of Toledo. Of the centuries of Visigoth rule little is left: some scattered capitals, a few broken columns, some fragments of carving. The principal remaining memory is that of a holy scholar who testified to the virginity of the mother of God and who became the city's patron saint. This was St. Ildefonso, whose memory El Greco was to glorify many times.

Toledo's militant faith resisted the most powerful conquerors and the longest reigns. Vanquished by the Muslims and annexed by the Saracen Khalifate, Toledo retained its churches, its privilege of freedom of worship, and its status as a Christian metropolis within the Muslim Empire. Toledo was never to bear the stamp of a Moorish city like Seville or Cordova. It also maintained its spirit of independence, its reluctance to submit to external control. It boasted of recognizing no other ruler or government than the faraway Sultan himself.

As the most important state in the Moorish Empire, Toledo also became a city of a thousand wonders. The Moorish chroniclers praised its fountains and waterworks, described its fairy-tale palace as a crystal pavilion rising from the centre of a lake with its interior lit by lamps of every hue. However great as architects the Moors had been, they left less to remember of their period of domination than they did memories of a time when their glory was in eclipse; this lived on in the work of their craftsmen, in the *mudejar* art. The churches they converted into mosques during their rule, such as that of Bib Al Mardom, were to testify to the permanence of the Toledan's Christian faith. An ancient building dating from the time of the Visigoths, it contained a miraculous Crucifix which, on the entrance of the Muslim troops, had been walled up by a faithful citizen with a lantern burning at Christ's feet. When Alfonso recaptured Toledo, the Cid's horse stumbled against the wall and the stones of the niche fell, revealing the Crucifix with the lantern still burning—after three and a half centuries. And the mosque which became a church once more was to bear henceforward the name of Christ of the Light: *Cristo de la Luz.*

The old bridge of Alcantara, a marvel of Mauresque architecture, had been swept away by the great flood of the thirteenth century; of the fifteen gates of the ancient city walls only one survived—the Puerta Antigua de Bisagra.

Perhaps stronger marks were left by the tormented presence of the Jews than by the long Moorish domination. To the legend which made them the founders of the city, doubtless confusing them with the first Phœnician colonists, another had been added, of a letter said to have been addressed by the Jewish community of Toledo to the Sanhedrin of Jerusalem in protest against the crucifixion of Christ.

After the fall of Jerusalem the Jews flocked into Spain. They brought with them, according to the Moorish chroniclers, treasures saved from the Holy City, the Table of Solomon carved from a single emerald, the Psalms of David written on leaves of gold in an ink made of diluted rubies. Toledo harboured every kind of legend. Within its walls all was amplified, shorn of its everyday, familiar features. But hatreds too became exacerbated there. Passions were appeased in blood. During the Moorish domination the act of a Christian renegade, who invited the nobles into his castle only to have them savagely assassinated, gave birth to the proverbial expression of "a Toledan night." There have been many cruel and bloody nights in Toledo. The persecution of the Jews began with the rule of the Visigoths and knew no respite save in the time of the Moors. The Jewish physicians were particularly renowned; their scholars translated Arabic works into Hebrew, Latin, and Spanish. Thanks to them the Middle Ages were nourished by a learning which would otherwise have been irretrievably lost; thanks to them Toledo became for long, even after the fall of the Moors, a centre for the distribution of a thousand-year-old knowledge, a meeting place between East and West.

One day held in high esteem, the next persecuted by an exasperated people, either fabulously rich or flung to an ignominious death, torn between pride and shame, the Jews with their ever-precarious and threatened existence had been the initiators of a science which subjected the unstable laws of human life to the permanence of the heavens, to the eternity of the stars. It was through the Jewish astrologers and their study of Arabic sources, reaching back into antiquity, that the Middle Ages received their initiation into this science; an initiation which was to live on and to dominate the West for a long time. The Jews also brought with them to Toledo an element of mystery which strangely became so much a part of the city that it seemed to be one with it. A Jewish scholar named Andreas had translated certain Arabic books on magic; the ground must have been so fertile, the time so favourable to mysteries that Toledo thus acquired a world-wide reputation as a centre of black magic. The supernatural gained ground with remarkable ease and persisted among the heirs of the magicians and the Cabbala; within those walls which had witnessed so much, everything seemed possible, nothing any longer caused surprise; out of the shadows cast by that harsh light men expected, according to the words of a poet, to see "either a saint or a lion" rise up at any moment.

This element of mystery lurking in the stones of Toledo possibly captivated Domenico Theotocopuli from the start and awoke in him something which had lain dormant in the rational and serene atmosphere of Italy. Having come to Toledo almost by chance, El Greco became spellbound by this city which had bewitched so many foreigners. No precise facts are known about the date of his arrival in Spain. According to subsequent research, he presumably spent a year and a half in Madrid before coming to Toledo; consequently he must have left Italy in 1575. Nor are there any clear indications as to his reasons for this journey. But the gigantic undertaking of the Escorial was the great event of the day, the highest hope of every artist in the world. Even old Giulio Clovio offered his services several times to Philip II, proposing to paint, amongst others, a picture of St. Lawrence, the patron saint of the Escorial, which he promised would be "a signal work." El Greco must have anticipated definite commissions when he embarked on his journey. He must have left Italy with pledges made in advance, for it would have been contrary to his nature, at once prodigal and prudent, to plunge into uncertainty, even if disappointment had been dogging him in Rome. Perhaps he was counting on the protection of Philip II, since he had been recommended to him by Titian. However, nothing is known of his activities during his stay in Madrid. Supposedly he painted some portraits and altarpieces, for in one of his later letters he mentions an advance from the archpriest of the cathedral.

While in Rome he seems to have got in touch, through Fulvio Orsini, with some Toledan humanists—amongst others with Pedro Chacón, who had been living a long time in Italy. Theologian, mathematician, historian, archæologist, and philologist, this man was one of those who had been commissioned with the reform of the calendar by Gregory XIII and he was regarded by his contemporaries as a living encyclopædia (*"perenne scientiarum flumen"*). With Chacón in Rome was Don Luis de Castilla, the illegitimate descendant of King Pedro the Cruel, and his meeting with El Greco was the start of a lifelong friendship. Don Luis was to look after El Greco's interests even after his death, for the latter appointed him to be the executor of his will. His first intervention in El Greco's affairs was in the name of his brother, Don Diego de Castilla, the dean of Toledo Cathedral and also protector of the convent of Santo Domingo de Silos, called El Antiguo. At the beginning of this decisive orientation in El Greco's life there occurred, at the end of the year 1575, the death of a very pious lady in the convent of San Domingo el Antiguo in Toledo. This was Doña María de Silva, who came from Portugal as a lady in waiting to Queen Isabella, wife of Charles V, and who retired into this convent after the death of her husband, Don Pedro Gonzalez de Mendoza, intendant of the palace. There she spent almost forty years and, in gratitude for the peace she found there, she bequeathed her entire fortune to the convent, for the reconstruction of its church, which was falling in ruins.

The dean of the cathedral, Don Diego de Castilla, was appointed as executor of her will. To carry out the reconstruction, he turned to the architect of the cathedral, Nicolas de Vergara, called *El Mozo,* who seemed the obvious choice. With him he concluded a contract at the beginning of that year, followed by another in which he engaged master masons to carry out the work according to Vergara's plans.

But there came a sudden change. Was it the new wind blowing from the Escorial and imposing an artistic conception more in keeping with the times, or was it rather the taste of the King? The Toledan architects built in a style which seemed to spring from the soil itself, a belated Gothic which could develop without transition into baroque— a kind of florid renaissance which drew its inspiration from all the scattered elements of the past: the exuberance of Mauresque ornamentation and a taste for arabesque close to Hebrew calligraphy. This highly ornamented style, which was to leave its mark on the cities of Spain, was chosen by the nobles and bourgeois for their palaces and houses, in harmony with the light of Spain which sharply chiselled every detail. But the official Renaissance style imposed on the cathedrals was of foreign inspiration and seemed to turn away from the indigenous work as from a provincial relation. Under the influence of that fanatic devotee of austerity, Philip II, classicism became more and more stripped and severe; the fashionable architecture of the day was haunted by the grandeur of bare walls. Its repercussions were felt in Toledo. The contract with Nicolas de Vergara was cancelled three months later, on the sight of his model, for which he was paid compensation. In May of the same year Don Diego de Castilla signed a new contract with the master masons, submitting other plans to them.

As a man conscious of his responsibilities towards the deceased lady, he did not wish to run the risk of entrusting the work to someone unknown; he therefore turned to Juan de Herrara, the architect of the Escorial. Herrara did not listen to any of the voices from the past which echoed in Toledo, nor did he let his imagination run away with him. He had come to architecture through mathematics and geometry; he had illustrated a learned Arabic work with geometrical drawings

and also attributed to him is a book on *The Explanation of the Cube
according to Italian Art*. He had a cold and precise mind, trained by
military discipline (he had served in Italy and Flanders as an arque-
busier in the Imperial Guard), and remained deeply attached to the
house of Austria, following Charles V into his retreat at San Yuste
Monastery. During these years when Don Diego was occupied with
the church of San Domingo, Juan de Herrera was in charge of the
rebuilding of the Alcázar in Toledo and drawing up plans for the Casa
del Ayuntamiento. The dean of the cathedral seized this opportunity.
He was so determined to do his best that he even exceeded the sum
bequeathed to the convent, providing the balance from his own purse.

Don Diego proceeded in the same way for the construction of the
great altarpiece destined for the church. He had first asked the man
he had close at hand, Hernando de Avila, the painter and sculptor
of the cathedral, to design the plans. But these no longer struck him
as being suited to the ambitious projects he had conceived for the convent church. He applied to Herrera, asking him to make a model for
the altar. El Greco's arrival in Spain, and his brother's recommendation, then induced Don Diego to entrust the newcomer with the whole
altarpiece, its architectural frame, carvings, and panels (Plate 21).

Had El Greco carried out architectural work in Rome? Had he already given proof of his abilities as a sculptor? There is nothing to
indicate any activity of this kind in the past, yet how is it possible to
imagine a novice in this field being invited to replace a man of Juan
de Herrera's reputation? That El Greco's self-confidence would have
led him to undertake the whole sculptural work without previous experience is an insufficient explanation. It is more likely that Don
Diego's brother had seen works of his in Rome of which no trace has
come down to us. At any rate, in September 1577, Don Diego de
Castilla signed a contract with Juan Bautista Monegro, a sculptor of
repute, who undertook to execute three altarpieces, the principal one
being destined for the high altar, according to the plans and models
of Meçer Domenico Theotocopuli, whose name henceforward took
on a Spanish ring. For the same main altarpiece Monegro was to execute a seven-foot-high custodial after El Greco's model. This detailed
contract, which laid down the order of the columns, the dimensions
of the architrave, the size of the bases, and the types of mouldings for
the frieze and cornice, also specified that fresh wood from the Sierra
de Cuenca would be supplied to Juan Bautista Monegro, who was to
execute the sculptures, in accordance with the models provided, by

16. St. Francis. c. 1570

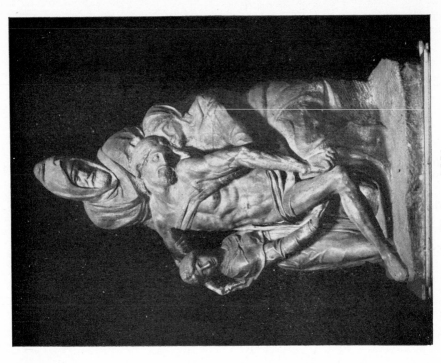

18. Michelangelo: Pietà. c. 1551

17. Pietà. c. 1575–77

20. Michelangelo: Last Judgment. 1536—41

19. Last Judgment. c. 1576—77

21. Altarpiece at San Domingo el Antiguo, Toledo. 1577

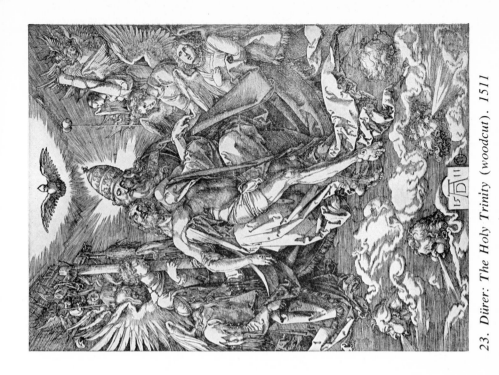

23. Dürer: The Holy Trinity (woodcut). 1511

22. The Holy Trinity (detail). 1577

24. *The Assumption of the Virgin. 1577*

25. *Titian: Assumption of the Virgin. 1516–18*

26. *Resurrection of Christ. 1577–78*

his own hand and without any outside aid in view of his well-known skill at carving and sculpture. El Greco, for his part, undertook "to paint all the pictures with his own hand, neither delegating nor being permitted to delegate them to other artists, because this work has been entrusted to the said Domenico in view of his reputation, as one eminent in his art and profession, and known for his personal ability which cannot be substituted by that of any other." El Greco further undertook not to take the pictures away from Toledo, nor to leave the city before he had completed them.

These clauses and provisions were typical of a contract concluded with a man whose arrival had been preceded by an immense reputation. Jusepe Martínez refers to it in his treatise on "the most noble art of painting."[1] He describes the arrival of El Greco in "the most celebrated and ancient city of Toledo," coming from Italy and calling himself a disciple of Titian. Although this treatise was written about a century later, Martínez could have had such details from his friend Velásquez, who greatly admired El Greco's work and whose father-in-law, Pacheco, had known him personally. But Martínez' taste, conforming to the conceptions of his own day, remained unresponsive to El Greco's particular vision and it was not without irony that he wrote of his beginnings in Toledo: "He came to this city with a great reputation, to such an extent that he let it be understood that nothing in the world was superior to his art."

El Greco quickly set to work to prove this superiority, of which he was fully conscious. In the same year of 1577 he executed the centrepiece of the high altar—signed and dated in Greek letters—"The Assumption of the Virgin" (now in the Chicago Art Institute) (Plate 24). As usual, in this transitional stage, El Greco, in spite of his self-confidence, resorted to borrowing whenever he particularly wished to succeed. Nor perhaps did he want to shock his Toledan patrons; he therefore confined himself to the classical and current composition and types familiar to them. He fell back on the firm ground of Titian's teaching. His "Assumption" all too clearly recalls the "Assunta" of the old Venetian master (Plate 25). Like him, he divided his picture into two spheres, the earthly and the supernatural. This division remains a purely formal one. The human beings and the angels are, as in Titian's picture, of the same bodily substance. The child's head peering over the arching clouds as if from behind a balustrade is a portrait,

[1]*Discursos praticables del nobilisimo arte de la pittura, c.* 1675, but not published until 1853.

just as the Apostles are; portraits and models used already in his previous works, such as the "Healing of the Blind Man" and the "The Cleansing of the Temple." El Greco's earthly sphere is all the more isolated in that the Apostles, as opposed to Titian's version, do not raise their eyes to the miracle taking place above their heads, but argue with eloquent gestures round the empty tomb. The Virgin herself is completely Italian, with small, feminine hands such as Pontormo painted, stretched out rather affectedly as if caressing the sky.

The clear, radiant picture, of a serenity rare with El Greco, a completely Italian serenity, discloses its Cretan origins only through its shortcomings. In the same way as the Italian painters El Greco tried to create depth by placing the sarcophagus on a slant, but his errors in perspective arrest the movement begun and the picture remains flat and confined to the foreground. El Greco must have been embarrassed by all that this picture failed to reveal of his true self. Contrary to his custom, he never returned to this subject.

To crown the altar, he painted "The Holy Trinity," now in the Prado (Plate 22), with the dead Christ in the arms of God the Father. For this composition he made use of an engraving by Dürer (Plate 23). And as if this formal borrowing, which he incidentally interpreted in his most personal manner, had influenced the whole spirit of the picture, a realistic note has crept into the body of Christ, a body of an anatomical and sculptural perfection rarely found with El Greco. Christ lies dead in all his Venetian beauty, his regular features barely touched by suffering. But the age-old lids lowered over the eyes of God the Father are contracted with grief, the eyebrows of one of the chubby angels are knit with pain of sorrow, and another with swelling calves already has the elongated Spanish head, flattened at the back, of El Greco's future angels.

From the same period of what seems to have been frenzied work (one or perhaps two years, 1577 and 1578) dates probably the "Resurrection of Christ" (Plate 26). Here too El Greco made use of what he had acquired in Italy: the elliptical composition dear to his Roman fellow-artists; the two lateral figures with their violent counterpoint of movement; the nude soldier seen from the back, an echo from Tintoretto; and the slender, almost elegant figure of Christ, with the perfectly modelled body whose gesture seems to imply barely more than a simple wave of farewell. But between the "Assumption of the Virgin" and this "Resurrection" something has happened, some element of emotion has crept into El Greco's art, as if he had rediscovered a part of himself. In this theatrical setting, between the cardboard rocks, a mystery takes shape, a struggle evolves between the earthly solidity of man and his awareness of the divine. The naked Apostle in the right bottom corner, curled up in heavy slumber, and the other one stretched out asleep by the empty tomb, form a striking contrast with the tall, naked soldier dumbfounded by the miracle, whose stupefaction is communicated to his dazzled comrade in a repetition of his gesture, in the ascending diagonals which lend movement to the rising figure of Christ. The picture, which seems to testify to the firm ground which El Greco probably felt beneath his feet, to a confidence newly acquired or recovered, is also a testimony of gratitude. In the left foreground, in his sacerdotal garments, is Don Diego de Castilla, included in the formal ellipse which embraces the miracle. This again is a realistic portrait looking up in half profile, with hollow temples, high cheekbones, upturned eyes, and a short upper lip; but it is also the precursor of all El Greco's saints who turn to heaven with violent fervour.

The two saints of the side wings of the high altar, which stood to right and left of the "Assumption," also appear to be portraits—portraits—portraits of monks or ecclesiastics whose expressions, however, harmonize so closely with El Greco's internal vision that they seem fully integrated with his art.

The body of "St. John the Baptist," with its gaunt, anchorite's anatomy, reveals the extent to which El Greco was familiar with Flemish painting. Those large, hardened feet; those prominently veined hands; those thin arms with muscles as tough as plaited rope; that broad, hollow chest; that collar-bone making a cavity of shadow in the powerful neck; all are of a realism barely transposed and would seem to have belonged to someone who posed for El Greco in a studio. Yet through its movement this emaciated body seems to be raised on to a higher, spiritual plane.

The companion to this half-naked anchorite is "St. John the Evangelist," or rather, according to a Spanish historian, St. Paul. It illustrates even better what was conscious and deliberate in this vision of the saints imposed by El Greco on the religious fervour of the Toledans. Draped in his ample robes caught up in folds around him, like a large and majestic pillar, he is the first in the line of El Greco's contemplative saints, of those intellectuals with furrowed brows, lost in contemplation as if alone in the world.

One of El Greco's rare drawings (Biblioteca Nacional, Madrid),

squared up ready for transfer to canvas, reveals how carefully he prepared his compositions, for it barely differs from the final execution.
This drawing is also revealing for its smoky texture, its fine cross hatching of shadows; it is the drawing of a man with an exclusively pictorial
vision, more preoccupied with the arrangement of the surfaces than
with the internal framework, the skeleton. A sensitive hand with long,
tapering fingers is held before the mouth, in the manner of solitary
beings who sometimes murmur the words they are reading out loud.
Even more characteristic is the other hand, holding a book as rarely
a book has been held, in an attitude that seems wholly personal to
El Greco: the forefinger is parted away from the others, which are
bunched together in a manner only possible for the very supple fingers
of an Oriental. Below the wrinkles furrowing the brow, above the narrow bridge of the nose, the eyebrows are knit in an effort of concentration from which nothing could distract this man, shut away with his
own thoughts.

Two other saints, painted in half length, probably a few years later,
also formed part of the high altar—the "St. Benedict" in the Prado and
probably the "St. Bernard" from the former Cheramy Collection—
though it is of a very inferior quality. These too are realistic portraits
—especially that of St. Benedict, with his pointed features and wide,
lopsided mouth, with twisted lips anticipating the sufferings that heavily drag down the mouths of those of El Greco's saints who were closest
and most personal to him. Painted, too, with a Flemish precision are
the crooks which these saints hold, crooks of delicate workmanship.
But this realistic treatment, which includes the wrinkled brows, the
tufts of hair spared by the tonsure, and the carving on the crooks, is
subordinated to the lighting, to the contrasts of light and shade which
mould the pictures into broad planes.

The most astonishing thing in the artistic balance sheet of San
Domingo is this quality of monumentality which El Greco achieved
with such ease, as if he had never done anything else before his arrival
in Spain than cover vast wall spaces with frescoes. Even if he had not
already given proof of his mastery of mural painting, architecture, or
sculpture, it all seems to have been ready waiting in him for a fulfilment both close and certain.

The arrogance which Jusepe Martínez mocked at a time when
appreciation of El Greco's art was suffering a long eclipse was merely
that great, inner self-confidence which filled this creator of tormented
saints. That derisive echo across the silence of the centuries perhaps

provides the very key to an understanding of El Greco: his conviction of his creative power, which nothing and no one could ever shake.

In the church of San Domingo el Antiguo, El Greco painted one other picture which is like a crossroads, a meeting point between Italy and Spain, between the traditional elements and the change which was taking place within him. This change was a rapid one. Two years at the most had elapsed since he began to work in Toledo, and if he still had recourse to borrowings, he was already recasting them in a wholly personal manner.

"The Adoration of the Shepherds" (Plate 27), painted for an altar in the right wing of the transept, clearly recalls Correggio's "Night"; yet he made use of this only as one would use a preliminary drawing or fragments of some picture painted in the past.

El Greco also drew on his own work: one of the shepherds surrounding the Child bears the features of his "Boy Blowing on Charcoal" (Plate 28). It was to his apprenticeship in Rome that El Greco owed the elliptical shape in which he set his composition. Yet, despite all these recollections and borrowings, everything that Italy had meant for him is abolished from this picture.

The ellipse of the composition, set on a slant, should open up depths in the background of the picture. In fact it merely creates a void and disposes the figures in tiers, as if they were placed on the steps of a staircase. The whole thing occurs in an undefined setting. Space has disappeared from El Greco's work and never again was he to try to correct this optical failing, the absence of perspective. As in Byzantine painting, there is no distance between the figures; in spite of their fictitious plastic quality they are separated from each other only by their outlines. Light remains the sole active agent bringing order into the picture. From now on light begins to eat into the substance of human bodies. Two angels, who appear on the extreme right of the picture under a thin crescent moon, are mere phantoms. And the glorification floating up above, although still composed of chubby little angels, is all flashing light and tongues of fire, an abrupt sunrise over the darkness of the world. To complete his message, El Greco placed in the right foreground the prophet Isaiah, the interpreter of the miracle, the commentator on the Scripture. The old man, looming up in half length from the frame, is seen against the light, set in a thin border of brightness. The candle he holds, which is his own private source of light, throws up his face, turned towards the spectator with a piercing gaze. It was typical of El Greco to have selected, as an intermediary between the believer and the miracle, this intellectual interpreting a passage from the Bible, who sternly scrutinizes the spectator to make sure he has been fully understood. Surely nothing could be more naïve than the tiny Child, the source of the light of the world; nothing could be more spontaneous in sacred history than the adoration of these simple-hearted men? Yet there is not the slightest trace of naïveté in El Greco's picture. No spontaneous outburst of faith acknowledges the miracles. Instead a process of thought, a reasoning based on Holy Writ. From the time of his earliest work in Spain, El Greco's cerebral quality becomes predominant. This quality was innate. It was not the outcome of his Spanish environment, but this environment released it in him, through an intimate concordance with the atmosphere of a place, the physiognomy of a town, or relations with human beings, a concordance which made it possible for a creative spirit fully to discover itself. This emancipation must have hastened thanks to that simplest of stimulants, personal happiness.

El Greco had completed the commission for San Domingo el Antiguo which had brought him to Toledo. He could have departed, instead of undertaking further commitments. Living conditions were difficult in Toledo. The town was overpopulated. When St. Theresa wished to settle there with a handful of nuns, she found accommodation only with the greatest of difficulty. The man who procured somewhere for her to live seemed an angel sent from heaven, and the fact of having found a precarious roof appeared to her a miracle.

The shortage of housing and the influx of foreigners had brought about a rise in rents and in the cost of food. "Toledo is costly but famous," wrote Lope de Vega. El Greco spoke no Spanish, or only a little. He was a foreigner passing through. Yet at a time when he was freed of his obligations and in a position to pursue the object of his journey to Spain, to return to Madrid, to show his worth at the court, and seek commissions for the Escorial, other more powerful ties bound him to Toledo.

It was probably during his stay in Madrid that El Greco had met Doña Jerónima de las Cuevas. She had relatives there, a brother or cousin married to a woman of that city. Her family, however, seems to have been Toledan in origin, though this name has not been found in the city registers. Toledan women enjoyed a reputation for great sagacity. As a contemporary asserted, "a woman here expresses more in one word than an Athenian philosopher in a whole volume." In addition to this sagacity, with which the woman who was to share the rest of El Greco's life must have been endowed, Doña Jerónima had also the heart-stirring appeal of her beauty. For El Greco she was to be all women, for from the moment of their meeting all the women saints he painted bore features derived from hers. It is from this persistently recurring woman's face that the constant presence of Doña Jerónima at his side is adduced.

El Greco seems to have had the same faculty for concentration in love as in his creative work, the same tendency to focus on a single object, the same taste for exclusiveness. Prodigal, even wasteful, on the material plane, he was thrifty, almost miserly where his affections, friendship, and artistic emotions were concerned, in the manner of men who mistrust their own capacity for self-abandonment. His faculty for an intense enjoyment of living, his taste for comfort, his need of luxury, went hand in hand with attachment to a single being or a single creative urge.

Almost all El Greco's early biographers have believed the portrait of "The Lady with the Fur" in the Sir John Stirling-Maxwell Collection in Glasgow to be the first trace of his meeting with Doña Jerónima. They have also concurred in seeing in this picture the last line of demarcation separating El Greco's Italian period from his Spanish one. But one of his more recent biographers has contested this traditional attribution, with the support of convincing arguments, since the celebrated portrait figured in the collection of Louis Philippe as being that of "El Greco's Daughter." However, neither its very smooth texture, painted with a miniaturist's care which does not linger over the details alone (such as the edge of the veil, or the fur, so marvellously painted that each hair almost corresponds to a thin stroke of the brush), but extends over the whole picture, nor the cold and forthright colouring accords with El Greco's technique, even at the time when he was adapting himself to the manners of Titian and Tintoretto.

The model with the pure oval face, large wide-opened eyes with their calm gaze, small but full mouth, and little pointed chin does not entirely belie the types of Virgin or Magdalen on whom El Greco bestowed the features of the woman he loved; but the spirit is missing. The beautiful face of the "Lady with the Fur" is quite devoid of emotion; her calm, almond eyes have nothing in common with the other's burning, typically Spanish gaze. If the portrait is by El Greco, then it is one of his early works, perhaps the portrait of some Greek woman, as one of his biographers would have it. In any case it is an effort at adaptation, successful but transient to a technique of careful detail and to that Italian serenity and detachment which he never quite learned how to master.

Doña Jerónima's first appearance in El Greco's work is perhaps in the "St. Veronica" holding out the sudary of Christ (Plate 29) in the San Vicente Museum in Toledo. She has a high, arched forehead; her face is broad and yet enormous eyes extend almost to the temples under thick eyebrows; long lashes and heavy lids droop over a sombre, burning gaze which bears witness to her origin. The nose is long and slender; the cheeks narrow sharply to a pointed chin; the mouth is small, with the thin bow of the upper lip compressed on to the swelling lower one. This face is far from the ideal of classic beauty, yet its irregular features, with the mouth too small for the too large eyes, are infinitely mobile. One feels it to be open to every emotion, almost transparent, reflecting its full capacity for feeling. In all the Madonnas and Magdalens to whom Doña Jerónima lent her features one finds turn by turn her tender sorrow or her ecstasies.

Historians, who have searched in vain through the archives for documentary proof, have nonetheless assumed, thanks to certain indications, than Doña Jerónima was of superior social rank, even belonging to the nobility, and enjoyed certain wealth. Yet these vague gleams of light shed by competent scholars only darken the mystery which overhangs the relationship between the young woman and her artist. Doña Jerónima became El Greco's mistress very shortly after their first meeting. Their son, Jorge Manuel, was born in 1578. Nothing seems to have stood in the way of El Greco's marrying the woman he loved, above all the mother of his son. Jorge Manuel remained his only child. He loved him passionately. He painted him at every age: as an adorable little page, as a graceful youth, and as a mature man, even arousing the indignation of the ecclesiastics by the persistence with which he depicted his features on every possible occasion. He loved him blindly, even deceiving himself as to his potentialities, his artistic gifts. He acknowledged Jorge Manuel from his birth and gave him his name. Yet most careful research in the Toledan church registers has failed to provide evidence that El Greco married the mother of his son. No contemporary mentions the presence of a lawful wife in his home. Their liaison and this child born in sin must have caused a scandal; the religious zeal of the Toledans implied a deep respect for the bonds of marriage.

In Spain faith joined forces with morality to safeguard the integrity of the family. As opposed to Italian tolerance, this country brought home, even to the most illustrious of bastards, the irregularity of their birth. The famous Don Juan of Austria, an illegitimate son of Charles V, was brought up for a long time in ignorance of his origins. Only Philip II's passionate regard for the memory of his father allowed Don Juan to enjoy the privilege of his rank. But Philip himself remained implacable towards all errors of conduct and imposed his own strict morality on his subjects. He himself never acknowledged his own illegitimate children. The Inquisition watched over family morals. Did El Greco, in that time of austerity, enjoy perhaps the indulgence granted (not without contempt) to artists, dissolute bohemians, and all those who lived on the fringe of society? Even during his first years in Toledo, when he possibly did not yet mix with the elite of his day, his patrons were high-ranking church dignitaries, the deans of the chapter, and local notabilities. In spite of everything he imposed on this city, in which the Church was all-powerful, his unlawful wife and his child born out of wedlock. There was in him a fierce need of independence, which would not yield even to a great passion. He may also have had a liking for defiance, the pride of a man to whom everything was permissible and who gloried in trespassing beyond fixed bounds with impunity.

This innate pride also formed an element in the understanding between the man and the place. All the testimonials, however few they may have been, combined to exalt the reputation which preceded his arrival in Toledo, and this was only confirmed by his haughty demeanour. A humbler or more hesitant man might not perhaps have been able to take up such a leading position from the very start. A high degree of self-awareness was a familiar idiom to the Toledans. Everything in that city exuded pride—the pride of all the races that had succeeded each other there and which, even when vanquished and persecuted, lived on amidst the continuing evidence of their past greatness.

The Moors and the Jews had either been driven out of Spain or forced to adjure themselves in order to carry on a precarious and threatened existence. Yet, with its entrance of four horseshoe arches and its golden-brown stone, the magnificent Puerta del Sol still proclaimed the greatness of the Moors. Probably erected by Moorish masons after the reconquest, it appeared as the triumphal monument of a ruling race.

It did not matter that the synagogues had been converted into churches; it did not matter that those of Santa María de Bianco and of the Assumption (El Transito) served, in El Greco's time, the first as an asylum, the second as a home for the order of Calatrava; they still bore the stamp of Moorish art at the height of its glory and a long inscription in Hebrew still proclaimed on the walls of El Transito that the Jews of Spain had erected this place of worship of "a strong and mighty arm," that they rejoiced in the divine mercy which had enabled them to find amongst themselves judges and princes to deliver them from their enemies and persecutors, and that God was with them and with Samuel Abulafia Halevi, "a man of peace, powerful amongst all, and a great builder."

There was above all that pride of faith triumphant which expressed itself in Toledo in a spectacular manner, as in the church of San Juan de los Reyes, for example, with its immense single nave, its wealth of decoration, and heavy rusted chains hanging from its walls—the chains of Christians released from Moorish prisons, a reminder of the humiliations of the past which exalted all the more the abounding glory of the present.

For the Cretan, who had spent his youth in Italy and who was familiar with both the splendours of Venice and the grandeurs of Rome, this particular defiance expressing the Toledan past was the discovery of a new world. It was a revelation he seems to have assimilated slowly, which only gradually penetrated him and his work. But it was also a revelation of himself and a kind of emancipation. It almost seems as if this astounding new quality confronting him, which perhaps at first put him off his stride, became slowly familiar to him, not in the way in which one grows accustomed to a sight never seen before, but rather as if he were rediscovering something he had forgotten, something which was his, although it had never belonged to him.

The first works he painted in Toledo are like pages from an autobiography in which he might have described how he became imbued with an unfamiliar atmosphere and how he stepped out to embrace what was offered to him.

El Greco had not yet completed the altarpiece for San Domingo el Antiguo when, in 1578, the same year as his son's birth, he was commissioned to paint a picture for the cathedral. This picture was destined for the vestry of the sacristy. Its subject—"The Disrobing of Christ"—was peculiarly well suited to the place. This commission, like the one for San Domingo, seems to have had its origin in Rome. Garcia de Loysa, canon of the cathedral, had been one of the Toledans staying in Rome, and there he must have seen amongst the pictures El Greco kept in his Roman studio a version of "El Espolio" (perhaps the panel on wood which used to be in the Justi Collection in Berlin) or one of the replicas El Greco later took with him to Spain.

Amongst the marvels of architecture Toledo boasted the cathedral was by no means the least spectacular. It does not soar up to pierce the sky like the Gothic cathedrals of the north; rather does it form a huge, massive cube, as if it found difficulty in separating itself from the soil it dominates. Only the tower—one of the two completed— rises up triumphantly with its famous bells, each weighing two tons, whose summons are said to be audible even in Madrid. And the vast precincts of this cathedral enclosed a whole world. Stored within it was a cross section of all that Toledo stood for. All the town's scattered wealth had taken refuge there; the passage of generations echoed through its vast nave and chapels; its history was unfolded in inscriptions on every door; each altar, each pillar, almost each railing and stall had a tale to tell.

Like everything else which formed part of Toledo, the cathedral was a source of legends. It claimed to have been founded by St. Eugene, the city's first archbishop. Converted into a mosque under the Moors, it was reputed to have been wrested from the Muslim cult through the courage of a queen and the cunning of a Moor, who appeased the ruler's anger. In actual fact the first stone of the cathedral was laid at the beginning of the thirteenth century, during the reign of Ferdinand III of Castile.

Its plan was ambitious from the start. But Toledo had no indigenous art other than the Mauresque, and no artists capable of expressing grandiose dreams in stone. The King and the Archbishop of Toledo called upon the most renowned builders of cathedrals—the French. The man who drew up the plans for this glorious building is known only by the humble name of Maître Martin. He set to work in Toledo, following the examples which were familiar to him, in the Gothic style of his age and country. Moreover the very thing required of him was an example of a most Christian art, in protest against the Mauresque influences which dominated the art of Spain. But the Frenchman who came to Toledo and those who came with or after him—just like El Greco three centuries later—gradually yielded to the spirit of the place. The Spaniards, who had as yet no native artists to give expression to their inordinate pride and militant faith, imposed their own vision on the foreigners. A certain Pedro Pérez, mentioned as one of the builders of the cathedral, was perhaps merely an assimilated Frenchman, Pierre le Pierre. As the cathedral rose, the pure French Gothic almost imperceptibly took on a Spanish character.

When El Greco entered its immense nave (the cathedral was surpassed in size only by those of Milan and Seville) he saw Spain at work, assimilating foreign influences until they became her own. The apse and the ambulatory, with its vaulting of rare perfection, constructed by means of alternating triangles and rectangles, are in the purest Gothic style of that epoch, but the windows of the triforium already show the influence of Mauresque art. Saints in hieratic poses surmount a pillar dedicated to the memory of the legendary Moor in pure *mudejar* style. The beautiful tomb of the Alguacil, Fernand Gudiel, dating from the thirteenth century, is in the Arab style of Granada, and *mudejar* also is the porch of the chapter house, built in the sixteenth century.

Apparently hostile elements are reconciled, as if they had found a common denominator. Even the parts which are not Mauresque, but French Gothic or Italian Renaissance, have become exuberant and rich, an unexpected efflorescence. Each century has added its tribute of precious materials, alabaster, coloured marble, jasper, silver, or gold, the first gold to come from the New World. The alabaster is carved like lace; the marble pillars are covered with reliefs as if embroidered; and these patterns are repeated in the embroideries on the sacerdotal vestments. This superabundance of ornamentation, of arabesque decoration, denotes a horror of emptiness typical of Mauresque art and of Oriental art in general.

This horror of emptiness, this conjuring away of space, was one of the first powerful influences to affect El Greco. This encounter with Mauresque art in Toledo became decisive for him in the most curious way—that peculiar way he had of absorbing impressions which corresponded to something he already knew, and of which he became aware only circuitously. There is no formal borrowing, no faintest reflection of what he had seen, no trace of imitation in his art. It was a more subtle and more profound influence. His vision remained deliberately Occidental. He knew that he had left home to emancipate himself from the art of the *madonneri,* to escape from a trend which led back towards an ancient past. But below the surface of these Occidental forms of composition he had adopted the Orientalism of Toledo appealed to the Oriental in him. The European inspirations, reconsidered in Toledo with a semi-Arabic mentality, were interpreted by him according to a Byzantine code.

At the same time other influences were at work on him, but these too steered him in the same direction. Amongst the marvels of the cathedral with which he was then becoming familiar there were also the choir stalls, the most ancient of which, carved by Maese Rodrigo, illustrated exploits in the liberation of Granada from Moorish invasion, an event almost contemporaneous with the carver's work. This intrusion of topicality into holy places, effected by a humble artist, almost an artisan, may well have emboldened El Greco, more or less consciously, to include Toledan society amongst the attendants at the miraculous burial of Count Orgaz. He drew further powerful inspiration from the stalls of the cathedral, but this time from those carved some fifty years later. Even though he had found no indigenous school of painting in Toledo, so that he felt himself to be the unrivalled master; even though Toledan art appeared to him as some sort of luxuriant foliage, he saw one powerful artistic individuality emerge from it, with a distinct contribution of his own. This was the sculptor Alonso de Berruguete, who, fifty years after Rodrigo, was commissioned, along with Philippe de Bourgogne, to carve the high stalls of the choir (Plate 30).

In Toledo, El Greco also saw Berruguete's altarpiece of the Visitation in the church of St. Ursula, and his tomb of Cardinal Juan Tavera. Berruguete had been one of Michelangelo's best pupils; he had been dominated by the master's inescapable presence, but he had also adopted the skin-deep realism, that manner of probing the sculpted surface peculiar to Donatello. On his return to Spain he retained as much from his Italian masters and inspirers as he needed for his own personal interpretation of the human body. As an Occidental, Berruguete had assimilated much better than El Greco the Italian vision, the relationship between bodies and space, and the mechanics of movement. A sculptor first and foremost, he had a three-dimensional vision; even his bas-reliefs have the plasticity of high relief. But his own struggle was also a struggle against form, against the density of his material, even against beauty, which could mask an inner turmoil. The means by which he achieved intensity of expression were not the same as El Greco's. His saints have heads too large and too square for their rather thick-set bodies, with prominent cheekbones and jutting jaws. But already the great wind of the baroque sweeps through their flowing garments; their eyes surmounted by circumflex accents of grief are raised to heaven, and their mouths are opened to frame either a prayer or a cry of despair.

El Greco, that borrower who in fact never assimilated anything, and who was henceforward to tread an increasingly lonely path, had perhaps only one direct forebear—this sculptor who had died more than twenty years before his arrival in Spain.

It was in a powerful suggestive atmosphere, and as if driven by a purpose quite different from that which had motivated him hitherto, that El Greco once again took up the theme on which he had worked in Italy—the disrobing of Christ, "El Espolio" (Plate 32). When El Greco first thought of portraying this subject, Michelangelo's shadow still weighed heavily upon him; no doubt then the "Martyrdom of St. Paul" was uppermost in his mind. When he resumed it in Spain, he used certain elements from his earlier pictures, the elliptical composition which threw the principal character into relief, the contrasting figures in the foreground, such as the soldier trimming the cross, the representation of Christ and the still-Venetian colouring. The most surprising thing about this picture for the cathedral, however, is the fact that, within the short space of time that had elapsed since his arrival in Spain, El Greco had already forgotten the teachings of Italy. The picture is painted as if he had before him, not a canvas, but a bas-relief. Everything takes place on a single plane. The ellipse of the composition straightens out towards the top of the picture into the triple vertical lines of the heads pressing in behind the head of Christ. From the formal point of view it is incredibly clumsy, after having singled out the figure of Christ through his purple robe of mockery, to allow his head to be submerged in the welter of other heads, all aligned on the same plane and in identical relief. But El Greco knew—he had learned it astonishingly quickly in Toledo—that he could engender by means of a variety of expressions an emotional upheaval far more intense and of a superior quality to the effect produced by a formal opening up in depth. The moving wall of heads rising up behind Christ sets him off as effectively as the night sky pierced by lances which crowns the picture. This surge of heads displays the whole gamut of human stupidity, vulgarity, and hatred of the incomprehensible. One pallid individual shakes his fist in rage just by the right shoulder of Christ; another, with a foxy face, points an accusing finger at him from the back. But it is not only human beasts that El Greco depicts; they are not all examples of moral decay, as the Flemish realists would have painted them. El Greco's contempt of humanity—and this surge of heads is painted by a misanthropist—was more subtle. He depicted a random crowd made up of the good and the bad, the brutal, the witless, the sly, the indifferent, and the noble, but a crowd easy to incite against anything beyond its mental grasp.

In order to measure El Greco's knowledge of human nature it is enough to analyse these heads, each of which is a finished psychological study. From the formal viewpoint the picture is chaotic. But it is painted by a philosopher, a disillusioned one. Its internal arrangement, following the laws of logic in human behaviour, is rigorous and inevitable. Here is the tragic night, a terrible epitome of the drama. On one side of Christ is the brute with the stubborn forehead and squat, almost misshapen, chinless face, the blind instrument with powerful muscles. On the other the knight in his magnificent steel armour, standing so close yet so indifferent to Christ, with his hands in its iron gauntlet elegantly folded on his hip, gazing into the distance, absorbed in something quite unconnected with the, for him, unimportant incident taking place beside him; he is the brain, the organizer, and his thoughts are far removed from the torture.

As a counterweight to the surge of heads up above, the three Marys stand down below in the left foreground—three heads set in recession, expressing emotions ranging from frozen grief to the fascinated horror with which Mary Magdalen's half-hidden profile is turned towards the executioner drilling into the cross.[2] A gesture of rare psychological subtlety also counterbalances the clenched fists and pointing, denunciatory fingers. Mary Magdalen, who cannot take her eyes off the instrument of torture, gently pushes the Virgin aside, as if seeking to spare her the horrible sight. And this gesture, made with a hand of remarkable, almost translucent, delicacy against the Virgin's dark mantle, is strangely similar to that of Christ. The first and fourth fingers are spread apart, whilst the two middle ones are joined, in a gesture which it is not easy to repeat and which, with El Greco, served as a secret signature.

This picture, painted by a consummate master of psychology, is also a masterpiece of pictorial art. From the viewpoint of colouring "El Espolio" is a firework, but one of those fireworks let off to conclude a period of festivity or to celebrate a departure. With those reflec-

[2]El Greco borrowed the figure of the executioner from Dürer's woodcut "The Erection of the Cross" (Kleine Passion), as pointed out by Dr. Frederic Antal in Zum Problem des Niederlaendischen Manierismus (Kritische Berichte, Jahrgang 1928/29).

tions of purple and trails of gold El Greco took leave of the torrid, xanthic colour shade of the Venetians. This picture painted for the cathedral brought a period of evolution to an end. It did so in a manner customary with El Greco, not by an abrupt change, a clean break, but by the introduction of new elements among the old, a gradual encroachment, like a slowly rising tide.

"El Espolio" had an enormous success. El Greco eagerly set about satisfying his clients' demands. Seventeen replicas of this picture are known (one of which belonged to Delacroix), all more or less close to the original, either from his own hand or products of his studio. The last full-sized and definitive version seems to have been the one now in Munich. The variations to be found in some of the replicas are concessions made by El Greco to theological objections raised by the chapter of the cathedral. This was a time of militant and mistrustful religion, when anything which was not a strict interpretation of the Gospels was suspected of concealing some dark heretical design. Several members of the chapter, inspired by particular zeal, were shocked by the fact that this Christ (who furthermore lacked His crown of thorns and whose face was stained by neither blood nor tears) was overshadowed by the heads of mortals. They also rose up against the introduction of the three Marys so close to Jesus, as their presence is not mentioned in the Gospels.

These theological quibbles were strangely mixed up with a sordid quarrel over money. On June 15, 1579, "El Espolio" being finished, the chapter, following its custom, appointed experts to value the picture. These included Nicolas de Vergara, architect and sculptor of the cathedral, and the painter Luis de Velasco. El Greco, for his part, appointed as experts the Toledan sculptor, Martínez de Casteñeda, and Baltasar de Castro Cimbrón, a well-known painter from Murcia. In order to reach an agreement as quickly as possible, an assessor was nominated a few days later, whose decision was to be final and irrevocable; this was Alejo de Montoya, a very famous Toledan goldsmith and official assessor for all the products of his craft. One of the experts appointed by the chapter, Nicolas de Vergara, must have had a grudge against El Greco, since he had been taken off the work on San Domingo and replaced by Herrera. Yet both the cathedral's and El Greco's experts agreed to pronounce in his favour, declaring that "the merits of the picture are so great that it admits of neither price nor evaluation," but that, taking into consideration the value of a similar work of that time, the price should be 900 ducats, at the rate of 375 maravedís per ducat. The chapter was indignant over this assessment, which it apparently had not anticipated, and found the valuation "excessive and beyond reason." It was at this stage in the quarrel over the price that the chapter took notice of the theological errors and demanded the suppression of certain figures and details, which no text corroborated and which "obscured the meaning of the holy scene." The decision now rested with the arbiter, Alejo de Montoya, who, on July 23, declared that "after having seen the said painting, he found it to be the best he had ever seen and that, if it were to be assessed, taking into account all the qualities, apparent in its manifold parts, one would have to value it so highly that few, or none, could pay for it . . . but that, in view of the nature of the times, and of what was customarily paid in Castile for the paintings of the great masters, he found that he should and did order that the said Garcia de Loysa pay, in the name of the Holy Church, the sum of 3,500 reals to the said Domenico Theotocopuli." As for the objections to the presence of the three Marys, he prudently left the decision to theologians well versed in this matter. In spite of this enthusiastic praise and the result of the arbitration, the quarrel over money continued. El Greco seems to have been embittered by the behaviour of the chapter. He had learned from Titian to insist on a fair evaluation of his work. He kept silent and did not deliver the picture. No doubt the chapter was unaccustomed to facing such a high degree of artistic conscience. On September 23, El Greco was summoned to appear before the mayor of Toledo. This was the first time he measured his strength with the authorities in a foreign country hostile to newcomers. He had already been living in Toledo for two years. The woman who shared his life was Spanish. Had he lived in such isolation, had he concentrated so deeply on himself and his work that he had not taken the trouble to learn the country's language? Or was it an Oriental's sense of caution that made him declare that he was unfamiliar with the Castilian tongue and ask for an interpreter? At any rate he appeared before the tribunal in a suspicious frame of mind, like a man scenting a trap in every question and arming himself with arrogance. He refused to reply to questions concerning his private life—insidious questions which tended to give the commission for the cathedral an accidental character, so as to lessen its importance. When he was asked if it were correct that he had come to Toledo to execute the altarpiece of San Domingo, El Greco replied that he was under no obligation to say "why he had come to Toledo" and that the questions had no bearing on the affair in hand. But the dispute grew acrimonious. Instead of debating the price, which lay within their jurisdiction, they again turned to attack the liberties which El Greco had taken with the subject. He was ordered to change whatever was unseemly in his picture, to suppress the embarrassing contiguity of the three Marys and to "set them apart." Behind these demands there was now more than just the civil authorities: there was the shadow of the Inquisition. There was also the threat of imprisonment if he persisted in his stubbornness. El Greco knew the danger to which he was exposing himself. He took fright. At the final injunction he replied on the next day that he was ready to suppress everything they desired. He was weary of the dispute and only desired to be finished with it. In this moment of lassitude he seems to have prepared a version which took the wishes of the chapter into consideration. But besides the theologians, there were amongst the cathedral authorities men of sound enough artistic judgment to recognize the difference between the original composition and the new, mutilated version. The appreciation of the experts and the enthusiasm of the arbiter must have been known in Toledo and must have impressed even the most obtuse of the theologians. The original picture assumed the place for which it was intended. Even if El Greco was offended by the machinations of the chapter, his future relations with this body improved, doubtless for the very reason that he had won his case over a point so vital to his conscience as a creative artist. In March 1582 the chapter commissioned from him a frame worthy of his work. The repercussions of "El Espolio" were tremendous. From the moment the picture was set up in its place, the enthusiasm of the connoisseurs and the fervour of the faithful made it seem increasingly precious. Perhaps the chapter forgot that they had haggled with the artist and harshly criticized his interpretation. At any rate they no longer disputed the price of the carved frame. It was moreover typical of the conditions of artistic life in Toledo, of its predominantly plastic vision, that sculptors were far more highly paid than painters—the heritage, perhaps, of a past whose memory was perpetuated there in stone, a tradition handed down to these militant Christians by the Arabs and Jews, who gave no credit to painting. At any rate El Greco was paid much more for the carved frame than for the picture: 200,000 maravedís. A polychrome relief in wood, "The Handing of the Chasuble to St. Ildefonso" (Plate 31), seems to have formed part of this sumptuous frame. Comparison of this with El Greco's painted work is most instructive. This heir of Byzantium, of a planimetrical vision, was eager, perhaps as a challenge to Michelangelo, for his sculpted work to be considered equal to his painting. Yet this first preserved example of his work as a sculptor merely attests to his struggle with the material. Executed several years after the emancipation from his Italian past represented by "El Espolio" (the commission for the frame dates from 1585), "The Handing of the Chasuble" reveals all his initial dependence on his contemporaries, such as the Roman Mannerists or the Flemish realists. Certain secondary elements are common both to El Greco's painting and sculpture—his manner of crowding figures together in space, his horror of emptiness, and also such details as the clouds in scrolls, the row of little angels' heads with conventional wings and such realistic faces that they seem like portraits. Realistic, above all, is the head of the old man, St. Ildefonso—that bald head standing out in high relief. This agitated group (an agitation that is purely formal) not only reveals how far El Greco conformed to what he had already seen, but also hints at a future orientation which would have been, not his own personal evolution, but the road which culminated in the baroque, following the trend of his time. Had El Greco, in the first place, devoted himself to sculpture, he would have followed the direction taken by the other schools of his day, instead of progressing along his own, solitary path.

"El Espolio" and its consequences—the dispute and the commission for the sumptuous frame—marked the end of an important stage in El Greco's life: the stage of acclimatization. He had put down roots into the Toledan soil. Perhaps he himself did not know how deep they already were.

A signed picture, "Christ on the Cross with Two Donors" (Louvre, Paris) (Plate 33), seems to conclude this first Toledan period. The head of Christ resembles that in the final version of "El Espolio." The body is inordinately elongated—the beautiful, emaciated body of an ascetic, with very thin arms and protruding ribs. El Greco had left far behind him those Italian Christs with their ample forms and glowing flesh, expiring in beauty on the Cross. This Christ has suffered in the flesh. His slender, bloodless body is stretched out like a tendon which has quivered in response to all that torments a distraught mankind. Even when nailed on His instrument of torture, He has not found the peace of death. He seems to be shaken by a spasm, as if in haste to ascend to heaven. And the sky, against which the solitary cross is set, is stormy, filled with dark clouds like huge wings upborne by a mighty wind and fringed with lurid light—the promise of a

day to dawn after the night of the drama. Two donors pray at the foot
of the cross. It has been supposed that they are the Covarrubias brothers. But these highly realistic representations correspond neither in
their features nor in their age to known portraits of the two brothers.
They are undoubtedly two Toledans. One is a priest, his hands folded
in prayer, with a trustful and pious expression; the other, a nobleman with a strong profile and well-groomed hands, the right one
pressed fervently to his heart, the left turned outward with one finger
raised as if in animated discussion, a strange gesture which seems to
call for an answer.

This "Christ on the Cross" with its two anonymous donors against
a stormy sky is like a balance sheet of El Greco's sojourn in Toledo,
which could have ended the very next day, had his hopes for an important royal commission materialized. It is also the herald of a
spiritual adventure, of the creative blossoming of one whom none had
preceded and whom none was to follow.

THE founding of the Escorial has been interpreted by
some as an act of contrition, of repentance, in order to
make amends for the atrocities committed by Philip II's troops when
they destroyed a small convent after the capture of St. Quentin. The
King is said to have promised to re-erect the convent in Spain. Repentance and regret, however, were never the chief impulses of this
fanatic, who made offerings to God with conscious pride in so doing.
In fact the Escorial was conceived as a memorial to the victories won
against the French on St. Lawrence's Day in 1557. Of this initial
conception all that remain in the plan of the basilica are the four
giant pillars connected by powerful arches supporting the dome and
lantern which are still known as the "triumphal arch." Contrary to
the legend the deed of foundation states: "We are building the
monastery of San Lorenzo el Real as a dedication to the blessed St.
Lawrence, as a memorial to the favours and victories which we began
to receive of God on his Day."

Indeed this victory was so dazzling and the peace treaty of Cateau-
Cambrésis which sealed it in 1559 so favourable to Spain, that the
Duc de Guise exclaimed to Henri II: "Sire, if you did nothing but
lose for twenty years, you could never lose as much as you have given
away with one stroke of the pen."

But the Escorial was not only (perhaps barely any longer) a memorial to victory by the time it began to take shape. The first stone
was solemnly laid on August 20, 1563, by Philip II, who never did
anything gratuitously or spontaneously. "It should be noted," wrote

Father de Sigüenza, "that in the same year, and almost the same month, the last stone of the sacred Council of Trent was finished and laid."[1] In the few years which had elapsed since Philip II learned at Cambrai the news of the great Spanish victory over the French, he had also come to regard himself as the defender of Christianity. He felt himself to be, not only the King of Spain, paying homage to the Almighty and the saint who protected him, but also the guardian of a church both menaced and militant at the same time. The Escorial became, according to Sigüenza, "an alcázar and a temple" where "the holy dogmas and laws were to be made eternal and obeyed forever."

Philip II (Plate 36) was thirty years old at the time when he decided to perpetuate the memory of his victories. For two years, since the abdication of Charles V, heavy responsibilities had burdened the shoulders of one who up to then had been but an obedient son, the docile instrument of another's power. But Philip had never been young, perhaps never even a child. He had doubtless inherited from his father the disposition which led to Charles V's numerous adventures; he was much loved by women and even roused his first wife, the ageing Mary Tudor, to passion. Some years earlier Titian had revealed his character as far as was possible in a state portrait—thick, sensual lips with hints of brutality at the corners; troubled eyes, ringed with tired shadows. The year Titian painted him was perhaps one of those rare ones when the youth he barely knew returned to him for a brief spell on foreign soil, free from family restraints. The childhood of this grandson of Mad Joanna was spent in the shadow of the father he so passionately admired and behind whose powerful figure he ceaselessly effaced himself. Once, when his son Don Carlos flung the insult of bastardy in the face of Don Juan of Austria, he provoked the retort: "At any rate, my father was worth more than yours." When Carlos asked his father to punish this insolence, Philip merely replied: "But that is the truth, my son." The son of Charles V could not be fully understood, the motives governing his behaviour would be much harder to decipher, if one failed to take into account this adoration of his father, which only increased and deepened throughout the long years of his reign.

This rare, formidable, and terrifying presence in Philip II's childhood was combined with the icy coldness which emanated from his mother. An eyewitness has described life in this family in the Emperor's absence—the meals presided over by the Empress amidst silent cour-

[1] *Historia de la Orden de San Jerónimo*, by José de Sigüenza (1544–1606), poet and historian.

tiers, sitting stiff, intimidating, isolated in a pool of silence. Everything seemed to conspire to turn the pale, fair-haired little boy into a lonely recluse. One particularly strict tutor made him adopt that mask of docility to conceal all the stubbornness which could not be given free rein. But the most fatal influence was undoubtedly the teacher who had charge of him from early childhood, and who was the least suited man to awaken humane feelings in the future king of a great people. His name, Siliceo, he invented for himself, to symbolize the qualities he admired. Hardships, and pride in having overcome them, had withered him both physically and morally. His contemporaries describe him as thin and bony, with a face like tanned leather broken into countless wrinkles. As a self-made man, he prized above all the virtues to which he owed his success, such as conscientious, stubborn, exact work and concentration on a single goal, to the exclusion of everything that might divert him from his path. As he could take no pride in his origins, this ambitious man fell back on his national and racial superiority and suspected Jews and Moors everywhere. When he became Archbishop of Toledo, he decreed the exclusion of their most distant descendants from all benefits of the Church. Under the aegis of this pedantic, provincial scholar, driven by dim grievances, the future sovereign of a vast realm containing so many different nationalities and races learned to speak fluent Latin, but, unlike his father, who spoke several foreign tongues, knew hardly any of those used by his subjects. It was to this son of the people that the fair, blue-eyed youth with the light skin of Nordic races, in whom the lantern jaw of the Hapsburgs suppressed all other racial characteristics, owed his proud awareness of being a Spaniard, all the keener perhaps because even his physique differed from that of the grandees and the masses of Spain. Events combined with his national pride to make this son of the Holy Roman Emperor solely a King of Spain.

His mother, fanatically pious, shut away in her mystical asceticism, shaped his religious outlook, an outlook which the uncompromising Siliceo merely reinforced, backed up with reason, coupled with mistrust of everything which seemed to diverge from the narrow path. Of all the feelings of which Philip II was capable mistrust had the strongest hold over him; this he owed to Siliceo, as well as his racial hatred, his horror of anything which had the least resemblance of heresy, a hatred and horror which made him a great lay inquisitor. It was between his first conception of the Escorial as a temple of victory and its building as a religious alcazar that the inherited faith of Philip II, deep rooted by

his education, took its militant turn. From being heir to the throne of
Spain, as he was at the time of the war with France, he had meanwhile
become the husband of Mary Tudor, who, at the age of six, had been
betrothed to his father. This marriage was dictated, not only for reasons
of state, from desire for a powerful military alliance against France, but
also for religious reasons, from the need to create a bastion of defense
against the rising tide of Protestantism.

For the first time Philip found himself on foreign soil which was
hostile from the start, facing the organized resistance of an heretical
movement. Philip regarded burning at the stake as a sacrifice pleasing
to God. Charles V, however, who remained first and foremost a poli-
tician, advised tolerance. His own confessor pointed out that the English episcopate had failed to find in the Holy Scriptures any reference
which would have authorized a man to be burnt at the stake for his
convictions.

But the acuteness of the religious struggle in England and the hostility of the people towards foreigners prevailed over a conciliatory
policy. Philip's dark mood was perhaps also conditioned by his disappointment in this marriage with an ugly, jealous, prematurely aged
woman and her hysterical pregnancy—a disappointment felt also by
his courtiers, who had hoped to make their fortunes in England. Philip
was soon able to write to his sister, Juana: "I have always favoured
the punishment of heretics such as is now being administered with such
ease in England."

The experiences of his English marriage influenced his decision to
make the Escorial into a fortress of Christianity. They also determined
his future policy, his conviction that the souls of his subjects were his
own property. They seemed to have released in him this strain of
cruelty which led later to the Spanish adage that with Philip II it was
but a short step from the smile to the dagger.

As the years rolled by, in the wake of new experiences, other motives
joined the principal idea which inspired Philip in his grandiose project.
The Escorial became the escapist dream of a man who dreamed but
little in his life. The burdensome inheritance imposed on him by his
father contained also the load of an entirely new conception of absolute monarchy. Charles V, a calculating and methodical psychologist,
was aware of the need to surround the sovereign's person with an aura
of unique prestige, of elevating him above the reach of mortals, of
creating around him a circle of respect not to be penetrated by the
haughtiest of his subjects, in order to maintain control over a realm

as vast as was his kingdom. He was fascinated by the sumptuous ceremonial of the court of Burgundy, with all its colourful pomp, its asso-
ciations with mediaeval chivalry, its ideals of life on a higher plane.
When Charles V reached the peak of his power, he decided to introduce this ceremonial into Spain by adapting it to the psychology of
both the Spanish people and the grandees. Like a demagogue of today
who employs every means of technical advancement to impose on the
masses a glorified version of his own image, Charles V resorted to the
most ancient legends and superstitions in order to lend support to his
might, to the point when he himself came to believe that the ruler was
invested with a personal magic, with the power to heal, as had been
attributed to kings of old.

On Spanish soil the etiquette of the Dukes of Burgundy became
sombre and rigid in adapting itself to this world of archaic conceptions
based on countless interdicts and superstitions deeply rooted in national history. This ceremonial, introduced only towards the middle
of the sixteenth century against the opposition of the grandees, soon
became an integral part of Spanish life. Its numerous rules expressed
the desire to intimidate, but also the idea that the royal person was very
precious and vulnerable. He could be approached on the knees only,
like a holy altar, to receive a glass of water or a napkin which had to
pass through countless hands before it reached him. It was on bended
knees that the tablecloth off which he ate had to be folded. His bread
was kept locked in a metal box. A physician had to taste every dish
and drink served to him, to ensure that it was not poisoned. The King
had keys to open every door, but never touched them; doors were
opened and closed for him by a high dignitary of the court, even on
his nocturnal visits to his Queen. Though never alone, he felt increasingly lonely among the fifteen hundred people who formed his court,
surrounded by an icy silence which weighed oppressively on the numerous assembly of gloomy phantoms stiffened into hieratic postures,
a silence which could not be broken save by the King himself.

A man as haughty and at the same time as self-conscious as Philip II
felt at ease in this atmosphere of deification through terror. Charles
V's political testament strengthened the natural distrust of his son. In
this voluminous document of almost 10,000 words, the Emperor, when
he sensed the approach of death, warned his son of favourites, recommended him never to let any of his councillors gain ascendancy over
him, to practice the art of deception, and to guard against any strong
affection, even for those who stood closest to him, to confine contact

with his sisters to unavoidable cases of emergency, and to limit his
conjugal relations. As an obedient son, Philip II succeeded so well in
creating an icy protective belt around him that he came to resent the
presence of human beings more and more. He left Toledo for Madrid,
then still a small town on which he hoped to impress his personality
with greater ease. But there were still too many people around him
living independent lives; it was disgust with the spectacle of life which
led this fanatic of isolation to make the Escorial the very embodiment
of his escapism.

Philip II spent a long time searching for a suitable site for this
monument which was to serve so many ends. He appointed a commission which for years explored the surroundings of Madrid. This
commission was formed, not only of specialists to find quarries and
water in sufficient proximity, of architects and master builders, of
physicians to study the climate, but also of scholars and philosophers.
"The King," said Father de Sigüenza, "was looking for a site which
gave uplift to his soul and support to his pious meditations." This
land was finally found, deserted and imposing, on a plateau of the
Sierra de Guadarrama, the site of an abandoned iron mine, covered
with iron dross (*scoria*) which gave it its name—El Escorial. It was
this iron soil which seemed to give its imprint to the building. The
quarry, called the Iron Pounder, supplied beautiful smooth grey
stones, not unlike steel; "all even in colour and durability," wrote the
chronicler of the Escorial, "they maintain their uniformity to such an
extent that the whole vast building seems to be cast from one piece
cut out of the rock."

It was at the moment when he conceived the Escorial as a self-sup-
porting retreat (the foundations of the basilica and the monastery were
already laid) that Philip came to realize the inadequate dimensions
of the project. He intended the monastery for the Hieronymite order,
partly out of devotion—they watched over the Emperor in his retire-
ment and assisted him in his last hours on earth—and partly out of
calculation, because there were a number of experienced architects
among the fathers. In his initial project he planned the monastery to
house fifty monks, but for the royal residence he henceforward envisaged this number did not suffice. Work was stopped. But Brother
Antonio de Villacastín, a rough, sensible man in charge of the building operations, reassured the King that the foundations were strong
enough to bear the monastery even if it were built twice as high. The

number of monks was doubled as well, and finally the building housed 150 persons, including the lay brothers.

All the initiative for this building sprang from Philip II himself, who regarded it as his life's work; he never asked for advice. Himself an amateur painter, he considered himself fully qualified to decide over a gigantic work of art; the outrageous admiration of his courtiers reassured him as to the infallibility of his taste. Philip II became a Spaniard by education, especially in his prejudices, but a Spaniard without roots in history. The face he forced on to the Escorial was a protest against the Spanish past, against a taste formed throughout centuries by a succession of races. This fanatic of austerity repudiated everything which could have reminded him of the contributions of the infidels, the enemies of Christ; he loathed the exuberance of their art, which was for him a tarnished inheritance. His dilettantism was attracted by the grandiose, the heavy, the unadorned. His despotic taste, which he believed to be daring, was in fact conservative. Distrusting innovations, he liked everything approved of by the established authorities.

In his time the art of Italy and neo-classical architecture became triumphant. The first architect of the Escorial invited by the King was a Spaniard—Juan Bautista de Toledo—who had studied in Italy and worked on the construction of St. Peter's under Michelangelo. He had also worked in Naples on the Viceroy's invitation, where he built the royal palace and the castle of St. Elmo. But his plan for the Escorial Church did not satisfy the King, who thereafter invited Italian architects to submit new plans, which he studied most carefully, only to accept the most orthodox one, designed in the rigid arrangement of a Greek cross, by a military architect from Naples named Paciotto.

The final destiny of the Escorial did not take shape, however, until after the death of Juan Bautista de Toledo, when Juan de Herrera became its chief architect. During the preceding years the project had undergone its final transformation in the King's mind. Years of mourning widened the vacuum around him. His disgraced, rebellious son, Don Carlos, died in prison. In the same year of 1568 he lost the enchanting Elizabeth of Valois, whom he married before she blossomed into womanhood. It was at her premature death that he was seen to weep; the only time in his life, because he who believed in his royal vocation was not to show any human emotion. The young Elizabeth, called Isabel la Paz by the Spanish, seemed to take with her the peace which had reigned in the land and also the little colour and warmth

still left in Philip's life. It was this recent loss which drew him closer
to the dead, for whom he professed more attachment than for the living. In his will, drafted at San Yuste, Charles V called upon his son to
build a tomb worthy of the royal family. Thereafter Philip enjoined
his chief architect always to bear in mind that the monument was to be
erected "to the greater glory of God, and in honour of our Holy Mother
Church, to serve at once as monastery, temple and tomb." In order
to fulfil his threefold destiny the King called on him to see that the
forms were simple, the whole building severe and noble without ostentation. Philip II found in Juan de Herrera the man for this work; in him
devotion went hand in hand with mathematics, and militant faith with
temporal pride. Henceforward the granite monstrosity which was to
become both monastery and necropolis grew rapidly on the foothills of
the Sierra de la Guadarrama. The gigantic, rectangular, rock-coloured
building seemed to have been conceived by the same mind as the
pyramids erected by the Pharaohs in the desert.

In the last instance, it was the dead who triumphed over the living.
Philip II brought home the bodies of those who were close to him.
Funeral processions passed through Spain, palanquins hung with black,
amidst legions of monks, knights, princes of the Church, and high
dignitaries of the Crown. The remains of the Emperor laid to rest in
San Yuste, of the gracious Elizabeth and her child in Granada, of the
Empress in Tordesilla, of the Infante Don Juan and his first wife in
Valladolid, of his royal aunts the Queen of Hungary and Doña Le-
nora in Estramadura were all conveyed to the Escorial in the end.

The feverish activity at the building site of the Escorial could have
been mastered only by a born organizer, a tough son of the people
who was able to cope himself with all manual tasks, such a one as
Antonio de Villacastín. Philip ceaselessly harried both builders and
masons to carry on the work "with fury." The undertaking swallowed
up more and more money. The basilica alone cost 500,000 ducats.
Fray Antonio kept his accounts well. The total cost of the building was
soon to reach three million ducats. The people began to murmur
against the new and heavy taxes imposed to cover it. In the wake of
the funeral processions superstitious rumours and new legends sprang
to life, aided by the elements, storms, and fires. The lonely site became a propitious one for apparitions. The harassed workmen professed to have seen the nocturnal vision of a phantom dog howling
round the Escorial.

Philip II, however, pursued his work unaffected by the complaints of the people and the warnings of his courtiers, like a man obsessed by a single aim. The walls were hardly raised before he began to think about their decoration. Less than a year after the first stone of the monastery had been laid he commissioned Titian to paint a large composition of the Last Supper for the refectory. The Spanish artists working in Italy were recalled to their homeland. A pupil of Titian, the dumb monk Juan Fernández Navarrete, called *El Mudo,* who had left Spain twenty years before, was appointed court painter. In the year following the issue of the charter of the Escorial he began to paint pictures for the monastery and church.

Always on the quest for established celebrities, Philip also invited Vasari, but he was too old and tired to accept this honour.

While in Madrid and in spite of his supporters El Greco does not seem to have succeeded in obtaining commissions for the Escorial. Yet he must have received some vague promises for future employment, for at the time his move to Toledo was merely temporary. Maybe he would have stayed even longer in his retreat at Toledo had the King not gone himself to that city to celebrate Corpus Christi. On June 11, 1579, he arrived there with the entire royal retinue, the Queen, Doña Anna, the Infantas Isabella and Catherine, his nephew the Cardinal Albert, and a numerous court. Toledo was anxious to receive the ruler by whom it had been deserted as sumptuously as possible, to prove to him, the Queen, and the Princesses that it offered more distractions than his new place of residence. Toledo prided itself at that time in possessing the foremost dramatic authors and actors. The Church itself readily employed the great local actors, or those who came from abroad, to take part in the mysteries performed on feast days. Thanks to them these performances in which sacred texts were blended with secular entertainment were not only enjoyed by the masses but also appreciated by the educated. The dignitaries of the Church could not receive the court better than by providing a sample of the perfection of the Toledan theatre. They engaged an Italian actor named Curcio and his company to perform a mystery play for the King and his family on the feast day. According to the chroniclers, the Church was not closefisted; the Italian received 50,000 maravedís for his performance.

Philip II stayed in Toledo until June 20. Mystery plays apart, he was shown all that had been created during his absence in the domain of the arts. The altarpiece of San Domingo el Antiguo was finished. So was "El Espolio," but it was during the very week of the royal visit

that the valuers were debating its price and it had not yet been delivered to the cathedral. Towards the middle of June a meeting must
have taken place between the King and El Greco, perhaps the one and
only encounter between these two men, each of whom embodied a
different aspect of his epoch, but one of whom was the most powerful
sovereign, whereas the other was but a local celebrity, a foreigner who
had come to Spain in search of his fortune.

Philip II was dominated by his governing idea, the building of the
Escorial. While in Toledo he must have cast his sinister and mistrustful
eye round to see what he could find to promote his pet project. He
carried off from Toledo the artists who seemed to him most suitable.
He found there the Italian sculptor Pompeo Leoni, son of the sculptor
Leone Leoni, a pupil of Michelangelo who in an outburst of temper
had disfigured an engraver in the service of the Farnesi, was first condemned to death, then pardoned, and spent several years in the galleys.
Pompeo had already left Rome before El Greco arrived there. He himself was involved in conflicts with the Inquisition and had to spend
some months in prison in spite of his royal protection. Since 1571
he had been working intermittently in Toledo on an extremely important commission obtained from the chapter of the cathedral—
the marble and bronze sarcophagus of St. Eugene.

These two artists, united by memories of an atmosphere once familiar to both of them, both speaking the same tongue, both removed
to a city so disconcerting for foreigners and both possessing an artistic
past which eclipsed their present, established a relationship based on
deep and solid affection. The portrait of Pompeo which El Greco
painted, now in the Stirling Collection in Keir, Scotland, bears witness to this friendship. He painted it with the symbol of what he considered to be his friend's major work, the portrait of Philip II.

The work for which Pompeo was commissioned by the King was of
such importance that the artist did not complete the sarcophagus, but
signed a contract for a sumptuous altarpiece for the basilica designed
by Herrera. This was to be 100 feet high and to cover the entire *chevet*
of the Capella Mayor, for which he was to execute 120 pedestals and
capitals and 13 bronze statues.

The King's visit and the royal commissions bestowed on two of El
Greco's friends finally brought about the opportunity for which El
Greco had been longing. Just then a vacancy occurred at the Court
of Spain. A few months prior to the King's visit to Toledo, El Mudo
died. The dumb monk's art achieved such intensity of emotion that

it makes one forget his Italian apprenticeship; it is more Gothic than
Venetian in feeling. El Greco was hoping to succeed him. The picture
he painted at that time had all the qualities of the work of an applicant
anxious to display his abilities. He seems to have sounded the terrain
and to have received useful indications as to Philip II's taste. He knew
that the sovereign who was to decide his fate liked Italian art, but he
also heard of his predilection for Bosch's fantastic visions. In the picture by which he hoped to win the King's favour the most heterogeneous
elements were blended with devotion. This picture is known as "The
Dream of Philip II" (Plate 34)—one of those traditional designations
which, although incorrect, conceal a hidden meaning. It reveals that
if the King ever had inclinations to dreams (or nightmares) these
might have produced similar images. In fact the picture has none of
the incoherence of a dream—such as could have been expressed by
El Greco—or the imagery of a vision; it seems to be more one of those
rational allegories so much favoured by the Italians. The subject—the
adoration of the name of Jesus—may have been suggested to him by
the very feast day which the King celebrated in Toledo. In the first
descriptions of the Escorial it was referred to as a "Glorification." Perhaps El Greco also took advice from the theologians with whom he associated. If so, it must have been a Jesuit who made suggestions to
him, for the anagram of the name of Jesus painted in the centre of the
halo is the symbolical sign of the Society of Jesus which also figures
on the front of their first church, built in Rome. The text followed by
El Greco was taken from the Epistle of St. Paul to the Philippians
(Chapter II, 9–10). "Wherefore also God highly exalted him, and
gave him the name which is above every name; that in the name of
Jesus Christ every knee should bow, of things in heaven and things on
earth, and things under the earth."

This text envisages the coexistence of three spheres united in adoration; it implies the grouping of three zones, divided either in depth or
horizontally, as adopted in Italy to interpret the visions of Dante. But
nothing could be further removed from the traditional Dantesque
grouping than the vision of El Greco. In his composition, based on a
single division, he seems to recall his Byzantine past. The upper half
of the picture is reserved for heaven, with gigantic angels in the foreground who, in their vigorous flight, disappear under a heavy cloud.
In the lower half earth and hell stand side by side on the same plane.
The earth is a small island, defined by the crowded figures surrounding it, by the distant heads fading into infinity. Right in the foreground

is a figure who was once believed to be the Emperor Charles V,[2] kneeling in his yellow, ermine-collared robe, raising his bald, white-bearded head to heaven in a gesture of ardent prayer. To his right is the stiff, dark figure of Philip II, his gloved hands joined in prayer, his gaunt profile unperturbed, with lacklustre eyes, kneeling on sumptuous rugs and cushions—a King who, even in prayer, does not betray his emotions. Among those kneeling are a pope and perhaps St. Maurice and St. Lawrence, all fervent advocates of mankind. This group, with the athletic bodies, muscular arms, and short heads of the Venetian type, particularly stressed in the figure of the warrior, is still very close to Italian art. A surge of muscular bodies, daringly foreshortened in violent Michelangelesque poses, disappears into the jaws of a monster—a glaring discrepancy between the realism of these whirling bodies and this representation of hell reminiscent of centuries-old visions, of the nightmares by which Byzantium had been haunted. In his Modena triptych El Greco had already employed this same motif. These old memories had been revived by a recent event, the discovery of the huge jaws of a whale landed on the shores of Albufera. The people, always hungry for mysteries, were deeply impressed by this and Philip II had it dispatched to his study in the Escorial devoted to natural history.

Over the floating line dividing heaven from the other two worlds in "The Dream of Philip II" rises the phantom arch of a gateway through

[2]In an article by Professor Anthony Blunt (in the *Journal of the Warburg and Courtauld Institutes*, Vol. 3, 1939–40), it has been convincingly shown that the figure in the right foreground does not depict the Emperor Charles V but the Doge of Venice. If this is so, the picture is probably an allegory of the Holy League brought about by Pope Pius V, who reconciled Spain with Venice. The League was formed in 1571 against the Turks and its greatest achievement was the victory of Lepanto. It is known that the Doge of Venice, the Pope, and Philip himself ordered several paintings to commemorate the battle; two paintings by Titian, now in the Prado, allude to it. In El Greco's painting the figure of Philip is beyond doubt a portrait; the figure of the Pope resembles the aged Pius V closely enough; the Doge is presumably Lodovico Mocenigo, who held that position at the time of the Battle of Lepanto. A similar configuration of the three rulers appears in an engraving published in *Habiti d'Huomini et Donne Venetiane, by Giacomo Franco*, Part II, entitled *La Città di Venetia*, 1614, which reproduces a painting in commemoration of the victory. This engraving is reproduced on Plate 35 by courtesy of Professor Anthony Blunt, who discovered it since the publication of his article in the *Warburg Journal*. In the engraving the three generals, Don Juan of Austria, Marcantonio Colonna, and Sebastiano Venier, stand behind their sovereigns. This confirms the suggestion that the three other figures in the left foreground of El Greco's painting represent the same characters and not St. Maurice and St. Lawrence. It is therefore possible that the picture may have been painted to be hung near the tomb of Don Juan, whose body was brought back from Flanders to Spain in 1579. (*Translators.*)

27. *The Adoration of the Shepherds. 1578–79*

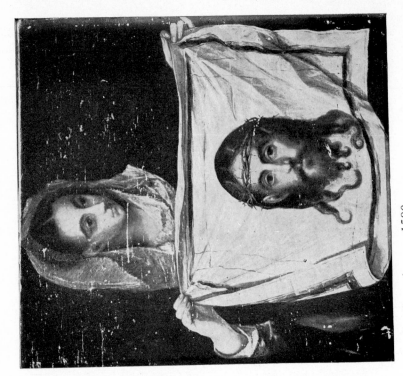

29. *St. Veronica. c. 1580*

28. *Boy Blowing on Charcoal. c. 1574–76*

30. *Berruguete: High stalls of the choir in Toledo Cathedral (detail)*

31. *The Handing of the Chasuble to St. Ildefonso. 1585*

32. *El Espolio. 1579*

33. *Christ on the Cross with Two Donors. c. 1580*

34. The Dream of Philip II. c. 1580

Lega fatta tra il S.mo Pontefice Pio V Filippo 2.° Re di Spagna et la Ser.ma Rep.ca Veneta l'anno 1571.
Capitani furono per Sua S.tà M.Antonio Colonna et morse Vice Re in Sicilia per la Maestà Cattolica
Giouanne d'Austria et morse Gouernatore in Fiandra per la Ser.ma Rep.ca Sebastiano Veneroti no.° Duce in Veneti
Franco forma con priuilegio

*35. Engraving from an unknown painting in commemoration of the Battle
of Lepanto, published in Venice in 1614.*

36. *Titian: Philip II, painted at Augsburg in 1550.*

which tiny human beings are fleeing from a lake of fire or blood: could this be a vision of Sodom in flames? Other scarcely defined human phantoms seem to stand in despair on an elongated isthmus: are these souls in purgatory anxious for salvation?

These episodes inserted as side lines to the main plot, in the manner of the narrative art of the Middle Ages or the illuminations in holy books, are in contradiction to the realistic presentation of the figures in the foreground, to their Italianate, sculptured bodies. This is as far as the Western perspective of El Greco went. He did not and never was to know how to depict events spread out either in space or time by any means other than those used by Byzantine and mediæval artists, by reducing them to a minute scale, to islets of tiny beings bordering too closely on figures of normal height. "The Dream of Philip II" is still the work of a miniaturist. Glowing colours, scintillating yellows, rich reds, appear in isolated, independent brush strokes applied with such daring that they shocked contemporaries. Father Francisco Santos refers in his description of the Escorial to a "Glorification" by El Greco as "the best picture he ever painted, although lacking in colour harmony."

El Greco took great pains to satisfy his royal patron. The replica in the Stirling Collection is perhaps an earlier version—much advanced and well finished. He did in fact succeed in rousing the interest of Philip II, who commissioned him to paint an altarpiece representing "The Martyrdom of St. Maurice and the Theban Legion" and El Greco was confident that this would be followed by a number of important commissions. The subject was very close to the King's heart. It reflected his self-sacrificing devotion, his refusal to compromise, and also his contempt for human life. In that year, 1580, when he commissioned El Greco to paint this picture, the isolated world of his choice became even more gloomy. He withdrew more and more from human contacts, as if haunted by his conscience. This scrupulous administrator of his heritage, this model bureaucrat, must have admitted to himself in the loneliness of his study that he had failed in his task. The Netherlands had seceded from the kingdom. The heresy which he strove to stem seemed to draw new life from its cruel suppression. On St. Bartholomew's Day the French Ambassador found the King "more delighted than by all the good fortune and happy events which had hitherto been his share." Without destroying the unassailable dogma of the sovereign's infallibility which was his *raison d'être* Philip could not even put the question to himself of whether a policy of tolerance would not

have better served the kingdom he had been given to rule. This conscientious chronicler, who made notes of every paper and document
passing through his hands, could not fail to perceive that the realm of
twenty-three crowns united in his person was crumbling both from
inside and out. This most powerful of monarchs wrote at that time: "I
cannot consider without grave concern the present disequilibrium of
the Exchequer. What an outlook for my old days, if God should grant
me a long life, since at present already I live from day to day, not
knowing how I shall live through the next or how to obtain all my
wants." But after the fashion of all tormented souls, he gave way to a
wave of violence even outbidding the past, as if he wanted to silence
his own secret doubts. His financial worries and his permanent need
of money led him to practice a certain tolerance towards the Jews
whom he forced along the road to salvation. A contemporary chronicler
describes how a rabbi baptized by Garcia de Loysa was greatly honoured by the King: "It is said that he has great wealth and that this is
the reason why he is always in the wake of the court, or the court is
in the wake of him." But Philip II soon abandoned all caution as unworthy of him. The statesman who read every report so carefully was
well aware of the detrimental effects on Spanish economy of the expulsion of the Arabs. Yet after a revolt in Granada, quickly suppressed,
he forbade Don Juan to treat the rebels with clemency. He had them
banished to the northern provinces. They set off "greatly depressed,"
wrote Don Juan to one of the King's councillors, "because at the time
of their departure the rain, snow and wind were blowing with such
fury that daughters would have to abandon their mothers, husbands
their wives and widows their children by the wayside. One cannot deny
that the spectacle of the depopulation of a whole kingdom is a most
disheartening experience."

Philip II remained unmoved by all admonishments and took a decision contrary to all moderate counsel. The impenetrable belt of
terror which he created around himself discouraged everybody from
volunteering further advice. "There was a borderline," wrote one of his
chroniclers, "over which none of his intimates dared to trespass, for
had they done so they would have broken their necks." According to
contemporary accounts, the most experienced generals began to blush
and tremble in the royal presence. Even the dignitaries of the Church,
who were confident that they could rely on the King's respect, learned
to their cost the risk of abusing the deference due to the throne. Cardinal Espinosa, who enjoyed the highest privileges at court, was called

a liar when he dared to contradict the King. He died a week after his disgrace and it was rumoured that a word from Philip II was enough to kill a man. He came increasingly to resent anything which could have affected his lonely grandeur. This personal resentment seemed even stronger than his deepest convictions and most urgent political consideration. The fate of the kingdom was subordinated to his own prestige and after the victory of Lepanto even the fate of Christianity was relegated to the background by this maniac for prestige. When the Pope demanded the continuation of the battle, in order to eliminate the Turkish menace once and for all, he ordered Don Juan to keep the Spanish fleet in Messina harbour. Don Juan was too successful, his reputation had grown too dazzling, he was much too spectacular a figure, who imposed himself vividly on the popular imagination as the last of the knights-errant. The death of Don Juan and the murder of his lieutenant, Escovedo, by Antonio Pérez, the King's private secretary, who claimed to have acted on the King's instigation, form the most sinister conspiracy among all the dark mysteries of history. Philip II, whether an instigator to murder or the victim of one of the few he trusted, had to suffer from the loss of an ever-victorious general —even if he desired his death—whose presence always brought a refreshing breath of air into his barren life.

Henceforward he seemed to belong more to the dead than to the living. The subject he chose for the altarpiece to be painted by El Greco was in fact a eulogy of death: the Theban Legion, dispatched by the Emperor Maximilius to fight the Christians beyond the Alps, who refused to obey his orders and were condemned to death (Plate 37). This scene of mass murder, this violent spectacle with its thronging crowds, its groups of daringly foreshortened bodies, which would have tempted Tintoretto, was depicted by El Greco in a novel and most personal manner. According to one of his biographers, Jean Cassou, he chose to paint one of the most tragic, must culminating episodes in the story as a simple discussion. In fact, in the centre of the picture, St. Maurice is debating with the Roman captains. It is a debate conducted by force of reasoning, with gestures inferring a peaceful mood—raised forefinger, palms outspread—as if the final argument of death were nonexistent. St. Maurice, lifting his right arm and dropping his left in an elegant gesture, seems to argue as follows: "We are armed, but we shall not resist; we prefer to die. True, we are the Emperor's soldiers, but we are also the servants of God." The heroic stand of a martyr has seldom been understated with such discretion, such elegant sobriety.

The epithet "elegant" seems to be the most apt one for El Greco's treatment, even if it is unsuited to such a bitter tragedy. The discussion in the foreground seems to be conducted by men of the world with reserved gestures. The Venetian figure from "The Dream of Philip II" has become a Spanish nobleman as well as the captains and two spectators, inserted between the figures conducting the debate, who are more like portraits of contemporaries. The less El Greco's figures resemble the Italian types of his earlier paintings, the more elongated do they become. Their heads grow more narrow, with uncommon bone structures, almost without backs to their skulls, pointed profiles, and receding chins. There are strange, arbitrary discrepancies in the picture and the costumes are no less surprising than the anatomy. These Spanish noblemen are all clad in skin-tight garments, with the exception of the two spectators, revealing the full play of the powerful muscles of their chests and backs down to the sudden cavities of their navels. In fact they seem to be almost naked under this imaginary uniform, after the fashion of the holy warriors in Byzantine pictures. Were those saints, whose singularly naked thighs and legs were more like those of dancers, recalled by El Greco in order to display his knowledge of anatomy? Or did he wish to satisfy the King, of whose predilection for the beautiful nudes of Italian paintings he was aware? He even deprived the Roman soldiers of their uniforms. The legionary brandishing his sword has only his loins covered. The masses of martyrs submitting to murder are in the nude. This complete nakedness of powerful, muscular-bodied men who make no attempt to defend themselves symbolized for El Greco the principle of non-resistance, the passivity of faith. The picture is dominated by a single, most uncommon gesture: in the scene of collective martyrdom which on the left-hand side portrays the sequel to the debate in the foreground, St. Maurice stands over the decapitated body of his comrade, stretching out his powerful arms towards him, with his palms spread in so wide and open a gesture that this could only appear natural for the supple wrists and loose joints of an Oriental. St. Maurice still wears his tight doublet; he is still in possession of his sword, but these outstretched arms, these outspread hands, eloquently express the religious fervour of a man who has refused to protect his life at the cost of other lives, who incites death and also incites the living who precede him, for he is to die the last. His slim, vibrant fingers seem to express his eagerness to find salvation, if not joy, in death.

"The Martyrdom of St. Maurice" contains various styles of artistic expression. The celestial beings are closer to an Italian plasticity than the human figures. They resemble in their sensuous beauty the inhabitants of paradise as depicted in Venice. These rather womanly angels with martyrs' crowns but with robust thighs, who appear catapulted into space; these angels playing instruments comfortably nestling in a wedge of clouds as if in a rocky cavity; these leaping, curly-headed cherubs, all could easily have been painted by a Venetian master. Perhaps El Greco painted heaven as (so he thought) it appeared in Philip's dreams?

The composition of the principal scene, which balances the diagonal of heaven with verticals of figures, lances, and a banner on the right of the picture, is of a type familiar throughout the Italian Renaissance. The beautiful bodies of the martyrs remind one of the bronze figures sculpted in Italy. But El Greco also remembered his beginnings as a miniaturist. He inserted the two scenes of martyrdom—the scene of St. Maurice standing over the decapitated body and the scene of the mass murder of naked soldiers—not according to the rules of perspective, but by precipitately reducing the dimensions in the manner of the mediæval painters and illuminators. The painting also reveals an artist to whom the realism of Flemish art was not unknown: the magnificent workmanship of the sword, the gleaming helmets, the roots growing out of the cracked earth, the dead branch of a tree in the foreground, the flowers painted in the manner of northern still-lifes, the snake behind the stone, all seem to bear witness to El Greco's desire to demonstrate fully his ability to paint. The picture would be an odd assortment of all the different styles he was able to master if the magic light did not transform the manners of his distant beginnings, his recent past, and his present into a convincing unity of purpose. This clear-sighted man, always conscious of his ultimate aim, did not make such use of light on a sudden inspiration or by accident. From the very outset he was determined to immerse his painting in a flashing light of gold and blue, transparent and crystal clear, like the light that shines through stained glass.

El Greco ardently coveted the royal commission for which he had had to wait so long, and was most anxious to satisfy his patron. Yet his pride made him conceal his anxiety and he was slow to begin this picture. On April 25, 1580, the King notified the prior of the monastery that the painter Domenico Theotocopuli, residing in Toledo, had been commissioned by him to paint a picture; the work, however, was not progressing, for lack of money and paints. He therefore ordered that the artist be provided with money and the best paints for which he asked, especially with ultramarine, in order that the painting should not lack beauty befitting a work done in the King's service.

This order of the King reveals El Greco's method of work. Even before he started to paint, he had a vision of the finished picture; he knew that he would be needing a great deal of ultramarine to paint long, transparent shadows, with startling golden shades in the foreground, sharp red, and pale green strokes, all glittering as if caught in the powerful beam of a spotlight. By means of lighting alone he succeeded in producing a fictitious depth in this picture which lacks the depth of perspective. Through the play of interchanging colours he filled the static figures in the foreground with such animation that the fatal subject of this argument can be sensed in spite of the discreet and reticent gestures. It is this light which truly interprets his conception. It resolves the discordant and arbitrary elements and gives the figures and their gestures true meaning. The joy and enchantment of this light spreading over the picture conveys the deeper meaning of "The Martyrdom of St. Maurice" and transforms it, in the words of Ortega y Gasset, into an invitation to death.

El Greco was well aware of his accomplishment, although he reverted to means by which he hoped to flatter a taste which was alien to him. He signed the picture with neat Greek letters on a tablet held aloft by the arabesque of a snake. It would be difficult to find a prouder signature, as Camon Aznar, one of his most intuitive biographers, has said.

The pictorial success of this work, which is still in the Escorial, can well be assessed today by the fact that all pictures hung beside it appear opaque; even a Titian appears lustreless in comparison with the flashing of this crystal-clear light. It seems as if a new optical vision were born, but this was not recognized by the conservative spirit of the Escorial. El Greco painted the most appropriate picture for Philip II's necropolis, yet this royal dilettante with his backward taste was unable to comprehend that the picture expressed the hidden meaning of his own will, that he had found in El Greco the perfect interpreter of the conception which led him to build the Escorial. A prisoner of his age and its prejudices, he may have been repelled by such a varied assortment of elements and styles, by such an arbitrary interpretation of his chosen subject. He also may have been shocked by the almost complete nudity of the saints and by certain realistic details such as the snake in the foreground; this proud symbol may have scandalized the man who made the following stipulation in his agreement with El Mudo: "There should not appear in these paintings either cats or dogs, nor any other indecent beings."

Whatever his reasons, Philip II disliked "The Martyrdom of St. Maurice." Several years later Father de Sigüenza interpreted the King's displeasure as follows: "There is here a painting of St. Maurice and his soldiers destined for the altar dedicated to this Saint, by the hand of a certain Domenico Greco, who lives and paints excellent things in Toledo; it displeases the King, which is not surprising, for it pleases only a very few, although it is generally said that this is great art, that its author has wide knowledge and paints excellent things by his hand."

This concise statement sheds light on the eternal dispute over every innovation, on the accusations voiced against everything implying a breach with the established and familiar past. This picture was doomed to failure from the start. Philip II, who cast a spell over his age, may himself have misled El Greco about his faculty of comprehension, the limits of royal understanding. He could not realize that on the spiritual plane his true opponent was the King, who not only represented the reactionary spirit of his time but also the spirit of ignorance and mockery which in the centuries to come was to surround his work and bury his name in long oblivion.

"The Martyrdom of St. Maurice" was not to occupy the place of honour over the altar for which it had been destined. Philip II commissioned another painting of the same subject by Romulo Cincinnati, a choice characteristic of him. This pupil of Salviati, feeble and eclectic, had been working for the King for several years. He painted several frescoes for the Escorial, perpetuating the well-worn-out academic compositions of the Florentine renaissance. These pallid pictures evoke no emotion in the spectator and no devotion in the ardent believer. They merely have a reassuring effect through their lustreless formality. Cincinnati's name has gone down in history for the sole reason that he was preferred to El Greco. He was also to complete the fresco of the "Paradise" begun by the Genoese painter Cambiaso, called El Luqueto, who died in 1585. Fray Antonio de Villacastín referred to this succession with little favour. This son of the people had better judgment than his scholarly King and, as a deep-rooted Spaniard, his taste was formed by a long tradition. According to him, "Romulo arrived here looking very thin; we gave him the designs left by Luqueto. . . . I wish that this Romulo were a little more spirited; he seems half dead."

However, Fray Antonio was an obedient servant who did not dare to contradict his King. He did not intervene in El Greco's favour. A courtier above all, he did not even dare to mention the name of a man fallen into disgrace. In fact Philip II could not have had a very high opinion of El Greco's substitute: he paid him less than El Greco. He paid 550 ducats for the picture which still hangs over the altar, whereas El Greco received 800 for the painting which was relegated to some hidden corner of the Escorial. Philip showed a similar contempt for all the artists who worked for him. He also removed the centre of the altarpiece dedicated to "The Martyrdom of St. Lawrence" painted by Cambiaso and, on the recommendation of Pompeo Leoni, invited Federigo Zuccaro over from Italy, only subsequently to destroy the majority of his mediocre frescoes. In spite of his narrow taste he was not without some feeling for quality. Yet he was never again to offer such scope for El Greco's genius as would have been provided by the immense wall space of the Escorial.

In the autumn of 1584 the huge building was completed. Philip II had succeeded in achieving the object dearest to his heart, an object which in fact meant everything to him. He moved into an apartment next to the Capella Mayor which had a small window looking into the chapel and through which he could follow the services. Though overwhelmed with work, this monarch carefully supervised the sacristans who handled the holy reliquaries, and if they were not put back in exactly their right places on the altars, the King sent one of his officers to call the sacristans to order; if an officiating priest happened to omit a verse, he immediately sent word to the prior. The Escorial was to remain the one passion of this man who forcibly stifled every other capacity for feeling. Father Juan de Sepúlveda wrote of him: "He has no other pleasures or satisfaction except in living with his monks in his house at San Lorenzo. For him, to leave here means death or the severest form of torture. But for his great desire to attend to the government of his states, he would never leave it."

This sovereign, reputedly the richest in the world, lived in a whitewashed, brick-lined cell. He slept in a windowless alcove. He had no need of a view; he bore his own sightless world within him. He had small images of saints hung all round his bed, "so that he could see them whichever way he turned." He conducted the affairs of two continents from a small writing desk with a little shelf for his books, such as every monk had in his cell. He made notes on the documents piled up before him, in the margins and across the texts; his untidy handwriting, the mad flourish of his initials, covered the neat calligraphy of his scribes. Everything around him seemed to bespeak his ostentatious self-deprivation, to flaunt his austerity.

Yet the day the basilica was consecrated by the Papal Legate, on September 13, 1584, this ever anxiously calculating monarch indulged in a debauch of expenditure by having all four façades, the towers, and domes of the building illuminated. The sky glowed red, as from an enormous fire. The glare was visible as far as Madrid. It could be seen even in Toledo. It was from Toledo that El Greco could watch the glow rising in the sky. Just about a month before he had delivered his painting to the prior of the Escorial and at the same time had seen a great hope die. The very object of his journey to Spain had eluded him. With the collapse of his ambitious projects and this wound to his self-esteem was he to set off again on a new journey, as he had done after his setbacks in Rome, in search of a more understanding patron? He had come such a long way since he had left his native island. He was well used to travelling and to temporary domiciles everywhere and nowhere; a passer-by with no roots in the present. But he was no longer alone. There was the woman he loved, and the child who at that age had all the charm of the incomplete, with features as yet unformed, a still childish but already greedy mouth and a look of premature gravity in his eyes. There was also Toledo. Although El Greco was unadaptable in his heart of hearts, the town had set its mark so strongly upon him that he almost seemed one with it.

A portrait reveals just how complete and irrevocable this assimilation was—the celebrated portrait of the "Portrait of a Man with His Hand on His Breast" in the Prado (Plate 38). Historians agree in believing it to date from the same period as the commission for the Escorial. El Greco had been only a few years in Spain. But all Spain is already contained in this canvas. The court and nobility were still having themselves painted by foreign artists, or in the cold, official effigies of a technique borrowed from abroad. Suddenly this Cretan, who had served his apprenticeship in Italy, gave the Spanish nobleman a face which was individual yet so convincing that it was to stand as a symbol for centuries to come. The "Portrait of a Man with His Hand on His Breast" is dressed in the costume which Spain had managed to impose on almost the whole world—the black doublet with the very high collar, with its froth of precious lace, which also curls round the cuffs. At his side he carries one of those magnificently chased Toledan swords famous throughout the world. But the picture as a whole proclaims at a glance its Spanish character, as typical of the soil as of its time.

This archetype of a Spaniard had already entered the scene, had already been brought to life in works of fiction, but for his first appearance on canvas he had awaited El Greco's arrival and his first incarnation in the Prado portrait, which was to be followed by so many others. Yet it is scarcely an idealized portrait. It is realistic in the same sense as the Flemish portraits. The man is painted with a high forehead, thinning hair, slightly uneven eyes, with one more closed than the other, a markedly crooked bridge to his nose, and a sensual mouth, half concealed by a thick moustache. Very realistic also is the hand, with its fingers, too delicate in relation to its broad back, its wrinkled joints, and its finger tips, so thin that they barely leave room for the small nails. But the monumental ensemble tones down and co-ordinates all these minute details. The man is painted standing stiffly erect in a strictly frontal pose; his eyes meet those of the spectator as they must have met each man with whom he conversed in his lifetime— calm, lofty, and remote. He does not appear particularly communicative; he seems rather to be wrapped in haughty silence, but his hand is placed on his breast as if to affirm some fact of great importance, holding his heart as witness to some oath. If the pose is unusual, even stranger is the manner in which this hand is placed, with the two middle fingers joined together, whereas the others are spread out fanwise. This gesture is so uncommon that generations of historians have tried to decipher its meanings. Is it a ritual sign, only intelligible to the initiated? A gesture recommended by St. Ignatius Loyola in his *Spiritual Exercises?* "This consists, each time one falls into sin, in laying the hand on the breast whilst inciting one's inner self to grief."

But this gesture is not peculiar to the model El Greco may have had before him. It is his own personal property, heralded already in his Italian pictures, figuring in "The Cleansing of the Temple" and, above all, in the Christ of "El Espolio." The hand of the nobleman is the very hand of Christ, with its broad palm, tapering fingers, small fingernails, even the suppleness of the thumb. In the Christ of "El Espolio" this gesture, in a hand tied by a vicious cord, has a quality of pathos, as if summing up the very meaning of the drama. With the nobleman it assumes the function of an important communication, a personal avowal.

But who could this man have been, who addresses the spectator with such intensity of gaze and gesture, at once haughty and seeking intimacy? And how could El Greco have borrowed his hand before he had even painted him, in order to give it to his Christ? An increasing number of his Spanish biographers assert that the "Portrait of a Man with His Hand on His Breast" is his self-portrait. The psychological arguments in favour of this attribution are numerous. The major objection against it is the picture in the Metropolitan Museum considered to be a late self-portrait, in which the nose is much longer and descends in a point. But is the portrait in New York, supported as it is only by long tradition, really a self-portrait? From the psychological viewpoint the nobleman in the Prado is more convincing than the old man in the Metropolitan. But if the former attribution is correct, as one is tempted to believe, then the miracle of assimilation would be even more astounding. It is perhaps not so much a question of assimilation as of a strange affinity. El Greco, whether he painted himself as a Spanish nobleman or whether he painted someone else so typical of his country, knew that he was never to leave Spain, that he would remain in Toledo for the rest of his days. The failure of his efforts to win the royal favour had only sealed his bond with the city to which he had come by chance. The Escorial was to see no more of his works, with the exception of "St. Ildefonso," purchased by Philip IV on the advice of Velásquez, and his "St. Peter," also acquired much later, after his death.

The paths of El Greco and Philip II had crossed for a moment only to separate again for ever. El Greco was never to be summoned to paint the members of the royal family, or even any of the courtiers. Philip, who inspired such extreme and passionate opinions, was never to have the portrait which would have truly revealed his character.

An incident of apparently minor importance—that of a picture refused by a king with absolute tastes—had incalculable consequences. This, because it was in fact more than a simple incident. Philip II and El Greco could never have met within the vast enclosure of the Escorial. The fortress of Christianity remained a stronghold of the past, a monument of conservation, a gigantic tomb, not only for the dead who were brought there, but also for the living, for ideas, for the vital impulse which sustained a tormented humanity. The living faith drew its strength from other sources. The Escorial became more and more a shell, echoing with the prayers and Masses said at every altar, with the collective beseeching of God. But it was elsewhere and amongst other paths that souls advanced towards God; it was elsewhere that the saints were born, on whom El Greco, a foreign immigrant, tried to bestow a new face, to express the perfect communion of the blessed.

CHAPTER
SIX
THE ADVENT
OF THE MIRACULOUS

LEGENDS so overlaid the historical facts in Toledo that they even created their own brand of truth, more convincing than the evidence of reality; and legends which teemed round the palace or estate of the Marqués de Villena were amongst those most deeply rooted in the popular imagination, being supported by the statements of scholars and men of letters. The situation of this property inside the walls of Toledo helped to gain credence for the dramas attributed to it. A steep street led up to it through the old ghetto, the *Judería,* which still bore the stamp of that semi-clandestine life and whose inhabitants, with only a few exceptions, remembered that they must always be fugitives, ready to change their place of exile, with their material possessions reduced to what could easily be carried away. Here the streets grew narrow, the houses drew closer together, as if rubbing elbows, and their façades became plain, denying themselves any ostentation, as if to form a protective screen for the wealth behind them. But the street, widening as it reached the top, also skirted the proud synagogue which Samuel Abulafia Halevi had built when he felt himself to be at last secure and dazzlingly powerful under the protection of the King. He it was, too, who, scorning the warnings of the prophets and the customary caution of his coreligionists, built himself an opulent residence, the symbol of his own rise to fortune. There the people believed that he had hidden fabulous treasures and practised alchemy and black magic. The cellars, with their beautiful *mudejar* vaulting—perhaps the same or similar to that in the house known today as the *Casa del Greco*—had from the start aroused envy mixed with superstitious fear.

Samuel Halevi was so immured in his pride that, according to contemporary accounts, he died of indignation when King Pedro the Cruel had him tortured, to make him confess the hiding place of his treasure. And these underground vaults, abettors of mystery, had preserved their secret of fabulous gold and magic practices.

Remaining true to this reputation for the supernatural, legend claimed Samuel Halevi's successor to have been a magician no less famous, the great scholar and wizard Don Enrique of Aragon, without the slightest proof that the rich aristocrat of the court of Don Juan II ever resided in this property. Only the logic of the miraculous, it would seem, brought him to this spot.

The first certain fact is the donation of the palace by King Enrique IV to Don Juan Pacheco, Duke of Escalona, first Marqués de Villena. Its reputation, however, still clung to it. A meeting place for witches and magicians in the popular imagination, the palace was also the chosen scene of spectacular events. One very convincing tradition has it that when the Constable Bourbon came to Toledo after the Battle of Pavia, on the order of Charles V, the finest palace in the town, that of the Marqués de Villena, was assigned to him as his residence. As a faithful servant of the Emperor, the Marqués de Villena submitted to the royal command, but with rage in his heart at seeing his home besmirched by the Constable of sinister repute. He left the house with his entire family and staff. At the first opportunity, when the Constable was absent from Toledo, the palace was set on fire at all four corners, and ancient woodwork, furniture, tapestries, priceless treasures, and works of art went up in flames. Spreading from Toledo right across Spain, news of this feat of ancient Castilian honour travelled as far as Italy. The great Italian historian, Francesco Guicciardini, described in detail how the palace "infected by the Bourbon's infamy and thenceforth unworthy of habitation by men of honour" was purged by the flames.

Yet no Toledan historian of the time mentions this sinister deed. On the contrary, the chroniclers who give detailed accounts of the Constable's arrival in Toledo also specify that it was at the palace of the Conde de Cifuentes that he resided during his stay. It would simply appear that the popular imagination dreamed so vividly of being able to avenge an insult, the scene lent itself so well and the proud Marqués de Villena seemed, according to a contemporary historian, so clearly suited to be the hero of such an exploit that the event took shape without any proof to support it.

Towards this second half of the sixteenth century the huge property, so difficult to maintain, began to fall into ruins; it became a group of buildings known as the *"casas del Marqués de Villena"* and was rented out in apartments both large and small.

On September 10, 1585, El Greco signed a lease with the Marqués de Villena's bailiff. The apartment he rented was disproportionately large for a man who seemed to live on the fringe of society. He chose the most sumptuous of the apartments, *"el quarto real,"* with an entrance hall, corridors, a room at the foot of the stairs leading up to the floor on which he lived, and a kitchen which was, as the contract specified, the former main kitchen. It was the apartment of a man who liked to have space around him, large rooms permitting both freedom of movement and seclusion, and who also liked to entertain numerous friends and had long dreamed of living in a palace.

The apartment was also excessively costly for an artist, who had suffered a recent setback and who had just missed an important commission. It cost 596 reals a year, a considerable sum for that time, whereas most of the apartments in the building brought in an annual rent of 50 to 100 reals. But in El Greco's case this extravagance was possibly just his own personal way of reacting to failure, a challenge to fate, a desire to prove both to himself and to others that he was far from regarding himself as beaten. Amongst the other artists, often needy, competing for commissions and treated with disdain by their noble or ecclesiastic patrons, this move provoked both indignation and envy, as if El Greco had thus escaped from some vague brotherhood of mediocrities. Many years later Jusepe Martínez still caught echoes of the consternation aroused by his unconventional mode of life; many years later he noted with disapproval that El Greco was in the habit of squandering the money he earned.

The large apartment which El Greco rented also represented for him a definitive understanding with Toledo, a pact concluded forever. All his love of the city was expressed in this choice of his. From the site of this building Toledo was to be seen at its best. If, later on, El Greco was to paint the city as one paints the portrait of a beloved woman, it was because he had watched it for a long time from the most favourable vantage point and in its most becoming light. The lease, which enumerates the rooms he occupied, also mentions a view over the steep bank of the Tagus. The vistas over Toledo, the details of its architecture, the curve of the river, the silhouette of a tree which he was later to introduce into his pictures were a daily sight, familiar objects which fascinated him and found their way into his holy scenes almost against his will, as if they belonged there by their own right.

Today the Paseo del Tránsito covers the site of the former palace. Across the street which borders it to the northeast was the ghetto and there, skirting the façade of the synagogue, stood another large property called the House of the Old Duchess; this site is now occupied by the house known as the Casa del Greco. This ancient dwelling has been reverently reconstructed, but in fact El Greco never inhabited it. However, its cellars and courtyard are doubtless similar to those of his house, a well also being mentioned in his lease; the big fig tree could have stood in his garden; the remains of *mudejar* decorations and even some Hebrew inscriptions might well have rubbed elbows with an analogous relief of a cross surmounting a globe, to ward off the evil spirits of the place. The Casa del Greco, with its suggestive atmosphere, is one of the major triumphs of the ascendancy of legend over historical truth in Toledo.

At this time, after finally settling in Toledo, El Greco took into his house an Italian who seems to have accompanied him to Spain or joined him shortly after his arrival there. Francisco de Preboste, who was then about thirty, was to play in El Greco's life that leading role which is so often assumed in the shadow of a creative genius by a lesser but competent and clever man who can be trusted blindly. He is sometimes referred to as his servant, but, following the Italian custom, he was also his pupil. No signed work of his is known, but he must have been a faithful copyist of his master and a large number of replicas are undoubtedly by his hand. His personal gifts seem to have been sufficiently appreciated for him to have been entrusted later on with an important work which he was to share with El Greco's son. He was so successful in winning the confidence of clients, and the support he received from his master earned him such respect that, in the event of a large commission, he was entrusted with "carrying out and having carried out any altarpiece or works of painting of any kind, as well as of architecture."

But it was less in his talent, which must have been that of an imitator crushed by a powerful personality, than in his gifts as a negotiator, in his skill as a businessman, that El Greco placed his trust. There is no document in El Greco's career which does not mention him, no agreement which does not bear his signature, no negotiation from which he is omitted, always with full powers granted him by El Greco and legalized before a notary.

As if he had exhausted in his youth all his ambition to see distant lands, his desire for novelty or change, El Greco gave up travelling and with rare exceptions never left Toledo again. It was Preboste who undertook to negotiate with clients in other towns and who went as far as Seville to sell his master's pictures. This man, who was almost El Greco's shadow or other self, but shrewder and with a keener commercial sense, must have often been painted by El Greco, who liked only familiar faces and endowed his saints with the features of those close to him. This Italian factotum must have appeared in many religious compositions; one of the numerous unidentifiable portraits is doubtless his. But the disrepute into which El Greco's work fell after his death, the shadow which for a considerable time blotted out his memory, also engulfed this subsidiary figure, who was nevertheless so important in his life and whose name persistently recurs.

When El Greco installed himself in the palace of the Marqués de Villena, he already had many acquaintances and some trusted friends in the city. By now he could speak Spanish. A document reveals that, in May 1582, he was summoned by the Tribunal of the Inquisition of Toledo to act as interpreter for a compatriot accused of secretly practising the Muslim religion. He was still referred to as "a painter residing in this city" and "a native of the city of Candia." He swore to interpret well and faithfully everything which occurred at the hearing, what the criminal said, and what the Lord Inquisitors replied, and to keep it secret under pain of excommunication, pending a heavier penalty.

Although El Greco had already heard a fair amount about the activities of the Inquisition from his friends and from Pompeo Leoni, who knew its prisons, this was the first time he faced the formidable tribunal by which he had already been threatened, although not on the criminals' bench. His faith was above suspicion—the mere fact of his being summoned proves this, and he was later to be called upon to portray the Grand Inquisitor himself—but this experience possibly strengthened his natural mistrust and perhaps led him to narrow the circle of his artistic vision even more than his innate disposition required.

The Holy Office was particularly vigilant over newcomers to Toledo. The Moors, converted and disguised, had lately flocked there, as if in response to a password which spread rapidly among those menaced. A council which met in 1580 declared the danger of this immigration. A special control was set up. Even their private lives were watched;

they were denounced merely for having exchanged a few words in Arabic, sufficient proof that they had reverted to their former errors. It was the foreigners who were in the first place accused of bringing with them the virus of heresy. The Toledans, who to begin with had given the Holy Office a scant welcome, from now on boasted that no citizen had figured in the recent trials and *autos da fé*. In this city which was at once hospitable (for it owed much to foreigners) and xenophobe through pride, suspicion fell easily on those who differed, whether in their habits or their behaviour, from natives of Toledo.

Heresy was tracked down in its most harmless guises, bringing to light the practice of forbidden cults, the menace of Protestantism, the activities of pious sects seeking a way of escape, a short cut to God, amidst the upheavals of the age, and which the Church counted amongst its worst enemies. In fact, through that predilection for the supernatural which was her traditional heritage, Toledo was fertile soil for mysteries, a quicksand for the feet of a foreigner. The very house El Greco inhabited had served as a meeting place for the *Illuminati* of Toledo, recruited from amongst the nobility of the town. These *Alumbrados,* tormented by a thirst for the absolute and shunning all human intervention in their communion with God, preached complete self-abnegation and demanded that a destitute man should refrain from trying to help himself so as not to impede the action of the Almighty.

The Holy Office of Toledo was the most feared in the whole of Spain. In the *auto da fé* which took place in 1580, people accused of the widest variety of crimes were burned at the stake, including four bigamists, false witnesses, blasphemers, a necromancer, Judaists, Muslim renegades, Lutherans, and eight men guilty of various heresies. The *autos da fé* opened in the square of the Zodocover, where two stands were erected, one for the authorities and local nobility, the other for the penitents and criminals. After the verdict the Holy Office withdrew and handed the condemned over to the civil authorities, who led them outside the town, to the square of Cristo de la Vega, where the stake was lit. Its flames were a sufficiently eloquent warning for every foreigner to feel that danger lay in wait for him.

El Greco who was at once highly mistrustful and highly sociable, seems to have been particularly cautious in his choice of friends. His first contacts were probably with the Greeks who, like himself, had come to Toledo in search of a wider field of activity, a more remunerative occupation, or simply a roof over their heads. One of his patrons and protectors, Garcia de Loysa, employed a compatriot of El Greco's, the Cretan Antonio Calosynas, who was also a physician and a poet, to copy famous manuscripts. Thanks to his deep humanist culture El Greco from the outset stepped straight into an intellectual circle. Later, on the occasion of a dispute with recalcitrant clients, the fact that he had "many friends" in Toledo was stressed. One of his first friends was Don Diego de Covarrubias y Leiva, a man of great repute, both jurist and theologian, who was already an archbishop at the age of thirty-five and President of the Council of Castile, from which he advanced to the presidency of the Council of State. The great achievement of Don Diego's life, however, was his contribution to the decisions of the Council of Trent, where, thanks to his rare ability, the honour fell to him of drafting the final degree on the observance of the reforms prescribed by the Council. A man of vast knowledge and a tireless worker, who never under any circumstances let himself be separated from his books, he was regarded as the most outstanding personality in the country. Possibly El Greco had known him in Rome, or in Madrid soon after his arrival in Spain, for Don Diego died in 1577. Did he paint him in Italy? Is the little portrait in the Greco Museum, which specifies that Don Diego was sixty-two at the time, the work of his hand? The treatment is too hard and severe, even for a painting of 1574. About thirty years later El Greco was to take up this portrait again—whether his own work or another's—and reproduce it faithfully, down to the smallest detail, with its sacerdotal vestments, the cap with the white hair curling stiffly out below it, even the precise line traced by the ribbon from which the cross on his chest hangs (Plate 40). But this posthumous portrait was painted by the genius for revealing human character that El Greco had in the meantime become. It was a resurrection. In place of a high dignitary who had been dead for over thirty years El Greco painted a man of compelling presence, in the full intellectual vigour that had been his. Instead of the apotheosis of one deceased, El Greco painted a living man, as if he had him before his eyes. He even painted his physical defects, including a small growth by his eyelid, in the same way as the Flemish would paint a wart. In spite of this realism the long and earnest face emanates such an impression of authority that, even without the surplice, one would know him to be an ecclesiastic, just as one would know him to be a man of importance.

This portrait is also revealing for El Greco's independence in relation to his model. It mattered little to him whether he painted a dead

or a living man, for, even if he lingered over such accidental details
as a growth of the skin or the ruggedness of a beard, he painted a
portrait of the inner spirit, endowing it with an intense vitality which
was both his own and that of his subject. It was this specific approach
of his which gave his sitters a vague family likeness, a common air
of austere spirituality.

Don Diego's brother, Don Antonio de Covarrubias, was of the same
intellectual mould. He owed his reputation above all to his profound
humanist culture; he was regarded as the greatest Latin and Greek
scholar of the century. But he was also a philosopher, jurist, and
theologian; he had followed in the wake of his elder brother's career,
attended the Council of Trent, been a member of the Council of
Castile and, in 1580, was appointed canon of Toledo Cathedral.

At the University of Toledo, which prided itself on having no equal
save at Bologna and Salamanca, Don Antonio was held in particular
esteem, being regarded as an oracle (according to a contemporary
witness) by all the learned men of every faculty. It was easy for such
a man to give his friends standing. The fact that they spoke a common
language and that, thanks to El Greco's humanist culture, they could
discuss problems dear to them both, was bound to create a bond of
friendship between them. But Don Antonio, like his brother, had also
inherited a great interest in the arts. Their father, Don Alonso de
Covarrubias, had been a noted architect, who drew his inspiration
from the indigenous art, from the exuberant plateresque[1] style. From
early childhood both brothers had associated with painters, architects,
and sculptors and knew how to judge artistic values for themselves.
Don Antonio became El Greco's staunchest friend, a friend for life.

El Greco painted him, too (Plate 41), with all his spiritual distinction, less severe, less intransigent than his brother, a weaker personality; but an expression of goodness is reflected in his face. There is
also a touch of humour in the rather weak, uneven eyes, with the
attentive look of a deaf man. The mouth is half open, as if listening
to what the ears can no longer hear or repeating the words read on
another's lips. El Greco succeeded in translating, not only his sitter's
infirmity, but also his manner of overcoming it. A contemporary witness records that Don Antonio, although he had totally lost his sense

[1]*Plateresque:* The term used for late Gothic architecture in Spain—corresponding to the Perpendicular style in England. It derives from the Spanish word
"platería," thus implying the elaborate ornamental character of silver-work repeated in architecture.

of hearing, talked to everyone on every topic of interest so exquisitely that none left him without being filled with the deepest admiration.[2]

Probably from this same earlier period dates the portrait of a doctor in the Prado with the ring on his thumb which in those days was the symbol of the medical profession (Plate 39). This is believed to be a portrait of Don Rodrigo de la Fuente, who, according to Cervantes, was the most famous physician in Toledo. It recalls the great state portraits such as Titian painted: the full, dark green gown gives him a monumental quality and his bearing and gestures are those of an important person. Rodrigo de la Fuente was also a poet and consorted with the scholars of his time. His long face, better suited to a reassuring, benevolent expression, seems tense with intellectual effort. But behind the state portrait El Greco also depicted the man's personal weaknesses, his physical shortcomings. His red hair is turning grey and his flesh is lymphatic, marked by disease; the eyelids are heavy, the eyes lustreless, the mouth displays a forced amiability. The majestic expression of these essentially undistinguished features is perhaps the result of disease or the proximity of death, which was to come to him in 1589 and which El Greco had already perceived hanging over him.

El Greco, the *émigré*, was the predestined painter of the elite of Toledan society with whom he consorted. The opportunity of a major work arose at a moment when he was ready to meet its demands wholeheartedly.

The palace of the Marqués de Villena was situated in the parish of San Tomé. Established in the heart of the ghetto at the time of Toledo's recapture by Alfonso VI, this parish was one of the richest in the city. But its church, dedicated to the apostle St. Thomas, became far too small for the faithful and began to fall into ruins. It was then that Don Gonzalo Ruiz de Toledo, Count Orgaz, Protonotary of Castile (the inscription in the church lists all his titles), who wished to be buried in this church, made important gifts in gold and silver to the parish for its reconstruction. In the hour of this pious nobleman's death a great and rare miracle occurred, as the tablet relates: St. Stephen and St. Augustine descended from heaven to bury him with their own hands. The parish of San Tomé, with its little rebuilt church, was as proud of this miracle—which took place in 1312—as if it had occurred on the previous day. An historian of El Greco's time

[2]Antonio Covarrubias died in 1601. According to Goldscheider, the signed portrait reproduced on Plate 41 was painted after his death, between 1601 and 1609, presumably from a preliminary study made at an earlier period.

specified that it took place in the presence of fifteen witnesses. But these witnesses had long been dead and, as the inscription engraved on the dark stone emphasizes, men are fickle and forgetful, unlike the inhabitants of heaven, who know how to display their gratitude. Thus it was that the citizens of the town of Orgaz, who had been ordered by Don Ruiz to pay the rectorate an annuity and to supply the poor of the parish with cattle and poultry (seventeen chickens precisely), wine, and firewood, had refused to pay this tribute "in the belief that this title had become void through the elapse of time." A trial was held before the court of Valladolid which the parish won in 1570, after spirited pleading by Don Andrés Núñez of Madrid, the vicar of San Tomé, and Pedro Ruiz, its major-domo, as the inscription also records.

Don Andrés Núñez was in fact an energetic man who knew how to defend the interests of the parish. Encouraged perhaps by the outcome of the trial, he felt it was a timely moment to refresh men's memories. The administrative council of the archbishopric of Toledo, of which he himself was a member, authorized him on October 23, 1584, to have a picture painted of the burial of Count Orgaz. The vicar of San Tomé himself belonged to that elite which had adopted the *émigré* artist. He was a friend of El Greco and a few years later was to receive, as a gift from him, a picture in which he figures as a donor.

By the time the archbishopric granted the authorization, El Greco knew that he would never now be summoned to the Escorial. He must have begun the preliminary studies right away, although the agreement was not concluded until March 18, 1586. By then his preparatory work must have been considerably advanced, for the big picture was already completed by Christmas of the same year.

Don Andrés Núñez was a man who knew what he wanted. In spite of his friendship with El Greco and his confidence in him he remained true to the custom of his age which prescribed in detail how the artist was to treat his subject. For the miraculous intervention the protocol ordained as follows: "On the canvas there must be painted a procession showing how the vicar and other priests read Mass for the interment of Don Gonzalo Ruiz de Toledo, lord of the town of Orgaz, and how St. Stephen and St. Augustine descended to bury the body of this nobleman, the one holding him by the head and the other by his feet, laying him in the tomb, whilst many people should be represented around it watching, and above all this must appear Heaven opened up to glory."

El Greco faithfully followed these instructions. He painted the saints with the gestures prescribed, the crowd looking on, and the opening up of heaven. As in all pictures depicting miracles, his task was to make this plausible and convincing, something beyond human experience, which at the same time could have been repeated on that day or the next for all whose faith was strong enough and whose actions were sufficiently pious.

As an heir to Byzantine tradition, El Greco was, so to speak, acclimatized to the miraculous; no need for him to imagine an upheaval in heaven before it could be made to intervene in the affairs of this world. Religious painting had long since lost that artlessness with which the primitive masters painted saints not wholly materialized, angels without bodies. With the new sense of reality, the science of three dimensions, painters had found a need for contrivances to enable them to distinguish between the human and the divine, contrivances such as space and light so that the two worlds could exist side by side. From the beginning El Greco believed in the miracle as in something so familiar that it posed no problem for him. "The Burial of Count Orgaz" (Plate 42) was the first escape of the art of that age into an intermediary world, suspended in time and space between earth and heaven, between reality and its spiritual transformation. The means by which he achieved this were not the fruit of scholarly and laborious research; they were the same as those employed by Byzantium to bring believers into communion with the saints. El Greco conjured away the earth with a contempt for reality inconceivable in a Renaissance painter. Nothing is shown of the scene of the miracle, of that church interior in which it was supposed to have occurred; in fact the figures in the foreground are cut off below their ankles, as if it mattered little to know how and on what they stood. But, although he eliminated the incidental of reality, El Greco did not paint a miracle occurring in an unspecified place or time, but one of his own age. A Toledan miracle in fact. The onlookers of 1312 are men whom he met daily in the street, most of them his friends. The fifteen witnesses of the miracle are in fact fifteen portraits lined up behind the scene with some less individualized faces in the row behind them. Later on the Dutch were to paint collective portraits, but they depicted a group of personalities assembled for some fortuitous occasion, each isolated in his sharply characterized individuality. The Toledans lined up on El Greco's canvas are also men of varying ages, from the youth whose lips are barely shadowed by an incipient moustache to the old, white-

bearded man. They are either deeply moved or argumentative, sorrowful or rejoicing, but they all have an air of uniformity, as if they were
brothers or cousins. This is not only confined to their identity of costume, or to their being of the same social rank; El Greco's models are
of that curiously pronounced and similar, almost unique type produced
by the mixture of races on Spanish soil. They prided themselves on
their pure blood; they traced their origins back through many generations. A contemporary pamphlet written by Cardinal Francisco de
Mendoza y Bobadilla, outraged by the fact that his own nephew had
been asked for proof of the purity of his blood, maliciously sought to
prove that all the grandees of Spain, even those of the noblest and
most ancient families, had some Jewish or Arab blood flowing in their
veins. It was these assimilated elements that seem to have created this
characteristic physique—the long narrow faces, sharp noses with their
sensitive nostrils and sometimes pointed tips which, together with the
sallow skin and black hair, gave them a vaguely Semitic look. This
physical uniformity was even more accentuated by a traditional behaviour, by inherited rules and customs, a reserve prohibiting any
display of emotion. The dark figures are frozen in hieratic poses and
it is only through their hands that these impassive men can show their
inner confusion.

From the beginning, directly the picture became accessible to the
public, the Toledans were proud to see themselves in such a mirror.
They displayed the picture to foreign visitors and, as contemporaries
reported, many of the most distinguished men of the day admired it.

One feels that El Greco was in close spiritual communion with those
he portrayed. One feels that he was at his ease. Whether consciously
or unconsciously he was so imbued with his environment that he did
not hesitate to paint these portraits, to which he devoted particular
care, as if they were motifs repeated from some *mudejar* decoration.

By portraying his friends or patrons as witnesses of the great event
El Greco seems to have been showing his affection and paying a debt
of gratitude. The priest reading the responses on the extreme right is
Don Andrés Núñez himself, the inspirer of the commission; it is easy
to identify him from the embroidered medallion on his dalmatic, representing the Apostle Andrew. El Greco painted him with that almost
Flemish veracity characteristic of him at this period, with a bulbous
forehead, a few wisps of hair in the middle of his bald pate, a stiff
moustache, and muscles twitching in his gaunt cheeks from the strain
of his meditation. Next to him stands a nobleman with a long, narrow

face and thick eyebrows, whose glassy black hair descends in a sharp
point on his forehead and temples. One would guess him straightaway
to be a man of consequence, even were he not carrying the tall cross
which links earth with heaven. El Greco seems to have painted him
a second time; and this other portrait, now in Minneapolis, poses
another of those mysterious problems with which both El Greco's life
and art abound. The Minneapolis picture is at least ten, if not fifteen,
years later than "The Burial of Count Orgaz," not only because of
its more advanced technique, but also because of the cut of the beard
and moustache, and the costume with its fuller ruff characteristic of
the beginning of the seventeenth century. Yet the man is the same age
as the one in the picture in San Tomé. Was he a younger brother, or
a close relation? With his sombre and disdainful air one would judge
this to be less a portrait than the very incarnation of a Spanish hidalgo.

The old man with the white beard, shown in profile, is believed to
be Don Antonio de Covarrubias, although this identification is not
entirely convincing. The Count of Benavente is also recognizable from
his authentic portrait at Bayonne; the part he plays in the picture could
be compared with that of a chorus leader in a Greek tragedy. Bending
slightly forward over the body of Count Orgaz, his eyebrows raised
in amazement, he seems to reveal all that is unusual about the scene
taking place before him in the broad gesture of his carefully groomed
hands; with his precious gesture he expresses the perplexity of all the
onlookers.

The models for the "Portrait of an Unknown Man" in the Hirsch-
land Collection in New York and for that of a member of the Leiva
family can also be identified. Some of El Greco's biographers believe
the man with the fine, high, domed forehead looking over Count
Benavente's shoulder to be his self-portrait. This face, however, in no
way differs from the generalized type of Spanish nobleman; one could
even describe it as less personal and more devoid of individual characteristics than those of the other spectators. Yet it would not be surprising if he too wanted to be present at the great event, among the noblemen with whom he consorted as if he were their equal and belonged
to the same race.

He again expressed this pride of his by placing his son in the foreground, dressed as a young page, with one knee bent, holding a torch
in that strange manner, typical among El Greco's figures, of handling
objects as if wishing to deny their material presence. This young page
is the very embodiment of that earnest grace displayed by all children

endowed with outstanding gifts or destined for a great future. Jorge
Manuel was then about eight years old. El Greco, who liked to append
his signature in a spot chosen according to some code, the key of which
is still unknown, put a piece of white paper between the folds of his
son's garment; on this, however, he did not inscribe the date of the
picture's completion, according to custom, but the date of his son's
birth. Yet it was not a painter of childhood, easily stirred to tenderness
and wonder, who made this portrait. El Greco was not interested in
beings who were still developing, still prisoners of an unawakened
conscience. None of his clients or friends ever seems to have asked
him to portray a young son or daughter. His Infant Jesuses are the
least childlike of any infants set on a mother's knee. Their chubby
little bodies are more reminiscent of the *bambini* of Italian pictures
than of a living, newborn babe. They have grown-up faces, too grave
and often ugly with that touching ugliness which often stamps children
reared in poverty or prematurely faced with tragedy. El Greco moved
in an adult world of men of wide experience and women familiar
with sacrifice. The little page in "The Burial of Count Orgaz" is one
of the rare exceptions in his work. But even when painting this son
whom he passionately loved El Greco gave him an insistent look in
his large, wide eyes, and a small mouth afflicted by too much knowledge. It was through his own child that he introduced the miraculous
event into the picture. It is this boy who with his hand, the hand of
an adult, points towards the intervention of the saints. The Count of
Benavente expresses only the perplexity of the onlookers; the priest's
eyes are fixed on his missal; the two monks discuss together the meaning of the scene unfolding before them; it is the child who realizes
that those present are being privileged to witness a unique event in
their lives. El Greco in his creative work made each choice consciously,
with complete lucidity; this arrangement was deliberate and planned.
The priest in the white surplice, on the right, turns his back on the
mortal world, raising his eyes to a heaven invisible to the rest; with
open arms and outstretched hands he offers his breast to the divine
grace descending upon him. A child and a holy man are the truly
initiated ones. It is through the mediums of faith and innocence that
the saints make themselves known.

The miracle itself has materialized before the eyes of those present
and become part of them. The man being buried is dead beyond doubt.
The body of Count Orgaz is stiff under his rich armour; the saints raise
the rigid limbs, made weightier still by so much steel, with a visible

effort. The knight's head hangs awkwardly to the right; his face has a cadaverous pallor, that bluish tingue assumed by the skin of very dark men, further accentuated by the reflections in the armour; his lips are bloodless in his dark beard. This is not a man with idealized features, sunk in sweet slumber, all ready for the resurrection, after the Italian manner of glorifying the dead. As an Oriental, El Greco was used to discoursing with death. He had no fear of it; for him it was not one of life's kill-joys. It was easy for him to fall in with the feeling of the Spanish, familiar with the proximity of death. The spectators at the burial of Count Orgaz, the ecclesiastics who wished to glorify their benefactor, found it natural to see his body broken and weighing heavily on the arms of the saints. The supernatural breaking in on men's lives has become material; the laws of the earth, of gravity and rigidity, remain immutable. It is only through their colouring, through their golden dalmatics, that St. Augustine and St. Stephen stand out from the dark mass of the onlookers. And these dalmatics are heavy, bejewelled, embroidered, and braided, of a weightier material than the transparent surplice of the priest in the foreground observing the opening up of heaven. The hands of this priest, who epitomizes the feelings of the onlookers in a gesture of perplexity, reach out with all their corporeal insistence towards the empty space created by the body stretched out between the fingers of the saints. There is no distance between the event and its witnesses. To make the miracle plausible, almost tangible, El Greco brought all his immense pictorial means into play. Few great masters of his time could have thus depicted the reflections in the steel, the joints in the armour, the borders stitched with pearls, the relief of the braiding or the points of white lace against black velvet. But along with his gifts as a miniaturist he retained a taste for interlarding the main plot with subsidiary events. He used the embroidered panels and medallions on the dalmatics of the two saints to relate their own stories, so well known to the Toledans. In the stoning of St. Stephen, closely akin to the martyrdom of St. Maurice, he depicted the excited mob as tall, naked figures, as arbitrarily naked as the men of the Theban Legion. Moreover, he brought off the *tour de force* of simultaneously composing a picture in its own right while realistically painting the embroidery of an ecclesiastical garment. On St. Augustine's dalmatic are the figures of three saints, these, too, both embroidery and perfect pictures in themselves; they follow the hem of the garment and bend with the movement of the stooping saint. These pictures within the picture reveal a particular quality in

El Greco's art—the reconciliation of the miniature with the monumental. These figures of St. Catherine, St. Augustine and St. Paul, with their flowing robes, their clean outlines, and spare gestures, could be transferred, just as they are, on to a vast canvas, or else carved in stone to stand in some canopied niche.

The painter of "The Burial of Count Orgaz" had attained his full artistic maturity. He was in possession of every means of expression. He had even profited from his own limitations. The lower part of the picture is a complete victory over form and colouring. Even had he confined himself solely to that part, he would still have given rare artistic pleasure to its dazzled spectators. But it was not merely the material aspect of the miracle which appealed to El Greco. It is only in appearance that his picture consists of two distinct parts, seemingly almost detachable from each other. A mere glance at the copy of the lower part made by his son (which shows, incidentally, the extent to which he misunderstood his father's work) is sufficient to make one realize that the whole picture was, from the start, conceived as a unit, both in its formal and its spiritual aspects. The contract stipulated a "Heaven opened up to Glory." El Greco's patrons must have recalled those Italian apotheoses, crowning the picture like a firework display at the climax of a festival. For El Greco what was taking place in heaven was more important than events on earth. He allotted more space to the upper part of the picture than to the lower, and if the two seemed disconnected and lacking in any formal link—with the exception of the thin shaft of the cross—their internal interdependence is so marked that a division such as the one his son created is like a cut in living flesh.

Even the details of the scene on earth are arranged with a view to this overpowering heaven. One can see, for example, why El Greco shifted the body of the knight held by the two saints to the left. Thus his lips form the mathematical centre of the picture and it is from these lips that the angel collects the dying breath of his soul to present it to the divine grace. El Greco was sufficiently conversant with theological interpretations—he associated frequently enough with ecclesiastics well versed in such matters—to stress this point. This fair angel with its large wings and flying, wind-swept yellow draperies represents the beginning of the supernatural, in its divergence from the earthly vision. But to human eyes this vision is one and the same: men conceive the saints and the blessed with the familiar features of people

they know. The vault of clouds split open by the miracle is the same
one which they saw every day in the opaque sky.

Yet by the same means El Greco employed to paint braiding, lace,
or homespun he succeeded in altering the very substance of flesh before
one's eyes. The portraits of the spectators, that row of Toledans, have
as their counterpart in the upper right-hand section of the picture the
serried ranks of the heads of the blessed. Some of these seem to reflect
the features of the contemporary onlookers, to be almost their doubles.
Among them is a famous Toledan, the late Cardinal Tavera, whose
skeletonlike profile had been copied from his tomb. A portrait in the
second row, with protruding eyes and an underslung jaw, has been
thought to be Philip II. Yet these portraits are somehow dissolved and
distorted by the light which falls on them. Even the most individualized
face could hardly be confused with the most impersonal of the living.
And this light flows down from above, from a single source, the
Saviour, who Himself seems to be woven out of the radiance emanating from Him. By one of those contradictions which are, however, only
so in appearance, El Greco employed that same science of composition in depicting heaven which he seems to have scorned in the lower
part. Whereas he crowded the spectators together, in seeming defiance
of every law of perspective, with no space between them and dominated in an ill-explained manner by the two figures of the monk in
grey and the priest in his surplice, he gradually diminished the ascending figures of the saints and the blessed up to their culminating point.
The canon of the triangle, as preached by the Italian Renaissance, is
here clearly defined, rising up along the back of St. John the Baptist
to the head of Christ. From this apex the mathematical centre descends
straight as a plumb line to the angel, passing through the symbol of
the dead knight's soul held in the angel's arms. The division of the
clouds, which are like pearly sea shells, equally stresses the masterly
handling of the diagonals. As opposed to the crowded scene on earth,
there is a considerable space in heaven, through which blows a gust
of wind, carrying with it in its upward surge the souls of the dead,
saints and angels.

The lower part of the picture is static; a slight bend of the head or
a gesture of the hands barely interrupts the vertical hatching of the
composition. In heaven, on the other hand, all is movement and drama,
converging on the ultimate serenity of the divine welcome. El Greco
went back to Byzantine sources when he painted the knight's soul in
its newborn innocence, in the shape of an infant child. But this painter

of the supernatural lacked the naïveté of mediæal artists, who used
to paint a soul as a child in swaddling clothes. He was appealing to
the men of his day, whose vision had progressed. The soul of Count
Orgaz is at once a child and a cloud, just as are the little angels scarcely
separated from their pearly background. Byzantine, too, in tradition
is the figure of St. John the Baptist, the interceder for the souls of the
dead, kneeling before the Virgin with his left hand stretched out
towards her, his right palm turned outward with bent fingers as if he
held all the arguments in the knight's favour in the hollow of his hand.
The blessed have come crowding down to plead for him; they have
scaled the clouds with outstretched hands; a host of heads, now dense,
now thinning, converges on two angels swept almost horizontal by the
wind, who beseech the Lord. On the other side of the picture the Old
Testament prophets also intercede in his favour. David with his harp,
Moses with the Tablets of the Law, and Noah with his ark. St. Peter
emerges from the hollow of a cloud, holding his keys as no man ever
held an object, letting them dangle from his thin fingers as if they had
lost all weight in this celestial world.

Heaven in turmoil grows calm at the Saviour's feet. This fervent
and frenzied appeal to the divine mercy rises up towards Him in a
dual stream and casts itself into His outstretched, sheltering arms, as
into an eternal haven for humankind.

Corresponding to the way in which the ascent to infinity is arranged
from the formal viewpoint, the light marks the stages of bodily dissolution which culminate in everlasting serenity, in ultimate peace. The
face of the Virgin is bathed in a radiance no longer of this world.
Christ is of a transparent whiteness.

"The Burial of Count Orgaz" arose from the split between two
worlds. The Renaissance had been a period of great certitudes. Man,
freed from his obsession with original sin, from anxiety for the salvation of his soul, wandering between the pitfalls of the present and fear
of damnation, had forged himself a future on earth whilst at the same
time recapturing a distant past of serenity.

But the shifting of the balance of power, the changes occurring on
the political chessboard, the upheavals of social conditions, religious
schism, the wars of conquest and civil strife had hastened the end
of this cycle of man's understanding with himself. The present was no
longer solid ground under the feet of man triumphant. The present
was again bristling with pitfalls, with mortal dangers for the soul; the
monsters of temptation were stirring in their lairs. The Renaissance

had been a world complete in itself, unshakably secure in appearance. But this new anguish racking men's souls began at the point beyond which the man of the Renaissance in his certainties had not looked. It questioned the future of man on earth, a material future now grown precarious, and tormented itself over the future of the spirit. One by one the triumphs of understanding with the temporal faded away. But, as spiritual contents change more quickly than their container, the outward forms survived, the material conquests could be neither forgotten nor undone, even if their finality was questioned. The man whose creative vocation it was to give shape to all that disturbed the present expressed the anxieties, dreams, and nightmares of a troubled age by the same means which had served to proclaim yesterday's security. The plastic vision is the slowest to adapt itself. Man was created in God's image, but men, tormented by a desire to escape from a hateful earthliness, demanded something more than the divine depicted in man's image. This flight from the material, which found its way on to every plane of spiritual life, tended in art towards expression of a plastic form in place of imitation of the form itself. From this dissolution of form, from this quest for *expression,* a school of painting was one day to be born to which this gave its name. Working in isolation, El Greco was advancing towards a similar goal. This duality of vision which he succeeded in embodying was painted for a small church in a city soon to become a provincial town. Had it been painted in Rome or set over an altar in the Escorial, "The Burial of Count Orgaz," which in Toledo merely aroused the curiosity of visitors, would have influenced the creative vision of his time and perhaps changed its direction. But, instead of hanging at a crossroads, El Greco's work was placed in a cul-de-sac and was only to mark a rift between two conceptions of the world.

For El Greco himself the picture in the church of San Tomé also served as a dividing line between two creative epochs. In its lower part he broke away from what he retained of the Renaissance. He rid himself of the last Italian elements in the manner of a great creative genius, with a masterpiece; as if he wished to prove his own mastery to himself, he displayed it in all its perfection before casting it aside. There is virtuoso playing in this picture, playing for the pure pleasure of it, despite all its resolute seriousness. For El Greco himself "The Burial of Count Orgaz" was a boundary stone at a crossroads. It was the image of the road he had already travelled. It was also a foretaste of things to come, the herald of future progress.

Several other works by El Greco stand on the same border line. One strange picture, very close to the lower part of "The Burial of Count Orgaz," is called "St. Louis of France" (in the Louvre) (Plate 43). The King's armour differs from that of Count Orgaz, yet it is painted in the same way; the young page is not Jorge Manuel, but in this picture he plays a similar part, contrasting the freshness of youth with the gravity of maturity. In certain respects, such as its arrangement as a state portrait, the column in the background, the relationship between the two figures, the red drapery wrapped round the armour, and the treatment of the King's muscular arm, the work strongly reveals its dependence on the heroic representations of Roman portraiture. It even reveals it to excess. It smacks of an occasional painting. This spectacular king with his barbaric, almost Merovingian crown looks more like some pious Visigoth ruler, or the conqueror of Toledo, Alphonso VI. Some of El Greco's biographers have thought him to be the Most Catholic King. The picture does not resemble a devotional painting at all. The figure is not treated in the manner in which El Greco was treating saints at that time; it has the realistic quality of a portrait, with its bony face, long nose, prominent cheekbones, and deep-set eyes, too languid for the vigorous features. The King is clean-shaven, unlike the Spanish noblemen of the day. Indeed, with his silky chestnut hair and his fair skin with the same golden reflections as his crown, he does not seem Spanish at all. No document mentions this work of El Greco's. There is no evidence to indicate such an occasion as might have led to a commission of this nature. One is left to conjecture.

In 1587, about the date which might be given to this picture, Toledo again witnessed one of those great days which were to become rare in the years ahead. On April 26 the remains of St. Leocadia, the patron saint of Toledo, who had suffered martyrdom in her native city, were brought back amidst great pomp. These relics had been moved several times from one church to another, bitterly disputed in each case. For a while they had found a resting place in the Benedictine abbey of St. Ghislain in Flanders. The greatest collector of relics of his time, Philip II had persistently claimed them; the monks resisted at some length, but finally had to yield to the all-powerful monarch. Philip II wanted to celebrate the day on which the Virgin's remains returned to her native city with full and due solemnity. Toledo did her utmost to make it a splendid occasion. The Toledan Church was particularly adept at organizing such festivals. The King came from Madrid, ac-

37. *Martyrdom of St. Maurice and the Theban Legion. c. 1580–82*

39. *Don Rodrigo de la Fuente. c. 1582–86*

38. *Portrait of a Man with His Hand on His Breast.*
c. 1580

41. *Don Antonio de Covarrubias. c. 1601—09*

40. *Don Diego de Covarrubias. c. 1601—09*

42. *The Burial of Count Orgaz. 1586*

44. *Julian Romero with His Patron Saint.*
c. 1587–94

43. *St. Louis of France. c. 1587*

46. St. Dominic. c. 1595

45. Mater Dolorosa. c. 1580-90

47. *The Descent from the Cross. c. 1590*

50. *The Baptism of Christ.*
    c. 1595–1600

49. *The Resurrection.*
    c. 1595–1600

48. *The Crucifixion. c. 1590–95*

companied by his sister, the Dowager Empress Doña María, by the Crown Prince Philip, and the Infanta Doña Isabella Clara Eugenia. According to a contemporary chronicler, grandees were to be seen in dozens, parish crosses and bishops' crosiers in hundreds, and ecclesiastics of every rank in thousands in the procession which escorted the relics. They entered the town by the Bisagra gate and progressed slowly towards the sanctuary of St. Leocadia, in the Vega, where the relics were to be temporarily housed. Along the whole route magnificent triumphal arches were erected, adorned with statues, paintings, and inscriptions in Greek and Latin. Finest of all was the one in the Plaza del Perdón, the work of the illustrious canon Juan Bautista Pérez; the most extravagant, too, for, covered with statues of the Kings of Spain and the archbishops of Toledo, with "divers paintings," emblems, and allegories, it cost 7000 ducats.

Following the custom of an epoch insatiable in its pursuit of pleasure, the festivities lasted three days and nights: music echoed down the brilliantly lit streets, there was dancing in the squares, the grandees measured their strength in tourneys, and richly clad and masked noblemen made their way on horseback through the jubilant crowd. The celebrations closed with a bullfight from which the King alone excused himself, for, he said, "one should not mix the divine with the profane."

Could the picture in the Louvre have been painted for this occasion? Does it represent perhaps one of the famous actors of the day in the role of a king in one of those sacred plays for which Toledo was particularly renowned? Was it one of the "divers paintings" which adorned the triumphal arches? Its profane quality is all the more flagrant if it is compared with another, slightly later and also rather puzzling picture, the portrait of "Julian Romero with His Patron Saint" in the Prado (Plate 44). The cloak and the crown placed beside this knight who recommends his protégé to heavenly grace are both decorated with fleurs-de-lis and thus seem to identify him as the saintly King of France. If this is St. Louis, however, he has nothing in common with the portrait in the Louvre. This warrior is beyond doubt a saint. His face has not the same earthly quality as that of the King in the Louvre. It is dissolved by the light flowing over its idealized features; the brilliant eyes are ostentatiously raised to heaven with that fervour which informs all El Greco's saints. Whether St. Louis, as some maintain, the knightly St. Julius, as do others, or even the Byzantine St. Theodore, he is in any case not of this world. His protective gesture is typical of

El Greco. One hand rests lightly on his protégé's shoulder; the other, long and supple, extends one single finger, a finger which touches nothing, as if he were moved by such piety.

The knight in the Prado picture is a familiar creation of El Greco's art in its light-effects, gestures, and expression; the armour, identical with that worn by Count Orgaz, must have been painted from a model in his studio. This patron saint is not alone in giving the picture its accent of religious fervour. The Commander of the Order of Santiago, whom he recommends to divine mercy, is a posthumous portrait, but it has none of that earthly presence El Greco knew how to give even the dead. His idealized features are those of a Spanish nobleman; he is all prayer, the pure offering of a pious soul. As in the portrait of Vincentio Anastagi, an inscription on the column in the background provides information about his rank. In life Julian Romero el de las Azañas had been a valiant soldier; he was wounded in the attack on St. Quentin and on that occasion was made commander of the order. He died in Italy, as a captain of infantry, at the capture of Alessandria. Lope de Vega wrote a conventional drama about his exploits in which, like every true hero, he saved the life of Philip II and fought so victoriously against the French that he chased them out of Douai. El Greco transformed the valiant soldier, the man of action, into a contemplative who has turned away from worldly things and aspires only to eternal peace. He painted him kneeling, his great cloak spread out around him in broad surfaces barely shadowed by folds, a pyramid rising straight up to the prayer in his eyes. The cloak is of a spectral whiteness saturated with gold, which seems to be reflected in his bloodless face. In itself the group conforms to the monuments erected over tombs at that epoch. The light adds to its funerary aspect, as if a cold breath were rising up from the invisible flagstones on which the commander kneels. The picture could have served, in fact, as a sepulchral monument; it may have been commissioned from El Greco by Doña María Gaytán Romero, as a votive picture to be placed beside an altar, toward which the dead man and his patron saint raise their eyes.

El Greco seems to have found himself in difficulties at this time and perhaps did not scorn chance commissions. A year and a half after completing "The Burial of Count Orgaz" he still had not received his fee from the church of San Tomé. According to custom, the picture was submitted for valuation to two painter-experts, who assessed it at 1200 ducats.

For all that Don Andrés Núñez was a friend of El Greco's, the church found the price too high and asked for a new valuation. Two of the best-known painters in Toledo again examined the picture, with what was nearly always to be the result in El Greco's disputes with his clients: they found the price too low for the merits of the work and fixed it at 1600 ducats. The church bitterly contested the new price; it was now willing to pay the one which it had first found too high, but El Greco would not yield over what he believed to be his right, over what he knew to be the amount due to him. However, he was apparently so deep in financial difficulty that he had regretfully to leave his sumptuous apartment, promising himself to return one day. Yet he rejected a proposed compromise and insisted on being paid according to the second valuation, by writ of execution on the property and revenue of the church. The dispute was deliberately protracted in the hope of wearing down El Greco's patience and profiting from his financial embarrassment. But the church merely succeeded in exacerbating his pride. Intractable, he appealed to every available authority. He took the dispute before the Holy See, applying directly to the Pope. This quarrel between a painter and a small church threatened to assume exaggerated proportions. Friends seem to have stepped in, bringing home to him the consequences of his stubbornness and the considerable cost of the proceedings. Suddenly El Greco yielded, as if overcome by fatigue. To avoid "the expenses, losses and other damages and inconveniences" which continuation of the lawsuit would involve, the two litigating parties submitted, on May 30, 1588, to the decision of the council. El Greco withdrew his appeal to the Pope and the rector and major-domo of the church of San Tomé undertook to pay him the 1200 ducats of the original evaluation within nine days. At the time of receiving this money, El Greco was so crippled with debts that his creditors intervened at once and the church paid 65,190 maravedís directly to his supplier of canvases, 73,600 to his apothecary, and 1700 to one Francisco de Buendia. A creative triumph was frittered away in petty money troubles.

Yet, with time, appreciation of his work was spreading. In spite of the dazzling reputation which preceded his arrival in Toledo, El Greco had been compelled painfully to conquer his road to fame inch by inch. Nevertheless, at the moment when "The Burial of Count Orgaz" was at last winning him acclaim, an increased clientele, and a reputation beyond the bounds of Toledo, he was already preparing to forsake a path which would henceforth be easy, to abandon already proven means. For him a complete success meant a stage transcended.

Some works still gravitated within the orbit of "The Burial," among them another of those enigmatic portraits to which famous names have been attached, though none seems sufficiently convincing. It is the portrait of a youth in a private collection at the Hague, of which a second version used to be in the Nemes Collection in Budapest. Unlike the King in the Louvre, this picture falls halfway between a profane portrait and the effigy of a saint, even setting aside the sort of halo which was later added to one of the known examples. Moreover the existence of two versions confirms that this was one of the religious paintings of which El Greco's clients were in the habit of asking for replicas. The young man is painted in the same manner as the youth in "The Burial of Count Orgaz." From his gesture he seems to be taking the oath to obey the rules of the Society of Jesus, a gesture borne out by the deep and relentless gravity of his look. It would be easy to believe this young saint, so rapt and earnest, to represent Ignatius Loyola, the founder of the order, in person. But his features do not correspond to known portraits of the latter and there is a hint of timidity about the mouth quite alien to the great leader of men. Can it perhaps be a portrait of St. Aloysius de Gonzaga, as it is most frequently held to be— the young prince who joined the Jesuit Order in 1584 and died prematurely in 1591? Against this attribution it is objected that St. Aloysius de Gonzaga was not canonized until 1621, but could not the great revealer of human nature that El Greco was have painted this holy fervour before it was officially recognized? Could he not have painted a saint's soul before his canonization? And would not this explain all the ambiguity in the painting, half profane, half religious? It is also objected that, as a page at the court, the young prince lived in Madrid from 1581 until his death; but he could have accompanied the court to Toledo on many occasions, one of these being the bringing of the relics of St. Leocadia.

To the period of "The Burial of Count Orgaz" belongs a picture which reveals how close El Greco was to the spirit of the people in his quest for the most telling expression, for authentic emotion: the "Mater Dolorosa," of which two versions are known, one at Strasbourg (Plate 45) and one in the Prado. The pure oval of the face, tapering rapidly to the chin, is that of a young Spanish girl. She is not the Mater Dolorosa laying bare to heaven the seven sorrows of her crucified heart; she is innocence, still unaware of her destiny, submitting to be chosen for such suffering. The Virgin of Strasbourg could also be a portrait; she probably bears the features of the woman El Greco loved, but her roots reach far back into the age-old tradition to which he was heir. Whilst having before him the face of a young Spanish girl El Greco also recalled the *madonneri* of his native island, who travelled so far to paint their miraculous Virgins; his memory of them is reflected in the calm vertical of the elongated face, the pure outline of the blue mantle which frames the foaming white veil in its hieratic folds. The Virgin of Strasbourg is at once Toledo and Byzantium. She is the Byzantine Virgin of Mercy, translated into the idiom of a sensitivity altered by the course of centuries. El Greco adapted what was familiar and at the same time withdrawn from the cares of daily life in these miraculous Madonnas to the vision of his time. His Virgin's head is also set in that *mandorla,* or almond-shaped halo, which framed the heads of Byzantine Madonnas, but El Greco translated it into a calm white light emanating from the Virgin herself, into an inner radiance which spreads around her as if she had lost all earthly opacity. Her face is diaphanous; the shadows blue as if saturated with light; her white, luminous veil seems to have a lustre of its own, and it is this whiteness which by contrast gives the face its faint colour and still relates it to human flesh. The Strasbourg Madonna heralds all El Greco's saintly women who melt into spirit before men's eyes, retaining just enough substance to remain perceptible.

El Greco's deviation from his path, which began with "The Burial of Count Orgaz," was carried further in "The Descent from the Cross" (Stavros S. Niarchos) (Plate 47). Here El Greco painted Christ in death as he had Count Orgaz; His body is already stiffening and weighs heavily on the arms of Joseph of Arimathea and the Virgin. The picture's composition is a last echo of the teachings of Italy. Three figures are skilfully compressed into a pyramid, the base of which is formed by Christ's body, and in order to complete it El Greco had to force the curve of St. Joseph's back. But this internal structure and the anatomy of Christ's body, which still has a broad frame and muscular flesh, represent all that El Greco owed to his Roman past. The realism of the details, such as the gaping wound in Christ's side, down which the flow of blood has congealed, or the crown of thorns, and the pictorial virtuosity displayed in the pattern of a scarf, the transparency of the veils, or the dishevelled hair of Mary Magdalen, still belong to this period which El Greco was shortly to leave behind. The new harmony, the new intensity were achieved by the juxtaposition of two heads, of two profiles, which forms the culminating point of the picture, the kernel of the tragedy. The Mother, aged by grief, leans over the body of her dead Son. There is no spectacular despair in those almost frozen features. Her eyes are dry after shedding so many tears; her drooping mouth is silent. Her hand is cupped with infinite tenderness round Christ's head, which she gently draws towards her as if careful to avoid any abrupt movement. It is the last mute colloquy between the living and the dead, the last farewell made in the dignity of a loss too great for words. She can draw no comfort from this lifeless face, but her eyes fixed upon Him radiate the knowledge that for her He will never be dead. In the agonizing grief of parting there is also this ultimate certainty, the certainty of faith and of those who have deeply loved. The statuesque profile of the Virgin, purified by grief, is set in contrast to the beautiful, stricken face of Mary Magdalen, disfigured in the way that tears disfigure the faces of the young, still unprepared for suffering.

Despite the heights of emotion which El Greco attained in this "Pietà" he knew that as a whole the work was still uneven, still partly composed of borrowings. And as if he found this unevenness, this partial success, painful, he never repeated this theme, contrary to his usual custom. Never again were his Christs to die as men do; never again were his Virgins to suffer as do women who have given birth in pain.

With "The Burial of Count Orgaz" and its kindred paintings El Greco's miracles endowed with earthly substance came to an end.

POPE PIUS V declared that the Church of Toledo was the most distinguished in the world. It commanded a truly vast territory in the interior of the peninsula. Towards the end of the sixteenth century the diocese of Toledo comprised four large towns, 183 small ones, 320 villages, and 817 parishes. It ruled over more than 750,000 souls. It was possessed of immense wealth. Its jurisdiction extended even on to African soil. Its archbishop was, according to a contemporary historian, regarded as "second to the King, not only in rank but for the number of his vassals and important towns." It was a state within the State. But, like the whole Church of Spain, it held itself aloof from political movements and avoided any conflict with the temporal power. During the Reconquest the Spanish sovereigns had succeeded in obtaining from the Pope all the powers the princes of Germany and the Netherlands had demanded in vain. It was the Spanish monarch who appointed vicars and collected part of their stipends. Moreover he found the Church easier to tax than the recalcitrant grandees. But the Church also knew how to defend its prerogatives and, as did the Church of Toledo, oppose any interference in its jurisdiction on the part of the King. The Church of Spain knew itself to be less vulnerable than that of Rome. It knew its clergy to be more capable and less corrupt, and in closer, more direct contact with the masses, whom they did not repel either by a scandalous private life or by an ostentatious display of wealth. Schism had little hold over an edifice so solid, so powerfully sustained by the faith of the people. But faith was not nourished only by the lavishness of its cult and the strictness of its religious ceremonies. A great current, fed by the most varied sources, flowed through men's souls, lifting them above everyday things, above enjoyment of worldly possessions, subordinating the vain occupations of an active life to one of contemplation and final renunciation.

Toledo, crouching on her hill, protected from all outside interference by her ancient walls, by her buildings standing witness to her history, and by her position on her rocky foundation, was a place particularly apt for self-communion. This city was like a lustrous shell in which reposed the soul, "that pearl of the East," St. Theresa put it.

It was in Toledo that this saint, with only four nuns, founded her second convent, where the Carmelite rule was to be observed in all its primitive harshness. It was in Toledo that, in the same year El Greco came to the city, she wrote *The Castle Within* or *The Book of the Seven Dwelling-Places of the Soul*. The great radiance which emanated from her lingered like a trail of light in the memory of her contemporaries. She was regarded as a saint in her own lifetime, and found worthy of beatification immediately after her death. More than five hundred witnesses could testify to her virtues and to the countless miracles which took place round her relics. Her contemporaries knew that her passage on earth had been that of an exceptional being, inspired by divine grace. Barely three years had passed since her death when, in 1591, Don Ferdinand of Toledo, the uncle of the Duke of Alba, bequeathed a great fortune to help towards the cost of her beatification, which was as greatly desired by him as by all who had known Theresa of Avila. El Greco knew that, along the same streets as he, a saint had passed; that she too had lived on the banks of the Tagus, in the palace of the Dukes of Medinaceli, and that miracles had sprung up in her wake.

There was no antinomy in Toledo between reality and the saints who dwelt within their walls. Possibly the Toledans were unaware (or perhaps everything was known in that city of echoes) that, on the occasion of the quarrel between the Discalced or barefoot Carmelites and the Calced Carmelites, who were winning the day with the Grand Chapter at Piacenza, Father Juan de Yepes was abducted by Calced Carmelites of Toledo, led blindfold through the city, and thrown into a cell of their monastery overlooking the bridge of Alcantara. In this gloomy cell, his naked body flogged every night by the monks, reduced to ignominious fasting, St. John of the Cross forged himself a soul as far beyond the reach of the sufferings of the flesh as of its joys; but it

was also the soul of a poet. It was in Toledo that St. John wrote his
famous poem:

> *I know the fountain well which flows and runs,*
> *Though it is night.*

Father Juan's escape caused more stir in Toledo than his nocturnal
arrival. He was said to have been miraculously aided by the Virgin.
Like many others in the city, El Greco must have heard talk of it.
Perhaps they did not yet realize that once again a saint had passed
through their city. The father was still held to be unruly and a rebel
against the Church. One sometimes has the impression, as an historian
has said, that in those days it was a gamble in Spain whether a mystic
found himself treated as a heretic or a saint. The quarrels between
monks of different observances were savage. St. Theresa, who had no
idea where the Calced Carmelites had taken Father Juan, requested
Philip II to intervene, adding that she would prefer to know him "in
the hands of the Moors, from whom he would perhaps find more
mercy."

According to the historian of the Inquisition, Father Juan must
still have been pursued by the Holy Office as a Luminary in 1580, so
narrow and bristling with pitfalls was the path which this man, who
was to become the logician of Spanish mysticism, had taken in his advance towards God.

Nothing openly links El Greco with St. John of the Cross; there is
nothing to prove that their paths ever met. St. John had adopted the
attitude towards religious art prescribed by the Council of Trent. But
perhaps he himself was not too far removed from that reprobation of
the worship of images which formed part of the schism. In the third
book of his *Ascent of Carmel* he wrote: "For they are of great importance in Divine service, and very necessary to move the will to
devotion, as is evident from the sanction and use of them by our Holy
Mother the Church. . . . That is a reason why we should profit by
them to quicken us in our sloth." But he immediately set forth his
reservations: "There are many people who rejoice more in the painting
and decoration of them than in the objects they represent."

In his theoretical exposé, St. John of the Cross was still a prisoner
of contemporary vision. He was also typically Spanish. He declared
that, given that the Church pursued a twofold aim in employing
images, that it wished to honour the saints and also to move men's

hearts and quicken their devotion to them, "those which represent them in the most natural manner" should be preferred.

Nothing could be further from El Greco's vision than these saints represented "in the most natural manner." But, in fact, this realism which St. John seemed to demand was merely opposition in his mind to contemporary painting, with its idealization of the body. "That which tends to raise our minds to God . . . must not become food for our senses."

He also said: "The soul which is attached to a creature's beauty is supremely ugly before God." In *The Ascent of Carmel* he outlined with great care his conception of religious art. "Since images are given to us as a means to attain the invisible goods, we should not make use of them except as a means. . . . It is imperative, in fact, that the senses do not take away from the spirit what it receives, and that the statue or painting does not replace the invisible object to which we pray. What is beyond doubt is that the more a soul feels attachment and possessiveness with regard to an image or a material representation, the less freedom will it have to rise up towards God."

Great poet that he was, St. John of the Cross also had recourse on occasion to visual creation; he experienced a need to attain the invisible, although he doubted whether man possessed the means to do so. Once, when in ecstasy before the Cross, he saw Christ crucified before him, in the state to which His torture had reduced Him, covered with wounds, His bones dislocated, His body streaked with blood. The vision stood out so clearly that, when he came to himself, he drew it on a small square of paper with a pen and Chinese ink. The little drawing is like a concession, almost involuntary, to the representation of a great spiritual upheaval through imagery. The path he indicated for the faithful, that path of solitude (*camino de la soledad*) which led to the summit of perfection, circumvented the visual and deliberately divorced itself from it. The poet-saint said: "When you cease in one thing, you cease to throw yourself into all." One day, passing some luxurious houses which he was asked to admire, he explained: "We do not walk to see, but not to see."

Nevertheless he considered the art of interpreting the divine to be so high a mission that he wanted to exclude all who were unworthy of it. The mystery of creation seemed to him to be closely bound up with that of human behaviour. He once made the astonishing remark that the fabrication of images should be forbidden to artisans who were coarse and heavy.

El Greco may never have come close enough to the spiritual activity of St. John to be influenced by his thought, but he had enough friends amongst ecclesiastics and monks, who must have been drawn into Father Juan's orbit, to be to some extent impressed by him. He probably never met St. Theresa, but he aspired to some transcending of reality which the saint invoked with her visionary power: "That which I see is of a white and a red such as one never sees in Nature, which shines more strongly, with a greater brightness than anything the eyes may behold; I see pictures such as no painter ever painted, for which no precedent is known, but which are nevertheless Nature and life itself and the most gloriously beautiful things one can imagine."

In any case it matters little whether the influences of St. Theresa and St. John on El Greco were direct or not. Ideas, even in a period of restricted circulation, have a habit of being propagated through intermediaries, by more or less occult means, until they reach those in whom they strike a responsive chord. They are in the air, the rarefied air of those who walk the spiritual heights. They are also rather like those deep subterranean rivers which unexpectedly break through into daylight. Even if El Greco did not follow the path of renunciation traced by St. John, even if he did not deny himself the pleasures of this world, even if he was not unfamiliar with the joys of earthly goods, which bring anguish and torment to a heart in chains, he shared his desire to "penetrate deeper into density." Like him, he identified light wth God; the upward striving of the soul was, for him too, a rise above the shadows. The reflection of that living flame of love which illuminated the path of St. John of the Cross glows in El Greco's pictures.

There was no need, in the Spain of that time, for a direct relationship or influence for El Greco to have experienced that ardour of self-abnegation which flowed in a powerful current through the whole peninsula. Spanish mysticism, as expressed through the doctrine of the saints, poets, and visionaries of the time, was rooted deep in the country's past. The tradition of mysticism had come from the East. The Hispano-Muslim school of Shâdhili also exalted the virtue of renunciation; it too honoured contemplation and wisdom, and considered that God better revealed himself to the human soul in the night of anguish (*leyl al gabd*) than in the brightness of day. This doctrine was still alive, it was still a source of inspiration for those who responded to its call. When Father Juan finished *The Ascent of Carmel* in Granada, the celebrated Moorish woman of 'Ubeda was still teaching the mystical dogma of Islam there. She was ninety-three years old, but even her adversaries had to admit that she "had no equal in the world of learning for constructive ideas," that she was known to every nation and that people came to see her from all over the world, "so great was her power of divination." This mystical tradition, which formed a foundation to Spanish thought, was close to the Oriental soul which El Greco had preserved, to that Byzantine heritage in which so many immemorial elements had combined to build up a mystical universe.

El Greco was borne along on the current of his time; he was the subject of a general orientation growing ever more powerful in Spain. Nevertheless his revolutionary role lies in his extension of this trend into the sphere of the plastic arts, in his efforts to express, by means which were his alone, what seemed to withstand visual expression—"the invisible goods."

St. John of the Cross was perhaps still alive (he died in 1591) when El Greco painted a "Crucifixion" (Prado) (Plate 48) which he would not have disowned. This is a Christ as tortured as the one the saint saw in his vision; His body is emaciated, His arms of a knotty thinness, almost skeletal, His head too heavy for so frail a body and crowned with thorns which scratch His brow, whilst the blood gushes in a broad stream from the wound in His side and drips from His nailed hands and feet. But El Greco also painted earth and heaven moved to anguish over so great a death, so immense a sacrifice. The angels have sped down from heaven to collect the precious blood, not in the customary chalice but in the palms of their hands spread out in ecstasy. These angels are no longer either wholly women or youths; their bodies seem weightless; the most solid thing about them is their large, shining wings, which stand out against the background of a stormy sky flecked with lightning. The clouds and the angels' draperies seem to be of the same material and the same flashing light. One angel has slipped down to the foot of the cross to gather the blood dripping from Christ's feet in a sponge; it is seen from behind, daringly foreshortened, yet it seems to have no more consistency than a feather bent by the wind. On either side of the cross stand the Virgin and St. John, calling on the distracted heavens to witness their grief, while Mary Magdalen has fallen to her knees at its foot, from which she wipes the streaks of blood just as she once wiped the feet of Christ as a humble servant of the Lord.

This dead Christ crucified, this tortured being who has suffered in the flesh, has more bodily substance and is closer to a human being than the living who watch over him. The face which the Virgin raises to the cross is barely distinguished from the ample folds of her cloak. Her eyes are merely slits of shadow; her half-open mouth a bare touch of colour round a cry of despair; the sharply tapering oval of her face is a mere triangle of light. Her figure is elongated out of all proportion, as if she were already preparing to leave the earth and join her son. St. John, too, is like a slender watchtower rising up to the sky; his proportions are the same, exceeding the canon of elongation called for by the theoretician of the Mt. Athos paintings—the head to be one ninth of the length of the human body. He is so ethereal that he seems to be held together by his garments and drawn upwards in an ascending spiral like a column of smoke. His face is hardly more than a wavering gaze and a cry of pain; his head is thrown back, with the features so foreshortened that the nose is simply a sharp point and widely dilated nostrils. El Greco's saints have left the attributes of daily life far behind them, as if they had sloughed their skins. They are, in fact, intermediate beings, with still enough bodily presence to be recognized by the faithful but already subjected to the laws of heaven, which cancel those of earth. No one could have met this Virgin in the streets of Toledo, yet she epitomizes all the suffering ever felt by a mother, for all mothers destined to suffer from the death of a son. A St. John of flesh and blood could never have set his agile feet on that small, sloping piece of rock, but he too is only halfway to being human; the gestures of his hands, widespread but too supple, as if deprived of their joints, guide souls in torment towards the revelations of heaven.

Nor is the space in which saints and angels are grouped round the dead Christ of this world; that cross was never set up on any earthly Golgotha; it is some interplanetary place, mournful and shot with tragic flashes of lightning, waiting in anguish for the mercy announced by a few shreds of light.

This "Crucifixion" probably formed part of a large commission which had occupied El Greco for several years. In 1591, Philip II came to Toledo with the royal family to spend Holy Week. Was it during this visit that Doña María of Aragon, lady in waiting to the Queen, saw "The Burial of Count Orgaz," which had become one of the sights of the city, and the meaning of which she understood better than the King, to whom El Greco's work was so alien? In 1581, Philip II had made over to Doña María of Aragon certain lands in Madrid, on which to build a college for Augustinian friars. The college church would appear to have been finished in 1590, for in April of that year the first Mass was said in it. Did its pious founder then search for an artist worthy of the work she had undertaken, to paint its reredos? She seems to have been in a hurry to conclude an agreement, as if she knew her health to be poor or had a foreboding of imminent death, which in fact did overtake her in 1593; but the final contract with El Greco was not drawn up until 1596, by the jurists of the Royal Council of Castile, who were deputed to carry on the work.

In 1595, before he concluded this agreement, El Greco, after having had such painful experiences with his clients, gave full powers to an ecclesiastical jurist "residing at the court of the King, our lord" to represent him "in all causes and lawsuits, both civil and criminal." In 1597 a payment to El Greco for the altarpiece of 375,000 maravedís figures in the accounts of the administrator of Doña María's estate. The agreement he had signed further provided for an immediate payment of 500 ducats, another for the same amount on submission of the plans and "at the end of each year a further 1000 ducats." Although this annual income was payable to him under the guarantee of His Majesty, he had difficulty in procuring it and, at the end of the year 1600, authorized a confidential agent in Madrid to claim from Juan de Herrera, "treasurer" for the royal allowances, the rest of the sum due to him for the painting for the college of Doña María of Aragon, amounting to 2535 reals.

The few surviving documents are not clear as to the dates on which El Greco began and completed his work. The different pictures which were to form the altarpiece were doubtless spread out over several years. But neither is it known exactly which pictures were to form the whole of this work. A much later indication states merely that the altarpiece was composed of scenes from the life of Christ. If "The Crucifixion" formed part of it, it must have been one of the first pictures executed, for the body of Christ still harks back to previous works of a period already left behind. "The Resurrection" in the Prado (Plate 49) could have belonged to it as well. Here it is the body of Christ, slender and elongated, but, in its plasticity, still reminiscent of the nudes in the "Martyrdom of St. Maurice," which is closest to "The Crucifixion." This Christ, still echoing Italian memories, also recalls Byzantium, as if the various stages in El Greco's past were becoming more and more blended. This is apparent in the square halo and the feet set one over the other. Italian memories are noticeable in the incongruously naked soldiers guarding the tomb; one of them, still dozing, is clad only in a helmet; another in the foreground has a light, clinging tunic; they are men with muscular arms and legs and deep chests. Italian above all in its derivation is the reversed figure in the foreground, the enormous falling soldier who, with his powerful shoulders and arms, forms a broad base for the picture and who, according to the vision of the dawning baroque, leads the eyes upwards towards the white column of Christ's body.

But the plasticity of these entangled figures is purely artificial; they are not three-dimensional, their feet do not rest on solid ground; very typical is the manner in which the clothed soldier descends the steps; his feet, far too small for so huge a body, are wrongly placed on an edge which would surely bruise his heels. Arms and legs collide with empty space; there is no room for any display of their strength; the sleeping soldier seems to rest his elbow on the leg of the falling one.

But the picture hardly aims at making something that surpasses human understanding plausible or at portraying the reactions of men of flesh and blood to the extraordinary. It is the irruption of the miraculous into a world already transfigured by this same miracle, it is the internal upheaval embodied by an earth already shaken to the core, displaying its confusion in the face of heaven.

Having achieved this emotional intensity, El Greco disdained all that could have lent credence to the supernatural as an event in everyday life. Unlike his predecessors, he deemed it superfluous to illustrate the event with a tomb found empty on the soldier's awakening. The material evidence is negligible in face of its repercussions in the human soul. Everything is concentrated on man's striving to attain the inconceivable. It also reflects his instinctive self-defence against a power which abolishes his humble life, as in the case of the soldier armed only with his shield and sword, which he brandishes at Christ. All is resplendence, a whole scale of bedazzlement which draws every gaze upwards, and against which a hand or bent arm covering the eyes is no protection. These tormented, naked souls, who have borrowed a mere semblance of earthly presence from the Roman soldiers, these men who fall to the ground or who seem to follow Christ in His ascent, are dashing in pursuit of something that has eluded them, not of a body which has vanished from a hollow in the ground but of eternal truth, the blinding light of salvation. In this pursuit man stands alone, his crisis is individual and personal. No look questions another, no gesture reaches out to another, there is no mutual understanding. There are merely—as Jean Cassou, that subtle intrepreter of Spain, has put it—"soliloquies and outcries of beings struck by lightning." And above this whirlwind of confusion Christ rises, very calm and erect, towards

His natural place, His heavenly abode, already washed clean of all the outrages inflicted upon Him on earth.

The picture is painted as if against a background of gold; the naked bodies are like old gold; a saturated green denotes the residue of the earthly in this ascent towards the light.

One picture alone is known with certainty to have come from the church of the college of Doña María of Aragon: "The Baptism of Christ" in the Prado (Plate 50). Traditionally this scene should have been calm and idyllic, in contrast with the sufferings of Christ, and bathed in the peace of a rural atmosphere. But of this atmosphere El Greco left only a vague indication of some rocks and a stream, neither more nor less solid than the folds of the red tunic spread out by the angels above Christ's head like the red dais of a Byzantine sovereign. There is not a blade of grass on this bank, not a plant to show it is still on earth. With El Greco the supremely static scene became all movement, a joyful communion between an earth already freed from the laws of gravity and heaven. Christ's body is excessively elongated, as if he, like St. John the Baptist, wanted to place the greatest possible distance between this feeble indication of earth and the celestial orbit. The scene of the baptism was, according to traditional painting, a discourse between two men, sometimes witnessed by respectfully kneeling angels. But El Greco broke away both from its usual form and its iconography. Below the outstretched, muscular right arm of St. John, terminating in a far too delicate wrist, pouring water over Christ's head from a shell—a Byzantine motif—El Greco placed a childlike angel which stands between the two like a little torch with a green flame. This child-angel with fair, curly hair, a nose all nostrils, and arms far too powerful for its youthful features, points in ecstasy to heaven, and seeks to capture the gentle, faraway look of Christ. Angels, clouds, and dove form a frieze above Christ's head; they are all so insubstantial that it is difficult to say where a cheek ends and a cloud begins, or what is still the gleam of a curl and what is pure light. Just as all is agitation in "The Resurrection," every inch of the picture seems to be braced by the thrust of a strong wind, which bowls the rosy cherubs over and billows out the garments of the tall, winged angels. The narrow shape of the picture is even further reduced by two internal parallels which close together to frame the white apparition of God the Father with His tiny head and white beard like a veil, a barely visible sign of what it is beyond human eyes to see, a pledge of His fervour, a promise made to man, that his soul may aim even higher.

Most of El Greco's biographers regard "The Annunciation" in the Museo Balaguer in Villanueva y Geltru (Plate 51) as having formed part of the altarpiece. It was a subject dear to El Greco's heart. He tackled it very early in life and continued to paint it until his old age. A large number of replicas of it are known, for it enjoyed great success with his clients. The picture in the Balaguer Museum is full of the same pulsating life as "The Resurrection" and "The Baptism," an animation full of gaiety, a cascade of joy tumbling down from heaven to earth. Just as in "The Baptism," only the feeblest indications of the earth are left. Nothing but a step and a tall *prie-dieu,* on which lies an opened book. No other indication of the setting, no trace of architecture, not even those usual iconographic attributes such as the lily, to signify the *hortus clausus* (the enclosure of the soul). Like the majority of El Greco's saints of that time, the Virgin, instead of wearing her garments, seems to be supported by them. It is not clear whether she is kneeling or standing; her long robe makes a spiral base for her, rather like one of those columns said to have been brought from the temple of Jerusalem. This Virgin is very young, with the fragility of a child-wife. The oval of her face descends rapidly to a pointed chin which is too long; the long upper lip seems to quiver slightly; her eyes are bathed in light as if in belated tears. There is no apprehension or surprise in these features, on which the emotions flow like water over a smooth surface; her trusting eyes are raised to the angel, which looks down as if dazzled by such sweet innocence. It is an adolescent angel, its slender, dancer's feet set on a cloud, with a narrow, curly head flattened at the back, a sharp profile with a small receding chin, and wings so powerful that they could easily bear its large body. The angel makes the gesture which El Greco's predecessors habitually attributed to the Virgin—the arms crossed and the hands folded in towards the breast with the submissiveness of those chosen to be the instruments of destiny. The Virgin has spread out her hands in a gesture which El Greco bestowed on the favourite subjects of his creation.

Between the Virgin and the young angel a little heap of burning twigs sends up small flames to meet the dazzling rays which the dove pours down upon the Virgin in a shower of light. All heaven is descending on her, shining clouds with the not fully formed heads of cherubs scattered in wreaths here and there, more like the buds or petals of flowers than children's heads, mere indications of an intermediary world in which angels are still being born. Only heaven seems to materialize fully in the joy of this angelic annunciation; the clouds are thick with the bodies of rather androgynous angels playing celestial music. This angelic concert, with flute, cymbals, lute, harp, and viola da gamba, was painted by a man who knew each instrument and how to play it—and these instruments are more real than the hands which hold them and the knees on which they rest. Here light is synonymous with sound; the brilliant colours sing like clear notes of music; the scattered radiance seems to conform to a musical theme which one strives in vain to re-create and which El Greco must have heard when he composed his picture, harmonizing with this sonorous arrangement.

Filled with the same joy, the same scattered luminosity, is "The Adoration of the Shepherds" formerly in the Royal Palace in Bucharest (Plate 52). Together with "The Annunciation" and "The Baptism" in the centre it is supposed to have formed the triptych of the main altar in the Madrid church. The pictures differ, however, in their dimensions, both in height and width. One is reduced to conjectures based more on an internal harmony than on a formal dependence. These canvases could just as well have been intended for other churches as for the side altars of the college of Doña María of Aragon. A certain preponderance of detail in "The Adoration" might make this canvas appear several years earlier than pictures like "The Baptism" or "The Annunciation," so purified of earthly remains. But El Greco's evolution, from the formal viewpoint, did not follow a straight line; with him the purification was not strictly progressive; he turned back to realism after having abandoned it, following an inner logic hard to determine. He neither acquired nor abandoned anything definitely, as if he felt a need for self-renewal without, however, deviating from the final goal of his creative aspiration. The background of "The Adoration" consists of an architectural scene, contrary to the indeterminate setting of the other canvases. There is a ruined arch, a gateway which threatens to collapse, an empty niche, and an indication of a door which leads nowhere. There is also light foliage with no sign of how or where it is rooted. Beside the Virgin appears a donkey's head in the foreground and, lying on the rock, a shepherd's crook and lamb. But in spite of these signs of a simple rustic environment El Greco had travelled far from Correggio's "Night" and even from the narrative side to be found in "The Adoration" of San Domingo el Antiguo. The Child lying on top of a wicker basket is the source of the light spreading over the world. But He is no longer a child. Like the cherubs barely distinguished from the clouds, He is only hinted at, He is a shining light which has assumed the shape of a child's body on the lustrous white linen. The light also dissolves the face of the Virgin, a slightly more mature Virgin of "The Annunciation," with a sad, childish mouth and a heavy gaze; it also dissolves the face of the angel bending over the Child with crossed arms; it strikes St. Joseph full in the chest, and he abruptly draws back, his hands spread in the expressive gesture of an Oriental, as if he could not believe the evidence of his eyes. The shepherd kneeling in the foreground, so excessively tall that were he to rise he would dominate the whole picture, is the interpreter of the miracle singled out by El Greco from amongst the onlookers; he expresses the fervour of a humble man who has never been touched by doubt. But in the background, behind the Virgin, the discussion about the birth of the Child is carried on between two men, a shepherd and an old, white-bearded man, apparently a nobleman, who comment on the event with effusive gestures.

The composition is reduced and compressed into a shining ellipse which replaces a linear arrangement. It is a fountain of light rising up from earth towards the glory of heaven, where angels and *putti* whirl around a blaze of incandescent gold.

If the total number of the paintings destined for the church in Madrid consisted of six and not of only three canvases, it was probably completed by "The Pentecost" (Plate 53), which would in that case be the last in date, an indeterminate date but doubtless a late one. In July 1600 a Toledan carter was hired to transport the pictures to Madrid. A year later, with payment long overdue, El Greco sent Francisco Preboste to Illescas to collect the money from one of the administrators of the college who acted there as a collector of taxes on merchandise. But the whole altarpiece does not seem to have been completed until 1606, for in August of that year El Greco and the executors of Doña María's will appeared before a notary to reach an agreement on the valuation of the whole work and the sums still due to him.

If the picture of "The Pentecost" was intended for the college church, it must have been the crowning work, conceived as its apotheosis. The subject was not often treated in the iconography of the time, as if this presentation of the unreal, of the descent of the Holy Ghost, discouraged the timid. Titian had painted it in his picture in Santa Maria della Salute. He had also, as a prelude to the event, introduced figures seen from the back in agitated movement stressing their emotion. But with El Greco the two men are seemingly dumbfounded by the sound descending from heaven; their draperies float round their exaggerated figures, lifted by the rushing wind which fills the whole house. At the sight of these flames rising like separate tongues the old man has stumbled, losing his balance on the steps. The young man on his knees, with that narrow head planed flat at the back which El Greco often gave his young saints and adolescent angels, raises an outspread hand and an astonished forefinger towards the miracle.

The few steps in the foreground are all that El Greco retained as an indication of the setting. The architecture has been replaced by the arrangement of the human bodies, particularly skilful for El Greco, as if he wanted every possible accent to stress the miracle. An inverted triangle throws up the figure of the Virgin, set in the folds of her mantle as if in the almond shape of a Byzantine gloriole. Her oval face is flung back, pure as a mirror, to reflect the brightness of the Dove; the heads of the Apostles are strung out to right and left like the beads of a rosary, in varying degrees of dazzlement or reflections of her ecstasy. All these hands raised in offering are so many accents of emotion; only the Virgin's are clasped in prayer, as if she had better grasped the full significance of the event.

Of the Apostles one alone looks away from the ecstatic Virgin or the tongues of fire, an old man with a white beard, the same who was arguing in the background of "The Adoration of the Shepherds." The way in which his gaze wanders out of the frame is that of many painters who have depicted themselves in a holy scene, and one of El Greco's most recent biographers believes this to be his self-portrait. In that case it would be the portrait of a man prematurely aged, his beard white before its time, all the keenness of his senses having withdrawn into his eyes. Moreover it is the only head which is not foreshortened; it is visibly a portrait, if not of El Greco, then perhaps of a very close friend for whom he reserved a place of honour.

The skill of the composition is balanced by a rare refinement, a luminous richness of colouring. The garments of the old man in the foreground, with his high complexion, are of an intense yellow and the blue of shot satin; the man beside him, with silver reflections in his fair, curly hair, is wrapped in purple velvet over his russet-green gown; over the blue tunic of St. Peter, El Greco placed an orange cloak, and this purple, green, and yellow are all isolated, with no regard for the colours next to them, each chord struck violently without transition, without any musical link. But it is not only pure colour which is thus almost aggressively displayed; each tone is saturated with light, shot through with reflections as if by electric shocks; each scintillates as if it had caught fire from the flame from heaven. This inconceivable happening incarnated by wind and fire, denying itself to the eyes of man, was, so to speak, built up by El Greco out of scattered fragments of the visible; he dissolved the forms, broke up the harmony of the proportions, set the colours on fire, gave density to the light, and created a whirlwind with hands and folds of cloth, curls and clouds, all serving a single emotion, all reflecting the same dazzlement, the split kernel of the soul opening up to a visitation.

The centuries to come were to hold El Greco's creative purpose up to ridicule. One of his first biographers, Antonio Palomino y Velasco, the Spanish Vasari, writing in the first half of the eighteenth century, considered the paintings in the college of Doña María of Aragon to be particularly absurd examples, as much for the heresies of their drawing as for the hardness of their colouring. But his own age, the age of mystical saints, poetic visionaries, and crusaders for the faith, followed him at his quest for new forms of pictorial expression. The transformation of his vision was in harmony with the spiritual upheavals of the time and his contemporaries found it convincing, as if for them it fulfilled a deep need. Commissions flowed in from every side. In his studio his clients saw the pictures destined for the altarpiece in Madrid when they came to ask for altarpieces or religious paintings for themselves, and it was then, when his painting underwent that sudden etherealization so mocked by the critics of the following century that his success became really great.

Even if his clients were recalcitrant in paying, so that he often had to threaten them with proceedings and even pay the costs of litigation, El Greco was now once more in easy circumstances, as he had been at the time when he lived in the main apartment in the palace of the Marqués de Villena. There are no data about his financial position in the years following his abandonment of that sumptuous dwelling, but a document from the year 1600 reveals that El Greco was then paying a rent possibly even higher than the one he paid the Marqués de Villena, since, for the house he had leased from Don Juan Suárez of Toledo, Lord of Galvez and Jumela, he paid the latter's agent 2535 reals and a half, doubtless including arrears.

Among the commissions he received at the same time as the one for Madrid was the altarpiece of Talavara la Vieja. It was a Toledan goldsmith, Lorenzo Marqués, who obtained this commission for him, for his brother was vicar of the church, and on February 14, 1591, El Greco signed a contract with him for an altarpiece which was to comprise five pictures and possibly a statue of the Virgin. The architecture of the reredos is classical in design, with Doric columns crowned by a broad entablature surmounted by a pediment. But no one was really shocked by the fact that so severe a frame should harbour a "Coronation of the Virgin" with exaggeratedly elongated figures, saints with heads too small for their bodies and with features distorted by the light. Two of the Apostles, the two Saints John, as well as those saints who were especially dear to him, Francis and Dominic, painted in half length, were made attendants by El Greco at this coronation by the Holy Trinity.

The main picture is flanked by two saints, Peter and Andrew, stamped with that new feeling for the monumental which he now possessed, and which is closer to the vertiginous soaring of a Gothic cathedral than to the order of a classical temple. The statue of the "Virgin of the Rosary," regarded locally as a work of El Greco's, seems rather to be that of a Spanish sculptor of the following century.

From the same years also dates a commission for the monastery of La Sisla which provides information as to the prices El Greco was then obtaining. For a single canvas, a St. Anthony, he received an advance of 800 reals and, on August 28, 1595, Brother Martín de Villamil paid him a further 1200 reals, being the balance of the sum owed him by the convent.

At the same time El Greco's private clients were increasing in number, coming to him from every part of the kingdom. Only a few scanty indications remain as to this success, which was spreading in ever-widening circles. El Greco seems to have had a particularly faithful clientele in Seville. He was in touch with a famous embroiderer of that town, Pedro de Mesa, to whom he sent a whole series of "likenesses of paintings, canvases and other things" for him to sell there. From July 1, 1588, he authorized two "residents of Seville" to collect the moneys due to him.

It was particularly characteristic of the vision of the time that the market in Seville was above all one for popular art, for pictures intended for wide distribution. It was at Seville that soldiers, officers, sailors, and monks embarked for the great adventure of the New World, and they were glad to take with them the image of some patron saint, of the Mater Dolorosa, or of Christ on the Cross, to that land of pagans and unknown perils. At Seville there was a flourishing trade in cheap religious images more noted for their fervour than for their artistic merits. El Greco's success in Seville proves precisely how far his art was intelligible to the masses and not just to an elite, how far it answered the needs of simple and pious souls.

Something strange was happening at this time, a rare artistic phenomenon. El Greco would paint a saint, a Virgin or a Christ in absolute harmony with his inner vision, with strict fidelity to the laws which governed his creation. He painted them in solitude, with a spiritual struggle the painful tremors of which can still be felt, with a sovereign contempt for all that had been done before him, stripping himself of all he had learned from others. He worked, so to speak, in an artistic void; no contemporary artist drew on the same inspiration, stimulated him by rivalry, or trespassed on his own domain. He was fully aware of his role of an innovator, of a man venturing into unexplored territory. He denied himself any concession. It is known that he treated his clients with a haughtiness which seems to have been tolerated from him alone, with an arrogance which, in itself, proves how highly he was held in esteem and sanctioned by success. He refused to let his art stagnate on any pedestal of an acquired reputation. One could go so far as to say that it was enough for him to achieve an objective for him to abandon it immediately. With each new stage he must have baffled his contemporaries just as he was to baffle even the most understanding of his biographers. He denied himself the facile, the accessible, the pleasing, and the pretty. His painting increasingly took on the character of a challenge to all convention. He was to continue on his path alone. He was never to have a spiritual heir or a disciple worthy of his name. Each of his canvases seems to surround itself with a zone difficult to penetrate, like a gateway to mystery. But the moment a canvas, whether saint, Christ, or Virgin, was finished in that complete creative solitude, it set unsuspected chords vibrating. A client, whether of rare spiritual distinction or a simple man who must spend a large sum to acquire it, carried it off like some secret treasure, like some pledge of intercession—maybe an element of superstition contributed to its strange attraction.

Many of these pictures were lost during the two centuries when El Greco's work, especially his later work, was regarded as that of a lunatic—or at best a maniac who had squandered his rare gifts. These pictures, mocked by the connoisseurs, must have been relegated to attics or else disposed of like many other family possessions which offend the taste of the day.

The number of replicas of El Greco's pictures that survive, in spite of the disappearance of so many, proves how extraordinarily wide their distribution was. El Greco never hesitated to repeat them. Each canvas represented for him a completed creative process, an accomplishment in which there was nothing for him either to add or subtract. It never bored him to copy himself, so long as it was still of interest for him to return to some spiritual conflict sufficiently dramatic for his liking. In this facility for repetition he displayed also that long, hereditary patience which had perpetuated Byzantine compositions for centuries, the patience of all petrified civilizations, whether found in Egyptian sculpture or age-old Oriental decoration. For his eyes, accustomed to the same impersonal features, hieratic gestures, and ritual colours, his own tragic and turbulent saints, his colours slashed by light retained their character of freshness even after constant repetition.

Moreover he was not the only one to multiply these replicas in a frankly commercial manner. Preboste assisted him and, on the occasion of a sale in Seville for which he and El Greco gave authority, it was specified that "it concerns pictures which *they* have done." His son must have set to work at an early age, and still anonymous pupils helped him; but they were so dominated by his manner and he kept so close an eye on them that there is little difference between an original and its copy.

Trade with Seville, the only surviving evidence amongst so much lost, proved particularly profitable. Preboste sent pictures there and went himself to supervise their sale, doubtless when substantial orders were involved. The picture dealer does not seem to have justified the trust placed in him. In May 1597, El Greco and Preboste gave full authority to a certain Juan Augustín Ansaldo, a native of Genoa residing in Seville, to take over from Mesa all paintings as yet unsold and the money collected from previous sales.

One of the powers of attorney mentions pictures representing St. Peter and St. Francis. Of all the saints he ever painted the *poverello* of Assisi, the saint of his native island, was dearest to El Greco's heart. He portrayed him as one does a friend whose features are so familiar that they can be evoked in the sitter's absence. He painted him at every stage in his own evolution; each variation reflected his state of mind and was also a milestone along his path. Through the pictures of St. Francis alone and the ways in which they differ or resemble each other, the full course of his inner evolution can be deciphered. In fact there was such a discrepancy between El Greco's psychological make-up and that of the Italian saint that one wonders what could have inspired the proud man he is known to have been to cherish such humility. The pictures of St. Francis are perhaps projections of this antinomy, the outcome of an inner conflict. El Greco needed comfort, even ostentatious luxury, in which to create, and yet he loved this unassuming saint above all others. Amongst his acquaintances he looked exclusively for intellectual distinction, yet he was moved by this saint who sided with simple souls. He liked to show off his superiority, paraded his arrogance, sometimes flew into deliberate rages, living entrenched in his creative isolation, and yet he gave of his best when painting the saint who preached the brotherhood of all things.

The bond which united him with St. Francis of Assisi was perhaps akin to the influence exercised over him by the mystic saints of his time, a need which ran counter to his own nature, an escape from the life he had chosen, a taste for the impossible, or simply a persistent dream.

His contemporaries recognized the reality of this intimate bond. Pacheco conferred on El Greco the glory of having been the best painter of St. Francis known to his time, superior to the rest because he "conformed to what history relates." The same phenomenon occurred in the case of St. Francis as with the other religious subjects, but even more strikingly. He was the saint of great popular devotion, as if the tribulations of the age found solace best in him. In Toledo alone there were in El Greco's time three Franciscan monasteries, including the important one of San Juan de los Reyes, and seven convents. El Greco included a Franciscan monk among the onlookers at "The Burial of Count Orgaz." As his contemporaries recognized that he gave this saint his most perfect image, the demand for his pictures became ever greater. Their output developed into a small industry. The total number of existing pictures—authentic works, replicas retouched by El Greco himself, and studio copies—amounts to 128. The presentation of the saint varies according to the stage which El Greco himself had reached and eleven distinct types are recognized.

First the saint "painted in a natural manner," belonging to a series begun in Italy (Plate 16). A saint "not beautiful of body," as his disciples described him, with protruding eyes either raised to heaven or lowered under bulging lids, a wide forehead, hollow cheeks, and a receding chin concealed by a thin beard. He painted him according to his story, in the solitude of the wild mountains he loved, in the shadow of a cave, or under a turbulent sky. He painted him with

Brother Leo, and the Gospels for which he had sent him in search, kneeling before a crucifix, lost in deep meditation, bending over a skull which he holds in his hands.

During the years when El Greco's art was detaching itself from reality the image of the saint changed accordingly. It was re-created from within without any illustrative scenery, like El Greco's other works placed in an indeterminate setting. It was then that the images of the saint multiplied, in response perhaps as much to an inner harmony as to an increasing demand. The picture in the Hospital de Mujeres in Cádiz (Plate 54) probably dates from the time when he was completing the commission for the church in Madrid. St. Francis, clad in his humble, patched homespun, has fallen to his knees, his long body leaning forward, long since ready to receive the miracle. Behind him all is darkness; at the very top of the picture there is a faint indication of a rock and a hanging branch with leaves very like the ivy of which El Greco was particularly fond. Beside him Brother Leo (or Rufus), seen from behind, overwhelmed by the supernatural, raises an arm in stupefaction to heaven, from which he watches the beautiful, glittering flame descend on the body of St. Francis. This heavenly flame is the one source of light in the surrounding darkness, light refracted by the eyes of the saint, who half opens his mouth to drink it in, spreads out his hands to collect it, his palms already pierced like those of Christ. The flame is still in heaven, the witness is still dumbfounded, but the miracle has already entered the saint's body.

Belonging to the same period or slightly earlier is the "St. Francis in Meditation," one of the most popular representations of the saint, of which at least thirty examples are known (Plate 55). A picture particularly dear to the Spanish, who lived in close communion with death, who liked to be reminded of the vanity of this world and who enjoyed life, fascinated by its extreme frailty and the imminence of annihilation.

The treatment was an innovation for El Greco, his own personal invention. But perhaps it could have been born only on Spanish soil, could have sprung only from that epoch marked by the passage of the Ecstatic Doctor, St. John of the Cross. The St. Francis of these paintings—in the Brera in Milan, in the Colegio de las Doncellas Nobles, in the cathedral and the Greco Museum in Toledo, in the Prado and in many other places—knees on a rock, his pensive, heavy-lidded gaze fixed on the skull in his hands. He holds it as only El Greco's figures holds things—distantly, with a light touch, as if afraid of being subjugated by everything on which they lay their hands. Below him, seen in half-length and half-profile, is Brother Leo, his elbows leaning on the same rock and his hands clasped in prayer. His presence seems intended solely to contribute through this fervent gesture to the saint's mute colloquy with death. His hands alone speak with that eloquence, that sensitivity peculiar to the hands of El Greco's saints, and, if one could put into words what the saint's sad lips do not say, one would hear the question put by St. John of the Cross: "What then has death to equal my life of mourning; since the more I live, the more I die?"

As El Greco became surer of his ability to shift the limits of the visual, to render souls and minds transparent, as it were, the bodies and features of his figures became transformed from within, existing solely by virtue of the emotion which gave them life. And in the person of his favourite saint he risked the portrayal of that most sublime moment to which a human being can attain—communion with God —ecstasy (Plate 56). Nothing in common now remained between the saints of the Roman Mannerists, raising their weeping eyes to heaven with elegant gestures and placid faces, and this St. Francis in ecstasy, in whom El Greco gave the most poignant expression to that which eludes men's understanding and remains inaccessible to them. In the picture in the Hospital de Tavera in Toledo (which is probably El Greco's last version of his favourite saint) St. Francis no longer has a witness to his communion with the radiance of heaven (Plate 57). The skull with a crucifix is set before him on a stone, but he no longer questions it about the vanity of man's brief spell on earth. His tall body is inclined in the humility of the elect who submit themselves to the extraordinary. His head stands out from his hood, offering itself to the light with all that it still retains of human semblance. It is the head of a man on fire, consumed from within by the living flame of love; the flesh is eaten away to the bone, the withered lips no longer cover the teeth, the eyes are deeply hollow and so burning in their sockets that they have sunk in like those of a dying man. This face of one burnt alive is nonetheless transfigured by the light which filters down through the darkness, and this merciful radiance restores to its gaunt ugliness, its shrunken features, their share of celestial bliss. The outspread hands, marked with the stigmata and still trembling from the weight of so much love, render thanks for the promise of heaven, a promise of eternal rest, of an end to all torments, and the quenching of the thirst of those dry lips.

Nothing remains in this St. Francis of the gentle Italian saint who smiled at the springs and sang the praises of the sun; he is a sombre Spanish saint, ascetic and passionate, the forerunner of all the monks consumed by the flames of their own fervour, the spiritual father of St. John of the Cross, the visionary poet who sang:

> *That everlasting fountain is a secret well,*
> *And I know well its home,*
> *Though of the night.*

St. Francis of Assisi was to accompany El Greco the whole way along his creative path. The flames of his ecstasy rose up on the threshold of the waning century.

In the years when El Greco was undergoing his creative transformation and his patrons were increasing, other saints conceived in his own particular manner came to vie in popularity with the image of St. Francis. One picture greatly in demand, of which he made numerous replicas, was that of a saint who was very dear to him—Mary Magdalen, the beautiful, repentant sinner. Her image reached far back into El Greco's Italian past. She was also the longest to bear the stamp of Venetian inspiration, as if her beauty had protected her from the dissolution of matter growing ever more pronounced in El Greco's work. In her triumphant grace she even emerged from the shadows which oppressed El Greco later on. Palomino refers to a picture of her in the possession of a fervent admirer, an *aficionado,* and says that he never saw anything by El Greco's hand so exquisite and with such a wonderful feeling for colour. The first time the saint appears in El Greco's work (Museum of Fine Arts, Budapest) she is the subject of all the Italian influences he had experienced (Plate 58). She may even have been painted in Italy. Her background is a broad landscape, with the sun setting behind distant hills; her head is bathed in natural light, as opposed to the light which was later to descend on El Greco's saints out of the darkness. She has a short, nearly square face; her eyes, under straight eyebrows, look up to heaven almost in astonishment. One hand covers her naked bosom, whilst the other is opened questioningly over a skull placed on a book. These delicate hands, rather broad for their slender fingers and anticipating the grace of the eighteenth century, recall those which Jacopo da Pontormo gave his holy women and Madonnas. But this holy sinner, too flimsily clad and not fully repentant, a saint who is still of foreign inspiration, was endowed by El Greco with the same gesture he gave to the nobleman with his hand on his breast, as if it were a secret sign of his predilection for her.

Mary Magdalen's plump hand also has the two middle fingers joined together and the rest spread out like a fan.

She appears again among the pictures of the years when El Greco was painting "The Martyrdom of St. Maurice," still radiant with an almost carnal beauty, with wavy golden hair, a transparent veil drawn over the pearly whiteness of her bosom, and lovely, calm, folded hands (Plate 59). Only her neck, at once too long and too fleshy, anticipates in its serpentine movement that upward striving of El Greco's saints, their efforts to escape from their human condition. The upturned face is drawn in a perfect oval, dominated by the huge luminous eyes. The nose is too small; the mouth also, and childish, as if in its innocence it were a stranger to the spiritual upheaval reflected in the eyes brimming with tears. El Greco expended his most precious gifts on this well-loved saint; he cajoled her with all his pictorial mastery and even the smallest details seem to be painted with tenderness—the precipitous rocks behind her, the sky torn by clouds, a branch of ivy, its gleaming, metallic leaves with delicate veins and rough undersides painted with a miniaturist's care. It was with the same love of virtuosity that he painted the silken locks of Mary Magdalen's hair, which surrounds her brow like curling smoke, its heavy waves falling across her bosom and partly covered by the transparent veil which accentuates the divergence between the two materials by superimposing one over the other—the live, glittering substance of the hair and the dull weave of the veil. With equal virtuosity El Greco painted a skull placed beside the saint and, in front of it, a graceful glass vase which, while the skull can be seen through it, retains the lustre of its own curving surface.

El Greco was extremely fond of this effect of an object seen through a vase or transparent cup and, even had nothing of his survived except these still-lifes, often placed seemingly at random in his pictures, they would amply testify to the extraordinary quality of his craftsmanship. In addition to this saint incarnating sin and forgiveness at the same time, and of whom numerous replicas are known (including those in the William Rockhill Nelson Art Gallery in Kansas City, the parish church of Parades in Seville, and the Worcester Art Museum), El Greco sometimes depicted her in head and shoulders only, without any background, praying before a crucifix leaning against a stone, a composition similar to that of St. Francis. In the course of the years her flawless beauty underwent a change. Her expression grew more intense, as if her feelings had gained in depth. She became a saint more moved by repentance than transfigured by forgiveness. Her face lengthened; she had wept so long that her skin had lost its radiance and her face had become swollen with tears.

This repentance of the saints seems to have held a particular fascination for El Greco, as if he knew the torments of the treacherous flesh and the wild remorse after an act of weakness. His patrons must have shared his affection for saints who were violent in their repentance. Seventeen replicas are known of his weeping St. Peter (Oslo, Barnard Castle, National Gallery, London—fragment of the head only —and others) (Plate 60). Remorse sweeps like a squall through the saint's robust body. This is a man of the people with a labourer's arms, pronounced muscles and protruding veins, and a powerful neck taut as if with repressed sobs. His head, too small for his large body, is squat, as if compressed by foreshortening; his hair is thick; he has a coarse beard, a low forehead, and a short, jutting nose. With clasped hands St. Peter raises his eyes ravaged with tears to heaven; his eyebrows are contracted as if in an effort to comprehend what has happened to him. Darkness and rocks form the picture's background; as in the representation of the repentant Magdalen, a plant has grown from a cleft in the rock, a symbol of fidelity or hope. In the illuminated left-hand margin of the picture El Greco introduced one of those subsidiary episodes which often accompany the main theme in his pictures: with a few brief strokes he painted an angel which seems to have risen from Christ's empty tomb, and a woman descending the steep path holding a glass goblet which gleams in the semi-darkness, who probably represents Mary Magdalen.

El Greco also painted St. Peter and St. Paul together, with a striking contrast between their two physiognomies. Shown in three-quarter length, they are walking side by side towards a common goal. In one of the oldest versions (in the Luis Plandiura Collection, Barcelona) El Greco gave them a characteristic and moving gesture such as only he could have conceived: their right hands are laid one over the other, not palm to palm but wrist on wrist, as if the crossed hands belonged to the same person, that of St. Paul weighing heavier, more insistently, in St. Peter's, with its impulsive gesture.

These repentant saints also include a St. Jerome, and several replicas of this picture are known (National Gallery of Scotland, Hispanic Society of America, and others). The penitence of this intellectual saint is not so spectacular as that of St. Peter, the man of the people. He is not shaken by a storm; his emotions run deep and are betrayed only by the intensity with which he gazes at the crucifix he holds. He is surrounded by the attributes of his distinction—the book, the hourglass, even his cardinal's hat hanging from a rock. But the atmosphere of the picture is almost electrified; each object seems to irradiate a light of its own; the colours seem to change before the spectator's eyes.

The new world in which El Greco was now placing his saints was a twilight world, but one of those glorious twilights saturated with gold which light the sky until nightfall. It was in such a twilight that he painted "Christ Carrying the Cross" (Prado). A Christ closely akin to these repentant saints, with His face bathed in that same golden light which forms the square halo round His crown of thorns. He is all radiance, all flame. His tunic is of a dazzling purple; the Cross itself is so brightly lit that the wood turns from brown to red, not from a borrowed reflection, but as if it were actually glowing. The mantle half covering Christ gleams like steel; every fold glitters like a blade. Drops of blood have flowed realistically down from the crown of thorns, but the face is already wiped free of suffering; the Cross no longer weighs heavily on His delicate hands, one of which rests on the wood in that almost ritual gesture, with the two middle fingers joined and the others spread out.

This Christ, with His instrument of martyrdom, was a subject highly appreciated by El Greco's contemporaries: about twenty replicas of it are known. In the one in the former Royal Collection of Roumania there is a particularly striking contrast between the realistic minuteness of detail with which the long drops of blood or the crown of thorns, with one of its twigs newly broken are treated, and the way in which the hands are placed on the Cross with all the fingers spread out fanwise—hands which have lost the power to grasp.

Barely a few years—perhaps ten—had elapsed since El Greco had finished "The Burial of Count Orgaz." During these years his art had undergone the most profound transformation. It had come about progressively, step by step, surrender by surrender, like the path of an ascetic who, from renunciation to renunciation, wins victory over himself. He had deliberately rid himself of the most well-tried pictorial values, of the mastery he had acquired; he had destroyed, broken up, and crumbled the image of a familiar world. From the scattered fragments he had constructed his own private universe. His creations finally escaped from their bodily envelope. Behind the gaunt human face appeared the saint, the penitent, pure thought or feeling indicated by a convention of the features, just as a quantity is indicated by a number.

The age in which he lived, the artistic sensibility of the elite with whom he consorted, the burning, tortured faith of the masses all supported him in this effort. Whilst pursuing a lonely path, he could not, however, have worked in complete isolation, in the emptiness of a laboratory. He did not live like a hermit. He had to secure himself a material basis for his existence. He had to find echoes of admiration and esteem for his work. But this mysterious harmony between his age and his creative evolution did not last long. The few short decades following his death broke up that harmony so completely that every trace of it was obliterated. The meaning of his work was swiftly lost, and his aim became incomprehensible and absurd.

The one comprehended fact was that a great change had come about and that his work, as Jusepe Martínez wrote, had become so different from that of his beginnings that "it did not appear to be by the same hand."

It was in Italy above all that the writers of the following century were to wax most eloquent in their indignation against this flagrant rupture with the heritage of Italian art. One of them reproached him with having sought at all costs to break with any dependence on Titian and with having "changed his manner into another so ridiculous and extravagant that it is staggering to see how a man who had been such a good painter could, as the result of a sudden impulse, become so bad."[1] Lanzi, another celebrated theoretician, summed up what had happened to El Greco during these decisive years as follows: "He attempted a new style, but with the most disastrous results."[2]

A picture which possibly dates from slightly later concludes this period of profound transformation. El Greco had often painted his own patron saint, Dominic; he had painted him as he had done his saints in prayer, surrounded by an oppressive solitude, against a dramatically turbulent sky, in ardent and mute colloquy with the crucifix (Toledo Cathedral). In these pictures, at least six variants of which are known, the holy monk is clean-shaven and his face is carved into broad planes by patches of light and shade which lend his features a strange mobility. But there is also the "St. Dominic" in the San Vicente Museum in Toledo (Plate 46). The saint has fallen to his knees. His

[1] *Arcadia pictorica* (1789), by Don Francisco del Vega Preziado, Spanish painter and writer who lived in Italy.
[2] *Storia pittorica dell' Italia* (1782), by Luigi Lanzi, Italian archaeologist and art historian.

53. *The Pentecost. c. 1595–1600*

52. *The Adoration of the Shepherds. c. 1590–1600*

51. *The Annunciation. c. 1590–1600*

55. *St. Francis in Meditation. c. 1585–92*

54. *St. Francis with Brother Rufus.*
c. 1592–95

57. *St. Francis in Prayer. c. 1609–14*

56. *St. Francis in Ecstasy. c. 1595*

59. *St. Mary Magdalen. c. 1582–85*

58. *St. Mary Magdalen. c. 1580*

61. St. Jerome as a Cardinal. c. 1600–04

60. St. Peter Repentant. c. 1583–86

62. St. Joseph. c. 1597–99

64. *The Holy Family. c. 1599–1601*

63. *The Holy Family. c. 1592–96*

65. *Don Rodrigo Vázquez. c. 1594–98*

66. *Portrait of Manusso Theotocopuli (?). c. 1600–04*

dark, homespun cloak and cowl form a sort of heavy reliquary around him, one of those carved shrines in which the baroque preserved its relics. His white gown with its thick folds completely encloses his body like a deeply fluted column. The tilted face with its small, pointed beard is framed in the white-rimmed cowl as if nestling in a shell. The emaciated face is shrunken, reduced to lids lowered heavily over protuberant eyes, cheeks so hollow that they are mere skin stretched over bone, and a big, sad mouth whither all the life in this skeletal head has fled. This mouth, which has only just fallen silent, has been addressing the crucifix which he holds in his left hand. The other hand is raised to his breast, the fingers spread out fanwise, a hand once broad and strong but now as gaunt as the face, with fingers so thin and frail that they would snap at the least pressure and, like the mouth, trembling with emotion. Everything around the saint echoes his inner trembling. The low horizon has almost vanished, along with any indication of the earth. All the storms which had thundered round each of El Greco's Christs in agony have amassed their thickest clouds behind this kneeling saint. A golden twilight fringes their green opacity like flickering lightning. The dramatic sky, the background deepening with nightfall, even the robe glinting with reflections as if from electric shocks all reflect the emotions of the saint so deeply sunk in prayer. St. Dominic with his fervour rises up above a mass of dead forms like the dark flame of a spiritual victory.

CHAPTER
EIGHT
SECRETS
OF MEN
AND COLLOQUIES
OF SAINTS

PHILIP II was wasted away by disease, his withered body was racked by ceaseless torture. Every movement brought hideous agony. Jehan Lhermite, his manservant, had constructed a mechanical armchair for him, which permitted him to be carried without being too badly shaken. Yet an indomitable energy lived in this stricken body, a determined spirit which drew a gloomy delight from this very suffering, the secret feeling of victory that a sick but always lucid man has over those in good health. Every trial seemed to strengthen this armour of resignation he had forged for himself. He no longer disclosed his feelings at each stroke of fortune; he set his pride to conceal his fits of rage or humiliation beneath the impassivity of a saint or a hero. When he learned of the destruction of his invincible Armada, a fatal blow to his ambitions and a hideous mortification, he contented himself with remarking that he had sent the fleet to do battle with men and not with tempests.

He seemed to take refuge in his own suffering so as to avoid noticing the poverty of the country, to use it as a shield against the discontent of the people. "The truth is that the realm is completely exhausted," wrote one contemporary. "Hardly anyone has either money or credit, and those who have use it neither in trade nor in speculation but hide it, in order to live as economically as possible in the hope that it will last them until they die. Hence the universal poverty which reigns in every class. There is not a town or city but has lost a large part of its population, as is proved by the multitude of closed and empty houses, and the lowered rents of the few that are still inhabited." Amidst this

general stagnation, which also preyed on men's spirits and stifled all
initiative, those who retained a shred of energy left the country and set
out for the New World to seek their fortunes. Every vessel leaving for
America was crammed with Spaniards, now no longer conquerors but
voluntary and disillusioned exiles. Everything had shrunk, everything
had become reduced to a state of precarious preservation. The ruler
of a still vast kingdom had no money left at his disposal to satisfy
either his passion for building or his hates. The treasury was drained
so dry that Philip II could not even pay the reward promised to the
murderer of William of Orange in ready money. The King felt his end
to be imminent. In 1596 he fell gravely ill. But his fierce will, now
reduced to a desire to survive, triumphed once more over illness. He
recovered sufficiently to go and spend the months of May and June
in Toledo. It was to be his last visit to that city. He did not now stay
in the Alcázar, as on his previous visits, but in the cathedral close,
where he attended the High Mass held to celebrate his recovery. He
no longer seemed to take any interest in the artistic life of Toledo. He
was no longer occupied with his personal glory or the glorification of
militant faith. He did not abdicate as his father had done—his son
was too young and he knew him to be unfit—but he lived the life the
Emperor had led at San Yuste, a life which, in the words of the Florentine Ambassador, was more that of a monk than of a king. Philip II
prepared for death with the infinite care of a bureaucrat. He had
drawn up his will in 1594—an enormous document. He knew that his
improved health was only a temporary reprieve. When he left Toledo
in that summer of 1596, he knew he would never see his former capital
again. His last illness had only heightened his physical misery. But
he still watched over the affairs of the realm, making notes on the
documents submitted to him in that increasingly illegible handwriting
—the writing of a dying man or a lunatic—which zigzagged over the
margins and every blank space on the paper. His mind had not aged,
as one historian has said, because he had always been old. But his
strength was deserting him. The manservant charged with extinguish-
ing the candles would find him dozing late at night, with files on his
narrow bed and a paper in his hand. He was no longer accessible to
anyone. His enemies called him the Black Spider of the Escorial. His
armchair was placed in such a way that, without moving, he could see
through the door of his room into the church. It was in the Escorial,
where he wanted to live, that he wished to die. In June 1598 he left
the Alcázar in Madrid for the last time. He was borne on a litter. His

body was covered with ulcers. His flesh was rotting. A suffocating stench filled his narrow room. But a sort of pride in his mortification lived on in him throughout his most agonizing sufferings. At the most dreadful moment of his physical decay he summoned his daughter, the Infanta Isabella, and his son Philip, the heir to the throne, who was only twenty years old, and, before his horrified children, according to the description of the Emperor's ambassador, ripped off the sheet which covered "his stinking body, riddled with ulcers and crawling with lice" so that they should understand the vanity of all things human, the impotence of all temporal power, even that of an absolute monarch. In this attitude of conscious martyrdom Philip II died in September 1598.

There was apparently no link between this royal death and El Greco's life. There is no reason to suppose that the disappearance of the sovereign who so long ago had refused an altarpiece in any way affected his career. Yet there was a strange coincidence between his death and the moment when El Greco's success became really dazzling. Perhaps his fame had merely grown great enough at last to find eloquent echoes. Perhaps his popularity amongst anonymous patrons had at last awakened the interest of those whose approval established true fame. The fact remains that his portraits of people of consequence— after so many portraits of unknown men—were painted after the death of Philip II. Only then did celebrities, some of them the most eminent of his day, begin to talk about him. It was as if a great adversary had vanished, to open up the way for him and free enthusiasm from all constraint.

It may also be that in the same year in which Philip II died the support which El Greco received, this official recognition which came to him so belatedly, resulted from the fact that in July 1598 his first protector on Spanish soil, Don García de Loysa, was appointed Archbishop of Toledo. The latter, however, was to die in February of the following year. Yet El Greco's glory lived on after him; it was not a brief blaze due to high protection. This fame burst suddenly into his life. No longer did he need expert colleagues to bring home to parsimonious clients how odious their bargaining was. Gone were the parish priests or friends of friends who passed commissions on to him, and the picture dealers who sold his ecstatic or repentant saints in faraway places. Suddenly El Greco seems to have passed on to a different plane. In fact all that is known of his life and position up till then is provided solely by the evidence of his pictures and is therefore either

deduction or conjecture. Only these belated testimonials permit the
reconstruction of his past; it is to their eloquence that one owes the
few certainties about him. El Greco's life is like a dark tunnel penetrated, when it has almost reached its end, by a brilliant shaft of light.
Everything about it sorts itself out and falls into place in retrospect.
The riddle of his existence, the mystery of his creative power, would
have remained undecipherable for ever but for this final illumination,
this belated shout of fame.

Meanwhile, in 1597, El Greco had embarked on a major work.
Martín Ramírez, a devout Toledan, died, bequeathing his fortune to
pious works. Negotiations were entered into with his heirs to place
this sum of money at the disposal of St. Theresa for a Carmelite
foundation. But his heirs preferred to perpetuate the dead man's memory in a more spectacular manner. One of them bore the same name:
he was a professor of theology at the University of Toledo and probably more sympathetic to the glory of the Church on the temporal
plane than to mystical renunciation. He used the money at his disposal
to erect a chapel in Toledo. This chapel was built in the official style
of the period, in a purified neoclassicism like that of Juan de Herrera.
It was dedicated to the saint who was at that time held in especial
favour: St. Joseph. St. Theresa called him "the father of my soul."
The Jesuits dedicated a chapel to him in every church they built.
Martín Ramírez, the professor of theology, seems to have been a man
who kept up with his age. The chapel was completed in 1594. He must
have searched a long time for an artist to paint the big altarpiece in
accordance with his conception of what would serve the memory of
the dead man best and in the most dazzling way. It was not until 1597
that his choice fell on El Greco. On September 9 of that year he signed
a contract with him for the execution of three altarpieces, which El
Greco undertook to have finished by the Feast of the Assumption in
August of the following year—a very short space of time for so important a work. According to custom, the contract specified details:
the painting destined for the high altar was to comprise an image of
St. Joseph as its central panel, painted on canvas and surmounted
by a Coronation of the Virgin, with a saint on either side. The frame
was to be of carved wood, following the plans already made, and carefully gilded, and the said Domenico Theotocopuli undertook to see
that the whole was executed "in all perfection."

For a frame of classical severity El Greco painted the strangest saint
ever offered for the worship of the faithful (Plate 62). Here one is

far from the familiar St. Joseph of Italian painting, the old man of the people, the humble artisan singled out by the miraculous, often shown still working at his humble craft. El Greco's St. Joseph rises up like a giant, with a pilgrim's staff in his gaunt hand, as if setting out along a road which would be long and arduous. The elongation of his figure has attained a degree unusual even for El Greco. From his bare feet one's eyes soar up to a dizzy height before reaching the head, also very narrow and elongated. The body is just a thin column, with the robe coiling round it in spirals. The asymmetrical head is slightly bent, in the manner of very tall men who never draw themselves up to their full height. The uneven eyes, with long, swollen lids, are full of an inexpressible sorrow, the sorrow of solitary men beyond the reach of human affection. The Infant Jesus has rushed up to him, not a new-born babe, but a grown child, His little face stamped with that ugliness lent by premature gravity to childish features. He clings to the saint, stretching out His little arm as if trying to prevent him from going away, looking round with a mute appeal for help. The saint's large hand is cupped round the boy's head but held away, as if hesitating to touch it. The Child's distress and the saint's sorrow never meet; the appealing gaze of Jesus into the distance and that of the saint falling on Him from above pass each other by, as if to underline the fact that all human affection is the prisoner of an ultimate solitude.

Above the grief-stricken saint and the despairing Child, El Greco painted the exuberant gaiety of the angels whirling in the sky; one full-grown angel has hurtled down head first from above, and little winged ones cleave through the clouds as though through water, scattering garlands and flowers, armfuls of flowers which rain down on the saint. Above him there is a joyous heaven, but the earth on which he treads, the low horizon which deliberately increases his height, is the familiar Toledan landscape spread out round his feet. This was one of the first portraits of the well-loved town which El Greco was to paint. His affection for it is particularly marked. It would have been more natural to show the pilgrim saint walking through the countryside, with quiet roads on the horizon and a road before him and behind. The Italian painters always liked to give their pictures depth by means of a landscape with a ribbon of blue water meandering through it and a tree standing out against the sky—a background which echoed the picture's diagonals and made them recede into infinity. But the landscape round St. Joseph's feet has a life of its own; it plays no part in the composition; it is only there by reason of the pleasure El Greco felt in painting it. He must have known the surrounding countryside well and its hues would have enhanced the gaiety of the colouring, but he loved the city with his own peculiar exclusiveness of affection. El Greco was to be the first artist to be smitten with an urban landscape, the first to prefer the line of a wall to the curve of a hill, a house front pierced with windows to a rock, a steeple to a treetop. The landscape at the foot of this picture is also a kind of inventory in which the goods might be said to be classified according to a wholly personal scale of values. All Toledo lay before him, but, following his own preferences, he chose to paint the Bridge of Alcantara, the Alcázar, the cathedral, and the castle of San Servando. This landscape, painted with the patient care of a miniaturist, nevertheless remains subordinated (so great was El Greco's mastery) to the monumental side of the composition, to its almost architectural arrangement. This same mastery enabled him to resolve yet another of the picture's discrepancies—between the sadness emanating from the saint and the boy, and the gaiety of the colouring.

After the transformation of forms, that evasion of reality which had been the turning point of his art, El Greco proceeded to the transformation of light. It turned to crystal, it became steel, it cut through the picture right into the figures like a sharp blade. Colours were lightened to transparency, the former saturation with the old gold gave way to an icy clarity. From now on the last trace of acquired craft vanished. El Greco no longer first drew a sketch in bistre, ochre, or terracotta, as was *de rigueur* in Italian studios; he no longer primed his canvases with underpaint below his thickly laid-on colours. His long, flowing brush strokes seem almost improvised, the layer of paint is so thin that nearly everywhere the texture of the canvas shows through. Colours have acquired an independence of their own; there is no relationship, no reciprocal influence between them; they are like the colours of a stained-glass window. St. Joseph's tunic is the greenish blue of deep water, his cloak the gold of a setting winter sun; the Child wears a red tunic which only emphasizes the diaphanous pallor of His little face. El Greco's saints from now on were to live in a world of lunar brightness, where human beings would shiver with cold.

Faithful to his contract, El Greco painted "The Coronation of the Virgin" over the reredos, and in this familiar subject, recently composed for the church at Talavera, everything is again etherealized, losing its density so that even the shadows become pervious to the light.

Set in this same light, as if reflected by a glacier, is the "Virgin with

Saints" in the National Gallery in Washington. She followed on a whole
series of pictures of the Holy Family which enjoyed the same success
with El Greco's clients as did his ecstatic or repentant saints (Plate
63). His precursors had painted the Holy Family as an intimate scene
evoking family love. But El Greco's pictures no longer had anything
in common with the human hearth, with reality. They exhaled a strange
peace, a joy not of this world.

They are in part grouped round an object which, taken by itself,
would seem to be a link with everyday life—a bowl of fruit like the
one doubtless to be found in El Greco's house, just as must have been
the vase set beside St. Magdalen. Filled with fruit, it could have stood
on the table at every family meal. But its transparency, painted by a
virtuoso, is of the same ice-blue as the sky; the fruit with which it is
filled is of a gleaming yellow; and it is through this transposition of
colour that an object loses its identity, that it achieves the quality of
unreality. When painting one of his first Holy Families, El Greco remembered Leonardo's St. Anne and placed, or seems to have placed
(the postures are as vague as the setting) the Virgin on the knees of
her mother, whom he painted as young as her daughter. But this memory of a world of real shapes was only a fleeting one.

It is the Virgin's head and not St. Anne's which dominates the
picture; the face is drawn in an ellipse, with a domed forehead, great,
luminous, slightly uneven eyes, and a mouth pale in its young innocence. Her brown hair is covered with the lightest of veils, very close
in its texture and shading to the clouds above. Almost all relationship
between the figures is abolished, just as is all feeling of distance. St.
Anne is placed so close to the Virgin that her hair brushes her veil;
she has laid a hand on her shoulder, but her lowered eyes look down
past the Child. The Virgin herself gazes into the distance and, with her
tapering fingers which touch nothing, holds out fruit to her Son without
looking at him. The gaze and hand of the Child Himself seem to by-
pass the object. Only St. Joseph seems to see what he is looking at and
to touch the bowl he holds. The independence of the colours matches
the isolation of the figures. In the version in the Cleveland Museum,
St. Anne is wrapped almost snugly in a red cloak of the same cold hue
as the bright blue satin spread over the Virgin's knees, the deep blue
of a mountain lake. All the colours seem to adapt themselves to the
crystal bowl: all the surfaces are smooth, transparent, iridescent; the
shadows are tinged with green, the reflections are icy white, the flesh

tints of the Virgin and the Child remind one of frosted windows barely tinged by a pink light.

Down the years this theme, which El Greco never ceased to repeat, assumed an increasingly unreal aspect. In the picture in the former Royal Collection in Bucharest, for example, the Virgin's face is elongated and tapering with a marked tendency towards asymmetry. Another version in a Montreal collection shows a Virgin markedly Spanish in type, with a St. Anne whose face is now a mere triangle, so pointed that it barely seems to hold room for her features. She makes a curious gesture: her fingers are spread out as if she were sketching the time-honoured and ritual sign to ward off an evil spell. Another composition of the same subject confirms a strange tendency of El Greco, his habit of assembling scattered fragments of earlier pictures into a new work. In a different version of the Holy Family (in the San Vicente Museum in Toledo) the memory of Leonardo had faded away (Plate 64). St. Anne has resumed her traditional aspect of an old woman; she leans over the Child placed on His mother's knee, and it is John the Baptist, a completely naked boy (or rather the soul of a dead child) who holds the bowl of fruit, with one finger laid on his lips as if to impose silence. Here El Greco has given the features of the young St. Anne to the Virgin; the triangular, asymmetrical face, the mantle set slantwise over her head, in a way no human head could ever wear it and which is as distinctive a sign with El Greco as the half-opened hand over the heart.

The "Virgin with Saints" in the chapel of St. Joseph is closely akin to the last pictures of the Holy Family. She is very Spanish, but even more remote from the spectator, as if she were painted through a veil. The picture seems to take shape more through its stained-glass colouring, its blues, reds, and green-golds, than through its forms. Heads of little angels cluster round the edges of the gloriole, barely detached from the clouds, like fat bubbles of soapy water. The features of the Virgin, Child, and angels are as vague as faces in a dream and seem to draw out, fade away, and become interchangeable as one looks at them. The two holy women, with their heads hardly projecting above their overlong necks, with their low foreheads, receding chins, pointed noses, and air of androgynous angels, have just the bare signs by which they may be identified as saints. Their attributes of a lion, a lamb, and a palm frond (simple signs as well, if compared with the realities) have even more substance than they themselves.

The masterpiece of the chapel, however, was the picture of "St.

Martin and the Beggar," now in the National Gallery of Washington (Frontispiece). The originality of the composition, with all its novel elements, particularly noticeable in a man who rarely took the trouble to vary his subject matter but confined himself to renewing the same theme from within, was perhaps owing to El Greco's desire to keep in his patron's good graces by painting his patron saint, who was also that of the pious founder, with particular care.

The arrangement of the picture was determined by the proportions of the canvas, probably chosen by El Greco, the same as those of its companion picture (just over six feet high and only about three feet wide) and which in fact better suited a Virgin in the clouds than a scene unfolding on earth. Within this slender frame the seemingly large and heavy bulk of a white horse evolves. Its massive body is placed on a diagonal, so as to suggest a recession in depth, but this intention was abandoned halfway through, as if by a man who knew his limitations and had therefore ceased to be preoccupied by them. The horse remains in the foreground, as if the suggestion of a vague background were enough to identify it as a horse approaching from afar.

In painting this knight in his rich armour on a trotting steed El Greco no doubt had in his mind's eye Donatello's equestrian statue of Gattamelata in Padua or that of Colleoni by Verocchio, which he had so often seen in Venice. The time had come when recollections of the years spent in Italy were beginning to stir in his memory. He seems to have been one of those with delayed memories, who at different periods live certain sections of their past over again. On Italian soil he had turn by turn struggled against the memories of Byzantium, which reached back to his childhood, and succumbed to their hold over him; on Spanish soil he had tried to rid himself of all he had brought with him from Italy. But from now on he began to be reconciled to this already assimilated contribution, to recapture an important part of his life.

The image of a Venetian piazza and of a statue bathed in that pearly light, enhanced by the reflection from the unruffled water, was as vague as a memory so distant that one can no longer tell how far it is blended with successive evocations and present impressions. The atmosphere of Spain had worked a curious transformation on this image. This knight in his glittering armour is less akin to a powerful Italian *condottiere* than to the sad knight of La Mancha.

The time when El Greco painted this picture was also the time when Cervantes, harassed by the sordid cares of his existence and having tried in vain to take service in the Indies, "common refuge of the poor in heart," embodied in his hero all the impossible dreams, the tragic and grotesque bruises inflicted on a generous nature by the duplicity of reality. El Greco, the *émigré*, doubtless knew nothing as yet of the book which this crippled victim of the Battle of Lepanto wrote to escape the haunting presence of poverty and imprisonment, and which was not to be published until 1605; but the popular image of St. Martin which dwelt in people's hearts was transformed into the melancholy knight of a dream, through the same process by which the image of Amadis of Gaul, who at that time inflamed popular imagination, was turned into that of Don Quixote.

In the picture for the chapel of St. Joseph, St. Martin has become very Spanish in his armour of gilded bronze, enhancing a very slender waist and broad shoulders. A white ruff frames his pointed, slightly bent face, the rather asymmetrical face of a sad youth who is neither surprised nor moved by this encounter, as if he had been expecting to meet this incarnation of all the poverty in the world. The poor man pressing against the horse is also a very Spanish *pobre*. El Greco deliberately heightened the contrast between the splendour of the knight—the dazzling mass of the white horse, the gold embroidery, the fringed velvet, the crimson trousers, the shining boots in the gold stirrup, the finely pleated linen, the green-gold cloak—and the nakedness of the beggar. He did not even have the charity to give his poor man the smallest rag; he made him appear before the saint as naked as a worm. He is unmistakably half starved. His body, once that of a healthy man, has been reduced by privation to a state of emaciation, hollow-chested, with protruding ribs and gaunt arms and legs. These legs have been scratched and bruised along the roads and El Greco painted, with the same virtuosity as he did the gold embroideries, a wretched little strip of cloth wound round above the right ankle. The beggar is plainly frozen under the deep blue sky, in the icy light of noon. He holds himself as humble people do, with drooping shoulders, his long body leaning forward. But this Spanish beggar raises to the knight the trusting look of those who have never appealed in vain to generosity. There is no avidity in the gesture with which he has caught hold of the sumptuous cloak, a cloak in any case useless to the knight, flung idly over the saddle, and which the saint is in the act of severing with his sword.

El Greco painted a scene taking place on earth and not on an interstellar planet still in formation. He made it credible by the realism of detail. He gave it a well-defined setting. The horse advances along a road he knows well. This time it is the Toledan countryside, with its tawny rocks, the broken line of purple hills on the horizon and small flames of greenery spurting from the soil. But these are the immediate outskirts of the city, whose walls can be seen glittering like silver. In the foreground is the famous water-raising machine constructed by the Cremonan clockmaker Giannello della Torre, who had been Charles V's companion at San Yuste. Cervantes mentions it as being one of the wonders of the city. No stranger failed to admire it. A special medal was struck in honour of its inventor, Della Torre or Juanelo Turriano, as he was called in the land of his adoption. He was one of those many foreigners who had been captivated by Toledo. He had not followed the court to Madrid in spite of all the commissions he might have hoped for. He had remained in Toledo, near his work. When El Greco arrived there, the machine known as "the celebrated contrivance of Juanelo" had ceased to function and Della Torre was about to construct another, more powerful one. El Greco seems to have been amazed by this skill of a mechanical genius which could supply a town deprived of water. In actual fact the celebrated contrivance was only a slight help against this dearth. Its yield of 162 hectolitres was insufficient for the needs of a large population. The water carriers—the *aguadores*—mainly Frenchmen, continued to draw water from the Tagus and hawk it through the city on the backs of animals. Jehan Lhermite, during his visit to Toledo in 1596, found the machine very costly and calculated that there was "not a jug of water but must cost the King more than one real." Besides the machine stopped working for lack of operators at nighttime, on feast days, in winter, and "when the river rises." For El Greco, however, Juanelo's contrivance was a symbol of the city, a feature on the face of a beloved, and he placed it in the foreground of a picture painted with particular care.

Yet even if the scene takes place on familiar soil, El Greco was anxious to show from the start that this cavalcade of a saint was not a real event. But neither is it a miracle which occurs; it is an act of charity, a virtue of men as well as of the saints, which El Greco depicts like a fairy tale. The evasion of the everyday image commences immediately in front of this familiar landscape, where the white legs of the horse, which should in principle bear the burden of a heavy body but which seem almost weightless, are set on the ground beside the ruddy legs of the poor man, excessively elongated, emphasizing the upward sweep by their multiplicity of parallel lines. And these horse's legs, too wavy in outline, as if they were quivering, appear more like some reflection in water than a direct image. Solidity grows with height; the horse's body becomes more substantial, the realistic details multiply. There is, at a certain height in the picture, a striking advance towards realism; the horse's head, painted in careful detail, has nothing in common with its insubstantial legs, but its eye has an almost human look, so understanding that it seems to share in the saint's generosity.

Like most of El Greco's commissions, however, this fairy tale, with its iridescent colouring, suffered a painful aftermath of sordid squabbles over money.

Dr. Martín Ramírez started a lawsuit, contesting the price asked of 31,328 reals, which he claimed to be exorbitant. El Greco persisted in demanding what he considered his due, although he was once again in pressing need for money and could not even pay the relatively small sum of 1053 reals which he owed for canvases until he himself was paid. An expert was summoned from Madrid to value the work. Agreement was not reached until the end of 1599, when the valuation corresponded to the price demanded and Dr. Martín Ramírez undertook with his person and goods to pay the money in two parts, in September 1600 and January 1601.

The altarpieces whose price had been contested by the administrator of the chapel were, however, admired from the moment of their completion. The story of St. Martin was particularly popular. El Greco must have repeated it for private clients, for about eight replicas are known, spaced out over several years, one of the closest to the original being in the former Royal Collection in Bucharest.

From the first the main picture was regarded as a masterpiece. In a book devoted to El Greco's client, the "venerable servant of God, the model priest, the distinguished lawyer and apostolic preacher, Dr. Martín Ramírez de Zayas," Brother Alonso de Zayas, probably a relative, refers to the three altarpieces which stood over the three altars of the chapel of St. Joseph and which were highly esteemed and of great worth, being the work of "that Greek, El Dominico, the Apelles of our time."

Although this eulogy was intended to honour Dr. Ramírez rather than El Greco, it reflects the fact that he was at last officially recognized. No member of the royal family, no grandee, no prince of the Church had yet sat to him for a portrait. Even the posthumous portrait of Don Diego de Covarrubias, which his brother, El Greco's friend, commissioned, dates at the earliest from the end of the century. All at once, as if with death of Philip II a ban had been lifted, they turned to "the Apelles of our time," to go down with him to posterity.

One of the most striking cases of this belated call for El Greco is the portrait of Cardinal Quiroga. Don Gaspar de Quiroga had succeeded as Archbishop of Toledo the unfortunate Cardinal Carranza, whom Philip II, breaking his royal oath, had handed over to Rome for persecution. Unlike his predecessor, a Dominican scholar with a world-wide reputation and too tolerant for his time, Quiroga was a man as much lauded for his resolution as for his prudence and even his apologists sometimes described him as cunning.

As Philip II's private counsellor, Quiroga had elaborated a project for the creation of an order of St. Mary of the White Sword, whose members must furnish proof of the "purity" of their blood and track down the impure, owing allegiance to none save the Grand Inquisitor. But Philip did not allow even the Inquisition to trespass on his royal prerogatives. He refused to sanction the creation of this order without, however, bearing any grudge against Quiroga for his zeal. As President of the Holy Office in Toledo, Quiroga exercised his high duties with all the severity of his character; particularly harsh towards the Moors, he instituted a special census of them and had their private lives closely watched. He even did what none of his predecessors had dared to do— forbid the teaching of Arabic, through which the humanist heritage had been able to survive. He died at a ripe old age in Madrid, in 1594. The portrait El Greco painted of him, the only portrait in profile known to be by his hand, is without doubt a posthumous one. In spite of its very poor state of preservation one can recognize the man as his contemporaries describe him, with his pallid face, abrupt manners, and mordant tongue.

Ecclesiastical justice and secular justice, El Greco painted the two facets of his time. Dating probably from the same period is the portrait of a man regarded as one of the greatest judges in the country, Don Rodrigo Vázquez de Arce, President of the Council of Castile (Prado, Madrid, Plate 65). Honest and implacable, he was held in such particular esteem by Philip II that he was entrusted with the most resounding and scandalous affair of a century which was not quick to worry over prompt justice—the trial of Antonio Pérez. Either by patience or intimidation he succeeded in extracting the secrets of the Princess Eboli who, in spite of the forbidding black patch she wore over her eye, had roused the passions of so many men of her time, even, it was said, of the King himself. Vázquez obtained proof that the King had been deceived by false evidence against Escovedo. The trial of Pérez was held *in camera*. The accused, although watched, still lived in his luxurious house, going about his affairs and receiving visitors as if protected by his impunity. But a thorough search enabled Don Rodrigo to discover the originals of Escovedo's dispatches, which Pérez had falsified, and also to prove that he had sold copies of the dispatches exchanged between the King and Don Juan of Austria to the rebels in Flanders. Don Rodrigo Vázquez was faced with the greatest conflict of conscience in his life. He had unmasked a traitor to his country, a virtual assassin, an established villain, who however enjoyed hidden protection and shared his secrets with someone very powerful. Yet he did not hesitate to assume his responsibilities before his contemporaries, passionately interested in the trial, and before history. In spite of the terror which the King inspired in all who approached him, and of his evident desire to hush up the painful affair, Don Rodrigo Vázquez resorted to extreme measures to get at the truth. The degree of Philip II's trust in his discretion may be judged from the complete independence he was granted in the proceedings. Transferred to Madrid, Pérez was submitted to torture. The man's stubbornness was as deep as his secrets. Not until the eighth twist of the rope did he confess to having arranged Escovedo's assassination, but he also confessed to having done so on the order of the King.

El Greco painted Don Rodrigo Vázquez in harmony with the inner image of a man who had not failed in a mighty task. His head is held erect, with that stiffness which is like an attribute of his office. That long and narrow head, with its pointed beard, does not at first sight seem to differ from those of the anonymous noblemen and intellectuals whose portraits El Greco had previously painted or whom he had made the witnesses of various miracles. Only a more accentuated lighting, a sharper relief, reveals what was unusual about this typical Spaniard, by way of personal characteristics or the nature of his office. His obstinate, almost square forehead forms an angle with his hollow temples; his cheekbones are so prominent that the skin is stretched tight over the bone. His long eyes are narrowed, as if from a habit of scrutinizing men who knew how to keep their secrets; they are insistent and mistrustful, but they never turn away. The wide, straight mouth must have been sensitive, but it has learned to clamp tight over irrevocable words. The elongated beard conceals a square jaw and a determined chin. There can seldom have been a smile on these features so composed from within, nor can they ever have relaxed, even in the pain of humiliation.

El Greco's portrait was doubtless painted at a time when Don Rodrigo Vázquez was at the peak of his career and power, before Philip III had come to the throne.

The young King needed money. The Count of Miranda coveted high office and offered him 80,000 ducats on condition that he was appointed President of the Council of Castile. Philip III used ill-health as an excuse to dismiss Don Rodrigo. It is, in fact, a man worn out, consumed by his task, that El Greco painted, as pale as if his blood had already drained away under his dull skin. But, to the arguments put forward by the King, Vázquez haughtily replied that the true motive of his dismissal was that he had always spoken the truth and served His Majesty in accordance with the obligations he had assumed. He did not live long after the blow delivered him by Philip III (he died in 1599), but in a Spain so sensitive to the safeguarding of honour Don Rodrigo Vázquez' reply remained a glorious affirmation of human integrity, a part of the national heritage. His dismissal also marked the caesura between the two reigns.

Toledo saw the young King within her walls for the first time in March 1600. Philip III toured the provinces and had himself acclaimed according to local custom. Barely a year before, he had married Margaret of Austria, and she accompanied him on his progress, for husband and wife never separated. The young couple were welcomed in Toledo by the *hermandad vieja,* that special police force set up (with a corresponding tribunal) to suppress crime on the highways. The policemen monks, covered by their dark cowls, with their banner unfurled, came out from the gates of the city to meet him and, following ancient custom, covered the King's face and hands with this banner. By this gesture they begged the sovereign to close his eyes to everything touching on the punishment of criminals, leaving this to the care of the brotherhood, and to close them also to mercy and let the *hermandad* watch over the safety of the fields and roads.

What the Toledans saw when the banner was raised was a face which, despite its strong Hapsburg characteristics, differed from that of Philip II as far as two human faces can. It was the face of a well-fed man, with the white skin of the sandy-haired, but with the high complexion of those who live in the open air, in contrast with the pallid skin of his father, which was the colour of plants that grow in the dark. And indeed the only two passions which ruled his quickly dulled body and lazy brain were gluttony and sport, particularly hunting. It was also a face whose expressions were only skin deep. The dying Philip II cherished no illusion about his son's qualities. On one occasion, overwhelmed by bitterness, he let himself go so far as to say to one of his intimates: "God, who has given me so many kingdoms, has not granted me a son capable of governing them. I fear they may govern him."

Philip III was doubtless born without qualities or gifts of any kind, but even the personal characteristics he might have developed had been stifled or, rather, burnt out of him with the red-hot iron of constraint. He was timid and, like all timid men, needed affection and esteem, and he knew himself to be as his entourage saw him—not a prince but the shadow of a prince. His pusillanimity was no doubt increased by terror of the fate suffered by Don Carlos. Like all weak men, he took refuge in the assurance given him by his position as heir to the throne, and resented the contempt of the King and his ministers all the more, in view of what he would one day become. The more Philip II withdrew behind the rampart of his icy solitude, the more his son needed to abandon himself, to let himself be destroyed, as it were, by confidence. One man alone seems to have shown him some consideration in his humiliated youth, and his gratitude found expression in an absolute and imbecile affection for him. This grandson of Charles V, whose first principle had been to mistrust favourites, this son of a father who had rooted all powers of affection in himself, was to place himself and his kingdom in the hands of Don Francisco de Sandoval y Rojas, Marquis of Denia, the future Duke of Lerma. From the beginning of this reign the Marquis of Denia managed to impose his creatures on the King and obtain favours for his relatives. It was his uncle, Don Bernardo de Sandoval Rojas, who succeeded Don García de Loysa as Archbishop of Toledo. He was to prove an ostentatious prince of the Church, arrogating to himself the same luxury as the grandees, interested in all that could further his own glory, in letters and the arts, a protector of Cervantes and the poets of Toledo. He was the man destined to inaugurate the new era now opening for the city, as yet without its knowledge, with the accession of Philip III to the throne—an era of almost exclusive domination by the Church, which increased as the civil power waned and during which Toledo lost all political importance forever.

The only characteristic Philip III had inherited from his father was his piety, expressed through strict religious observance, hatred of heretics, and intolerance. During the royal pair's stay in Toledo an *auto da fé* was held in their honour. It was on this occasion that El Greco was called upon to paint the President of the Holy Office, who came to Toledo to attend the arrival of the young monarch.

Don Fernando Niño de Guevara was born in the same year as El Greco, but looks aged before his time. His deep black beard is turning white; he has the complexion of a sick man, suffering perhaps from a liver complaint; his mouth is half open as if he found difficulty in breathing under the weight of his sacerdotal vestments. His eyes also seem to be lowered and, as he was a man who never chose to miss anything, he wears two-sided spectacles; but behind the lenses his eyes have remained piercing, incisive, unwavering, in spite of the sleepless nights he must have spent, for they are ringed with the shadows of fatigue.

El Greco painted him in his familiar surroundings, against a wall hung with embossed Cordova leather, with a door in the background, sitting in a type of armchair common at the time, upholstered in red velvet with big gilt nails, and with his red-slippered feet set firmly on the black and white marble floor (Plate 67). The Cardinal must have been short and squat, for he chose to be painted sitting down, holding as erect as possible a body too short for his long and unwieldy head. El Greco furthered his aspirations towards monumentality; he spread out the heavy watered silk of his vestments, pulling the cape to the left and arranging the folds in a wide fan so that they overlapped the chair. Don Fernando Niño de Guevara seems to be posing for his own monument, for, as he appears with this wide base and massive silhouette, he could have been sculptured in marble or cast in bronze, gilded, of course.

This portrait, in all its deliberate breadth, reveals the absurdity of the fantastic assertions, made in order to explain the elongation of his figures, that El Greco suffered from astigmatism. This portrait followed on the spiral ascension of St. Joseph and the disproportionately huge beggar beside St. Martin, and it was to be followed in turn by figures which recede ever further from the earth beneath their feet. El Greco's optical vision was evidently not the same for men as for saints. He painted Guevara as he was, omitting nothing, with his furrowed brow, the rings round his eyes, and his dry lips. He also painted him in his cardinal's dignity, only recently acquired; he painted the richness of the silk, the delicacy of the linen and lace, down to the fine needlework

over his hands, the white hands of a prelate accustomed to holding out
his ring for the faithful to kiss. The Cardinal must have been pleased
with what he would have considered the success of the composition,
an achievement of pictorial craftsmanship difficult to surpass. El Greco
was fully conscious of the honour which had fallen to him in painting
so important a personage. He made a preliminary study for the head,
which in itself is an elaborate picture and not merely a sketch for the
big portrait. But he did not only paint a man, or a prince of the Church.
He wrote a page of history. Perhaps unwittingly he drew up an indict-
ment. The square of the Zodocover, where the stake was burning, was
far from the palace of the Holy Office, yet it is as if El Greco could see
the flames reflected in the windows and playing over the Cardinal's
purple. Beyond doubt he saw them in the Inquisitor's eyes. Don Fernando Niño de Guevara was a man of high culture, the son of a distinguished and ancient family. He was on the whole moderate in the
exercise of his charge and said to be more tolerant than his predecessors. But this office had set its indelible mark on the man and made him
what he was. El Greco, through the individual, painted a function,
the terrible function of a judge. Even if nothing was known of him,
even if one was unaware that he was at that time President of the
Holy Office of Toledo and to be appointed Grand Inquisitor in the
following year, one would immediately realize that his role was a re-
doubtable one. Fear seems to hang around him and, even if he seems
to shiver himself, he makes those who see him shiver too. If he himself
breathed with difficulty, he must have stifled those admitted to his
presence still more. Even stripped of his purple and standing up, so as
to disclose his short body with its top-heavy head, he would have retained that piercing, rather sideways glance, those beetling brows, that
lined forehead of a man tense with suspicion, that haughty lower lip
beyond the reach of pity. Every muscle in his pale face seems to be
under control, to repress all emotion. One of his slim-fingered hands
dangles lazily, the hand of a prelate at rest, but the other, caught by
El Greco in a characteristic gesture, grips the armchair, tension playing under the skin—a restless and aggressive hand which betrays all
that the impassive face strives to conceal. Rarely, perhaps, has it been
given a painter to assemble so many internal images in a single portrait, to superimpose on that of an individual the image of a social
rank, the devouring hold of a function over a man. A slice of the history of Spain and of an institution can be read on these few square
yards of canvas. The terrible portrait of Don Fernando Niño de

Guevara remains more valid than the most eloquent testimonials, more instructive than volumes of partisan controversy. He sits in the cruel majesty in which El Greco clothed him as the prototype of the Grand Inquisitor, of an implacable judge who has stifled all human impulses in himself.

The very fact that El Greco was entrusted with this portrait bears witness to the fame he had at last acquired among the great men of his time. Yet his position remained a peculiar one. He was not to be summoned by Philip III as court painter any more than he was by Philip II. The Queen, whom he now saw in Toledo, with her regular and placid features weighed down by the Hapsburg chin, was never to be painted by him in her lifetime, though he was to commemorate her death. Only outstanding men of independent tastes seem to have called upon him. Contemporary witnesses stress the fact that he was as odd in his behaviour and remarks as in his painting. He himself seems to have been most exclusive in his choice of friends, consorting only with those whose artistic sensibility was akin to his own and who shared identical spiritual preoccupations.

This exclusiveness was confirmed by a striking example—his friendship with Gregorio de Angulo, doctor of the University of Toledo and town councillor, *regidor* of the *Ayuntamiento,* and a future member of the Royal Council of Naples. Dr. de Angulo was also a man of letters and a poet. Though in this he was probably no more than an enlightened amateur, an epoch much addicted to superlatives exalted his literary merits as if he were an exceptional genius. Though wanting in creative gifts, Gregorio de Angulo certainly had a genius for friendship; he must have had faultless taste, a feeling for quality, and moreover he was free from prejudice; he was rich enough to give active proof of his friendship for artists harassed by material cares, who amply rewarded him with their gratitude by preserving his name for posterity.

In his *Journey to Parnassus,* Cervantes described him as one of the most unusual minds of his time. Lope de Vega dedicated his comedy *Poverty Is not a Vice* to him. The kindness shown him by Dr. Angulo must have been considerable, for the poet's adoration of his patron became increasingly fervent. In his *Laurel of Apollo* he extolled him as a "Spanish Tibullus, a Toledan Horace, an eloquent and gentle Anacreon."

For El Greco, too, Dr. Angulo proved a staunch friend. He stood surety for him on many occasions; he "helped him in particular necessities." El Greco could turn to him on every occasion. When his grandson was born, it was Dr. Angulo whom he asked to be god-father. He borrowed money from him and died owing him a consider-able sum. But nothing is known of the contacts he may have made in Dr. Angulo's house, where his famous protégés were always made welcome. In this city whose pride alone prevented the realization that it was reverting to the status of a provincial town, the most illustrious men seem to have passed each other by without meeting or without attaching any importance to such meetings. In the restricted space of an age when tormented spirits eagerly sought each other out, in the confusion of a time of spiritual transformation, when a free creative outburst was hampered by innumerable difficulties, Spain knew the flowering of solitary geniuses whose paths never crossed. The artists who exalted their patron beyond all his merits never noted the light of neighbouring glories. Cervantes and El Greco must have met in the same room, must have taken the same streets in pursuit of their bound-less dreams; Cervantes must have prayed before the altar in the church of San Tomé and his eyes must have lingered on the pious Count Orgaz; at some crossroads Don Quixote had passed the sad knight, St. Martin; but not the slightest trace has remained of what could have been the great encounter of the century, a unique confrontation of the Spanish genius. In conceiving the most extraordinary figure with which the genius of one man has enriched human creation Cervantes left reality as far behind him as the ascending saints whose feet barely touch the ground, with their tiny heads vanishing into the clouds. A momentary reciprocal blindness must have played a part in this abor-tive meeting, some error in the switching of the psychological railway lines, to let such a supremely exceptional hour pass by unexploited.

Nor does El Greco seem to have had any contact with Lope de Vega.

It was in Toledo that Lope de Vega met his future patron, the Duke of Alba. He often returned there after leaving his service, sometimes staying for several weeks, sometimes for months on end, writing his plays (he once wrote fifteen acts in two weeks there), then setting off again following the movements of the theatrical company to which the beautiful Micaela de Lujan was attached. It was in Toledo that he settled in about 1604, with his wife and children, but also with Micaela de Lujan, whose seven children were only attributed to her long-absent husband in the eyes of the law. In Toledo he maintained two homes and two families. Was El Greco, so free from prejudice in his own private life, shocked by this behaviour? Despite the scandal such a mode of life could have raised Lope de Vega does not seem to have lost the good will of official circles. Toledo, ever seeking occasions for boasting, was proud to count him amongst the personalities of the city. When an heir to the throne was born to Philip III in 1605—the future Philip IV—it was Lope de Vega who was charged with organizing the festivities, who drafted the convocations and the announcement of the happy event, and who made the inaugural speech by virtue, it was said, of his being a Toledan poet, obviously the most experienced of those living in the city. Neither did the ecclesiastical authorities resent the disorder of his private life. In 1608 he was invested with the formidable rank of "domestic" of the Holy Office. The passionate and fickle lover, the never wholly repentant sinner, always ready to fling himself into some new adventure, to be consumed in other flames, and to proclaim his joys and torments to the world, sought refuge in religion, became a lay brother of the Franciscans and, on the death of his wife, took the cowl.

In fact Lope de Vega was a man who respected the temporal law, despite the liberties he took, a man in agreement with the precepts of religion despite his defiance of morality. His world, peopled with a countless throng of the most varied characters, was a closed one. Those seething emotions bubbled, as it were, inside a sealed vessel. He never felt the least doubt as to the eternal stability of the moral and social structure of his time. He never questioned the hierarchy which made him "lie like a dog" at the feet of a Spanish grandee. It would never have occurred to him to revolt against the despotic power of the King or the supervision of institutions like the Holy Office. The vast mirror in which he reflected his epoch was one of unconditional acceptance and discloses only positive images without the least distortion or the faintest recoil. If, in *The Duke of Viseo,* he described the terror which an absolute monarch spread around him, in which a mere hint of suspicion, one ill-chosen word, a parlour game, or a horoscope could destroy a man, no hidden criticism slipped into his presentation, none of his characters felt the slightest impulse towards rebellion. The blind fury of a despot was, on the contrary, exalted as a force of nature.

The rigidity of the social and moral structure was no hindrance for Lope de Vega; on the contrary, it was his security, his safeguard against pitfalls in his path, his refuge from his own nightmares. No spiritual anguish tormented him, no desire for escape made him look higher and further. His enclosed world was a conventional one. Perhaps he

was not made to understand El Greco's distortion of reality; this man
of overflowing imagination probably could not appreciate this way
of creating on a single plane, the plane of a man endlessly repeating
the same subjects with terrible concentration. He who had burned so
much incense before mediocre talents, who had opened the gateway to
fame for many who are known only today because he recorded their
names, never mentioned El Greco. Was his silence the result of incom-
prehension or of resentment? El Greco and Lope de Vega must certainly have met, but no trace of this has remained. El Greco may also
have been as unresponsive to Lope de Vega's work, with its blend of
emotions, its torrential outpouring of images and ideas, as the latter
was to his painting. He had made his own, clear-cut choice for a form
of literature as polished, precious, and hermetic as his own art, one
which expressed ideas often difficult of access and emotions which
were rare, subtle, and delicately shaded. As a well-read man, El Greco
opted for that esoteric poetry which abandoned the sources of popular
inspiration. The most famous representative of this school of poetry
was Góngora. Even if El Greco and Lope de Vega had been made to
understand each other, their relationship would have been marred by
the strange figure of Luis de Góngora rising up between them.

For the intellectuals of his time it was not in Lope de Vega's but
in Góngora's art that Spain found her true expression. These men,
standing at the literary crossroads and following the evolution of
thought from their watchtowers, expected Spain to succeed vanished
civilizations on the spiritual plane as she had on the material one.
One contemporary wrote that, "given the majesty of the Spanish Empire and the polish of her tongue, which is the closest to the Roman,
as the Roman was closest to the Greek, Spain's turn has now come
and it is in her that the heroic spirit destined by Heaven for this renewal must be sought and found." This phœnix of the muses, who was
to rise up from "the burnt-out ashes" of Homer and Virgil, who could
it be, who could one expect it to be "if we do not recognize it in Don
Luis de Góngora? What soul have we seen as heroic of this kind, or
what other should we expect to come throughout posterity?" It was he
who combined the most resplendent gifts of poetic art, "impetuosity
so great and such rapture of mind that, being overwhelmed by these,
his genius burst out to stir the whole world."

There was something of the *poète maudit* in Góngora. Unlike Lope
de Vega, he had found life easy. Success awaited him at every turn
of the road. Luis de Góngora y Argote was born of a noble Cordovan

family; he became a priest, but one who felt more at ease in worldly living than in the contemplation of faith. He was entrusted with a task suited to his rank and qualities as a diplomat: enquiry into the ancestry of those soliciting high ecclesiastical office. At the expense of the applicants he was sent all over the kingdom to investigate their "purity of blood," to make sure they were not descended, even remotely, from converted Jews or Moors. He loved music, bullfighting, amusements, and gambling; in his youth his want of assiduity in his religious functions earned him the reproaches of his superiors. But, as opposed to an "angel of light," he had become an "angel of darkness." With his sensitive and highly strung nerves he was one of those who go out to meet suffering, whose more or less consciously sought climate is misfortune. Everything he saw merely led him back to himself. He made his own tendencies the basis for his creative endeavour. He discarded the evidence of reality in favour of its spiritual essence, more solid and truer than anything transmitted by the senses. His early poetry is musical and accessible, but he rid himself of his mastery of words as consciously as did El Greco of his pictorial virtuosity, to pursue the rare, indirect turn of phrase, omitting articles to give nouns more weight and compressing his phrases as if, like El Greco, he were abolishing the surrounding space. With him everything is dense and painfully concentrated. When in a poem he spoke of a young man—"in his face little blood, in his eyes great darkness"—it might be a portrait painted by El Greco. For a creator as tense as Góngora the sensual virtuosity of a Lope de Vega was at once a challenge and an offence. The aristocrat in him was shocked at the pretensions to nobility of this son of an artisan; as a man who had never known a struggle for existence, he mocked the expedients to which a needy poet resorted. Lope de Vega's work and reputation were immense, whereas only a few poems of Góngora's were in circulation and no collection of them was to be published in his lifetime, though his poems and satires carried much weight. When Lope de Vega married the daughter of a rich Madrid pork butcher, the writers of the time, led by Góngora, applied themselves gleefully to composing puns on this alliance between poetry and pig's meat, the pen and ham. When Lope de Vega, already ageing, paraded his liaison with a very young woman, the most biting and calculatedly malicious verses by Góngora passed from hand to hand throughout Spain.

His personal hostility was enhanced by the animosity of a clique. For want of a war of opinion, unthinkable during this period of surveillance, literary battles raged. Veritable tourneys were held between partisans of the poets or of artistic trends. Two rival academies existed in Toledo and fought with verbal swords—the Count of Mora's, to which Lope de Vega belonged, and the one presided over by the Count of Fuensalida, which numbered twenty-three members, many of them Góngora's friends. Amongst them figured "the painter," without more precise details, as if there could be only one thus referred to in Toledo.

It is not known when and how El Greco knew Góngora, or how close their friendship was. The poet seems to have passed through Toledo in 1589. His admiration for El Greco was expressed in a sonnet in which he extolled in highly personal verses "the sweetest brush that ever animated a panel or gave life to canvas." After El Greco's death he exalted his name "with a greater pæon of praise than that of which the bugles of Fame are capable." In that precious style of his which, according to the taste of the day, appealed to all inhabitants of Olympus, he summed up what had for him been El Greco's relationship with reality, *la naturaleza,* and his creative transformation, that vision of the essence, the goal to which he himself aspired.

"Nature taught him Art, Art Study, Iris her colours, Phœbus his lights, if not Morpheus his shadows."

Two isolated creative artists had met and this meeting no doubt mitigated their solitude, at least for a brief while. Contemporaries had already recognized the kinship between them; one of the rare testifiers to El Greco's glory when, barely a few years after his death, it was already beginning to be eclipsed, spoke of the great painter who had been for the eyes what Góngora had been for the poets.

It was now, when his fame was spreading amongst the most exclusive scholars of his time, that El Greco seems to have had at his disposal means to return to the sumptuous palace of the Marqués de Villena. The apartment he rented on August 5, 1604, does not seem to have been the same one he had previously occupied. It appears to have been even larger and more luxurious; it may even have been extended by the addition of other rooms, of another apartment, to make it more imposing. It was still the finest wing of the house he rented—*el quarto real*—with the part giving on to the garden and the women's *patinillo,* the main kitchen, and what the lease called "the wide corridor down below." Twenty-four rooms in all, a seemingly exaggerated number even for an age which was not niggardly over space. The rent was very high—more than double what El

Greco had paid for his first tenancy, even taking the depreciation of money into account. But, as if this suite of rooms, which must have been vast, given the customs of the time and the fact that a great nobleman had built them for himself, were not enough, El Greco further rented in 1610 a supplementary apartment. This luxury to which he aspired, as if he had long been deprived of it, was not for him an outward sign of success but a definite need. The painter of saints in ecstasy, of monks wasted by asceticism, of repentant saints with a skull to remind them of the vanity of all this world's charms, never lived like a hermit. The large apartments he loved reveal a sociable, ostentatiously hospitable man. In his love of material things, those velvets, glass bowls, and flowers growing from clefts in the rock or falling from an icy sky, there is a diffuse sensuality which shines through even his harshest visions. There was no particle of contempt in him for the wealth and joys of this life. On the contrary, these were necessary to him to stimulate his sensibility; they formed part of his creative work, both beautiful materials and books, precious objects and vast rooms, a distant view and music. If he demanded a high price, if he profited from a picture's success by making easily sold replicas of it, if he haggled and prosecuted bad settlers among his clients, it was hardly out of avidity, in order to amass treasures. He even lacked that prudence which anticipates a rainy day, sickness or old age. The increasingly strict economy of his means of expression was only the mark of a creator and not a reflection of his nature. The dominant impression he left on his contemporaries was that of a spendthrift *par excellence*. In that sort of posthumous trial to which Jusepe Martínez subjected him this characteristic stands out first and foremost. "He was," he wrote, "as extravagant in his nature as in his painting." Above all it was the luxury of his dwelling that shocked his contemporaries. "He earned many ducats but he squandered them on the inordinate ostentation of his house," Martínez insisted. A great nobleman in spirit, El Greco lived the daily life of a highborn. He even went so far, says Martínez, "as to have paid musicians in his house, so that while he ate he could enjoy every delight."

Prodigality, never entirely comprehensible to sober and well-balanced men, was to do as much to earn El Greco the reputation of a mad genius as was his unprecedented painting.

Perhaps he himself felt an obscure pride in his reputation for extravagance, as if to wipe out the memory of a period of privation. He seems to have given his family and the friends who had remained in his native island the impression of a man who had made good and prospered, in the manner of those who, having ventured forth into the unknown, love to make the most of their success, to justify their action to their relatives. His eldest brother seems to have believed him to be the owner of a great fortune when he came to join him in Toledo, at a date not exactly known. There is no evidence as to the true identity of this Manusso Theotocopuli, who was about eleven years older than Domenico and who came to Toledo when already advanced in years and tried by life, to die there. Amongst the Cretans who bore the same forename it seems easiest to identify him with that Manusso who was a tax collector in Candia for the Venetian treasury between 1566 and 1583. Improvidence and the ways of a *grand siegneur* seem to have been a family characteristic. The tax collector from Candia must have mishandled money. Thrown into prison, he fell ill and obtained permission to be tended at home, where he remained under surveillance for several years. The portrait El Greco painted of his brother helps to identify him with the unlucky tax-collector mentioned in the Cretan archives in Venice, for it is the very image of a man who has suffered misfortune, full of bitterness, and with a permanent grudge against fate. Is it the portrait of an adventurer as well? Of a man who has led a dangerous life? For the Cretan archives also preserve traces of a Manusso Theotocopuli (or Theotocopulo) who, in the year of the Battle of Lepanto, offered himself with three of his compatriots to the Signoria as corsairs against the Turks. Had El Greco's brother been that experienced corsair before he was appointed tax-collector? His portrait in the Contini-Bonacossi Collection in Florence (Plate 66) hardly reveals an adventurous spirit. The delicate bone structure, the high forehead, and refined features do not belong to a man of action. But he wears earrings which, following an ancient Cretan tradition inherited from the East, were not so much ornaments as charms endowed with the power to protect their wearer from the hostile elements and in particular, it seems, from sand and wind. They had been worn longest by sailors most exposed to bad weather and apparently are still worn today. This earring worn by Manusso Theotocopuli might testify to his piratic past. He was at any rate a man who had led a difficult and turbulent life, and who was already defeated by fate at the time he took refuge with his brother. His look is subdued by grief, the insistent, almost contagious sorrow of one dogged by adversity. He died shortly after El Greco's second move into the palace of the Marqués de Villena, in December 1604, at the age of seventy-four.

His death certificate, in which his unusual first name is altered to Manuel and in which, instead of his patronymic, he is merely referred to as "the Greek"—Manuel Griego—concludes the passage of a pale ghost through El Greco's life, probably the last reminder of his distant childhood. Like all bereavements, his brother's death seems to have awakened faded memories in him. They emerged suddenly and found their way into his pictures—thin echoes reverberating as if in spite of him. They can be found in the "St. Paul" of the series of Apostles, most of which date from this period, a St. Paul far removed from the usual iconography of the militant saint, with the exaggeratedly elongated head of an Oriental and round, infinitely sad eyes filled with that sorrow which seems almost like his signature at this period. St. Paul plainly holds a sword, his obligatory attribute, but the painter of beautiful, chased hilts only hinted at an almost insubstantial weapon. The main accent of the picture is the letter St. Paul holds out in his fingers towards the spectator—the letter to Titus, first bishop and patron saint of Crete—as if El Greco now remembered with particular intensity that he was a Cretan.

About this period of his creative life he showed a special affection for painting two saints together, as if he were aware of his enhanced psychological penetration, in the juxtaposition, not of two temperaments, but of two spiritual doctrines. One of the first of this series, a prelude to this particularly striking dual harmony, is the picture of "St. Andrew and St. Francis" (Plate 68), discovered during the Spanish Civil War in the Convent of the Incarnation in Madrid, closed to visitors. Here El Greco attained the major canon of elongation. His previous saints are mere dwarfs beside these two gigantic figures. It is no longer an upward rising but levitation which tears them off the ground. The ascensional movement is emphasized by a whole cluster of verticals which leap upwards like the jet of a fountain—the bodies with their garments in rigid folds, the left hand of each saint so turned that it is merely a bunch of fingers or, rather, a hank of thin ribbons. The main accent of this fountainlike movement is given by the double cross of St. Andrew, tilted so as to leave hardly any space between the two arms, traversing the picture from top to bottom, conveying no feeling of either wood, weight, or density. Three quarters of the way up begins the dialogue of the hands. St. Andrew's has an exaggeratedly flexible thumb, with the palm turned outwards in the violent gesticulation of an Oriental. To this persuasive appeal the poor, emaciated hand of St. Francis, marked with the stigmata, replies with an unobtrusive gesture towards the breast with the fingers spread out fanwise, their tips so delicate that they seem to tremble, whilst the other, folded, hand completes this flowing movement of surrender. Higher still, on very long necks, float the two heads, the bold head of St. Andrew with its scattered beard and fleecy hair, and the gaunt, humbly bent profile of the Poverello of Assisi. The hands converse, but the lips are silent; their eyes do not meet; at this altitude of destiny each saint is alone, isolated in his communion with God, in painful concentration.

El Greco painted this double image with particular care. The stained-glass colouring, that crystal quality of its tonal values, links it with the altarpieces in the Chapel of St. Joseph. But at the same time he set out on a new path, following his habit of abandoning a stage directly he had attained it. And on this new path a personal memory lingered.

The horizon of the picture is very low, more a springboard for a leap into the clouds than solid ground. But for El Greco it was like a reminder of the sources of his inspiration which permitted him to fling his saints so high. Beside St. Andrew there is a sketchy landscape which is a residue of reality, a twilight ghost of Toledo. But in the centre and behind St. Francis there appears a mountain covered with snow, with an oddly shaped peak of luminous whiteness against an azure sky. People familiar with El Greco's work have claimed that this peak has the peculiar shape of Mt. Ida, whose glitter dominated the horizon of his childhood. The same peak recurs in a later image of two confronted saints, that strange dialogue between St. John the Baptist and St. Francis, painted at a moment when forms were breaking up, as if a great hurricane had blown through his pictures, and of which only the replica in the Prado is known, probably in part a studio work.

The same mountain, with its hollow flanks looking as if they had been scooped out with a spoon, this time in its summer aspect, its slopes planted with trees, appears in another double image of "St. John the Baptist and St. John the Evangelist." In this tormented background, in which violently lit clouds intervene in the dialogue, the horizon is less abrupt. With its restless lines it forms part of the debate; it is an argument by the same token as the captive dragon in the chalice. This picture was probably painted in the year of Manusso Theotocopuli's death. The mountain could be a vision of Mt. Ida seen from its most pleasing and verdant side, a nostalgic vision which rose up before El Greco's eyes as, on a winter's day, he watched his brother laid into the earth of his land of exile.

CHAPTER

NINE

THE MAGIC

OF DISSOLVED

MATTER

THE picture known as "El Greco's Family" (Plate 69), in the Theodore Pitcairn Collection, Bryn Athyn, Pennsylvania, is a curious one for its time, unusual above all for Spain. It is, in fact, a *genre* scene. In the centre sits a young woman with a cushion on her knees, sewing or embroidering. An old woman, wizened and tight-lipped, is knitting a sock. Her staring, red-rimmed eyes are long-sighted but with failing vision, for she wears a pair of dark spectacles which have slipped down her nose. These spectacles over which she peers might well look ridiculous on an old woman's face, but her profile, with the nose descending in a straight line from the forehead, very like that of the sorrowing Virgin in "The Descent from the Cross," is still imposing despite the ravages of age. The young woman wears an embroidered dress: the sleeves showing under the mantilla are covered with braid and end in delicate linen frills round her thin wrists. On her head she wears a ruche of pleated lace —costly lace, its points standing out clearly against the dark background. The old woman's head is wrapped in a silk scarf painted with meticulous care.

Beside these women are two maidservants, their rank indicated by the plain scarves wrapped round their heads. One of them, holding a spindle, attentively follows the work of her mistress; the other leads a tiny child, barely able to stand, in a rich frock trimmed with lace, its chubby face almost smothered in a ruche of lawn, wide-eyed, and with a seemingly amused smile playing round its lips. The scene is dominated by a cat perched on high, the most extraordinary cat ever to find its way into a picture, with huge eyes, more akin to an Egyptian goddess than to a domestic animal.

Despite the minute care devoted to the painting of lace, silk, braid, and frills the picture dates from El Greco's last period. The fingers are now mere tentacles, long ribbons, or filaments. The painting is probably not entirely his own work; it must have been finished by Jorge Manuel. It seems to represent his son's family; the young woman sewing is probably Doña Alfonsa de los Morales, Jorge Manuel's wife. She bears a striking resemblance to the portrait of a woman with a flower in her hair in the Stirling Collection at Keir, Scotland—the only portrait of a woman signed by El Greco, with the exception of the miniatures belonging to the Hispanic Society of America. This portrait antedates the family group by several years. The long face with the regular features is a Spanish type *par excellence*. It reflects that purity of still-innocent beings who wait, patiently and almost without apprehension, for what life has in store for them.

This face is very close to the portraits at Fayum, as if El Greco had drawn from a common source of inspiration to paint a young woman of his time, her calm gaze reaching him across the centuries. Over her swept-up chestnut hair is a ruche of lace and pleated muslin, which also surrounds her neck and falls over her shoulders like spiky foam—a scarf exactly like the one worn by the young woman in the family group. Some flowers are pinned on top of her hair, under the lace, one of which is strangely flattened out like a star—perhaps a fully opened lily, the symbolism of which would accord with the purity of the features.

It is not known when Jorge Manuel married the beautiful Alfonsa de los Morales. But in March 1604—the year of Manusso Theotocopuli's death—Gabriel, El Greco's first grandson, was born; he is doubtless the baby boy who figures in the family group. The chubby, amused child must have suffered from the lack of stability in the life of this family, here depicted during a momentary spell of peace. A few years after his grandfather's death he lost his mother, and his father set up a new home, from which he subsequently fled to the safety of a monastery. Barely seventeen years had gone by since the picture which preserved his childish awkwardness for posterity had been painted, but El Greco's fame had already become so eclipsed that in the xenophobe climate of Spain the youth found a foreign name with barbaric consonants hard to bear. At the age of eighteen the grandson of Domenico Theotocopuli repudiated the illustrious name

67. Don Fernando Niño de Guevara. c. 1600

68. *St. Andrew and St. Francis, c. 1600*

69. *El Greco's Family. c. 1605*

70. St. Bernard. c. 1603

72. *Jerónimo de Cevallos. c. 1604–10*

71. *Portrait of an Unknown Man. c. 1586–94*

73. *Coronation of the Virgin. c. 1603–05*

74. *The Cleansing of the Temple. c. 1600*

75. *The Cleansing of the Temple (detail). c. 1605–08*

76. *St. Ildefonso. c. 1603–05*

and adopted that of his mother, with its more familiar ring, possibly the name of some petty nobility, and it was as Gabriel de los Morales that he entered the monastery of St. Augustine in Toledo.

Was the old lady with the spectacles in the picture Doña Jerónima de las Cuevas, his grandmother? Her imperious features hardly recall those generally ascribed to the woman El Greco loved. Excessive discretion on the part of his contemporaries seems to have formed a conspiracy of silence around her. There is no evidence to show whether she continued to play a part in El Greco's life. But neither does any death certificate record her disappearance. Only this figure of an old woman sitting amidst her family poses the riddle of an elderly presence in his home. Could it be Catalina, the sister of Alfonsa de los Morales? It is known that she was taken in by the young couple and that she stayed on with her brother-in-law after her sister's death, even when he remarried. The difference in their ages, however, seems too great. And the old lady emanates undeniable authority. That way of peering over her spectacles was a habit, lest anything escape her; she watches over the young wife and the servants and, though strongly marked by both physical and spiritual suffering, her mouth has that tight line customary amongst those who give orders and know how to exact obedience.

The documents which preserve such silence over Doña Jerónima make it possible, on the other hand, to reconstruct Jorge Manuel's eventful life in detail. He early became closely involved in his father's activities. As a painter, he was his father's creation. Only an innate lack of concern seems to have saved him from being crushed by so forceful a personality. His mediocre gifts are confirmed by his ceaseless work as a copyist. Just where one would expect to find a personal contribution his limitations are shown up by the harshness of his colouring and the aridity of his drawing. Contrary to his friendly, inconstant, dissolute nature, his art had a certain firmness, a sort of hard core which resisted his father's progressive dissolution of forms.

The charming little page in "The Burial of Count Orgaz" must have worked in the studio at a very early age. On him El Greco imposed this vocation, which was perhaps not his true one, not only through the work to which he trained him, but also through the confidence which he prematurely placed in him. Jorge Manuel was only nineteen when El Greco made him share in a contract which he signed for the reredos of the high altar in the royal monastery of Our Lady of Guadelupe. It was an important commission and the contract gave El

Greco eight years in which to fulfil it. The price, also most impressive, was 16,000 ducats. In this year of 1597, El Greco must have felt worn out or ill, for the contract stipulates that, in the event of his death, Jorge Manuel and Francisco Preboste should carry on the work alone. He himself does not in fact seem to have contributed to the altarpiece; apparently Jorge Manuel was entrusted with it later on, together with the sculptor Giraldo de Merlo as architect, for the pictures were executed by another painter.

In the succeeding years the collaboration between father and son became increasingly close and active. In 1603 they both worked on an altarpiece destined for the chapel of the College of St. Bernard in Toledo. In February of that year Jorge Manuel received from the college an advance of 200 reals for this reredos, which, it stated, "my lord is to do." It was he, however, who was entrusted with the architecture, for the next year he was requested directly to execute a new decorative section.

It must, indeed, have been hard to reconcile an architectural frame designed in a neoclassical style still very much dependent on its time with the spirit in which the painting itself was conceived. The figure of St. Bernard rises solitary against a vast expanse of sky, a turbulent sky of a dark, greenish blue, streaked with luminous clouds like forks of lightning. There is almost nothing else in the picture; only the saint and the sky, both of the same density, of the same plasticity, as if they were engaged in secret colloquy (Plate 70).

At the saint's feet is a very low horizon, just a strip of earth to support a naked foot; on the left, in a hollow of the ground, the spectral outlines of a town and in front of it a hilltop with a strange silhouette fringed with gold, very similar to that of Mt. Sinai, which had haunted El Greco in his youth. On the right, balancing this dreamlike landscape, three mitres stand on the ground, painted with that loving care which El Greco sometimes lavished on objects.

The saint rises straight up from the narrow strip of earth to a dizzy height, as if supported by the heavy folds of his brown robe and thickly knotted cord. High up, perhaps three quarters of the way, a hand projects from a wide sleeve, a very small, gaunt hand, to grip a staff on top of which blazes, as at the heart of a sunflower, the anagram of Christ. The upward sweep culminates in the saint's head, on a neck so long and thin that it is bent as if this head were too heavy for it. Yet the head is tiny, as if it were already vanishing into the clouds, beyond the reach of human eyes . . . one of the strangest heads El Greco ever gave to his extraordinary saints. Of all El Greco's solitary saints St. Bernard seems the most lonely, the most conscious of his isolation; his is a sadness on the verge of tears. Around his soaring figure Jorge Manuel constructed a frame with a very deep arch, two columns with pseudo-Ionic capitals, an entablature and a light pediment—a frame which, after the disappearance of the College of St. Bernard, was transferred to the convent of St. Isabella de los Reyes, whilst the picture hangs today in the Greco Museum.

The governors of the college must have been pleased with his work, for in 1607 they asked him to make a design for the college gate for which he received a special gratuity.

While collaborating with his father Jorge Manuel mostly took charge of the architectural side. He also received commissions on his own account; he drew up plans for the rebuilding of the Casa de las Comedias, the Toledan theatre in which Lope de Vega's plays were performed. His plans were accepted and his work proved so satisfactory that in 1605 it was proposed to present him with a silver tray. In fact it was as an architect that Jorge Manuel, aided by his constructive sense, was later to secure a modest position for himself. In him the Eastern heritage became diluted; he could only himself assert in his work as a copyist. His Western vision also endowed him with a stronger plastic sense, which was to show itself directly he escaped from his father's artistic tutelage. He was also initiated by El Greco into the art of sculpture and in the registers of Toledo he figures as painter, sculptor, and architect.

Jorge Manuel was twenty-six years old when his son was born. Since "The Burial of Count Orgaz" El Greco must have portrayed him several times. Some of his biographers have thought they recognized the boy's features in those of the sad youth who, as St. Martin, rides the big white horse. There is, in fact, a strong resemblance and the age would also be right, for Jorge Manuel was nineteen at the time when El Greco was working on the altarpiece for the chapel of St. Joseph. El Greco even introduced this beloved son into devotional paintings, sometimes to his clients' indignation. But he must also have painted one or more true portraits of him. The "Portrait of an Artist" in the Seville Museum is catalogued as being of Jorge Manuel. It was painted after 1600, the year in which Philip III ordered by decree the wearing of those large, pleated collars that the Spaniards mockingly called *lechuguilla* (from *lechuga,* meaning lettuce). Judged by its technique, the picture cannot date much later than the beginning of the century. The model looks older than twenty-six or -seven, which was Jorge Manuel's age at the time. There is no striking resemblance with the little page of "The Burial of Count Orgaz." The eyes, with their straight eyebrows, are more elongated in shape; the mouth is wide; the upper lip long and curving. Could the boy's straight nose have developed into that prominent, hooked nose of the painter in the Seville Museum? Opinions remain divided. One of his oldest and most authoritative biographers has categorically denied this attribution. Indeed only the psychological image could perhaps be identified with the personality Jorge Manuel had developed. It is the face of a sensual, weak, and perhaps also dissipated man.

Moreover there is in the Prado a "Portrait of an Unknown Man" of the same period, wearing the same *lechuguilla,* who is so akin in type to the supposed portrait of Jorge Manuel that he might be his brother. He has the same soft features, velvet eyes, sensual mouth, and carefully trimmed beard; in fact he is a typical Spanish beau.

Comparison with the earliest portraits reveals all that the Seville one lacks in spiritual qualities. One of the most moving is the signed one of an unknown man in the Prado (Plate 71). This might be the personification of intellectual Spain rather than the portrait of an individual. It seems redolent of a long past, of experiences mastered, of deep meditation, subtle thoughts, and eloquent words. Seldom has a picture expressed so many qualities which one would have thought untranslatable into plastic terms. It is as if El Greco had been inspired by a strange understanding, a sort of affinity between himself and his model.

The portrait is painted with virtuosity and at the same time with minute care. The flying brush strokes are clearly visible on the canvas, but, despite this rapidity, this sort of fury of execution, nothing is omitted, neither the reflection of the little white collar which frames the already tired cheeks, nor the streaks of silver on the temples, the irregular growth of the beard. This portrait, seemingly improvised, was in fact carefully prepared; the same model's head on a smaller canvas (in an American collection) may well have been a preliminary study for it, a study as searching as the finished picture.

Beyond the distinction of the features and an extraordinary pictorial craftsmanship, there is this depth of emotion, this transfiguration operating from within, which gives the picture its strange intensity, its suggestive, indefinable quality. Through the mobility of expression a temperament, almost a characteristic mentality, is revealed. It is the face of a disillusioned man, of a sensitive nature too often hurt and rebuffed; his yellow-grey eyes seem saddened by all the ugliness he has seen. But he is also a man who has mastered his suffering and overcome his bitterness. He has not withdrawn into himself or taken refuge in his dreams; there is something deeply attentive about him, an air of concentration; his mobile features are clearly those of a thinker. The "Unknown Man" in the Prado is perhaps El Greco's most characteristic portrait, the one which remains uppermost in the memory, like a man's most prominent feature, expressing what is best and most personal in him.

From the same period as the picture in Seville, or shortly after, to judge from the enormous *lechuguillas,* date two portraits in the Prado which could scarcely differ more from each other. Identity of costume and the same spiritual climate often give El Greco's portraits an air of resemblance, as if he had stamped them with his own personality. But the two portraits in the Prado prove the extent to which he could efface himself before his model.

In the signed "Portrait of an Unknown Man" a soft, fleshy face rests almost slackly on the enormous starched ruff. The relatively small eyes have a satisfied look, the chubby cheeks are familiar with the smile which still lingers on the greasy skin, whilst the kindly mouth forces itself to reflect the gravity appropriate to the sitter's age and probably to his high rank.

The portrait of Jerónimo de Cevallos, the great jurist (Plate 72), is hardly less grim than that of Niño de Guevara. Like the latter, it displays the oneness of the man with his office. The carriage of the head is so emphatic that it seems to support the enormous ruff rather than to be supported by it. This is a militant jurist who could equally well have been a leader of armies. He has a square head, high cheek-bones, irregular features under the thick, brushed-up hairs of the grey moustache, and a wide, bloodless, twisted mouth. The tired eyes are also uneven, the right one being smaller and placed higher, as if fixed immovably in its socket, whilst over the left one, larger and more open, the lid droops limply. This man is formidable; he seems one to curb his rages and cultivate his grievances. Cevallos was a poet and formed part of the Count of Mora's rival academy to which Lope de Vega belonged, and it is possibly a sign of the high esteem El Greco from now on enjoyed that it was he whom Cevallos commissioned for his portrait.

The pictorial technique is highly developed; apart from the huge ruff one might think it had been painted by an Impressionist. This technique, so far in advance of its time, so out of keeping with customary painting—especially portraiture, as smooth as enamel— shocked El Greco's contemporaries. When, a few years later, Pacheco, Velásquez's father-in-law, stopped in El Greco's studio during his artistic "grand tour," he waxed indignant over these conspicuous, almost independent brush strokes which, seen from close to, seemed to collide violently with each other. He called them "cruel smears" (*crueles borrones*). And, with the sovereign contempt of a man so rooted in the present that he believed the vision of his time to be eternal and all evolution to be at an end, he added: "I call that working to be poor." Yet, despite his disapproval, he suspected this sureness of touch to have been acquired at the expense of great labour, of desperately hard work, and he was astonished that anyone should seek, as El Greco did, to make a show of facility in order to conceal how much work had gone into a picture.

When Lope de Vega referred to a skilled artist whose pictures, seen from close to, were nothing but smears (*borrones*), he probably had El Greco in mind. But El Greco had reached that time in the life of a creative artist when the scandal he has raised and which has hampered him for so long becomes one of the factors of his success. The majority of the named portraits, those of the celebrities of his day and those of the illustrious dead, date from this late period of his life. Does the portrait held to be of the Blessed Don Juan of Avila, who died in 1569 (Greco Museum), belong to this category of posthumous evocations? Yet it bears no resemblance to contemporary engravings of the supposed model. The most recent biographers even doubt its attribution to El Greco. But this portrait contains signs of approaching old age—a sagging of the flesh, a puckering of the probably already toothless mouth, the brittle hair, and that air of frailty which comes with age and which is so characteristic of El Greco, as if he felt pity or even tenderness towards everything that deteriorates and decays.

One of these moving portraits of old men is of a canon—formerly in the Royal Roumanian Collection—and it has been thought that the name of Bosius can be deciphered on the open book before him; this would probably have been Jacopo Bossio, the Italian historian, who was agent for the Order of Malta at the court of Pope Gregory XIII and the latter's historiographer. The work was conceived as a state portrait, in the manner of the Italian portraits with which the sitter was familiar. El Greco painted him standing, his hands resting on a book, with a velvet cloak with a fur collar lending fullness to his figure, which one can guess to be already grown thin and wizened by age, an erect head and the gloomy, rather mistrustful look that must customarily have been his. The material in which he modelled this face, by means of rapid brush-strokes and splashes of light, seems friable and porous, but this dissolution of the flesh only serves to emphasize the sitter's indomitable spirit, its triumph over the passage of time.

Closely connected with these portraits are various replicas of a devotional picture, "St. Jerome as a Cardinal" (Plate 61), in the National Gallery, London, so much so that one version bears an inscription, added later, to the effect that it is a portrait of Lodovico Cornaro, painted at the Biblical age of a hundred, in 1566. This attribution seems to be based solely on the human quality of the picture, for it bears no resemblance to the authentic portrait of Cornaro in the Palazzo Pitti. El Greco seems to have had a particular liking for the Greek St. Jerome. He also painted him repentant in the desert and made several replicas of the old man clad in cardinal's purple, endowing him with a rank which did not exist in St. Jerome's time. He seems to have wanted to combine the dignity of great age with that of high office. In fact the old man's head rises from the pyramidal base of his mantle as if set on a plinth. He seems to have that legendary age which the inscription attributes to the so-called Cornaro. This long, narrow head with its flowing beard could be that of God the Father enthroned in the clouds, were it not so marked by the cares of this world. The skin has the patina of old ivory; it is so dry that it is broken up into deep wrinkles and furrows. One of his immensely long hands—hands far too young for the saint's age—lies heavily across the book, whilst the other attentively follows the lines of the text, tracing them curiously with the thumb instead of the forefinger. Although the old man's head and mantle seem worn threadbare, his spirit has resisted the disintegration of the flesh. The replicas are identical in detail, even down to the folds of the mantle and the shape of the fingernails, but the saint's expression varies, as if El Greco had essayed different forms of this spiritual triumph. In the picture in London sorrow weighs heavily on him, a sorrow moved to pity; there is a sort of perplexity in the frowning eyebrows, and the searching eyes grieve over the human weaknesses which an infinite understanding is ready to forgive. In the face of the "St. Jerome" in the Frick Collection in New York anger accumulates in the frowning brows and the eyes have the gloom of despair; their searching glance is that of a judge. In the version in the Bayonne Museum, showing only his head and shoulders, the eyes are so uneven, so haggard with grief, that the saint appears to squint; his look is that of an old man with failing sight, yet his still passionate spiritual vigilance is undiminished.

These aged saints El Greco painted mainly at a time when he himself was approaching old age occupy a special place in his work. In the beginning he had striven to withdraw his saints from their brotherhood with men, to break their bonds with reality. But those he now painted are very close to portraits of men who have reached the end of their lives, as if the death already lurking in him had abolished the frontier between mankind and the blessed. Nevertheless they remain unmistakably saints, no longer thanks to the light which destroys their earthly surroundings, nor to the dissolution or distortion of their substance, but through the intensity of their presence, their way of transgressing their earthly state through their sorrow or ecstasy.

Very characteristic in this connection is the "St. Ildefonso," painted for the Hospital de la Caridad at Illescas (Plate 76). He was a familiar saint in Toledo, a relative of St. Eugene, a disciple of St. Isidore, and metropolitan of the city. Amongst the traditions and legends so rife in Toledo there was the very popular and widely believed one of how St. Ildefonso, after having completed a book on the virginity of Mary, saw the Virgin appear before him with his book in her hand, to thank him for his work. It is the bursting of the miraculous into everyday life, a confrontation with the supernatural to be painted on two planes, with different lighting effects to make it plausible, and thus El Greco himself would probably have painted it when he first came to Toledo. Now, however, he proceeded with astonishing audacity, brushing aside both iconography and legend. There was no further need for the external manifestation of the miracle. It takes place in the heart of the saint himself. El Greco's means of expression had now become so great that he could pass over visible evidence to achieve credibility, confining himself to evoking an inner, disembodied vision. In fact he painted the saint set more firmly in his daily surroundings than are the subjects of his portraits. When painting the Grand Inquisitor in his house he merely used the room as a background. On the other hand, he painted St. Ildefonso in a Toledan interior showing every detail, in a room which was probably his own in the Marqués de Villena's palace and doubtless one similar to those of his friends. An intellectual's study is reproduced in loving detail, quite contrary to his usual method which proceeded by omission, by suppression of accessories in favour of emotional intensity. Before a classical archway stands a large desk covered with red velvet, the panels of which are bordered with a fringe and joined together by standard passementerie motifs in gold braid. The saint's armchair is covered with velvet and the pointed knobs on its back are carved and decorated with a gold fringe—a chair typical of the period. At the back is a door, half open as if in expectation of a visit, and a wall hung with tapestry. Even the door hinges can be seen. On the velvet tablecloth lie a writer's usual paraphernalia—clearly a well-to-do writer, accustomed to precious stuffs, chased objects, and to being waited upon: a large book, a penholder, an inkwell, a sandbox, a small bell and, under his hand, the bound notebook in which the saint is writing. He has this instant broken off; the hand holding the pen has paused in mid-air whilst the other holds down the pages of the notebook. In place of the Virgin herself there is a statuette on a carved bracket, a statuette also familiar to Toledan homes, a reproduction of the Virgin of the Sagrario in the cathedral. This traditional mediæval statuette holds a tiny baby in its arms instead of a book, as the legend prescribed. The saint, who has stopped writing, looks up from his work, but it is not towards the statue of the Virgin that he gazes. This emaciated and bloodless profile, painted as El Greco painted his portraits of old men, seems to radiate light. The movement of the head, the opening of the weary eyelids, the quivering of the nostrils and the mouth, which reflects great happiness despite its drooping corners, are of such intensity that they make one believe in the saint's vision and participate in the miracle.

The "St. Ildefonso" for the hospital at Illescas represents one of the summits El Greco was given to achieve. In the Virgin's holy panegyrist he painted the very image of a man inspired. Perhaps no other painting in the history of art has so vividly captured the creative process. The saint's eyes reflect the invisible, his ears are strained as if the solitude were speaking. His features, racked by the torment of creation, have become smooth in the light which illumines saints and poets. The Illescas picture is also called "St. Ildefonso Writing to the Dictation of the Virgin." In fact it represents that facility of the inspired, which comes to them from outside, that state of grace which crowns the ecstasy of saints and the supreme moments of a genius.

With the commission for the Hospital de la Caridad at Illescas El Greco came to a great turning point in his artistic career. The

church of Illescas also rose on the sacred soil of legend. The image
of the Virgin it sheltered was, according to tradition, the work of
St. Luke brought to Spain by St. Peter himself, to be given to the
first bishop of Toledo. From Toledo, St. Ildefonso was said to have
transported it to Illescas in 636, when he founded a convent there
under the patronage of the Virgin. The church, which had been destroyed under the Muslim domination, was rebuilt on the founding
of the hospital. In 1592 two architects were entrusted with the work,
following plans probably drawn up by Nicolas de Vergara, chief architect of the cathedral. In 1600 the building seemed so nearly completed that the image of the Virgin could be transferred to the new
church. On June 18, 1603, a contract for the reredos was concluded
with El Greco and his son. This contract stipulated that the reredos
should be completed by August of the following year. El Greco received 1000 ducats as an advance on the whole work, which was to
be submitted to the valuation of experts. Dr. Gregorio de Angulo
figures in this agreement as his guarantor.

El Greco and his son were to execute the architectural framework
and the sculptures of this reredos, the centre of which was to harbour
the miraculous image, and to be crowned by a picture representing
the Virgin of Charity. For this frame (Plate 77) El Greco chose a
wealth of ornamentation which broke with classical severity; three
half columns on each side, highly projecting, like the cornice with
its strong mouldings, Corinthian capitals, and a broken pediment.
Extending the reredos, niches were let into the walls of the presby-
tery framed in Doric columns and containing life-size statues of the
prophets Simeon and Isaiah. Under a wide arch there was intended
to be an elliptical picture representing the Coronation of the Virgin
flanked by two circular canvases depicting the Annunciation and the
Birth of Jesus. In this setting, more evocative of the agitated surfaces
of baroque architecture than of the rigid order of Spanish classicism,
El Greco painted his centrepiece, "The Virgin of Charity" (*Madonna
Caritatis*). It is hard to believe that this picture (Plate 78) belongs to
the same period as that of St. Ildefonso, destined for the cloisters of
the hospital and in fact painted two or three years later. Here the difference in the material clearly separates the reality from the vision.
In the middle of an undefined space the Virgin floats like an agitated
cloud in her luminous robe. Her arms spread out her wide protective
mantle, but her weary-looking hands fall back and the cloak opens
by itself, following the laws of that universe of El Greco's in which

the bodies of the saints, clothing, and clouds all have the same consistency and weight. On top of this elongated body, just like a cloud
which the wind has lifted high into the sky, is set a little face, far
smaller than either of the limp hands, with the strangest features a
human being could ever dream of as belonging to the Mother of God.
A dream face, in fact, at once clear and blurred, with a wide forehead
and half-closed protruding eyes, descending rapidly to an abnormally
narrow chin. This face is thus seen abruptly foreshortened by those
who, taking refuge below her mantle, raise hands clasped in prayer
and imploring eyes towards the Virgin. These men are portraits of
El Greco's friends and relatives who, mingled with little angels, crowd
into this warm and charitable shadow. A subsequent dispute revealed
that among those which he elected to place under the Virgin's protective mantle was a portrait of his son—and presumably one of his
friend Dr. Angulo as well.

To this vertiginous ascent of the Virgin of Mercy corresponds her
Coronation, in an ellipse which is a mere hole in the sky (Plate 73).
Like the artists of the baroque, El Greco adopted the viewpoint of
the spectator looking up in wonder. But, unlike those of the baroque,
he avoided giving shape to the heavenly spectacle by means of daring
foreshortenings, perspectives vanishing into depth, and that extension
beyond the frame which creates the illusion of ceilings and walls torn
open. There is no artifice or *trompe l'oeil* to give the spectator the
naïve sensation that he merely has to hoist himself up to that fictitious
opening in the wall to consort with the angels and the saints. El
Greco's little angels also jostle each other amongst the clouds and
take perilous dives into them as if into a whirlpool, but these *putti*
have never been formed into children's bodies, they are part of a wave,
they are all air and light; the angelic heads set between their wings
are bubbles rising to the surface, particles of iridescent cloud. The
Virgin, who raises her hands in prayer towards the crown which floats
above her, is seen from below, with her neck excessively elongated
and her forehead almost vanishing. The head of God the Father is
also sharply reduced; light and shade sculpture Christ's features as
summarily as those of distant faces; but these laws of reduction and
distortion incurred by distance have nothing in common with those
of earthly space and perspective. Within this ellipse heaven reigns
supreme. The most tangible things in the picture are the clouds, which
have parted like a curtain just enough to reveal the jubilation of the

celestial sphere. "Coronation of the Virgin" has in fact the suddenly arresting quality, the unforeseen shock, of a revelation.

The picture appears improvised. It seems to have been painted in a trance, under "dictation." Nevertheless, like all the work of a cerebral man in full control of his emotions, it is the outcome of mature reflection and calculation. This often minutely careful preparation of what appears to be joyfully haphazard creation or even capricious distortion is revealed in a particularly instructive manner in the picture in the Epstein Collection in Chicago, which was probably a preliminary study for the Illescas canvas and in which the same arrangement, the same shock of the unexpected, is to be found.

An heir to the Byzantine tradition of the static and immutable, El Greco had had to travel a long way before realizing that movement in an increasingly rapid rhythm corresponded to the fundamental change in artistic sensibility. The Byzantine saints who waited behind a curtain of incense for the approach of the faithful, their waiting through eternity barely interrupted by a hieratic gesture, had become alien to the anguish of El Greco's time, to that frantic desire for escape, knocking at the very gates of heaven. But this spiritual turmoil which baroque painting was to interpret through entangled bodies, contorted limbs, and muscles straining with gigantic effort became with El Greco discarnate matter, swept along by a whirlwind, as fluid as a wave, as slight as all that flies or floats, as unstable as if it were constantly to transform itself before our very eyes.

With El Greco light now became the principal agent of movement, and dramatic in itself. Hitherto it had been a dissolver of forms, a uniting or disuniting factor; from the Illescas paintings onwards it became his principal means of expression. He seems to have grown anxious, as if he felt that he would never achieve the ultimate message of his art. His pictures became a battle between light and shade, violence broken up into clots of radiant or opaque matter which attract or repel each other in an apparently arbitrary fashion to form, here the likeness of a face or the curve of an arm, there the indication of a hand or the flowing line of a robe. Through this new medium El Greco recomposed all the subjects which he had treated hitherto. The "Annunciation" of Illescas, inscribed in a circle, is a whirlwind; the angel is nothing but the crest of a wave or a rising column of air; it floats above the Virgin, who raises her tiny head towards it, blurred by the bright light of heaven.

"The Birth of Christ" is painted with the same luminous violence.

The Child's body is almost transparent; according to a recent biographer, it has already become the Host. Here the interpreter of the miracle, a figure El Greco was always fond of, is St. Joseph. He has become a giant clad in flashing blue, and he holds his large hands out towards the Child in a strange gesture showing astonishment and expectation confirmed at the same time.

The work for Illescas also ended in sordid disputes. The initial valuation was made in August 1605 by a painter and sculptor, both unknown, on the request of the hospital administrators. They assessed the price of the reredos at 17,576 reals and the material used for the gilding of the woodwork at 9226 reals. As always in wrangles over money objections of a different, mainly theological, nature were raised in order to disparage the work. One could easily imagine the administrators being repelled by El Greco's conception, but curiously enough they do not seem to have been shocked by what was daring and revolutionary in his vision. On the other hand, they highly disapproved of the intrusion of contemporaries into the immediate proximity of the Virgin and requested El Greco to suppress these portraits with *lechuguillas* and replace them with other figures "more seemly for such a place." To these objections and to a valuation too favourable to his clients El Greco replied through his lawyer, Dr. Narbona. But his own voice speaks haughtily through the legal statement. This valuation, he said, did not even pay for the gilding of the reredos and the chapel, although it was the best and most perfect to be found in Spain; and the architecture, sculpture, assembling, and painting were of the same outstanding quality, so that "each thing in itself is worth the sum at which the whole has been assessed."

All those who came into contact with El Greco never failed to stress his power of concise reasoning and the biting quality of his remarks, and the refutation of the valuers appointed by the hospital bears their stamp. It was evident, he said, that they had proceeded with biassed feelings, for, when called on to determine the value of a work, they had started to censure it, to find faults in it to the extent of raising objections to the presence of contemporaries beneath the Virgin's mantle, and it should be noted that they had found indecent something that was customary throughout the Christian world.

Neither side was prepared to yield. They appealed to the Council of the Archbishopric of Toledo, which appointed two other valuers, a sculptor and a painter; but these were in turn violently repudiated by the hospital as being in connivance with El Greco, for both were

Toledans and frequenters of his house. In September 1605 the hospital suggested another valuation for the reredos, amounting to a total of 48,934 reals, adding a whole list of imperfections. According to them, it was badly assembled, the paintings were placed in such a way that they were invisible, one of the prophets blocked the view of the altar from the place where His Majesty was accustomed to hear Mass, the chapel was gilded down to the floor, the angels above the high altar must be suppressed because of their shape, the statues of the Virtues, instead of being carved from massive wood, as agreed, were made of wood so light that it would rot within two years and (the hospital always reverted to its major grievance) El Greco's own son appeared in the picture with a very large *lechuguilla* amongst other known people. The Council of the Archbishopric of Toledo appointed two further valuers who, in their assessment of January 26, 1606, refuted the arguments of the Illescas authorities point by point. According to them, the tabernacle was very well made, of good wood which would last "in perpetuity," the prophet in no way impeded the view, the painting was good, done in oils with the "necessary craftsmanship," the portraits were "an honest thing" and as for the objection that they wore ruffs, this was the most natural way in which to characterize them as men in prayer, for otherwise they might be mistaken for saints.

This exchange of documents is revealing of the mentality of the time, but now and then one seems to catch an echo of the ironical and condescending voice of El Greco himself, and his happy gift for repartee. Thus, to the objection that the reredos should not have been gilded down to the ground, its defenders retorted that if the gilding had been stopped higher up, as was demanded, it would have created the effect of a sacerdotal vestment which descended no further than the knees.

Having thus disposed of the critics, the valuers assessed the whole reredos at 53,333 reals. The administrators of the hospital were vexed to see the experts side with El Greco and reproached them with being "intimate friends of the opposing party"; they appealed to His Holiness and the Apostolic See. To put an end to a dispute which threatened to become interminable, the Council of the Archbishopric decided to reduce the price to 42,000 reals. But the hospital was obstinate and appealed to the Chancellery of Valladolid. Before so much ill-will and bad faith the council decreed rigorous measures—another proof of the high esteem El Greco enjoyed in Toledo, where, according to the allegations of the Illescas authorities, most men were his intimate friends—and ordered all objects of value in the hospital church, including the Virgin's jewellery, to be seized and deposited with a notary in Illescas. Meanwhile the hospital once again voiced its objections to the portraits and sent its prior in search of a good painter in Madrid to replace the picture of the "Virgin of Charity." The case was heard by the Nunciature in Madrid, where El Greco was represented by Francisco de Preboste. The Nunciature, however, declared the litigation to fall under the jurisdiction of the government of Toledo, whose council was appointed to deal with it. The initial valuers, who had been the originators of the trial, were once again cited by the Illescas administrators, but, on their repudiation by El Greco, with the council's approval, the hospital sent for experts from Madrid, amongst whom was Pompeo Leoni. The trial now took a turn which threw the hospital into confusion. The arbitrator it appointed in the last instance valued the altarpiece at 784,878 maravedís. Final agreement was ratified in May 1607. The lawsuit had been long and painful for a man who referred in every document to his advanced age; he even alleged himself to be seventy-five years old, although he was only sixty-six at the time. The trial had wide repercussions: for the artists of the epoch, treated in an offhand manner by their clients, it had been the awakening of a new artistic conscience. One man alone, with all the daring of an innovator, had won his case against powerful authorities, thanks to the stubbornness and tenacity with which he had defended the autonomy of the creative artist. From the status of a mere craft painting passed to that of artistic independence. Every artist in Spain, even if he had never seen a picture by El Greco, knew that he was no longer isolated, that he could find prudent friends and impartial experts who would declare themselves in his favour. A precedent had been established. Every struggle against artistic servitude was to refer to it in the future. The case was quoted for the first time in a memorandum published in 1639 by various men of letters and legal experts in favour of the abrogation of taxes on works of painting. The famous Spanish biographer Palomino wrote at the beginning of the eighteenth century that all those exercising an artistic profession "must render eternal thanks to Dominico Greco" because he had broken the first lance in defence of the immunity of art with such success, and he added that all the legal disputes which had taken place since El Greco won his lawsuit had been based on the judgment given in the Illescas case. At Illescas itself they did not really grudge El Greco his victory. The notion of honour, so alive in Spain, had been enriched by that of artistic integrity. El Greco could have come out of this lawsuit with the notoriety of a disagreeable, ruthless litigant; but even in the eyes of the ecclesiastical authorities he acquired still greater esteem. The monastery of the barefoot Franciscans at Illescas ordered from him a picture of the Virgin for the altar dedicated to her. It also ordered two tombs for the monastery's founder, Don Gedéon de Hinojosa, and his wife, Doña Catalina de Velasco—two large marble monuments adorned with pilasters, and with statues, which have since disappeared, of praying figures in its niches.

Having reached this new phase in his artistic evolution which began with the Illescas paintings, El Greco reconceived the pictures he had done before and reshaped them in the light of his modified vision. He talked much of his advanced age, yet he worked as if he were on the threshold of a period in which he could still accomplish everything and achieve this, for him decisive, transformation.

In this spirit of a message still to be transmitted he again took up the subjects which had tempted him all his life. Like all those who have reached a high level in their existence, who have acquired great inner certainties, he glanced back at the life he had lived, with all that was incomplete and unfinished in it. He relived his youth, with all its influences, but also all its as yet unfulfilled promise, with particular intensity.

One of these subjects, which ran like a red thread through his creative life, was "The Cleansing of the Temple," as if Christ's struggle against the baseness and cupidity of men evoked personal feelings in him. The first repetitions of this subject probably date from shortly before the Illescas works (Plate 74). These pictures are revealing for what El Greco retained from the works of his youth and at the same time for the new elements he introduced, revealing also of his fidelity to himself, that manner peculiar to him of maintaining a certain constancy of form whilst radically changing its spirit. Taking up a picture once again after a lapse of more than thirty years, a more impatient artist would have, so to speak, rewritten the tale, altered the composition and the figures. Perhaps there was in this fidelity and constancy a nostalgia for the past; perhaps he only now realized how much it formed part of himself.

El Greco retained the oblong shape of the first version, which he had since used only rarely, as well as the setting. He made no attempt to transplant the tale on to Toledan soil; the scene takes place in Italy, with a vista through an archway of a street lined with palaces, under an Italian sky. The same figures are present, almost without exception: the young man seen from behind, warding off Christ's blows with his arm; another with a naked torso; the frightened woman; the old man seated in the foreground; the men gesticulating in argument; even the woman with the basket. The most astonishing thing about the picture is El Greco's ability to change it from within, so to speak, in the bearing of the figures and the spiritual intensity of the event. The scene is reduced and concentrated round the principal group; one's eyes no longer stray towards the high capitals but stop at the two symbolical reliefs in which El Greco, with his taste for stories inserted into the main plot, painted Adam and Eve driven from the garden, with the amazing diagonal movement of the angel, and Abraham's sacrifice. Formally and spiritually the figures are centred round the anger of Christ, who has descended into the midst of the crowd like a column of light, as if borne up by His flashing red robe. This new concentration on the essentials no longer tolerated indifferent onlookers such as the woman with the child, departing with her back turned to Christ; in the late version she is replaced by a woman bearing a basket on her head, advancing from the abridged colonnade, and she too is discussing with a broad gesture what has just occurred. The late version is also marked by the suppression of certain details. Gone are the beautiful naked legs and full bosoms; the draperies cover the shoulders and the bodies lose shape beneath their heavy, flowing folds.

"The Cleansing of the Temple" in its late version was a great success with El Greco's clients. Six good quality examples of it are known, apart from studio replicas. But, in spite of this success, El Greco knew that he had not yet reached a final solution. Perhaps he did not feel the recasting of the old material to be thorough enough or the drama sufficiently intense, for he took up the subject once again in the picture for the church of St. Ginés (Plate 75). In accordance with his taste for elongation he now changed the shape of the canvas; he also transformed the setting, accentuating, as he did in the Illescas altarpiece (to which this is closely related), its restless opulence, the projection of the columns, the piercing shadows, the impact of the light. The St. Ginés picture reflects that interest in architecture which was beginning to play a leading part in El Greco's work and which certain biographers have attributed to the influence or collaboration of his son. "When, in works attributed to El Greco, an architectural detail is unduly emphasized, one may suppose it to be a contribution made by Jorge Manuel," wrote Elizabeth du Gué Trapier. In letting tall niches into the surface of the walls and placing in them a reliquary or a statue El Greco seems to have reverted to the first versions; but there is a quarter of a century of radical change between the early statues, inspired by the school of Athens, and this nude, excessively elongated Adam. In fact this architecture, unlike that in his Italian pictures, was not a memory of things seen so much as an expectation of things to come, an anticipation of a future style.

Perhaps El Greco, stimulated by the presence of Jorge Manuel, had begun to dream again of building churches and palaces. He who had so readily juggled away space, deprived men and saints of any definite surroundings, and removed the earth from under their feet to place a vast sky overhead henceforward led them back into settings of his own time or into the palaces of his dreams.

His architectural anticipations culminated in the settings he gave to the pictures of "Christ in the House of Simon," pictures slightly later than the canvas of St. Ginés and, in fact, its logical conclusion. These pictures give some idea of the goal he was pursuing, of what he would have liked to achieve had he constructed interiors and chapels. In one version, in an American private collection, he set the scene in a room in Toledo, with a ceiling richly ornamented in the *mudejar* manner. Another, in the Winterbotham Collection at Burlington, Vermont, U.S.A., which apparently bears traces of repainting, is the dream of a reconciliation between East and West, which he had hinted at by placing that Arabic ceiling above Christ's head (Plate 79). Simon's guests are gathered under the portico of a strange, circular building. The arch under which the table is placed rests on plain pilasters with rather flat cornices, as if they were drawing back before the opening of the archway on to the fantastic. In this vista a classical portico stands next to an Oriental dome crowned by a tall minaret. Through a strange symbolism to which El Greco alone held the key the Crescent floats high in the sky just above Christ's head.

Apart from the strangeness of its architecture the picture is typical of El Greco's new purpose. The subject itself occurs very late in his work. Perhaps he only took it up in place of another, more grandiose one which, oddly, he never tackled. Of all the moments in the drama of Christ there was one amongst those most frequently painted in Italy of which no sufficiently plausible version is known to be credited to El Greco's hand: "The Last Supper."

Did he feel the tragedy of the betrayal to be beyond his means of achievement? Yet in the feast in the house of Simon the drama is already present in all its intensity; it breaks out, both when compressed within four walls and under the open portico. A whirlwind of emotion spins round the small table, which is the only centre of stability, a break of emptiness in the midst of violence. And this, moreover, is all it is. It is not a real table; never could fourteen guests have found room round it, just as, with their gigantic bodies, they could never have stood up without striking the ceiling or even touching the high curve of the arch. On the faces assembled under the portico falls a light (apparently from above) as violent as a hailstorm, rescuing a half profile from the shadows, picking out a head on an overlong neck, animating a glance, or throwing up Judas against the darkness. El Greco painted Judas as a giant in the foreground; across the table a dialogue is held between him and Christ, who, like Judas, has raised one hand with the palm turned outward, while the other rests on the table with the third finger stretched out in a characteristic gesture. But these are no longer entirely hands; neither are those of the disciples, who take up their Lord's dialogue with his adversary in chorus— sketchy gestures, finger tips suspended in the air or, rather, question marks made from the thinnest of fingers, which sometimes also act as hyphens. The disintegration of the human element into simple signs merely emphasizing the basic features, into sketches of movement as symbols of revolt, here clashes with the solidity of the walls or the sharp outline of the cornice. But this contrast seems to form part of El Greco's new pictorial conception, in which reality is only retained sometimes as a frame and sometimes in accessories. In these two versions he varied the recollections of the earthly; the table set under the *mudejar* ceiling is strictly bare; several objects are scattered on the one in Burlington, but there is only one plate and one knife. This detail illustrates how far El Greco's contemporaries, although accustomed to the realism of their still-lifes, were ready to accept a single plate and knife for fourteen guests, just as they adapted themselves to disembodied saints.

This abandoning of form everywhere where it is not indispensable to interpret the scene demands an effort on the part of the spectator to supplement what has not been painted, just as a listener has to supply the meaning of a significant silence. El Greco consciously appealed to this sensibility of the onlooker; he does not even seem to have envisaged the possibility of its absence. When he spoke of his own liberated vision, he did so with contempt for all those who were careful to paint everything, to say everything, to create the illusion of reality. Several years later, when Pacheco came to see him, El Greco was to surprise him as much by his attacks on classical art as by his criticism of Aristotle. Through Pacheco's vague vocabulary and the summary indications he gave of this important conversation El Greco's conception takes shape, at least in part. For Pacheco the real success in painting was to create that illusion of three-dimensional form which he called relief. "Many excellent painters," he said, "have done without beauty or grace, but none without relief." He admired Michelangelo, Caravaggio, and Ribera first and foremost, and it was with their plastic qualities in mind that he asked El Greco which he found more difficult, drawing or colouring. Colour, replied El Greco without hesitation—to the astonishment of his interviewer, although he stated resignedly that such an opinion was not surprising in a man as accustomed to paradoxes as El Greco. He was, however, deeply shocked when, talking of Michelangelo, whom he regarded as the father of painting, he heard El Greco say that "he was a good man but he couldn't paint."

In his creative certainty El Greco had thrown off the hold of Michelangelo which had weighed so heavily on him in his youth. Perhaps his reconciliation with his own past could only come about when he had overcome his hate-love for Michelangelo and freed himself through friendly contempt.

Amongst the works which fully epitomize El Greco at this time is the "Christ on the Mount of Olives" (Plate 80). The subject appears only late in his work, as if he had not cared to risk it until quite sure of his means. He tried it in several compositions, one oblong and another upright, adopting the latter as the final solution. In accordance with the growing importance he attached to colour the canvas is a fairyland vision. It is night and heavy sleep has overcome the Apostles. From an opaque background a beam of light has strayed like the tail of a comet to cast a luminous belt round Jerusalem. But in the shadow which encompasses the three sleeping Apostles colours burst out like yellow and red flames darting through the ashes. The Mount of Olives has become an enchanted garden.

The splendour of the colouring so dominates the picture that one has to ignore it in order to realize the skill of the composition, following El Greco's own private rules. The three crouching Apostles are set in a half ellipse, forced into it, their bodies (in so far as they have any) compressed; the heads of St. John and St. Simon almost touch, whilst St. Peter sleeps with his arm arched above his head, as no man ever slept. An invisible wind has bellied out their garments like sails; the folds rise up, curve after curve, in a series of truncated ellipses towards the one which engulfs them. But this calculated rhythm is offset by a rectangle which El Greco set above the ellipse in the manner of a frame dividing the two zones, a frame composed of bare branches with a few sparse leaves, a freshly cut tree trunk and an olive branch at Christ's feet, of the same symbolic value as the ivy, emblem of fidelity, beside St. Peter. They are painted with such virtuosity that they alone seem to represent reality in the picture.

In comparison with the size of the Apostles the scene above diminishes abruptly, as if set at a high altitude. Christ has fallen to His knees before the angel approaching with the chalice, and the folds of His red robe are like a whirlpool of blood around Him. As if thrust by an invisible wind, He sways towards the angel, which is nothing but a white cloud borne on large wings, the bowing of a far too small head, a vehement gesture holding out the chalice.

The Mount of Olives, with its strange peak, pointed and bare, to which just a few tufts of flowers still cling beside a thin, naked branch, recalls the Mount Sinai familiar in Byzantine imagery. In the far background El Greco, with his love for subsidiary tales, painted a minute and spectral group of soldiers advancing with lighted torches.

This late composition was at once accepted in all its mysterious intensity. The numerous replicas of it testify to its success, at least eight being known. Some of them are still in the churches and chapels for which they were painted, proving the extent to which the faithful of that time comprehended and felt close to this cloudlike angel and this Christ swaying like a blood-red reed in the violence of His prayer.

Storms are frequent over Toledo. One day lightning blazed through El Greco's studio, but it did not strike.

Of his life the most important events are unknown; in fact nothing is known of his great joys or sorrows. But henceforward he was famous, and there was now a poet at hand to marvel over this mercy from heaven. In a sonnet "On the Lightning Which Penetrated an Artist's Room," Fray Hortensio Paravicino hymned the wrath of Jupiter, who, envious of "the larger life" with which El Greco's brush challenged him, wished to destroy the studio; but the lightning recoiled, dazzled, before the colours illuminating the walls.

A stormy sky was as familiar to El Greco as the lightning which slashed the clouds and with which his saints in ecstasy seem to hold secret colloquy. Of the city he saw from his windows, he knew every curve of riverbank, every tuft of tree, every hollow, just as he knew every rising street and every building, from humble roofs to proud watchtowers on the city walls, or the steeples pointing to the sky. This landscape was not blurred by daily familiarity; habit had blunted neither his keenness of vision nor his affection: these, on the contrary, grew even more intense with the years.

One day, perhaps the same day that Paravicino was visiting him, he saw Toledo under a stormy sky and at the same time illuminated by an invisible sun. The drama in the sky formed one with the city. Was it a real storm he painted, an outward and fleeting phenomenon? Or did the landscape itself give birth to this heavy sky with its jagged clouds, to satisfy the need of a mysterious unity? As in a portrait dominated by some characteristic expression, with the features subordinated to that factor which best reveals a human being, Toledo was painted from within, in a revelation of its own particular quality (Plate 83). El Greco was telling Toledo's story, unfolding it in detail. But he did not simply relate what he saw, with its accidentals or accessories, common to every city. He did not describe it as an eyewitness, but as a novelist, who transforms his experience into a work of art. The "View of Toledo" was a deliberate choice made perhaps according to the degree of his affection, certainly according to the laws of an order which he imposed on the rolling landscape. This order was so powerful that El Greco adopted it even in the shape of his canvas. He who preferred upright pictures and who could easily have fitted the soaring city into a tall frame, spread it out with its hills, groves, coiling roads, and zigzagging paths, as if seeking to imbue it with the mighty breath of a nature lying still untamed at its gates. Patient historians have pored over this tale of Toledo to discover all that El Greco failed to note in it. They have observed that the tower on the Alcantara bridge, on the city side, was square and not octagonal as he painted it; that the river does not twist so sharply to the right; that instead of the groves halfway up there are only sand and tussock. They have also said that, from the city's wealth of buildings El Greco selected the castle of San Servando, the Alcázar, the cathedral, perhaps the palace he inhabited and that Bridge of Alcantara he so often crossed, at the expense of the rest. But these patient studies contribute neither more nor less to this hymn to the city than do philological observations to the music of a poem. El Greco painted Toledo as he painted his holy pictures; his approach hardly differed at all from his customary one at that time as seen, for example, in the drama of Christ on the Mount of Olives. The city rises from a base of superimposed ellipses, like the folds in the robes of the sleeping Apostles. It rises up as if borne on the crest of a wave. The hills are in fact akin to waves, with their shadowy hollows, the transparent light on their ridges; and the stone of the buildings is like grey foam which turns green in the shade and gleams in the light. Both the soil and the buildings have the specific weight of fluidity of foaming water, thus giving a very real city, perched on its hills, the quality of an aquatic spectacle. Yet the picture contains everything a contemporary visitor might have taken away as his impression of Toledo—the tawny earth showing through the brilliant grass, the slate-coloured rocks tinged with mauve, the Arabic or Gothic character of the buildings. But in spite of this exact material

likeness the city is just as disembodied as El Greco's saints, notwith-
standing their braided and embroidered robes. The buildings and towers might be made of spun glass; they have that quality of cut glass
which is not entirely transparent but one of light imprisoned. Like his
devotional pictures, the view of Toledo is in the process of evolution.
It forms and dissolves before one's eyes; the luminous green of the
hills rises up to assault a tragic sky; pointed up by its shadows, it ebbs
and flows back and forth. Somewhere through a rent in a cloud light
filters down, to be the victor in the drama being played out.

It is through this movement imposed on an essentially static view
that El Greco conveyed that feeling of mystery peculiar to Toledo,
its own special magic. But, apart from the transformation he worked
on the spectacle of a city, the subject itself was a strangely daring one
for its time. In those last years especially El Greco multiplied evocations of Toledo in his pictures; they are like snatches of a confession
scattered throughout his works and, with advancing age, they become
as poignant as farewells.

But these fragments of things seen were customary among the artists
of the time, who liked to endow the men or saints they painted with
something of their own memories or dreams, but always as a setting,
always in the background, subordinated to the main theme. In the
best cases this background has a suggestive quality; it is the extension
of a state of mind or the echo of some emotion. Landscape *per se* was
not yet a subject for painting. For El Greco to have chosen it as such
reveals a lifelong love of nature, probably innate, bound up with that
taste for solitude often developed by highly sociable beings. This love
was not, however, an isolated trait peculiar to him. A revaluation of
nature had also taken place in literature. The Spanish mystics exalted
life in places far removed from human activity. In his *Spiritual
Canticle* St. John of the Cross sang of solitude as a refuge for wounded
love and a guide towards the heights of communion with God. He sang
of the mountains, the wooded valleys, the babbling streams, and the
whispering of the amorous breezes. The anguish of the age, the over-
whelming responsibilities of a life becoming materially ever more difficult and morally ever more disturbing, set up a vast movement of
escape towards the peace of renunciation. Throughout the reign of
Philip III a growing number of men and women turned to the Church
as a refuge and sought peace in monasteries and convents.

The number of hermits increased considerably throughout Spain.
Men who had enjoyed every worldly honour and success withdrew to

wildernesses where nature, though harsh, with freezing winters and scorching summers, seemed to them better than the best of men.

El Greco himself also once painted a picture in praise of holy solitude (Museo de Valencia de Don Juan, Madrid), a strange picture exalting the hermit life of the Camaldulians, whose landscape has been thought to depict the valley of Batuescas, dear to the hermits. It apparently belonged to the brother of Niño de Guevara, the Grand Inquisitor, and is not unlike a votive picture, commissioned perhaps to render thanks for a spiritual healing.

Glorification of the hermit's life was an inspiration alien to El Greco. He loved cities. He loved Toledo. Thanks to this love the first autonomous landscape in the history of art from which men are absent happened to be an urban one. The deliberate audacity of El Greco's choice is typical of this period in his creation. He was at this time reconsidering his whole work and subjecting it to revision. Like so many who have worked hard and with overexclusive concentration, he realized all he had missed, all that was still lacking in his art. Perhaps, harassed by material needs, he had concentrated too much on exploiting successful themes; perhaps he had not felt sufficiently sure of himself to tackle new subjects. At an age when the creative vision often begins to fail El Greco's horizon extended and acquired new vistas. There came a deepening, a remoulding of what he had already stated, accompanied by a diversity which he had never had before, by a renewal, as if he were still on the threshold of life. But there was also the impatience of an old man anxious to express himself in the fullest possible way, which incited him to break through the narrow circle of his inspiration. Certain subjects he tackled at this time were as much an advance towards the future as a return to and a reconciliation with his own past. Amongst the memories of Rome which in the meantime had lost their last taste of bitterness, there powerfully arose one which in his youth had been a focal point of artistic interest—the tragedy of Laocoön. Ever since the antique statue had been reclaimed from the soil of Rome in 1506, it had been a source of inspiration for generations of artists. Instead of waning, interest in it grew even greater as men lost their inner certitude and their peace of mind crumbled away. Laocoön's torment seems to have acquired a new significance, to have become a reflection of their own anguish. Bramante had already invited sculptors to present a wax model of the re-erected statue which was to be cast in bronze; characteristically it was a Spaniard, Alonso de Berruguete, who won this competition. François I himself had been so impressed by the antique group that he had sent Primaticcio from Fontainebleau to Rome to reproduce it in bronze.

The "Laocoön" painted by El Greco was the only one of those mythological subjects so popular in Italy he ever evoked (Plate 81). But doubtless such themes were not in demand in Spain, at any rate not this legend as he saw it, for the inventory drawn up after his death mentions four replicas, two large and two small, which do not appear to have found purchasers. Seldom has a classical fable been treated in a spirit so alien to its subject, almost in direct opposition to its traditional plastic meaning. If El Greco still recalled the group he had seen in Rome (Plate 82), the memory had become transposed, the impression assimilated and reshaped in his own manner. He retained nothing of the sculptural composition, of the bodies welded together in their agonized embrace, bound by the serpent's coils into a terrible unity. Nor did he retain that feeling of Greek tragedy, of man defying fate with his utmost strength. It is the work of a painter who had never experienced the intoxication felt by artists of the Renaissance as they saw antique statues emerging from the soil.

It was typical of El Greco's almost anti-plastic feeling that, on a large canvas, he broke up a group conceived as a pyramid and dissolved its confused entanglement into several distinct elements. The protagonists in a common drama are as isolated as possible, each facing his destiny alone, in the presence of the gods, who are barely interested spectators. It was also typical of El Greco that he gave his Laocoön the head of an old man, taken, incidentally, from the same model as he used for his St. Peter. This old man no longer struggles like the Laocoön in the group from Rhodes; he has fallen like a felled tree trunk and the serpent coils round him so loosely that it scarcely seems formidable at all and it is hard to see the mortal danger lurking in its tiny head. This great, fallen body is akin to the "Dying Gaul," but still more to the river gods which inspired Michelangelo's figures adorning the Medici tombs. Italian memories seem to have flooded over El Greco as he painted this picture, and to have led to one of Laocoön's sons, already dead, being painted head down, and to the other, still standing, being given a body closer to a martyred St. Sebastian than to a pagan youth. The disembodied mythological deities seem far from gods taking revenge for an insult. In El Greco's composition the naked youth seen from the back plays that part of interpreter which he so often used in his holy scenes. The disparate elements which go to make up the picture are, however, united according to the laws which at that time governed El Greco's compositions, his own peculiar rhythm. The space between the waving verticals of the two standing figures on the right and the spiral of Laocoön's struggling son on the left is filled with broken curves, with movement leading in sharp zigzags from one apparently isolated body to another. The landscape in the background repeats this jerky rhythm. Although El Greco, faithful to the legend, introduced a minute Trojan horse into this background, he did not scruple to show the whole of Toledo behind this scene of Laocoön's death, or, rather, a selection of the city's buildings made according to his own preferences. Here can be seen the Bisagra Gate with its escutcheon; the Alcázar, the tower of San Tomé church which sheltered his "Burial of Count Orgaz"; the city walls; and the calm, undulating hills. The turbulent sky is governed by the same rhythm and the colouring adds to this movement, to give the picture its strange unity. The clouds are flesh-tinted, whereas the young gods seem to float away like clouds.

This search for a new rhythmic arrangement, like the adoption of new themes, shows an activity in El Greco defying the exhaustion of an already worn-out organism. A Spanish historian was later to note what tradition had passed down to him: El Greco was never idle, even in his old age. This activity was not a blind groping, a confused advance towards outlets as yet unexplored. Everything that seems arbitrary or enigmatic in his art, especially in his late works, was, on the contrary, the calculated result of long meditation and formed part of a carefully elaborated system. It is only at first sight that El Greco appears spontaneous, driven by his inspiration, improvising according to the whims of creative joy. His work reveals how cerebral a painter he was and a belated witness confirmed this fact. When Pacheco came to see him about this time, he was dazzled by his keenness of mind, psychological insight, and swift repartee. He realized from his talk that these flashes of eloquence formed part of a whole carefully constructed system of thought. At the end of the conversation Pacheco concluded: "He was a great philosopher."

El Greco was not content to dazzle his contemporaries with his conversation; he perpetuated the system he had elaborated in writing. Following the fashion of the day, he wrote treatises on painting, sculpture, and architecture. These would have provided the key to his work, but, with the darkness which soon after engulfed him, his manuscripts did not seem worth preserving for posterity. The inventory made by his son mentions "five manuscript books on architecture, one with drawings," but no treatise on painting. However, the haste with which Jorge Manuel made this inventory may well explain such a summary account.

To the multiplying testimonials of these last years could be added a portrait, to complete the image of this man—a portrait believed to have been painted by El Greco of himself (Plate 84). Jorge Manuel's inventory indeed mentions "a portrait of my father in an ornate frame." The attribution of this portrait in the Metropolitan Museum (formerly in the Beruete Collection) is based on a long tradition. There is also, as Camón Aznar has perceptively observed, a note of intimacy in the picture, as if it depicted someone very close to him. But is this sad, dejected face really the image of a great man? These round, staring eyes under arching eyebrows, almost stupefied, with their limpid but wandering gaze—can they be those of a painter who followed so very personal a path? The dominant expression is that of a highly garrulous man who has not yet finished telling his tale of woe and feeling astonished over what has happened to him. His high, pointed forehead is bare, his temples narrow and sunken; his sharp nose descends to a wide, half-open, moistly gleaming mouth—the mouth of a man who talks easily and too much. Rarely can the phrase "a speaking likeness" be applied more aptly. Could El Greco's psychological portrait coincide with this old man's revelations? His most recent biographers have questioned this identification. To the spiritual improbability is added one small material fact. The costume dates from before 1600. The technique seems to indicate the same. But in about 1590 El Greco was only fifty years old, whereas the sitter looks much older. Recent biographers suggest that it could be a portrait of his brother. There is, however, little in common between the delicate features of the old man with the earring generally considered to be Manusso and this man, so eloquently disconsolate. It was doubtless some friend of El Greco's, who often looked at him with those candid and anxious eyes.

This portrait in the Metropolitan Museum only deepens the mystery surrounding El Greco's true face. Is it to be found in the nobleman with his hand on his breast? Or in the captain in "The Martyrdom of St. Maurice"? It seems psychologically certain—and it is psychological certainties which often prove decisive in El Greco's work—that he painted himself in the guise of one of the Apostles, in the series on which he was then embarking. The "St. James the Less" in the former Herzog Collection in Budapest (Plate 85) is thought to bear his features. It is unmistakably the head of an Oriental. And the keenness of the gaze, inward-looking and strangely dreamy, credits it as a portrait of El Greco, above all in view of the pride reflected in the face, that mouth expressing a contemptuous superiority, which is believed to have been typical of him. All the supercilious remarks noted by his contemporaries, either voicing the high opinion he had of himself or calculated to impress them, would seem natural to that sensuous lower lip, firmly compressed beneath the upper one, drooping with disdain.

Another of El Greco's biographers has thought to recognize him in the portrait of "St. Luke" in Toledo Cathedral (Plate 86). Indeed it would be no surprise to find him portraying himself in the guise of the painter of the Virgin. The two attributions do not contradict each other. A gap of several years—perhaps a decade—separated the two paintings; the two heads have the same elongation, the same high forehead, long aquiline nose, and protruding lower lip. St. Luke's eyes are wide open and uneven, as if he had a squint. But they differ above all in expression. St. Luke seems to be deep in some melancholy dream; his head is bent, not as if gazing into the distance, but as if listening. The Apostle identifies himself by means of a large, open book turned ostentatiously towards the spectator, like Giulio Clovio proudly exhibiting his masterpiece. Similarly to El Greco's old Croatian friend, it is as a miniaturist, as an illuminator, that St. Luke displays the miraculous image on the page of his book facing some text. The image in itself is strange. El Greco must have recalled those Byzantine icons which claimed descent from the first image of the Mother of God painted by the Apostle. But this veiled Madonna, with the Child giving the benediction in her arms, is more akin to the Sienese Madonnas than to those of Byzantine iconography. The most characteristic aspect of the picture is, however, the gesture of St. Luke, who holds the brush as if he had only just finished painting the image. Even if El Greco did not portray himself in the guise of this Apostle, he surely gave him his own gesture and perhaps even his own hands. The saint holds the thin brush as if it were a pen; just, in fact, as St. Ildefonso is holding his when the miraculous inspiration interrupts his writing. And if St. Luke is not El Greco himself, he at least reveals the manner in which El Greco painted, like a door half opened into his studio.

The cycle of Apostles to which these two presumed self-portraits belong formed part of the progressive widening of his vision. He painted one or another of the Apostles throughout his life. One day, however—encouraged perhaps by some commission—he decided to paint a whole cycle of the Twelve Apostles with the Saviour. From the viewpoint of financial success the idea proved excellent. At least nine different series are known, painted down the years as if in response to urgent demands. For El Greco these disciples of Christ represented twelve states of mind, twelve spiritual attitudes, twelve variations of the same surrender to a mission. The one common element in these imaginary portraits is their total abandon. Each figure reveals an inner debate, the form of which varies according to his age or temperament. This debate has been going on for a long time and the portraits El Greco painted are its final outcome. Each Apostle is taken, not at the outset of the revelation made to him, but after a time of acclimatization to it, after a spell of living in enlightenment. They are no longer entirely human beings; their features are transfigured, dissolved, adapted to something greater. They come to us from afar, bearers of their own personal truth, but since that truth is one alone, they are in a sense brothers, with that similarity of beings deeply marked by a common experience. Young or old, light came to them in the same hour.

In El Greco's work the cycles of the Apostles represent the successive stages of his own evolution, like milestones along his road. They spread out over approximately twenty years of his life. Several series have been dispersed. They differ in size; some of them depict only the heads and shoulders of the Apostles, others are done in half length, doubtless according to the clients' financial means. The first ones date from about 1590, or perhaps a little later.

A subject so circumscribed would appear to leave little scope for variation. Yet El Greco introduced into these pictures a diversity and variety, not only of spirit, but also of attitudes, attributes, and colouring, so much so that from cycle to cycle the same saint appears each time as a different man.

Each series was naturally determined by its focal point, the picture of the Saviour. Two of the earliest versions are the representations of Christ in the Galleria Parmeggiani at Reggio nell'Emilia and in the Prado (Plate 87). This *Salvator Mundi* clearly recalls that of Titian, but in a manner typical of El Greco's way of remembering things in recession, superimposing one memory on another, as in a palimpsest where the old texts appear ghostlike under the new. Christ's features might still be called Venetian, up to a point, were they not enclosed within hieratic rectangles or extended rhomboids. The square shape of the halo is repeated within the frame of long, flowing hair by the

pointed forehead, high cheekbones, and cheeks tapering sharply down
to the chin. This Saviour could by Byzantine with His emphatic
angles and hieratic gesture of benediction were not His features slightly
asymmetrical, His eyes uneven, His nose twisted to one side, with all
the touching, profoundly human quality inherent in this lack of
symmetry. This Christ is calm and sad, with that ancient sorrow,
fostered by all the sufferings of mankind, by the cruellest agonies of
expiation, but which has already risen above its capacity to suffer, for
only the faintly irregular mouth droops in pity.

The Saviour in Toledo Cathedral (Plate 88) shows how far El
Greco had advanced within the space of a few years. This Christ is
Spanish in His sombre majesty, rising up in the certainty of salvation
to give His benediction to the world. In this spirit He is closer to the
Byzantine Christ, triumphant against a golden background, than, for
example, the bewildering Saviour from the collection of the Duchess
of Parcente, more akin to the one at Reggio. But the pictorial quality
obliterates any possible remnant of a traditional heritage in this
Christ. El Greco's brush attacked the canvas with an almost furious
energy, splashing streams of colour all over it; with one broad stroke
it emphasized the fall of the flashing green mantle, enclosed in one
sweeping curve the folds piled up on the arm with their silver reflections, and charged violently over the red robe with its white highlights.
The novelty of this technique corresponds to the revision of the traditional gestures. Like His predecessors, the Saviour of the first series
rested His folded hand on the globe. The *Salvador* of the cathedral
lays His very elongated hand on a globe placed extremely low down,
or, rather, lets it fall like an object drawn to the centre of gravity; and
this gesture, with the thumb held in close to the opened fingers,
seems to reassure this little globe: protected by His long palm, no
harm can come to it.

Toledo Cathedral contains a complete cycle of Apostles painted
probably around the year 1604 in the same Impressionist technique.
The Apostles pursue their colloquy with Christ with eloquent, Oriental
gestures. Some are born talkers, like St. Batholomew, who brandishes
his book as evidence of the Scriptures, his palm turned outward, the
thumb spread out widely from the mobile fingers which seem to
enumerate his arguments, in the manner of every Greek who ever carried on a debate in a public square; his fleshy mouth is still chewing
over his last words, chewing them with difficulty, as if twisted in the
effort. Some are more firmly earth-bound than others, like "St.

78. *The Virgin of Charity. c. 1603–05*

77. *The Altar at the Hospital de la Caridad, Illescas.*
c. 1603–05

79. *Christ in the House of Simon. c. 1608–14*

80. Christ on the Mount of Olives. c. 1608–14

82. *Laocoön. 40–20* B.C.

81. *Laocoön. c. 1606–10*

84. *Portrait of a Man (self-portrait?). c. 1599–1609*

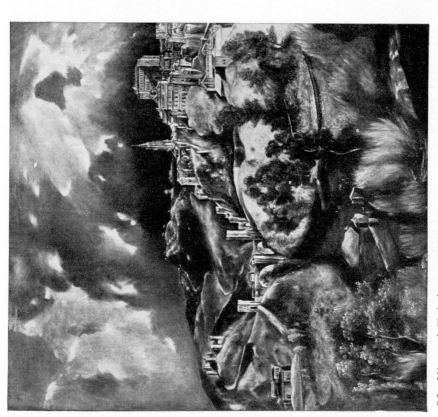

83. *View of Toledo. c. 1609*

86. *St. Luke. c. 1604*

85. *St. James the Less. c. 1595–99*

88. *The Saviour. c. 1604–09*

87. *The Saviour. c. 1596–99*

90. St. Bartholomew. c. 1604–09

89. St. John the Evangelist. c. 1604

Thomas," with his robust neck, impassioned head, and eyes consumed with their own fire, and with his broad hand raised in an immemorial gesture of doubt. There are also the resigned ones, like "St. Andrew" in his old age, as if imprisoned behind the bars of his immense cross. There are those whose faces are lined by contemplation, spreading out their hands as if allowing everything to slip through their fingers.

In the first rank of these master dialecticians is one of El Greco's most remarkable creations, "St. John the Evangelist" (Plate 89). There is something like affection in his manner of painting this young Apostle, a feeling of wonder at the most precious substance of which this almost androgynous youth is made. The saint's face is drawn in a sharply pointed triangle; his wide forehead stands out clearly under the heavy mass of dark, curly hair; his long nose descends in a straight line, as in a Greek statue; his mouth is small, like the mouth of a young girl, tremulous in expectation. In his right hand he holds a magnificently chased gold chalice in which writhes a winged dragon, which also looks like the work of a master goldsmith. In the splendid version in the Prado, El Greco placed the saint before a stormy sky, against which his green garments stand out, with russet tints like autumn leaves and a rose-coloured cloak shot with silver light.

Several years passed, while other cycles of the Apostles were painted, scattered examples of which are known. On reaching the last years of his life El Greco painted a cycle probably destined for the church of the Hospital of Santiago, whence it comes. This cycle was unfinished. It is painted as if the artist were in a great hurry to complete this last revision of an important work, but also sure of himself, so fully in command of his craft that he could dispense with drawing, to splash his Apostles directly on to the canvas with energetic strokes of the brush. The backgrounds are mostly opaque and sombre, as if to avoid any distraction from the main accent; the robes are composed in powerful masses, in flat surfaces, as if they were to be transposed into mosaics. Owing to this disposition in broad planes and to certain hieratic gestures, these Apostles are closer to their Byzantine origins, to large-scale mural decorations, than their predecessors. The Saviour, very elongated with His angular white aureole, clearly reveals this affiliation. But as if within a rigid frame their faces decompose, their hands seem to flow and thin out into trickling fingers. Their features take shape according to their expressions the moment one looks at them. A cloud solidifies and assumes an almost human form, only to melt again into shreds. St. John the Evangelist is reduced to the mere triangle of a quivering face; his mouth is twisted to one side in a smile quite devoid of gaiety. Yet nothing in this evolution of forms could be imputed to the feebleness of old age, to a failing of sight or touch. For example, the letter which St. Paul holds in his fingers seems to tremble, so uncertain is their grasp. Yet his sword is painted with the same clarity, down to the minute relief of the blade and the chasing on the pommel, as that of the nobleman with his hand on his breast.

These contrasts between indefiniteness and finished detail reveal how much El Greco deliberately suppressed, omitted, and submerged in vagueness. Thus St. Peter appears to have almost dissolved, in his extreme old age: his eyes have sunk deep into their sockets, one of them being half veiled by its lid, and his toothless mouth has caved in, yet threads of silver gleam with minute reflections in his curly hair, as do the keys he holds in his hand, a hand so revealing of El Greco's dual optical vision, often appearing in the same canvas. The hands of these saints are, as a rule, the most typical. A small square of canvas showing the long flowing palms and threadlike fingers would suffice to identify it as his work. But even in the pictures in the Greco Museum, in which this fluidity reaches its peak, El Greco seems to have suddenly remembered that St. Peter was only a humble fisherman with the big hands of a labourer, and it was thus that he painted them, with their thick wrists, broad backs lined with prominent veins, heavy thumbs, and square nails. As if to compensate for the sunken features and coarse hands El Greco clad this prince of the Apostles in a scintillating blue tunic with a yellow drapery which is like a cloak of gold, a great, captive blaze of colour.

Even now, towards the end of his life, El Greco was still in the springtime of his creative power. One would think that after painting so many series of Apostles he had said all there was to say, that he could only vary their attitudes or secondary characteristics imperceptibly. Yet suddenly, in this last series, an entirely new conception of St. Batholomew emerged (Plate 90). He had painted him several times, holding the Gospel, with his face in torment. But his St. Bartholomew in Toledo is the image of an Oriental Christ. A greatly elongated face is set in thick curls falling to his shoulders, with a long, silky, flashing beard, thick eyebrows, heavy lashes, brilliant eyes, a thin, aquiline nose, and a haughty mouth. This face is drained, as if all the colour had fled from it, leaving satin reflections on the drawn skin; a face seen in a lunar light, standing out spectrally from the sombre cloud of hair. It floats above the white garments—a white mantle over a white tunic—which are an amazing *tour de force,* with all the wealth of nuances which can accumulate in the shadows of white materials. El Greco's pictorial mastery surpassed itself in this monochrome painting, in which even the hands are composed of the same lunar substance. And, as if to complete this hallucinatory apparition, St. Bartholomew brandishes in one hand a knife of flashing steel, whilst in the other he holds a red-haired demon on a chain—the only spot of colour apart from the background—a demon with the grinning face of an ape, its eyes protruding from their sockets like snails.

The picture of St. Bartholomew stood in its white phosphorescence outside all known artistic conceptions, outside its time, at once immemorial and never before seen on canvas, carried out with an audacity which remained unequalled until quite recent times, a unique purpose, a taste of the absolute.

Side by side with these series of Apostles, these twelve variations of an inner colloquy, El Greco also pursued his dialogues between his gigantic saints. Following his new conception of movement, his quest for headlong rhythm, this dialogue became a drama, a collision of light and shade, with a jagged sky, an earth moving beneath the saints' feet, eyes that measure each other, and hands that answer each other. It was thus that he painted "St. John the Evangelist and St. Francis," with their eyebrows contracted in grief, in a picture in the Prado which is not entirely by his own hand but doubtless a studio copy reduced in size from a large canvas.

With the same feeling for drama he painted the confrontation of "St. John the Evangelist with St. John the Baptist" (Jesuit Church in Toledo). He left a greater space between them, which is filled with the sky and a burnt-ochre landscape, with a few smudges of greenery. This sky is not only a witness more or less involved in the intimate debate; through the formation of its clouds it takes part in the colloquy, as if all nature were moved to add its word to what the two saints have to say to each other. The naked body of St. John the Baptist, with the gaunt anatomy of an ascetic, is framed by a cloud, which surrounds him with shadow as if to emphasize his relief. The clouds have also played with the garments of St. John the Evangelist, to the extent that one can no longer tell where their folds end and where the light materializes. High above the earth the two heads stand out from a hollow in the clouds—the one, that of an adolescent who is almost an angel, with its tiny, half-opened mouth; and the other, that of a man who has greatly suffered, who is so consumed with inner fire that all

his strength has fled into his enormous, passionately sad eyes. Rarely
has a saint, even a saint painted by El Greco, been so overwhelmed
by pity as this herald of Christ as he fixes his burning eyes on the
youth, whose head droops like a wilting flower.

The same intervention of the sky is to be found in the large picture
of St. Peter painted for the church of San Vicente in Toledo and now
in the sacristy of the Escorial (Plate 91). It is almost a tussle between
the elements and the saint, so gigantic that he can well stand up to
them. He has risen very high above human lives, on to a peak which
dominates the blue mountaintops, glittering with snow on the far
horizon. His bare feet, which have already travelled so many roads,
still quiver as if in haste to set out once again. The sky with its torn
clouds descends on him like an avalanche: the wind lifts his ample robe
of burning yellow, like molten gold, fills it and flattens it, striking
flashes of light off it and piercing it with shadows.

From the writhing column of the body, arched against the falling
sky, emerge hands with bent wrists—long, aged hands so quivering
with sensitivity that they seem the embodiment of spiritual tension.
The heavy keys dangle from the finger tips, which barely retain them,
painted with that virtuosity El Greco lavished on objects, they are the
one sign of solid matter in a fabulous world of garments made up of
streams of lava, torrents of clouds and light breaking over the saint's
head like a wave.

One day this picture was to become El Greco's posthumous revenge
for all that had been denied him by way of official recognition during
his lifetime, for Philip IV bought it on the advice of Velásquez for the
Escorial, where "The Martyrdom of St. Maurice" was still relegated
to a secondary position. Also on Velásquez' advice Philip II's grandson bought, from the same church of San Vicente, the "St. Ildefonso"
(Plate 93), believed to have been painted for its altarpiece as a companion picture to "St. Peter." If there were no other proof of this persistent dual vision of El Greco's, one would date this picture several
years earlier, perhaps as a contemporary of "The Burial of Count
Orgaz," in which the saints are materialized in their heavy gold dalmatics.

St. Ildefonso, however, surpasses these in magnificence, in the
wealth of ornament, and minuteness of execution. If some of El
Greco's pictures are like stained-glass windows, this one is like a
shrine, a piece of a goldsmith's enamelled work. On that heavily embroidered dalmatic, that braided chasuble, that damask and brocade

El Greco lavished the most precious hues on his palette—pale silver and gold, fading rose and pearly reflections. The crook doubtless faithfully reproduces the costly work of some contemporary goldsmith, with that miniaturist's taste which El Greco preserved when even the features of his saints were lost in the ardour of their communion with heaven.

Unlike the saints swept up in the vortex of their own will, St. Ildefonso is motionless, as if petrified in his stiff garments. But between the finely wrought shrine of the dalmatic and the mitre which crowns it, itself also fashioned like a custodial, an aged face reflects that humanity of great old men which for El Greco was comparable to saintliness; against the glitter of precious stones the face is livid, the features crumble, the thin eyelids are lowered over weary eyes, but a peaceful smile seems to play around the mouth.

This old age of which he was such a peerless painter had descended on El Greco himself, prematurely, it seems. He gave those who approached him an impression of great age; he referred to it himself; he even seems to have been rather coy about it, as if he wanted to stress the contrast between the feebleness of his body and the strength of his creative spirit. A sick man, he could apparently move only with difficulty, aided by a stick. But in spite of old age and sickness he retained all his touchy pride and irascibility.

An anecdote describes how he intervened one day in a quarrel between his favourite disciple, Luis Tristán, and the monastery of Sisla. Tristán is said to have demanded 200 ducats for a "Last Supper" painted for the church, but the monastery, like all El Greco's clients, found the price too high. In spite of his poor state of health El Greco is then said to have gone himself to examine the work on the spot. The story runs that he flew into a rage with his disciple, threatening him with his stick for having asked too little for so valuable a work. The anecdote is false, but it has that psychological truth which makes use of imaginary facts in order to arrive at a genuine portrait. It also illustrates the relationship between El Greco and his pupils.

From the beginning of the century his studio had continuously grown in importance; orders poured in and his pupils also increased in number. But although El Greco had a studio and pupils, he never had a school. His art could not be passed on. His inspiration could not be communicated. His pupils learned the craft from him and copied his works, the more faithfully, perhaps, the less they comprehended their spirit; but they did not even assimilate his passion, the boldness of which was beyond their timid temperaments. Luis Tristán seems to have preserved a fleeting impression of El Greco's art so long as his master was alive and stimulated him by his presence. But the moment El Greco was no more the small flame died. He remained a painter of portraits which indicate above all what El Greco was able to pass on to him by way of solid technical training. It was his most superficial side which his pupils appropriated the most easily—his love of detail, his taste of a miniaturist, that virtuosity which dazzled his contemporaries and which continued to be admired even in the time of his eclipse. One of his first biographers, Palomino, echoed this in the way one repeats a widespread opinion: "What El Greco did well has never been done better; what he did badly has never been done worse."[1]

It was the intrusion of still-life into his work that his disciples imitated best, like Luis Tristán in his portrait of a theologian against a background of bookshelves. Several future painters of still-lifes *par excellence* frequented his studio, such as Alejandro de Loarte and above all Pedro Orrente, known as the "Spanish Bassano." The earliest traces of him in Toledo date from about 1600; he became particularly attached to El Greco's son, who later asked him to be godfather to his two children. It was typical of El Greco's influence on those who came to him that the majority of his pupils turned out to be excellent draughtsmen. Even those who had only a few years' apprenticeship in his studio, like Antonio Pizarro, who appeared in Toledo in 1603, or the future Dominican monk, Juan Bautista Mayno, owed their reputations to their feeling for construction and conscientious draughtsmanship. Nevertheless these pupils, however close they lived to El Greco, perhaps under the same roof, and however much they copied his works or had a share in the large commissions, have remained anonymous and lost in oblivion.

El Greco was sixty-six or sixty-seven years old when he undertook some particularly important commissions, as if, in spite of bad health, he had many years ahead of him and an old age as active as that of his master, Titian. One of these commissions was the altarpiece in the church at Titulcia, Bayona (Madrid Province). As usual Jorge Manuel was entrusted with its architecture, and he was soon joined by the sculptor Giraldo de Merlo for the sculptural part of the work. The altarpiece was dedicated to the saint El Greco painted in a particular

---

[1] *El Parnaso español* (1724), by Don Antonio Palomino de Castro y Velasco, 1653–1725.

radiance: Mary Magdalen. But after having conceived the design of the reredos and probably that of the principal panels El Greco left the execution of these to his son. In the almost inevitable lawsuit which followed it was Jorge Manuel who was described as the painter of the altarpiece. The strangest picture among the five scenes from the life of Mary Magdalen is the saint's assumption—the first female nude known in Spanish art prior to Velásquez' "Rokeby Venus." Yet this nude, doubtless sketched by El Greco himself, is as devoid of all sensuality as a female nude could be. The body is rather fleshy, but its contours are androgynous and the flesh itself livid. Jorge Manuel, by emphasizing the modelling, lost all that graceful, flowerlike quality which El Greco used to confer on the repentant saint. Four of these pictures are to-day in the church at Titulcia. The fifth seems to be the "Christ in the House of Simon" (Hispanic Society of America) based on a work by El Greco. In the other pictures—*"Noli Me Tangere,"* "Jesus in the House of Mary and Martha," and "The Angel Appearing to Mary Magdalen"—Jorge Manuel must have also transposed his father's works, with that peculiar plastic quality of his, into a chiaroscuro which was perhaps Orrente's contribution. Unlike his father, Jorge Manuel was not impervious to outside influences; he felt more and more the impact of that current of realism which had been developing in Spanish art, primarily in Seville under the promptings of Francisco Pacheco, to culminate in the first manner of Velásquez.

El Greco himself was devoting his efforts at this time to a work of which he was particularly anxious to make a success: the high altar and side altars of the church of the Hospital of St. John the Baptist. The administrators knew his habit of delegating extensive commissions to his son and the contract, signed on November 28, 1608, was amended a few months later, on May 19, 1609, when El Greco received his first advance of 30,000 reals on account of his work "of assembly," gilding, and sculpture, by a clause stipulating that he must take charge of the work himself, having been selected as "a man so excellent in his art."

El Greco's connection with the hospital went back several years. It had begun in 1595, when he was commissioned for a richly carved and gilt tabernacle, the custodial habitually found in all Spanish churches. It comprised statues of the four doctors—St. Ambrose, St. Augustine, St. Gregory, and St. Chrysostom—the Twelve Apostles, and Christ resurrected, the last of which is believed to have been recovered in a statuette 18 inches high, one of the rare examples of El Greco's sculptural work which has survived (Plate 95).

Three years later, however, the work was still unfinished as a whole, as can be learned from El Greco's disputes with the hospital administrators, who, like all his clients at that time, contested his demands and appealed to experts who considerably reduced the price asked. But El Greco insisted on a countervaluation, in which a well-known Toledan goldsmith took part. The dispute dragged on until the day when the sculptor Sigüenza was called in as an arbiter and, "in view of and considering the goodness, art, perfection and skill displayed by the said custodial, the particular care necessary to overcome the manifold difficulties arising from such a work," he valued El Greco's work at 25,000 reals. Despite these squabbles over money El Greco remained on excellent terms with the hospital. As soon as he had obtained moral satisfaction, with the gesture of a *grand siegneur* he reduced his claim by 9000 reals "out of the great devotion he bore the Hospital" and "out of love for the said lord administrator," Salazar de Mendoza.

The Hospital of St. John the Baptist was a pious foundation made with an almost royal magnificence by Juan Tavera, one of those princes of the Church of a spacious age, when Rome and Toledo vied with each other in splendour. He enjoyed the personal friendship of Charles V and was invested with the highest honours his country could bestow on him, both secular and ecclesiastic. After having been Archbishop of Seville and Toledo, he was elected a cardinal and was in turn President of the Council of Castile and Grand Inquisitor. An upright man, whose sense of justice and prudence were much praised, he was also a patron of the arts, a Maecenas for artists such as Covarrubias and Berruguete. He led the life of the most ostentatious princes of the Church during the Renaissance. Apart from a huge domestic staff he had forty pages in his service, all of them sons of distinguished families. If need be, he could muster whole armies; he aided the building of churches with his vast resources, and enriched Toledo Cathedral with its finest monuments. The Hospital perpetuated his name after his death in 1545, for it was also known as the Hospital of Tavera. When its administrators decided to order the sumptuous altarpieces, they also thought of paying their debt of gratitude to the Cardinal by commissioning El Greco to paint a portrait of their late benefactor. But this great prelate, who had done so much to perpetuate his name with splendour, does not seem to have had the desire to preserve his features for posterity. Whether through a lack of personal vanity, prudence, or perhaps an obscure feeling of secret discord between his physique and his aspiration, this man, whose protégés included the best painters and sculptors of his time, had never, according to Salazar de Mendoza, allowed his portrait to be painted. The hospital possessed only the death mask taken by Berruguete, which it put at El Greco's disposal. The administrators seem to have known of his talent for resuscitating the dead, for bringing the departed back to life. This time, however, it was not an old portrait of a living man he took for his model, but a mask which faithfully retained the imprint of all the ravages that recent death can work on a man's face. El Greco made no attempt to obliterate these, to soften the harshness of the already decomposing features, to suppress all that illness and final exhaustion had engraved on it. He even added what he knew to be the pallor of a dying man, when the cold sweat dries on his face and the bloodless lips sink in over a toothless mouth. The only life with which he infused this death's-head is in the eyes he substituted for the closed lids, perhaps in conformity with all he had heard of the man. The intensity of their gaze is particularly remarkable in this already absent face; they have an appeal at once passionate and sad, with the sadness of those who know they will not be understood. With one long hand laid on a book beside his cardinal's biretta, the same hand which El Greco gave to his St. Jerome, Tavera waits in patient disdain, with this hallucinatory gaze which is like an appeal from beyond the grave.

Perhaps El Greco was particularly well qualified to express this invocation of perpetuity at a moment when he himself feared to see his strength fail him. The works he agreed to complete for the hospital within a space of five years progressed but slowly. He had the altarpieces constructed in his studio, in accordance with the taste of the administrator, who was opposed to the *plateresque* style, which he defined as "Gothic work." But on El Greco's death, well after the five years had elapsed, only scattered pieces—a spiral column and roughly sketched pictures—were found.

The only canvas he seems to have finished was "The Baptism of Christ" (Plate 94), which is perhaps not entirely by his own hand. Just over ten years separate this last "Baptism" from the one in the Prado. The ascensional movement, the whirlwind of the jagged forms in the Prado picture, would seem impossible to surpass. Yet the picture in San Juan Bautista reveals the road El Greco was opening up for himself in order to increase the intensity of emotion even further. Comparison of the two pictures is all the more instructive in that the

scheme of the composition is the same, with the same interplay between heaven and earth and an almost identical grouping of the principal figures. The numerous changes were all bent in the same direction, towards the vertiginousness of the ascent, the frenzied yearning
to shake off all earthly bonds. From now on the fusion between earth
and heaven is absolute. The beginning and end of the drama of salvation have united. This Christ still kneeling on a rock, leaning towards
the shell, already reflects Christ returning to heaven. In the Prado picture the angels had spread out red garments above His head like a
royal dais, but also like a dividing line between His passage on earth
and His return to the Eternal Father. El Greco's increasing awareness
of the goal he was pursuing no longer permitted these horizontal
divisions. The verticals are like powerful springs which are released
directly they touch the earth. The angel with the upraised arm com-
municating the miraculous to heaven has no longer fallen between
Christ and St. John; it forms a pendant to the equally gigantic saint,
with its green robe with orange lights arranged in spirals emphasizing
the upward movement. Its former place has been taken by a kneeling
angel, a column of fire-reddened smoke. The formal and spiritual
density El Greco achieved in this painting no longer tolerated empty
spaces between the figures or glances that avoided each other. A piece
of red cloth fills the space between the fair angel and Christ, and it is
between these two that a mute colloquy takes place, that the ultimate
agreement is sealed.

   In the same spirit of increased density, of immediate communion,
El Greco now placed the Dove directly above Christ, with its rays of
light pouring down like the water on to His head. God the Father no
longer sits enthroned in a still vertical, a calm white light above the
whirling angels. Turned in profile, He faces His Son, gently inclining
His head as if to echo Him. The clouds, like a vortex spinning in two
directions at His feet, seem to suck in the saints and angels, drawing
up the agitation of heaven to converge on high. This heaven is the
most dramatic that El Greco ever painted. One angel, right at the top,
has plunged so violently into the clouds that only its thrashing legs
can be seen. Nothing could be added to this celestial tempest, from
which the angels' heads emerge like the reddish crescent of a moon
showing through a cloud, in abrupt foreshortenings flung back so far
on long necks that only the nostrils or flashing eyes are visible, whereas
their hands wave like fans or young palm fronds.

   "The Baptism of Christ" was to remain El Greco's sole contribution

to the work of the Hospital of Tavera. Its slow progress, despite his
"love for the said lord administrator," was not alone caused by his
failing health, which must have been particularly tried by the fever
of his increasingly tormented pictorial conception. It was also caused
by the numerous commissions he then undertook, as if he were still
at the height of his powers. Official recognition, which had so long
been delayed, henceforth courted him persistently. In place of the
private clients and the administrators of chapels and churches, it was
the city authorities, the Ayuntamiento, or municipal council, who
came to him for the first time, now that his talents were at last recognized. During the council's deliberations, one councillor declared that
he regarded El Greco as "a man skilled in his craft," while another,
one of his passionate admirers, maintained that he was "one of the
most outstanding men known in this art, both inside and outside the
kingdom," adding that the judge, the *alcalde mayor,* shared the same
opinion.

This appreciation was doubtless influenced by a friend so devoted
and faithful to El Greco as Dr. Angulo, for it was he who was appointed, at the end of 1607, to conclude an agreement with El Greco
for an altarpiece destined for a chapel in the church of San Vicente,
which was administered on behalf of a pious foundation by the Toledan Ayuntamiento. For this El Greco received his first advances
at about the same time he received those for the Hospital of Tavera,
and undertook to supply the paintings within eight months. Nobody,
however, seems to have taken this clause seriously, for six years were
to elapse before the completion of the altarpiece. From now on El
Greco appears to have been too "eminent" for his clients to dare to
nag him with their impatience.

Furthermore the municipal council took him off this work for an
important occasion. The Queen, Margaret of Austria, had died. She
died, like so many Queens of Spain, while giving birth to her fourth
son, Don Alfonso, whom the Spaniards, with a rather macabre apt-
ness, called "the dear" because he cost his mother her life. But in this
Spain so overshadowed by the reign of Philip III her death created a
deep impression. Exhausted by long wars, the country at last knew
peace abroad, bought at the cost of heavy sacrifices, a time of truce
which should have allowed her a breathing space. But, urged on by
his councillors, Philip III, who during his reign had learned neither
to think for himself nor to consult competent and disinterested ad-
visers, took advantage of this truce to fling himself into disastrous

enterprises. In his religious fanaticism he regarded himself as his father's heir and felt completely sure of himself. At the beginning of this rule the distressed state of Spanish finances had imposed some moderation on him. To pay for the luxuries in which he and his favourites indulged, he had decreed an embargo on gold and silver, whilst doubling the value of copper money. The sole result of this measure was a sharp rise in the cost of living and the disappearance of silver coinage, whilst copper counterfeits of gold coins flooded the country. To palliate this monetary disaster, Philip III had accepted gifts of gold and silver from Portuguese Jews and agreed to enter into negotiations with the Moors. But after the peace concluded with England, James I sent him the secret correspondence exchanged between Queen Elizabeth and the Spanish Moors as proof of their unremitting conspiratorial activities. As soon as the truce signed with the Netherlands, combined with the eclipse of the English threat, permitted the release of the fleet, Philip and his councillors decided, in the autumn of 1609, to expel all the Moors from Spain. Crammed into large sailing boats, the Moors were allowed to take away with them only what they themselves could carry. Abruptly torn from a soil to which they were passionately attached, they saw themselves deprived of the fruits of a lifetime's labour. In each village only six old men were permitted to remain, to teach the new settlers the cultivation of the soil. Spanish historians disagree as to the number of Moors expelled; some estimate it at 300,000, others at a million.

This expulsion bled Spanish economy white and the country was never to recover from it. But it won the approval of the masses and even gained sympathy for the King. The Moors were hard-working, sober, miserly, and had an expert knowledge of the land they tilled; they played no part in wars and sought neither refuge in monasteries nor fortunes in America; they were content to consolidate what they had so painfully acquired. The Spaniards knew there was land to be distributed and places to be taken over, but they apparently did not realize the hard work involved and the shortage of labour. All the disastrous consequences, for industry and agriculture alike, soon became evident. In addition to the expulsion of the Moors war, the lure of new continents, emigration to America and the Philippines, and the flight into monasteries had reduced the population by one third within the space of barely twenty years. At the same time life became more and more expensive and the cost of staple foodstuffs leaped to disastrous heights, one *fanega* (1½ bushels) of beans, which cost 272 maravedís in 1555, reaching a price of 612 maravedís in 1605, whilst a *fanega* of corn doubled in price.

The Cortés of Castile, convoked in 1611, registered alarm at the state of the country, the sharp decline in every sphere, the increasing discontent of the masses, and the revolt of the grandees, who, conscious of their ancient glory, saw the foundations of their power threatened. There was a sort of poison in the air, a progressive deterioration, with regret for a past irretrievably lost mingled with a desire for renewal. The Cortés protested vehemently against current vices and abuses and demanded a restriction of public expenditure, above all that of the royal family, reform of excessive taxation, and a purge of corrupt officials. They also requested that ecclesiastical powers should be reduced, the number of monasteries diminished and the jurisdiction of the Inquisition confined to religious questions. All these accumulated grievances centred round the King's favourite. The arrogance of the Duke of Lerma, who felt himself to be all-powerful and knew that nothing was denied him, who wanted to monopolize and do everything himself, made him, in the eyes of the Spanish, "an enemy of virtue and truth and a friend of all licentiousness."

A party of malcontents was formed at the court itself amongst the young courtiers, led by the Duke of Lerma's own son. He even influenced the King's confessor and won over the Queen and Prince Philip. The favourite's favourite, Don Rodrigo Calderón, Marqués de Siete Iglesias, was the first to be sacrificed by the King, as being an underling within easier reach. Then the Queen died, and her death was imputed to Calderón's revenge. A rumour spread that Margaret of Austria had been poisoned. Mourning for the Queen assumed the form of a protest against a hateful regime.

The city of Toledo had also suffered from the country's general decline; her greatness now merely consisted of memories and regrets, under a King who no longer showed her the same courteous respect his father had done.

The Ayuntamiento of Toledo paid even more magnificent homage to the dead Queen than it was wont to do for living sovereigns or the relics of saints. El Greco was commissioned to erect a monument in the ambulatory of the cathedral in celebration of her funeral, and this monument was to be more costly than the one which Monegro was charged with building after the death of Philip II. El Greco conceived it in harmony with the elevation of the Gothic vault under which it was to be placed and his own taste for the ascensional: it was 110

feet high and 40 feet wide. This upward movement was achieved by
the superimposition of several structures, which converged towards
the top and were surmounted by statues. Kings in armour were succeeded by virtues and angels with trumpets, set in niches or over the
archways, right up to the final drum surmounted by a cupola, which
was in turn crowned with a lantern over which floated an angel ten
feet high, holding the imperial crown. These statues were completed in
El Greco's studio by Jorge Manuel, who signed a contract with some
carters who undertook to transport "figures and other things" from
the Marqués de Villena's palace to the cathedral. Both monument and
statues were made of wood, but, according to the custom of the time,
they were painted in perfect imitation of stone. The monument was
regarded as the "finest ever constructed in the city." But unfortunately the Toledans were given little leisure in which to contemplate
it, for it stood in place for only a few days.

Philip III had loved his wife, in so far as his inertia could be affected
by emotion; husband and wife never separated, yet even her death
could not bring him to abandon his programme of customary diver-
sions. Away hunting at the time, he did not even return to Madrid
to attend his queen's funeral. One wonders if, despite his obtuse mentality, he fully realized how much this exalting of the Queen, the supposed victim of his favourites, implied a condemnation of himself,
and if this resentment rebounded even on the homage they were preparing to render her in Toledo. At any rate a dispute over protocol
broke out between the Cortés of Castile and the city authorities. The
solemn celebration in the cathedral was revoked. Barely a few days
after its erection the monument on which El Greco and his son had
expended so much labour was hastily dismantled on the order of the
King. El Greco, who had never been summoned to paint any living
sovereign or member of the royal family, saw even his efforts in honour of a dead queen destroyed. The composition of this wooden monument is known only through the dry vocabulary of the official contracts, but a poet was at hand to extol what he saw under the vault
of the cathedral. Fray Hortensio Paravicino wrote a sonnet in praise
of the monument El Greco made in Toledo in Queen Margaret's honour; he invited the curious visitor contemplating this royal monument
to admire "the Greek miracle" which had torn the sun, on which Margaret's gaze was henceforth fixed, from its restless course, from its
region of pure fire, so that her face could absorb the shimmering lights
of heaven.

WHILE El Greco was working for the Hospital of Tavera, Toledo, of whose fascination he never wearied, lay spread out before him. At the same time he probably had long talks with Dr. Salazar de Mendoza, the hospital's administrator. It was presumably through Don Antonio de Covarrubias that El Greco came to know Don Pedro, "first Penitentiary Canon of the Holy Church of Toledo," for it was Don Antonio who, in 1601, recommended Salazar de Mendoza's book, *The History of the Life and Deeds of the Saintly and Beloved Monarch, Philip III*, for the royal imprint. Don Antonio extolled the amount of work expended on this book, the author's zeal, and the style he employed for so varied a heroic subject, all of which had given great satisfaction. The book was plainly written by a courtier full of blind flattery excessive even for those days, but it was hardly a commissioned work. In the letter which accompanied it Salazar de Mendoza complained of having devoted the best years of his life to its preparation and spent all his patrimony on it. Philip III does not seem to have paid even his panegyrists. Possibly the administration of the hospital was offered to him as a recompense. If Don Pedro thought he would win the King's favour with this book, he was mistaken. The work was not published until much later, in 1771, together with a history of the reign of Philip IV by Gil González Dávila, who called himself the chronicler of both kings.

Instead of procuring the post at court to which he must have aspired Salazar de Mendoza became, at best, a provincial notability, just as El Greco was for many years a purely Toledan celebrity. Perhaps, like El Greco, he had been captivated by Toledo. The two men seem to have discussed what the city meant for them, what was permanent and was transitory about it, and how the hold it had over men's souls could be epitomized in a symbol, according to the taste of the time. The picture El Greco then painted has not the unity of a spontaneous work, of a single purpose, but seems rather to be the outcome of long discussion, or a project incorporating a great many suggestions. The learned doctor was unfamiliar with pictorial problems: El Greco had to initiate him into the mysteries of perspective, backing up his explanations with the evidence of his work. The big picture in the Greco Museum called "View and Plan of Toledo" (Plate 97) is known to have belonged to Dr. Salazar de Mendoza.

There is in the picture indeed a plan of Toledo, very clearly drawn, doubtless by Jorge Manuel, which is being unfolded by a young man; a plan which, like all town plans, is an abstract, devoid of heart and soul. But these El Greco introduced, using the young man as one of his habitual commentators. This young man in the foreground is a strange apparition. It has been thought to be a portrait of Jorge Manuel, but he was much older at the time. It is certainly not his son, and not even a portrait. El Greco never painted a human being of flesh and blood like this, nor even a saint, when he allowed one to appear in human guise. He is a symbol, difficult to decipher. Could this young Spaniard embody the spirit of the city, revealing its permanence through the features of eternal youth? He leans back so as not to obscure the landscape spread out behind him. A ghostly apparition with the greenish-white face attributed to phantoms, his features are almost transparent, unstable, ever ready to dissolve; his velvet costume is of the same subdued green that dominates the whole landscape. One might say that the whole picture was painted on a silver ground, just as the primitives used to paint on a gold one.

Forming a pendant to the young man, set farther back in the picture, is a nude beside a large bowl of fruit and an overturned amphora —a nude painted all in gold, a distant memory of those river gods which the Italians, inspired by antique statues, cast in bronze at the bases of fountains. But this nude is more curled up than the river gods usually were. Did El Greco, a cerebral painter nurtured on the subtlety of the Greek dialecticians, have the waves of the Tagus in mind when he painted this bronze god with his legs drawn up almost at right angles to his body and his knees level with his head? In the centre

foreground a large patch of white shaded with blue is surmounted by
an important building, the Hospital of Tavera. In a long inscription
traced by his son El Greco explained, as one does to those ignorant
of pictorial laws, that he was compelled to present the hospital in the
form of a model and taken out of its topographical surroundings because otherwise it would have been concealed by the other buildings.
He added that, having adopted this method of presentation, he preferred to show the building from its most favourable aspect instead
of the façade which would have been visible from the same viewpoint
as the rest of the picture.

The city falls back in a semicircle behind the three main elements
in the foreground. El Greco, who had so often painted Toledo, picking out certain quarters and buildings as isolated features, as emotive
factors, here made a careful balance sheet of the whole city, as if
anxious to omit no detail of its amphitheatrical construction, its encircling walls with their towers, its piled-up roofs, terraced quarters,
monuments, and hovels. Toledo appears here as an inventory drawn
up by a conscientious man; an architect charged with making a model
of a city in relief could not have proceeded otherwise. Yet even if this
fidelity was his primary intention, his love of the city transformed a
balance sheet into a glorification. The buildings are painted with the
care of a miniaturist who noted the number of stories, the projection
of the towers, and the shadows they threw; but they are also painted
as the spirit of what they represent, almost transparent against the
blue sky. The city is at once as he saw it and as it might have appeared
in dreams to men tormented by nostalgia. On this canvas El Greco
lavished his brightest and most delicate colours, as he did on the
dalmatic of St. Ildefonso. Against his own taste for the vertical, to
which the city lent itself so well, he composed the picture in broadly
horizontal lines.

It was typical of all the elements of which El Greco's art was formed
that he combined several disparate ones in this picture plan: memories
of a classical deity, young Spain, and the Virgin. For it is the Virgin,
rewarding the fidelity of a Toledan, who completes the apotheosis of
the city. In the midst of jubilant angels she offers the chasuble to St.
Ildefonso. In the second half of the inscription El Greco patiently explained, again in the way one spells out a text to illiterates, why he
only sketched this "story of Our Lady" in the sky, for, so he said,
"they are heavenly figures, like lights seen from a distance, which,
however small they are, to us appear large."

This interpretation of the real and the imaginary, particularly apparent in this view of Toledo, was keenly felt by his contemporaries, above all by those whose art also aspired to conquer nature, as Fray Hortensio Felix Paravicino remarked of El Greco's works. Fray Hortensio was one of the most eloquent voices of his time, one of the most resounding clarion calls in support of El Greco's fame. He was particularly fitted to command attention thanks to his qualities, rarely to be found combined in the same man; an ease which made him shine in the world, a spiritual distinction which assured him the esteem of the most exclusive literary circles, and the hold he had over many souls as a Dominican preacher.

Paravicino was one of those born to dazzle. His contemporaries used to relate how, at the age of five, he already astounded scholars with his knowledge of Latin. He was only twenty-one when he was appointed a professor at the famous University of Salamanca. He possessed great theological ability and was also a well-versed Humanist; above all he had the fluency of those whose knowledge is always at the tips of their tongues at any given moment. But he was also opposed to facility and avoided cheap effects, always seeking for the *mot juste* to express a lofty thought, the rare word which best conveyed a shade of feeling. In an age intoxicated by high-sounding language and in a tongue which lent itself especially well to verbal flights, Paravicino imposed on himself a rigid discipline of speech corresponding to his horror of the instability of ideas. He compressed his style and framed his images with such precision that they seem wrought in metal, thus achieving such a density of ideas and expressions that hardly any air can pass between them. His eloquence, the warmth of his voice, and his imposing presence imbued his sermons with vibrant life, making them comprehensible even to those who found him hard to follow and who accordingly felt highly intelligent at being able to share in his exaltation. This great preacher was also a poet who wrought his sonnets like a jeweller; their turns of phrase, in their hammered richness, relate them in fact to the work of baroque goldsmiths. His new style, deliberately hermetic and combining calculated daring with moving sincerity, created a great stir and exerted an even greater influence on the literary expression of his time, an influence perhaps out of proportion to the importance of his work. Unlike the Spanish mystics, he had made his spiritual home in the world; there was perhaps even a touch of affectation in the way in which he insisted on the right to enjoy the good things of life.

Despite the difference in their ages the painter and the poet were made to get on together, sharing the same tastes, the same horror of the facile and obvious, and the same artistic tendencies, in which images and expressions accumulated so thickly that there was no space left empty on a canvas and no possibility of a vague word or an approximation in a sonnet. It is not known when El Greco became closely associated with Fray Hortensio Paravicino. Perhaps he had already met him on the occasion of Philip III's first visit to Toledo, for, as court preacher, Paravicino accompanied the King on his travels. Paravicino was definitely in Toledo in 1611 but, according to Spanish historians, there is no trace of his presence there either in the previous years or in those to come. He attended the festivities in memory of Margaret of Austria, when he delivered a sermon typical both of his precious style and of the means employed by all those gifted with eloquence to fire the imagination of the masses, to stupefy them with repetitions. "Germany is weeping because Margaret is dead; Bavaria is weeping for the loss of Margaret; Spain is weeping because Margaret is no more. The faithful weep because Margaret is dead."

During his stay Paravicino also took part in the poetical jousting organized in honour of the dead Queen by the Count of Saldaña. It was then that he saw the funeral monument erected by El Greco and celebrated it in a sonnet. El Greco's portrait of him probably dates from this time, although Paravicino says in the sonnet he dedicated to El Greco that he was twenty-nine years old, which would place it in the year 1609.

The portrait in the Boston Museum (Plate 96) is at any rate of a man who achieved fame very young. A touch of adolescent freshness still lingers in the face, which is perhaps one of the most moving to be found among El Greco's portraits and surely one of the most eloquent. El Greco painted a friend, a man he knew so well that he captured him in the fleeting expression of a moment. The portrait appears spontaneous, with that immediacy which animates a sketch or an unfinished picture. Yet this impression is deceptive. Despite his familiarity with his model El Greco made a preliminary study of the head and shoulders (in a private collection in Madrid). Fray Hortensio scarcely resembles those Spanish noblemen with their long heads extended even further by goatees whose type was immortalized by El Greco. He has a big head with a wide forehead, made even wider by his dark, bushy hair. Under the straight, thick line of his eyebrows his almond-shaped eyes seem to be gazing at the spectator without seeing him, so absorbed are they in some dream. Contrary to the usual persistent stare of El Greco's models Fray Hortensio's eyes look inward, as if he were self-sufficient, as if he drew all his strength from himself. His face is almost triangular, accentuated even more by his fringe of beard. The sensitivity visible in the almost quivering nostrils is also present in the fold of the eyelids, which have just contracted, and in the wide mouth with the strong lips, so mobile that the words just uttered seem to linger on them. But these lips also betray a hint of suffering at their corners, the early suffering of those who are easily wounded or rebuffed and who have not yet learned how to arm themselves with contempt for everything inflicted on them. El Greco did not paint his friend as a man abundantly favoured by nature and destiny, nor yet as one easily in harmony with himself, and still less fortified with pride like the magistrates and noblemen in his Spanish portraits. But around this face, which might be that of a romantic poet, and around these spirited hands, he deliberately constructed an imposing frame corresponding with the man's social position and personal importance. The picture is composed in breadth and this is accentuated by the widespread arms resting on the arms of the chair, by the book placed slantwise in Paravicino's hand and by the square back of the chair itself.

From the start the portrait of Fray Hortensio Paravicino was regarded as a masterpiece. El Greco's first biographer already referred to "the famous portrait commendable on so many grounds." Paravicino himself dedicated a sonnet to it, in which he sang of the rival of Prometheus who, for a portrait, stole life itself. The reputation of Paravicino, who was also Philip IV's preacher, survived that of El Greco, temporarily in eclipse.

This was probably the last great portrait El Greco painted. His fame, which Paravicino extolled with such enthusiasm, was then at its height. Despite the old age and infirmities of which he complained this portrait was painted by a man in complete mastery of his craft, with a virtuosity which marked the corners of the eyelids with fleeting shadows and traced the curl of a sleeve round a wrist with one sweeping brush-stroke.

It was also painted with a human warmth which imparts itself to the spectator and with the full vigour of confidence. Despite the different nature of its subject it is imbued with the same clear and silvery spirit as the "View and Plan of Toledo." But it was also a departure from that luminous painting, the spiritual content of which is, if not

an affirmation, at least an assent. Something like rebellion, or perhaps despair, rose up in El Greco at this time. His colours darkened,
to harmonize with this dominant note of exasperation.

The difference in conception can be seen most clearly when he repeated the same subject—in the way in which he reconsidered it, in
order to bring it, despite a certain formal identity with an earlier version, into line with a comprehensive idea, even, one is tempted to say,
with his personal philosophy. One theme which turns up regularly
throughout his work, as if to mark its various stages, is that of Christ
on the Cross. It must have been one greatly in demand, considering
the countless variations of it known. It was naturally a subject easily
appreciated by pious clients. But it was also one which lent itself
better than any other to revision in that it formed the peak of a
spiritual upheaval, of the direst tragedy. From the version in the
Louvre (Plate 33)—one of the earliest known—onwards, these pictures of Christ crucified, like cries ringing up to heaven, are clearly
the products of the same state of mind, of the same atmosphere. The
drama lies in heaven, despairing of the earth, as much as it does in
the agony of the Saviour, the livid stormy light and the apocalyptic
setting. One would have thought this first Christ on the Cross could
hardly be surpassed in intensity. Yet there is the Philadelphia picture
of Christ crucified, elongated beyond all measure, with a Byzantine
head and with the Virgin and St. John at the foot of the Cross. This
was probably the picture commissioned on August 25, 1606, for the
chapel of Los Ubeda de San Ginés in Toledo. The Virgin's face, contracted with grief, is half hidden by her mantle. She appears to be
placing her hand on St. John's neck in a strange gesture, like someone
groping in agony for support, for some human warmth to which to
cling, a gesture probably unique in the whole of Christian iconography. It is towards her and not the Cross that St. John turns his androgynous head. On the other side of the Cross lies a view of Toledo,
a ghostly vision haunting the fringes of the night. Along a road cut
into the hillside on which the city stands horsemen gallop on white
steeds, these too phantoms of the night. At a dizzy height far above
the city and the figures of the Virgin and saint floats the head of
Christ.

"The Crucifixion" in the Cincinnati Museum (Plate 92) is unat-
tended, alone with the night. The livid light blurs his body and softens
its tremulous outlines; it is a mere shaft of light in the surrounding
darkness. But this body does not hang lifeless; it is not already pre-

paring to ascend like the one in the Louvre. It writhes, as if seeking to tear itself from the Cross in one last, despairing effort. This is the Christ of *"Eloi, Eloi, lama sabacthani,"* flinging back His head, with staring eyes and teeth bared in the grimace of a dying man reluctant to leave the earth. This Christ on the Cross, still imploring that the cup of bitterness be withheld from Him, is set in the heart of Toledo. At the foot of the Cross lie odd, scattered bones, skulls and crossbones, and frightened horsemen ride away with their banner like tiny ghosts. The city is at the same time Toledo and Jerusalem. A large Oriental dome rises up beside a Gothic tower. One day, when El Greco was no more, Jorge Manuel was to erect a cupola exactly like this one over the Mozarabic chapel, which daringly crowned an octagonal Gothic drum with a Renaissance dome. Although the picture is signed by El Greco, Elizabeth du Gué Trapier believes it to be the work of Jorge Manuel because of this cupola, which was not completed until after El Greco's death. Perhaps it was, in fact, added later, yet it could also be the dream of an old man who always dreamed of architecture and which was realized by his son.

Although physically weakened at this time, and doubtless haunted by thoughts of approaching death, El Greco never abandoned his creative struggle. He was still spurred on by an urge for renewal, expressing himself in the revision of old, familiar themes as much as in the addition of new ones. It was now that he painted the strangest of all his extraordinary pictures—"The Opening of the Fifth Seal" (Plate 98). Large as it is, the picture in its present state may well be only a fragment of an even vaster composition, cut down possibly in width and most probably in height (where it must have converged on some celestial apparition). El Greco was now about seventy. To his friends he appeared worn out. Yet, as if wanting to force himself to a superhuman effort, he embarked on the most hallucinatory scene a mortal ever dared to tackle, a vision of the Apocalypse. The great Day of Wrath has dawned over the world. St. John announces it in prophetic ecstasy. He is as gigantic as his message, the eruption of a power capable of penetrating the terrors of the future. Even were this figure of visionary emotion all that had survived of the picture, one would realize at once that the rest of it must have depicted some very great and awe-inspiring event.

St. John has fallen to his knees, as if overwhelmed by what he has been granted to see. Were he to rise, his head would brush the stars. His gesture is the one familiar to El Greco's interpreters of the miraculous: both arms raised to heaven with outspread hands. But no other is filled with such elemental power, such surging impetuosity, like a volcano in full eruption, crowned with tongues of fire terminating in the little flames of his ceaselessly quivering fingers. His head is a mere swaying oval, his eyes and nostrils mere holes, his mouth a mere twisted groan.

The prophet sees this day of terror dawn over the darkness of the world, on which the graves have opened to deliver up the souls of the martyred. El Greco's martyrs float over the ground like ethereal spirits: even those who are kneeling, even those who do not yet seem fully released, with their naked, earth-coloured bodies, stretch up towards the dark clouds as if striving to blend with them, like columns of smoke wavering in a passing breeze.

The nudes in the centre of the picture, men and women with an androgynous figure amongst them, are scarcely avengers crying with a loud voice to the Lord. They stand calm and confident, waiting for their white robes, and their slow and tranquil rising contrasts strangely with the prophet's announcement. Even the three men on the right, impatiently reaching up towards the white material the cherubs are bringing to them, are scarcely rebels. Their ghostlike bodies have something plaintive and insistent about them, but, unlike those who claim amends for an injury or an injustice, they are sad, with a resigned sadness as if they had never lived. Bodies of men who have never known a woman, for they are virgin; bodies of women spotless before the throne of God; the elect amongst the 144,000 that were signed, hastening towards the Mystical Lamb on Mt. Sion, which probably formed the upper half of the original picture.

El Greco's apocalyptic vision is not the fiery red one of the nights of wrath, of the trembling earth, vengeance washed away in the blood of the Lamb, and the violence of total destruction. It is hardly even a nightmare. It is a hallucinatory dream, like a walk through a thick fog, colliding with the ghosts of all that has not been—vain torments, regrets, stark reminders of all that life denies and always will deny. The true meaning of this apocalyptic vision remains a mystery, but, whatever it may have been, it responded to an infinite desolation, to the indescribable and resigned anguish of a man already face to face with death.

From now on El Greco lived shut away in a *tête-à-tête* with his work. Francisco Pacheco, who was at this time making his great artistic pilgrimage to preserve the features of all the celebrated men of his day, stopped in Toledo in 1611. The portrait he drew of El Greco has been lost, but his account of his visit remains the only complete testimony that has come down to us, the only detailed description of the surroundings in which El Greco lived, the sole authentic record of an actual conversation.[1] This vivid fragment of El Greco's daily existence is, thanks to its uniqueness, a light cast back on his life, and through the singularity of all that Pacheco saw and heard, as illuminating as a revelation.

El Greco was too ill to be able to do the honours of the house in person. It was Jorge Manuel who showed Pacheco round. He saw a hall which served at the same time as a museum and as the warehouse of a commercial enterprise, in which all the pictures El Greco ever painted were to be found reproduced in small sizes for the benefit of his clients, who had only to choose from the samples presented to them. This precaution, taken by such an excellent manager of his own art as El Greco, explains the number of replicas and their fidelity.

Pacheco found this procedure "beyond all praise"; he seems to have been overwhelmed by everything that distinguished El Greco's methods from those of the other painters whose studios he had visited. If El Greco had learned from Titian his skill at exploiting his own products, he seems to have borrowed other facilities of his craft from Tintoretto. In his house Pacheco saw models sculpted in wax which he used for his paintings. The angels in their soaring flight, the diving cherubs, and other details of the celestial spectacle were doubtless derived from these wax models which, as with Tintoretto, must have been suspended from the ceiling, swaying between bright lights and dancing shadows.

If El Greco's methods seemed odd to Pacheco, he was even more struck by the conversation he had with him. The old man, though he no longer stirred, even to show a guest round the house, still preserved his impressive appearance, his caustic, mordant wit, and the pride with which he knew how to make the most of himself even in the days when his reputation was not yet established. Pacheco was dazzled by the immense variety of El Greco's interests. Going to visit a painter, he found in fact a studio organized with a view to the best possible exploitation of his works. But El Greco talked. He talked like a man who knew how to manipulate words, how to construct and co-ordinate his thoughts, and who, even in a language which was not his native tongue, revealed himself as the heir to a centuries-old dialec-

[1]Francisco Pacheco: *Arte della Pintura,* Seville, 1649.

tic. Pacheco was astounded by the ease and brilliance of the formulas
he employed. And he discovered, hidden behind this brilliance, both
sound scholarship and a surprising knowledge. He realized that the
art of this "great philosopher" was based on a strict aesthetic system.
El Greco had probably not lost that malice with which he loved to
dazzle and disconcert his listeners. Pacheco, firmly entrenched in his
contemporary vision and ideals, was startled to hear him speak con-
temptuously of the "ancients," of Aristotle and, above all, of his idol
Michelangelo. Probably later, when he was beyond the reach of El
Greco's personal fascination, this strange talker seemed to him peculiar
in all respects. It was his pictorial craft he felt himself best equipped
to attack. Accustomed to painting with a surface as smooth as enamel
and revealing no trace of the brush strokes, he was shocked by a technique which admitted long streaks of colour, vigorous texture, and
those visible slabs of paint which created an illusion only from a distance. His indignation increased when he found that these "distinct,
disjointed colours" were introduced on purpose and that their lack of
harmony was deliberate. Blind to all artistic sensibility other than his
own, he reproached El Greco with striving to give an impression of
virtuosity, of facility, where it was really a question of laborious hard
work.

Pacheco's account of his visit to El Greco reflects his perplexity:
one can feel how torn he was between the certitudes he brought with
him on entering the house and the impressions he received there,
which deeply shook him. Being a well-balanced man, he soon came
to terms with himself in which his rooted convictions won the day.
But he was an artist and possessed that artistic honesty which would
not permit him, after the event, to falsify impressions received. When
composing his *Treatise on Painting* he wrote: "In spite of all we have
said elsewhere regarding certain of his views and paradoxes, we cannot exclude Dominico Greco from the number of great painters, after
having seen certain things by his hand, so revealing and so alive (according to his manner) that they equal those of the best of men."

Pacheco's visit was probably the last occasion on which El Greco
was able to dazzle a caller. His strength was failing. He was in no fit
state to fulfil his contracts either with the Hospital of Afuera or with
the Ayuntamiento of Toledo. Was it a heart attack which got the better
of his hard-working tenacity? His handwriting, that beautiful script
like copper plate, with which he signed his pictures in Greek letters,
became heavy and sluggish, as if traced by a trembling hand. He was

also struggling with grave material difficulties. He no longer had with him his faithful intermediary, Preboste, who knew so well how to market his works in Toledo and the other cities of Spain. Preboste's signature is found for the last time at the foot of an agreement which reflects the absolute confidence El Greco had in him and which dates from the spring of 1607. Did he die before his master, although much younger than he? The registers of the parish of San Tomé, to which the property of the Marqués de Villena belonged, contain no mention of his death. He was sufficiently well known in Toledo as El Greco's representative for his death certificate or traces of his survival to have been preserved had he stayed on there, even apart from his master. Nothing is known of him after that spring of 1607. It is more likely that he simply returned to Italy; yet the reasons for such a departure are unknown; it must have been abrupt, perhaps after a breach which put an end to so long a collaboration, for the most plausible explanation would be his failure to get on with El Greco's son. Just as Preboste seems to have been industrious, reliable, self-effacing, and economical, so Jorge Manuel appears to have been unreliable in character, unstable in his work, and prodigal with the money he earned and also with his father's. A few months after El Greco's death he was no longer satisfied with the house, which he kept on, although he described it as *"capaz,"* and rented an additional room; he possessed a great deal of furniture (including twenty chairs) and employed at least three servants.

This son of whom El Greco was so inordinately proud never submitted to the discipline of work and merited the trust of his clients only so long as his father was alive. After the latter's death he gradually let himself drift, as if the brakes imposed on him by his education and his father's example were released one after the other. When his wife died, three years after his father, he remarried: he had a large family and was faced with increasing financial difficulties. He did not fulfil the obligations he had contracted, failed to carry out the works entrusted to him, and cheated his waiting clients, supplying them with works by his father which he subsequently took back, sometimes by means of a lawsuit. For many years his father's name seems to have protected him. El Greco's devoted friends came to his aid: Dr. Angulo paid his debts and stood surety for him. But a time came when the regard felt for him weakened, when he had worn out the best of wills by his abuse of a great name. The administrators of the Hospital of Afuera were among the most patient and understanding of his clients, as if they felt a great debt of gratitude to El Greco. They waited years for the construction of the reredos begun by his father, whose original plan seemed too severe and rectilinear for the new conceptions of the baroque, and which Jorge Manuel was to adapt.

He always managed to invent fresh excuses to avoid work, whilst at the same time he signed new contracts in order to collect advance payments. Regarding the most important commission he received, in the year of his father's death, for the façade for the Ayuntamiento of Toledo, the mayor of the city complained about the slow progress of the work, whereas Jorge Manuel claimed to have been most assiduous, to have spent his own fortune and that of his friends in order to carry the undertaking through, without having received what was due to him for the work. However, the workmen, who had not been paid, grew angry and succeeded in having him sentenced to prison. He pleaded the size of his family and took refuge *"con su casa poblada,"* with his numerous household, in the Hospital, thus escaping from material difficulties too great for his scatterbrained nature. Indeed the hospital sheltered him for several years, but, even living on the spot and on charity, he made little progress with the altarpiece. His father's friend was no longer there to protect him. In 1622, on the complaint of the new administrator, the *alcalde mayor* of Toledo ordered Jorge Manuel's arrest; but he seems to have anticipated this move or to have been warned by his friends, for he fled, and the bailiff, not finding him at home, contented himself with seizing and removing his furniture and pictures. A year later Jorge Manuel, still in flight, his studio abandoned, requested that the order of arrest put out against him be revoked. But this request does not seem to have been complied with, for, in the autumn of the same year, a new seizure was made. However, he succeeded in recovering his position, for in 1625 he was appointed *maestro mayor* of Toledo Cathedral and put to work on the Mozarabic chapel. But he soon seems to have found himself once again in financial difficulties and in dispute with his clients. He was just over fifty when he died, in 1631, worn out by a struggle for existence for which he was ill-prepared by his youth and exhausted by the dissipated life of a spendthrift, as if the one thing he inherited from his father was his ways of a *grand seigneur*. After his death his children's tutor, who was also his second wife's cousin (Jorge Manuel married again for the third time), interceded with the authorities to obtain the release of the sequestrated furniture and above all of the pictures, which were stored in a place for which the family had to pay rent and where they were deteriorating day by day. The great hope of a devoted father, who began life in his shining wake, ended in this pitiful image of a man hunted by the police and of pictures "wasting away," as the official document put it, the majority of them probably painted by El Greco himself.

But at the time of his parting with Preboste, El Greco did not know or perhaps did not wish to know that he could not trust blindly in his son, as he had in the Italian. He seems to have believed that certain characters grow stronger in measure with the trust placed in them, that they rise to the demands made upon them. Barely a month after concluding the agreement in which Francisco Preboste's name figures for the last time El Greco signed another in which Jorge Manuel was granted the widest, most unconditional authority El Greco ever gave. Now that his strength was failing, Toledo saw in Jorge Manuel his artistic heir. The city did not regard the latter as a foreigner; he was given honorary posts which never seem to have been offered to his father. In 1611 he was appointed major-domo of the brotherhood of the Holy Sacrament in the parish of San Tomé, which held one of its meetings in the Marqués de Villena's palace, in that sumptuous apartment which Jorge Manuel, together with his wife, his wife's sister, and his young son, shared with his father.

At this time he was basking in reflected glory. The monument El Greco constructed for the funeral celebrations of Queen Margaret of Austria had left a deep impression on the minds of the Toledans. El Greco and his son were well known by the monks of San Domingo el Antiguo, who prided themselves on having given him his first commission. In 1612 the monks appointed Jorge Manuel to construct for them "a monument for Holy Week." They who had haggled so bitterly with the father made no attempt to bargain with the son, according him straightaway the price of 11,000 reals. The monument was never built. The monks, after waiting patiently for five years, finally rescinded the agreement.

The commissions Jorge Manuel accepted in his father's name as well as his own brought money into the house. The advances El Greco received were considerable. His house was a museum; it was also, at the prices paid for his pictures, a gold mine. The first inventory drawn up immediately after his death by Jorge Manuel mentions 110 paintings by him, 10 copper plates engraved after his paintings, with 10 engravings printed from each, 100 plaster models, about 100 wax ones, and 50 drawings. In a later inventory much more carefully prepared, at

the time of Jorge Manuel's second marriage, as many as 241 paintings
are listed. Perhaps Jorge Manuel deliberately confused his own with
those of his father, so greatly increased is the number, whereas 16
pictures specified in the first inventory do not here appear, as if in
the meantime they had been sold. These inventories give a picture of
a studio in full prosperity, of a painter still in demand despite his age;
they mention 15 pictures roughed in and 20 portraits begun. There
were also plans for building schemes and a treatise on architecture,
doubtless already prepared for publication, with drawings to accompany the text. In this private museum there were even 100 engravings by other hands. The list of pictures, drawings, and plaster or
wax models sufficiently explains why El Greco needed twenty-four
rooms to live in.

Yet Jorge Manuel's inventory of this large apartment in the "royal
quarter," which one would imagine to have been sumptuous, suddenly
reveals an inexplicable poverty. The very image of desolation rises up
between the terse lines of this brief list. In the twenty-four rooms there
were only eight chairs, two candelabras, and one brazier. One thinks
of how cold it must have been in the long winter evenings; one pictures
the old man taking refuge in his meanly lit bedroom. The kitchen alone
appears to have been adequately furnished and here the rest of the
family seems to have lived, with María Gómez, the old servant who
remained in El Greco's service for twenty years and looked after him
until his death. This deserted apartment must, however, have once
been splendidly furnished, as witness the "pavilion": a crimson velvet
dais with panelling, costly furniture, a writing desk covered with
leather, doubtless the embossed and gilded leather of the period, cupboards, one of them very large, sideboards and tables which must
henceforth have had the effect of things saved from the wreckage of a
life. The rest was in keeping with this strange picture of poverty. The
inventory records eight napkins and two towels, as if the linen, once
worn out, could not be replaced. Yet plenty of room had been allowed
for piles of reserve linen, for there were two linen presses and a large
chest of five drawers. All these were as desolately empty as the apartment itself. By way of personal linen the old man possessed only three
shirts; he now seems to have had only one spare suit, whereas he had
once been accustomed to dressing luxuriously and even with ostentation—that velvet cape, for example, to which a sword and belt belonged, to complete the image of a Spanish nobleman.

This almost deserted apartment, these poor remains of a worn-out life, which contrast so strangely with the red velvet dais and chased sword, were still housed alongside what had been the great luxury of its time, El Greco's library. The walls of this one room, in which he seems to have lived from now on, were still lined with books, from which El Greco would not part even though the last towels had fallen to pieces and he barely had a clean change of shirt. The first inventory mentions 27 Greek and 67 Italian books. None of those El Greco had brought with him from his native island and which must have accompanied him throughout his travels seems to have been missing at the hour of his death. He had continued to buy books all through his life, specializing in architecture; according to his son, he possessed nineteen works on this subject. Herrera's book on the Escorial, which he had in his library, was not published until 1590, and a book on perspective by Lorenzo Sirigatti was only published in 1596. El Greco was passionately attached to his library and his friends knew of this passion. Don Antonio de Covarrubias presented him with a Xenophon. His were valuable books, yet none was used to satisfy the urgent needs of the household, to alleviate this apparent poverty. Between the two inventories the number of books diminished, and Jorge Manuel was to continue to sell them, as he sold the pictures. When, a few years later, he made his own inventory, only twenty remained of the ninety-four Greek and Italian books. But until his death El Greco watched over them like a miser over his treasures.

One might think that Jorge Manuel possibly exaggerated this gloomy picture of a barren interior and even tacitly appropriated part of what belonged to his father (which would conform with his furtive nature). Yet he listed every book and painting, the values of which were greatly beyond those of a napkin, a shirt, or a chair. There is other evidence of El Greco's destitution. The rent for that luxurious apartment had not been paid for years, apparently not since 1608; in the August of 1611 the demands of the Marqués de Villena's administrator became pressing: El Greco and his son undertook to pay part of it from sums they were due to receive from the Hospital of Afuera. As for the rest, Dr. Gregorio de Angulo, that staunch friend in need who was present at the signing of this pledge, stood surety with his person and all his property. In addition to the guarantees afforded by one who was then a municipal official (*regidor* of the Ayuntamiento of Toledo) Dr. Angulo also lent El Greco money: he came to his aid "in the particular needs he encountered," as El Greco put it himself in a document dated

May 1609, in which the artist and his son acknowledged debts contracted with Dr. Angulo amounting to 5859 reals. Yet in August of the year 1610, while the rent for the preceding years does not appear to have been paid, Jorge Manuel on his own account rented four more rooms in the same palace, as if he found himself short of space.

El Greco's life, overcast by deep shadows into which only a few revealing shafts of light occasionally penetrate, this life so full of contrasts and contradictions, ended on a note of deepest enigma, with an image of an old man huddling in an almost empty room before a solitary brazier. Behind the door of this room stretched the succession of huge rooms with their walls covered with paintings, shelves of plaster and wax models, and cupboards filled with countless portfolios of easily marketable engravings; and the studios with their porphyry slabs on which to mix the paints, their three workbenches and parts of altarpieces, columns, and carved cornices. There can be few images in history as striking as that of a man who borrowed money, deprived himself of the bare necessities, and yet who refused to part with a work of art, to accept perhaps a starvation price, and who preferred to see his furniture taken away by creditors rather than sell a book.

In this twilight of mystery El Greco awaited his end. He bethought him of a tomb worthy of a life he had always tried to live proudly. With his peculiar fidelity, with his memory which attached so much importance to the successive stages of his life, El Greco's thoughts turned to that church of San Domingo el Antiguo which saw the beginning of his career. On August 26, 1612, Jorge Manuel signed a contract with the convent of San Domingo, represented by its Abbess, its Mother Superior, its deputy Mother Superior, etc., through which he acquired a vault under one of the altars in the church on a payment of 3600 reals. He further undertook (and pledged his father, who ratified the agreement in November of the same year) to erect a reredos above the vault at their own expense. The vault was ceded to them as a tomb for El Greco himself, his family, and his descendants, "for always and for ever."

As if reassured by having provided for a death worthy of his reputation El Greco recaptured a taste for living and for work. His health improved. He took advantage of a respite to begin on the work contracted for at the end of 1607 with the Ayuntamiento of Toledo, for which he had already received an advance. In this contract for an altarpiece for a chapel in the church of San Vicente it had been expressly stipulated (the Ayuntamiento knew his habit of delegating work to his son and pupils) that all the work to be done by brushes should be by his own hand and none other. The altarpiece had first been trusted to Alessandro Semino, an artist of whom nothing is known today, who died whilst at work on it. The plans he had made were immediately modified by El Greco (with the agreement of the administrators). Following his taste for elongation, the reredos was heightened by four and a half feet, representing "a fifth part of the whole." El Greco's clients had foreseen everything with the minute care of bureaucrats; they demanded that the painting be executed, not *al fresco*, in tempera, but in oils, so as to be "more serious and enduring." Doubtless conforming to the wishes of the pious donor, Isabella de Oballe, the altarpiece was dedicated to episodes from the life of the Virgin. The main panel, the first to be finished, represented the "Assumption of the Virgin" (Plate 99). Even if El Greco was then a condemned man profiting from a momentary respite, his creative power hardly reflected his physical debility. The picture is a triumph of the spirit over the flesh, a personal victory just as much as an unsurpassed glorification of this triumph in general terms. This Assumption, built up all in length, is like a rising tornado, a desperate straining for liberation from all earthly contingencies; it is a flight through space, accompanied by the beating of great wings and culminating in celestial beatitude. All the *Assuntas* above Italian altars, including that of his master Titian, seem to draw up all the weight and density of things on earth below; they resemble mere scenes of acrobatics compared with this true flight of bodies freed of earthly substance and no longer of this world. Despite its wilful distortions, infinite elongation, and compressed and crowded space this Assumption strikes one as being completely natural and the only plausible one. In so far as it depicts a miracle one feels that this one really occurred; one knows that this Virgin of El Greco's ascended joyously into the bosom of eternity, just as one knows that these angels really live in heaven and are blessed with wings. El Greco's art had attained an ultimate degree of persuasive power. Here there is no further division into two spheres to mark the miraculous event, no point of departure for the Virgin's ascent, not even the crescent moon which still supported her assumption in San Domingo el Antiguo (Plate 24). Comparison of these two pictures, one of the first and one of the last he painted on Spanish soil, is sufficient to grasp the direction of his evolution, to define his creative purpose. It is hard to believe that they are by the same hand. Between

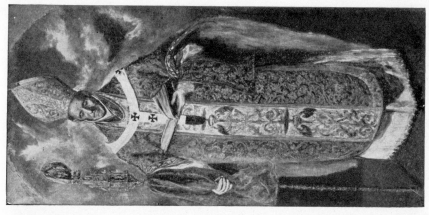

93. St. Ildefonso. c. 1606–08

92. The Crucifixion. c. 1602–10

91. St. Peter. c. 1606–08

94. *The Baptism of Christ. c. 1608–14*

96. *Fray Hortensio Felix Paravicino. c. 1609*

95. *The Saviour. 1598*

97. *View and Plan of Toledo. c. 1609*

98. The Opening of the Fifth Seal. c. 1610–14

99. *Assumption of the Virgin. c. 1608–13*

100. The Visitation. c. 1608–14

101. The Betrothal of the Virgin. c. 1613–14

the two, thirty-six years had elapsed. Thirty-six years of Toledo, with all that they had stimulated, clarified and liberated in him. When El Greco was no more, his friend Paravicino thus summed up the meaning of those years: "Crete gave him his life and his brushes; Toledo a better fatherland, where he began, with death, to gain eternity."

Like all human beings and particularly creative minds, El Greco sometimes took detours to arrive at his goal and often lost himself in an impasse, but few men, few artists, have been so true to themselves, so eager to find themselves with the least amount of wasted energy. Perhaps he was endowed with that power of exclusive concentration which is a form of endurance, the gift of refusing to let himself be distracted or delayed by concessions. The singularity of his painting, his quest for successive means of expression, may have misled people as to the strictness of his conception. Certain aspects of his art may appear arbitrary, in turn fascinating or forbidding, and very often hard to fathom. But comparison of these two canvases reveals the extent to which nothing in his work was left to chance or eluded his purpose. Every inch of the picture from the Oballe chapel is an affirmation of the same principle, displayed by all that is present and all that is lacking in the altarpiece from San Domingo. No human being or saint in human guise now marks the earthly orbit or creates a link with the Virgin. It is the low horizon of Toledo which defines this earth, vanishing as if into an abyss; an already rather ghostly Toledo, the last song El Greco was to compose in honour of the city and all that he loved in it, with the castle of San Servando at the back, the Bridge of Alcantara, San Juan de los Reyes, the cathedral, and that hill on which the clouds cast their shadows. The one reality left in the picture is a large bunch of lilies and Jericho roses, liturgical emblems, but also tokens of everyday life, the proof of a miracle that has taken place on earth and much more convincing, for example, than the patently empty tomb in the San Domingo picture. The balustrade of clouds marking the base of heaven in this first Assumption seems a facile device beside the angel of San Vicente flying up from the earth. It is this angel which gives the signal for the ascent, like a great wind sweeping clouds, angels, and the Virgin up to heaven. Unlike the San Domingo painting, still full of gaps through which empty space percolates, the one from San Vicente is crowded and almost breathless with movement.

The Italians (and El Greco with them) had painted the Virgin foreshortened, a vanishing figure slipping out of sight like all material objects placed at a great height. The San Vicente Virgin rises up,

ascending through eternity, drawn out in her azure gown like the reflection of an object on water, stretched out like a shadow. Finding
her hard to follow, the eye draws support from the shining folds of
her robe. It takes its bearings from the angels which accompany her
escape, waving verticals as gigantic as herself. The San Domingo
Virgin is enthroned amongst angels, still women or youths, the one
celestial thing about which is that they are more graceful than human
beings. The San Vicente Virgin has already ascended into her true
element: the angelic musicians have welcomed her with their celestial
music: the Dove, with its emphatic eagle flight, has admitted her
within the orbit of its radiance. The San Domingo Virgin has spread
out her arms and raised her graceful, feminine hands; the San Vicente
Virgin has strangely large hands folded over her bosom, but they are
less hands than shreds of cloud tossed in the wind. The face of the
San Domingo Virgin is abruptly foreshortened, already less distinct
than that of the Italian Virgins whose type she has borrowed. The San
Vicente Virgin has no features left except for those which the light has
thrown up with the aid of fleeting shadows.

Between the two pictures a change had taken place which was like
a revolution in artistic perception. El Greco had opened wide the door
to all that the future was to experience; he had replaced knowledge
of an event, its pictorial narrative, by a direct appeal to the emotions,
by a drama in perpetual progress. From the formal viewpoint he had
broken the harmony of the proportions, subjugated space, and built
up his own personal universe from elements of reality.

And he was alone, quite alone in undertaking this artistic revolution.
His audacity seems all the greater for the fact that he had nothing to
back him up in his purpose, that he provoked no echo, not even feeble
imitations. The great innovators in art, even the most revolutionary
of them, even those who departed most from the present and who
aimed the highest, knew that on the steps they were cutting, so to speak,
in a glacier another would set his feet; even men like Masaccio,
Leonardo, Michelangelo, and Rembrandt had more or less direct
disciples who followed in their wake. But El Greco knew himself to
be isolated. He knew his art to be unassimilable. "He had few disciples," wrote Martínez, "for they did not care to follow his doctrine,
which was so capricious and extravagant that it was only of use to himself." Perhaps, like every creative artist, he hoped, even against all
likelihood, that he would still find an heir. The picture from San
Vicente was in a sense his artistic testament. He announced its com-

pletion on April 17, 1613. It was the last picture he had the strength
to finish.

For the same reredos he also painted "The Visitation" (Plate 100).
The agreement stipulated the inclusion of this subject in honour of St.
Elizabeth, the founder's patron saint. Did the picture in the Dumbarton
Oaks Collection in Washington perhaps form part of this reredos? Was
it a sketch for the large picture or an unfinished painting? In any case
it poses a disturbing problem, the last riddle of El Greco's art. His
mastery of composition here reached its peak. No other of his canvases displays such skill in the distribution of large masses and the
juxtaposition of rigorously circumscribed planes. He seems to have
recalled that "Visitation" by Jacopa da Pontormo which he must have
seen in Italy, in which the two figures, conceived as two immense
blocks, confront each other with the Virgin's delicate hands creating
a link between them. But here there is nothing of the youthful grace
Leonardo's pupil gave the Virgin in contrast to her heavy body. El
Greco had long ceased to aspire to beauty; he had long since broken
all bonds with things seen and even with summary indications of them.
The two holy women no longer have faces. That of the Virgin is a
vanishing profile; that of St. Elizabeth is hidden in the shadow of her
mantle. At first sight one would think that it must be a sketch. But
behind the saints there is a door of the purest classical style, like all
those constructed by Juan de Herrera. It plays an important part in
this new amplification to which El Greco subjected the miraculous.
It is done with great care. The old man's hand never trembled while
painting the relief of this embrasure, the volutes of its consoles and the
studied gradations of its projecting cornice. The arch on which the two
saints stand, as if on a bridge, is of a similar character. Did El Greco
first paint the setting, to be followed later by the holy women, whom
he left unfinished? For him such a procedure was hardly normal. The
door forms part of that reality which situates an event, by the same
token as the lilies and Jericho roses in the "Assumption." The problem remains unsolved: is it an unfinished picture or a new conception,
representing featureless saints in a realistic setting?

Another picture, "The Betrothal of the Virgin" (former Royal Collection of Roumania) (Plate 101) is closely related to this altarpiece,
although there is no mention of it in the contract made with the
Ayuntamiento. As with the "Visitation" this was the first time El Greco
approached this subject. It is as if he had promised himself to extend
his range with all the themes he had not hitherto tackled. This, too,

is a meeting of phantoms in a realistically defined setting. The feet
are invisible, but the robes sweep a floor inlaid with a pattern of black,
white, and grey marble tinged with green as if lit by a ghostly light.
Behind the group hangs a grey curtain concealing the Holy of Holies
in the temple, also very realistic with its folds which convey the density
and fall of cloth. Before this curtain are heads lined up in a level row;
in the foreground, the Virgin with her blue mantel, the colour of faded
turquoise saturated with pearly reflections. Facing her stands St.
Joseph in a green garment turning to gold in its folds, under a yellow
cloak with coppery shadows. By a device of the composition (the garments trailing over the marble) the two saints appear taller than the
rest, especially the Virgin, with her tiny face inclined in profile. A high
priest has joined their hands together in a way that two hands were
never joined, for St. Joseph has taken hold of only two of the Virgin's
slender fingers. The high priest is garbed in white and his golden dalmatic pales to silver. He is very old. Beneath his white mitre is a
wrinkled face, its flesh almost transparent and worn away like a stone
grown porous through exposure to rough weather. His eyes are so
deeply sunken that it is difficult for him to see out of them. His beard
is like whitened lichen. Behind him stands an onlooker who might
easily be the portrait of some contemporary with his velvet costume
contrasting with the draperies of the saints. He too is an old man—
bald, with a silvery beard, a still-dark moustache, and a thin, aquiline
nose—an old and sick man. His skin is leaden and livid, but his gaze
is still insistent, challenging the spectator. In all likelihood El Greco
painted himself in this manner typical of all painters, staring out of
the frame. This would be his last self-portrait, with its strangely sad
expression, as if he knew it was to be his farewell. Three sketchy
figures lined up against the grey curtain complete the picture, or,
rather, its harmonies of broken colours—faded rose, evanescent gold,
and greenish white. The work is in fact unfinished: St. Joseph's left
hand is still unpainted.

"The Betrothal of the Virgin" was the last picture El Greco ever
painted. He seems to have wielded the brush until his dying breath.
If the "Assumption" was completed in April of the year 1613, to be
followed by two further pictures, he must have spent at least several
more months at work. Then, suddenly, his strength deserted him, possibly in the middle of his work, possibly at the very moment when
he was about to add St. Joseph's missing hand. This attack which laid
him low was the last one. He could no longer hold either brush or pen.

He felt his end to be imminent. He who seems to have been ill and worn out for some years past, as if in colloquy with death, yet who two years before had taken precautions to secure for himself a tomb worthy of his life, suddenly realized that he had made no disposition with regard to the living. Now it was too late. He was no longer able to draw up his will himself. His hand was doubtless paralyzed, but he retained all his lucidity. On March 31, 1614, he sent for a public scribe. He had not enough strength to dictate his last wishes and make an inventory of his possessions. He entrusted this to Jorge Manuel. In "being ill and confined to my bed," he dictated to the scribe, "with a sickness with which it has pleased Our Lord to smite me," but in full possession of his mental faculties, the gravity of his illness prevented him from making a will befitting the service of God Our Father for the salvation of his soul and, to clear his conscience, he made all his authority over to his son.

The great philosopher, as Pacheco called him, the man who in his art had followed such a lonely path, spoke in the hour of his death like every dying Spaniard. He spoke a language which the scribe was accustomed to hear from a dying man. He affirmed his belief in and confession of all that the Holy Mother Church of Rome believed and confessed; he affirmed that he had lived and died as a good, faithful, and Catholic Christian.

In this hour of his death one name necessarily rose to his lips, the name of a woman who had probably died long since, when he named as his sole heir Jorge Manuel, son of Doña Jerónima de las Cuevas. That often blind and always rather poignant love for an only child also welled up in him through his dire exhaustion. In charging Jorge Manuel, who was present at this painful dictation, to draw up in his stead and at a given time the will which he could no longer make himself, he specified that this son of his was "a person of trust and of good conscience." He revoked all testaments, codicils, and powers of attorney prior to this day and instructed Jorge Manuel to make various pious bequests and donations in his name. The signature El Greco set under the deed drawn up by the public scribe is almost illegible.

Several witnesses were present at the drawing up of his last wishes, including two Toledans whose names do not occur in any other document referring to his life. Perhaps they were friends or simply neighbours. Two other witnesses had Greek names, as if El Greco, in these last hours of his life, had been anxious to hear the familiar tongue of his childhood and to see round him the faces of Cretan or Greek *émigrés* with whom he had never lost touch. After the great effort it must have cost him to put his affairs in order and his conscience at rest El Greco lay waiting for death. To those who saw him during his last illness he must have looked so worn out that they took away an impression of a very old man. His first biographer, who collected what his contemporaries could remember of him, asserted that El Greco died at the age of seventy-seven, though one would have thought him to be much older. In actual fact he was only seventy-three. Death did not delay long after the day when his friends and witnesses assembled round his bed.

In the death register of the parish of San Tomé there appears as the first entry on the fourth day of April 1614, "a little girl of eight months" followed by a no less laconic note, dated the seventh, stating that on this day died Domenico Greco, leaving no will. He had received the Holy Sacrament, adds the note, he was buried in San Domingo el Antiguo and he had donated candles. In the death register El Greco even lost his patronymic, which had been retained in every contract concluded with him during his lifetime.

He died like every other pious Toledan and was buried like every well-to-do Spaniard. His funeral was attended by the brotherhood of the Santa Caridad of Toledo, with its banner, the clerks of the church of San Tomé with their cross, and the brotherhood of Our Lady of Sorrows from the monastery of St. Peter the Martyr.

On the day of his funeral a Mass was said in the monastery of San Domingo el Antiguo, a sung Mass with deacon and subdeacon, vigil, and response, in addition to ten Masses for the repose of his soul said before the altars of St. Peter the Martyr and in the monastery of the Holy Trinity.

El Greco's death made a profound impression on the artistic circles of his time. His friend Paravicino seems to have learned of it far away. He knew it to be an irreparable loss. With his poetic foresight, which the immediate future was yet to deny, Paravicino summed up the meaning of El Greco's work, which was to remain without a successor as it had been without a precedent—"that the centuries to come will admire it without being able to imitate it."

El Greco was interred in the vault of San Domingo, the ownership of which he had long ago secured. Jorge Manuel seems to have done things well. He must have sold some pictures or collected advances in order to be able to give his father a burial worthy of him. El Greco reposed in a porphyry coffin. Góngora wrote a poem on this "tomb of Domenico Greco, that excellent painter":

> *Stranger, this glittering tomb of porphyry fair*
> *Imprisons now that master's hand, which drew*
> *On canvas or dull board with touch so true,*
> *As if the breathing forms of life were there.*

He too had a feeling of terrible loss. He realized the special qualities of El Greco's art, how far it had departed from the well-trodden path, to triumph over reality.

In memory of an illustrious inscription Góngora addressed the pilgrim at El Greco's tomb:

> *Pass on, but greet it first with reverent prayer.*

Despite all the precautions taken El Greco's tomb did not remain long in the vault of San Domingo, purchased by him for his family "for always and for ever." In 1617 Jorge Manuel's first wife joined him in what should have been his eternal rest. But soon after, something happened to disturb the peace of the dead. Jorge Manuel must have fallen out with the administrators of San Domingo, with whom he had failed to fulfil the contracts he had signed for the monument for Holy Week. The Church must have required the site reserved for El Greco's family in its work of reconstruction. In February 1618 the monastery asked for permission "to remove the bodies from the said vault, for Jorge Manuel to take them where he will." But no document has been found recording an exhumation or the purchase of a new tomb with the money which the administrators had to refund to him, assessing the vault at 46,923 maravedís.

Jorge Manuel's second wife, who died in 1629, was buried in the church of San Torcuado. Did El Greco's son also have his father's remains transferred to the same church? There is no evidence of such filial piety. Oblivion settled ever deeper round the life and death of El Greco.

At a time when this darkness was beginning to lighten attempts were made to reconstruct his life and a search was carried out for his earthly remains. Toledo, which made him so welcome during his lifetime, did not preserve the illustrious dead. The excavations made at the place where the vault should have been revealed neither a porphyry coffin nor any inscription at all. Only numerous remains of human bodies were discovered, some scattered about the ground, others mingled with the paving stones.

In his death El Greco rejoined the Toledans, the unknown, and the forgotten with whom he had lived.

ACKNOWLEDGMENTS

Acknowledgments are due to the following, for permission to reproduce the illustrations:

Alinari, Florence—Plate 18
Anderson, Rome—Plates 3, 9, 11, 14, 27, 40, 41, 70, 91, 93, 97
The Art Institute of Chicago—Plate 79
Bowes Museum, Barnard Castle—Plate 60
Braun, Mulhouse—Plates 2, 20, 22, 24, 25, 33, 36, 38, 43, 65, 71, 72, 80, 82, 96
Bulloz, Paris—Plates 34, 37, 42
The Cleveland Museum of Art—Plate 63
Dumbarton Oaks Collection, Harvard University—Plate 100
The Frick Collection, New York—Plate 15
Giraudon, Paris—Plates 23, 47
Graphische Sammlung, Munich—Plate 8
Hauser y Menet, Madrid—Plate 68
The Johnson Collection, Philadelphia—Plate 17
Arxiu Mas, Barcelona—Plates 16, 26, 29, 30, 31, 32, 39, 44, 46, 48, 49, 50, 51, 53, 54, 55, 57, 59, 62, 64, 75, 76, 78, 86, 87, 89, 94, 98
The Metropolitan Museum of Art, New York—Plates 67, 83, 84
The Minneapolis Institute of Arts—Plates 10, 12
Moreno, Madrid—Plate 77
The Trustees, The National Gallery, London—Plates 61, 74, 85
The National Gallery of Art, Washington—Frontispiece and Plate 81
Puytorac, Bordeaux—Plates 4, 5, 6, 19, 45, 56, 69, 90, 92
Vernacci, Madrid—Plate 73

Special acknowledgment is due to Señor J. Camón Aznar for his kind assistance in obtaining photographs from Spain and for the loan of a number of photographs from his own collection; to Mr. Edgar Hanfstaengl for his kind permission to make use of the photogravure reproductions from A. L. Mayer's catalogue; to the Witt Library (Courtauld Institute) for the assistance received in connection with the illustrations. We are also greatly indebted to Professor Anthony Blunt for his kind permission to publish for the first time the anonymous engraving in memory of the Battle of Lepanto (Plate 35).

BIBLIOGRAPHY

ARTEMIDOROS AUS DALDIS: *Symbolik des Träume* (Vienna, 1881)

ARTIGAS, MIGUEL: *Don Luis de Góngora y Argote* (Madrid, 1925)

BABELON, JEAN: *Jacopo da Trezzo et la construction de l'Escurial* (Bordeaux, 1922)

———— *El Greco* (Paris, 1946)

BARRES, MAURICE: *Le Greco ou le secret de Tolède* (Paris, 1923)

BARUZI, JEAN: *Saint Jean de la Croix et le problème de l'expérience mystique* (Paris, 1931)

BASCH, VICTOR: *Titien* (Paris, 1920)

BAUMEISTER, E.: *Eine Zeichnung des jungen Greco* (Münchner Jahrbuch der bildenden Kunst, 1929)

BELON, PIERRE, DU MANS: *Les Observations de plusieurs singularités et choses mémorables trouvées en Grèce, Asie, Judée, Egypte, Arabie et autres pays etranges, rédigées en trois livres* (Paris, 1553)

BERITENS, GERMAN: *El astigmatismo del Greco* (Madrid, 1914)

BERTRAND, LOUIS: *Philippe II à l'Escurial* (Paris, 1929)

BERUETE, A. DE, Y MORET: *El Greco, pintor de retratos* (Toledo, 1914)

BETTINI, SERGIO: *La pittura di icone Cretese-Veneziana e i madonneri* (Padua, 1933)

BLUNT, ANTHONY: *The Dream of Philip II* (Journal of the Warburg Institute, Vol. 3, Nos. 1, 2)

BRADLEY, JOHN W.: *The Life and Works of Giorgio Giulio Clovio* (London, 1891)

BREHIER, LOUIS: *La civilization Byzantine* (Paris, 1950)

BRUNO, R. P., DE JÉSUS MARIE: *L'Espagne mystique au XVIe siècle—Le Greco à Tolède,* Bernard Champigneulle (Coll. Documents d'Art et d'Histoire, Paris, 1946)

BYRON, ROBERT: *The Byzantine Achievement* (London, 1929)

———— *El Greco: The Epilogue to Byzantine Culture* (*Burlington* Mag., 1929, II, p. 160)

CALVERT, ALBERT F.: *Toledo* (London, 1907)

CALVERT, A. F. and HARTLEY, C. GASQUOINE: *El Greco* (London, 1909)

CAMÓN AZNAR, JOSÉ: *El Greco* (Madrid, 1950)

CANOVAS DEL CASTILLO: *Historia della decadencia de España desde Felipe III hasta Carlos II* (Madrid, 1880–1910)

CARGOL, JOAQUÍN PLA: *El Greco y Toledo* (Gerona, 1927)

CARVALLO, DR. J.: *Exposition d'art ancien espagnol* (Paris, 1925)

CASSOU, JEAN: *Cervantes* (Paris, 1936)

———— *Le Greco* (Paris, 1931)

CEDILLO, D. JERÓNIMO LÓPEZ DE AYALA Y ALVÁREZ DE TOLEDO, CONDE DE: *Toledo en el siglo XVI* (Madrid, 1901)

CHARBONNEL, J. ROGER: *La pensée italienne au XVIe siècle et le courant libertin* (Paris, 1919)

COCTEAU, JEAN: *Les Demi-Dieux: Le Greco* (Paris, 1943)

COSSIO, B. MANUEL: *El Greco* (Madrid, 1908)

———— *Lo que se sabe de la vida del Greco* (Madrid, 1914)

———— *Toledo* (Madrid, 1933)

COSSIO DE JIMÉNEZ, NATALIA: *Notes on El Greco's Birthplace, Education and Family* (Oxford, 1948)

DÁVILA, GIL GONZÁLEZ: *Vida y hechos de los señores reyes D. Felipe III y IV* (Madrid, 1771)

DEJOB, CHARLES: *De l'influence de Concile de Trente sur la littérature et les beaux arts chez les peuples catholiques* (Paris, 1884)

DVOŘAK, MAX: *Kunstegeschichte als Geistesgeschichte* (Munich, 1928)

ERLANGER, PHILIPPE: *Henri III* (Paris, 1948)

ESCHOLIER, RAYMOND: *Crees anciens et modernes* (Paris, 1937)

FIOCCO, GIUSEPPE: *El maestro del Greco* (Revista española del arte, Sept., 1934)

FOSCA, FRANÇOIS: *Tintoret* (Paris, 1929)

FRANCASTEL, PIERRE: *La contre Réforme et les arts en Italie à la fin du XVIe siècle* (Publications de la Société d'Etudes Italiennes, Paris, 1941)

GARCIA DE BLAS, ANGEL: *Parroqia de Santo Tomé* (Toledo, 1947)

GATES, EUNICE JONES: *The Metaphors of Luis de Góngora* (Philadelphia, 1933)

GERLAND, ERNST: *Kreta als venezianische Kolonie* (Historisches Jahrbuch XX, 1899)

GEROLA, GIUSEPPE: *Monumenti veneti dell'isola di Creta* Vol. III (4) (R. Instituto veneto di scienze, lettere et arti, Venice, 1908)

GOLDSCHEIDER, LUDWIG: *El Greco* (Paris, 1949)

GRAETZ, DR. H.: *Geschichte der Juden* (Leipzig, 1863)

GRAPPE, GEORGES: *El Greco* (Paris, 1948)

GRAY GRISWOLD, FRANK: *El Greco* (Privately printed, 1930)

GREGOR, JOSEPH: *Das spanische Welttheater* (Munich, 1943)

GUINARD, M. P.: *Saint François chez Greco* (Revue d'Histoire Franciscaine, January, 1925)

HADELN, DETLER, FREIKERR VON: *Bassano und nicht Greco* (Kunstchronik, 1914)

HARRIS, ENRIQUITA: *A Decorative Scheme of El Greco* (*Burlington* Mag., 1938)

HAUSER, HENRI: *La prépondérance espagnole, 1559–1660* (Paris, 1940)

IBARRA, EDUARDO: *España bajo los Austrias* (Barcelona, 1935)

JUSTI, CARL: *Miscellaneen aus drei Jahrhunderten* (Berlin, 1908)

KEHRER, PROF. DR. HUGO: *Greco als Gestalt des Manierismus* (Munich, 1939)

KYROU, ACHILLE: *La patrie du Greco* (Revue de Paris, 15, VIII, 1933)

LAFOND, PAUL: *Le Greco* (Paris, 1913)

LAFUENTE FERRARI, ENRIQUE: *Some Recent Discoveries* (*Burlington* Mag., December, 1945)

LAMBERT, ELIE: *Les procédés du Greco* (*Gazette des Beaux Arts,* Paris, 1921)

LEGENDRE and HARTMANN: *El Greco* (Paris, 1937)

LONGHI, ROBERTO: *Il soggiorno romano del Greco* (Arte, 1914)

LORCA, FEDERIGO GARCÍA: *L'image poétique chez Don Luis Góngora* ("Trois Conferences," Paris, 1947)

LOTH, DAVID: *Philippe II* (Paris, 1933)

MAGNONI, VALENTINE: *Il Greco* (Florence, 1931)

MALE, EMILE: *L'art religieux après le Concile de Trente* (Paris, 1932)

MALRAUX, ANDRÉ: *Les voix du silence* (Paris, 1952)

MARANON, DR. GREGORIO: *Exhibition Catalogue "Le Greco de la Crète à Tolède par Venise"* (Bordeaux, 1953)

MAYER, AUGUST L.: *El Greco und Bassano* (Monatshefte für Kunstwissenschaft VII, 1914)

——— *Greco in Toledo* (Zeitschrift für bildende Kunst XXII)

——— *Ein wiederentdecktes Spätwerk Grecos* (Zeitschrift für bildende Kunst XXXII)

——— *El Greco und das Hospital von Afuera* (Kunstchronik, November, 1922)

——— *Unbekannte Werke des Greco* (Pantheon, 1930)

——— *El Greco* (Berlin, 1931)

——— *An Unknown Portrait by El Greco* (*Burlington* Mag., 1940)

MEIER-GRAEFE, JULIUS: *Spanische Reise* (Berlin, 1912)

MELIDA, J. R.: *El arte antiguo y el Greco* (Madrid, 1915)

MENÉNDEZ Y PELAYO: *Historia de los heterodoxos españoles* (3 vols. Madrid, 1880)

MOLMENTI, P.: *La vie privée à Venise* (Venice, 1895–97)

NAVENNE, FERDINAND DE: *Rome, le palais Farnèse et les Farnèse* (Paris, 1914)

PALLUCCHINI, RODOLFO: *Il polittico del Greco della R. Galleria estense* (R. Ist. di Arte e Storia dell'arte, 1937)

———— *Some Early Works by El Greco* (*Burlington* Mag., 1948, I, p. 130)

———— *La période italienne du Greco* (Exhibition: Le Greco de la Crète à Tolède par Venise, Bordeaux, 1953)

PARAVICINO, FRAY HORTENSIO FELIX: *Oraciones evangélicas y panagéricos funerales* (Madrid, 1641)

———— *Obras posthumas divinas y humanes* (Madrid, 1641)

PASHLEY, ROBERT: *Travels in Crete* (Cambridge, 1837)

PERNOT, HUBERT: *Etudes de littérature grecque moderne* (Paris, 1916)

PERROT, G.: *L'île de Crète* (Paris, 1867)

PFANDL, LUDWIG: *Philipp II* (Munich, 1938)

PHILIPSON, M.: *Heinrich IV und Philipp III* (Berlin, 1876)

PILLEMENT, GEORGES: *La sculpture baroque espagnole* (Paris, 1945)

POLO, BENITO JOSÉ: *La catedral de Toledo* (Barcelona)

PORCELLA, AMADEO: *An Unknown El Greco: A Problem* (*Burlington* Mag., 1932, I, p. 276)

PROCOPIOU, G. ANGELO: *La peinture religieuse dans les îles ioniennes pendant le XVIIIe siècle* (1939)

———— *El Greco and Cretan Painting* (*Burlington* Mag., March, 1952)

ROSINSKI, X. XR. B.: *Wyspa Kreta: L'île de Crète préhistorique et contemporaine* (Lwov, 1925)

RUTTER, FRANK: *El Greco* (London, 1930)

———— *The Early Life of Greco* (*Burlington* Mag., 1932)

SABATIER, PAUL: *Vie de Saint François d'Assise* (Paris, 1899)

SALAZAR DE MENDOZA, DR. DON PEDRO: *Historia de la vida y hechos de D. Felipe Tercero* (Madrid, 1771)

SÁNCHEZ CANTON, F. J.: *Fuentes literarias para la historia del arte español* (Madrid, 1933)

———— *Dibujos Españoles* (Madrid, 1930)

SAN ROMÁN, FRANCISCO DE BORJA Y FERNÁNDEZ: *El Greco en Toledo* (Madrid, 1910)

———— *El sepulcro des los Theotocópulos* (Madrid, 1912)

———— *De la vida del Greco* (Arch. esp. de arte y arqueol., May–Dec. 1927)

SCHWEINFURTH, PHILIPP: *Greco und die italo-kretische Kunst* (Byzantinische Zeitschrift, 1930)

SERRANO, CARLOS: *Il bizantinismo del Greco* (Bul. del. sem. de Estudios de arte y arqueol., Valladolid, III, p. 119)

SEUPHOR, M.: *Greco* (Paris, 1931)

SIERRA CORELLA, ANTONIO: *Le Musée Saint Vincent de Tolède* (Mouseion, Sept., 1929)

SIPLE, ELLA S.: *The Boston and Cleveland El Greco* (*Burlington* Mag., April, 1927)

TALBOT RICE, D.: *Five Late Byzantine Panels and Greco's Views of Sinaï* (*Burlington* Mag., 1937)

TRAPIER, E. DU GUÉ: *The Son of El Greco* (Hispanic Notes, III, 1943)

———— *El Greco* (Hispanic Soc. of America, 1925)

VERD, YVAN-BENJAMIN: *Le Greco. Remarques sur la peinture et al folie* (Bordeaux, 1934)

VOSS, HERMANN: *Die Malerei des Spätrenaissance in Rom und Florenz* (Berlin, 1920)

VOSSLER, KARL: *Poesie der Einsamkeit in Spanien* (Sitzunsberichte der Bayerischen Akademie der Wissenschaften, 1936)

———— *Lope de Vega* (Revista de Occidente, Madrid, 1933)

WATERHOUSE, ELLIS: *El Greco's Italian Period* (Art Studies, 1930, I, p. 69)

———— *Catalogue of an Exhibition of Spanish Paintings* (Edinburgh Festival, 1951)

WEISBACH, WERNER: *Der Barock als Kunst der Gegenreformation* (Berlin, 1921)

———— *Französische Malerei des XVII Jahrh* (Berlin, 1932)

WILDENSTEIN, GEORGES: *Catalogue de l'exposition organisée par la Gazette des Beaux Arts à Paris,* 1937

WILLUMSEN, J. F.: *La jeunesse du peintre El Greco* (Paris, 1927)

ZERVOS, CHRISTIAN: *El Greco* (Cahiers d'Art, Paris, 1939)